DIVERSITY AND CHANGE IN MODERN INDIA
Economic, Social and Political Approaches

PROCEEDINGS OF THE BRITISH ACADEMY · 159

DIVERSITY AND CHANGE IN MODERN INDIA

Economic, Social and Political Approaches

Edited by
ANTHONY F. HEATH & ROGER JEFFERY

Published for THE BRITISH ACADEMY
by OXFORD UNIVERSITY PRESS

Oxford University Press, Great Clarendon Street, Oxford OX2 6DP

Oxford New York
Auckland Cape Town Dar es Salaam Hong Kong Karachi
Kuala Lumpur Madrid Melbourne Mexico City Nairobi
New Delhi Shanghai Taipei Toronto

With offices in
Argentina Austria Brazil Chile Czech Republic France Greece
Guatemala Hungary Italy Japan Poland Portugal Singapore
South Korea Switzerland Thailand Turkey Ukraine Vietnam

Published in the United States
by Oxford University Press Inc., New York

First published 2010

British Library Cataloguing in Publication Data
Data available

Library of Congress Cataloging in Publication Data
Data available

Typeset by New Leaf Design, Scarborough, North Yorkshire
Printed in Great Britain
on acid-free paper by
Cromwell Press Group, Trowbridge, Wiltshire

ISBN 978–0–19–726451–5
ISSN 0068–1202

Contents

Notes on Contributors

Mukulika Banerjee is Reader in Social Anthropology at the London School of Economics. She is completing a monograph (*Democracy: An ethnographic approach*) discussing the grass roots experience of democracy and political participation in village India (based on extended ethnographic fieldwork); among other things, this asks why poor illiterate people vote with such enthusiasm. In 2009, she directed a multi-sited study *Comparative Electoral Ethnographies* (funded by the ESRC) that provided ethnographic description of local practices during the Indian general election. She has published two monographs, *The Pathan Unarmed* (2000) and *The Sari* (with Daniel Miller, 2000), and an edited volume *Muslim Portraits* (2008) that presents portraits of ordinary Muslims in India. In 2007 she delivered the Barbara Ward Memorial Lecture at Oxford and is the Commissioning and Series Editor of *Exploring the Political in South Asia* (Routledge).

Tim Dyson is Professor of Population Studies in the Development Studies Institute at the London School of Economics. His research has included work on demographic time series, interactions between populations and their food supplies, the demographic transition and its wider consequences, HIV/AIDS and urbanisation, climate change, and the past, present and future population of the Indian subcontinent. With Cormac Ó Gráda he co-edited *Famine Demography* (2002) and with Robert Cassen and Leela Visaria he co-edited and contributed to *Twenty-first Century India: Population, economy, human development and the environment* (2004). He is a past President of the British Society for Population Studies, and he was elected a Fellow of the British Academy in 2001.

Dipankar Gupta is Professor, Centre for the Study of Social Systems, Jawaharlal Nehru University where he has been a Faculty member since 1980. Between 1993–5, he was Professor, Department of Sociology, University of Delhi and he has been a Visiting Professor at the Universities of Toronto, Strassbourg, Sciences-Po (Paris) and Lille. He was a Visiting Leverhulme Professor at the London School of Economics in 2003 and Woodrow Wilson Fellow at the Woodrow Wilson Centre in

2007. His latest book is *The Caged Phoenix: Will India fly?* (2009). Until 2007 he was co-editor of *Contributions to Indian Sociology* and he is a Member of the National Security Board and the National Media Authority. In 1998 Professor Gupta started the Business Ethics and Integrity Division of KPMG, India which he led till 2003; he was Senior Advisor to KPMG from 2004–7. During this period he personally audited or oversaw the audits of hundreds of companies, big and small, and also crafted Business Ethics and Business System Manuals for big corporate enterprises, both national and transnational. India's first ever *Business Ethics Survey* was conducted under his supervision in 2000.

Zoya Hasan is Professor at the Jawaharlal Nehru University and Member of the National Commission for Minorities. She has published widely in the areas of state, political processes, parties and movements in India and issues related to disadvantage, discrimination, and affirmative action. Her recent books include *Politics of Inclusion: Castes, minorities and affirmative action* (2009); *Quest for Power: Oppositional movements and post-Congress politics in Uttar Pradesh* (1998); *Unequal Citizens: A study of Muslim women in India* (co-authored, 2004); *Democracy in Muslim Societies: The Asian experience* (2007); *Parties and Party Politics in India* (edited, 2002). She is the Series Editor of *Critical Issues in Indian Politics*, Oxford University Press. She is presently working on a book tentatively titled: *Congress after Indira Gandhi: Limits of centrism in a divided society.*

Anthony Heath is Professor of Sociology at the University of Oxford, a Fellow of Nuffield College and a Fellow of the British Academy. His research interests cover social stratification, ethnicity, electoral behaviour and national identity. His most recent book, *Unequal Chances: Ethnic minorities in Western labour markets* (edited, with Sin Yi Cheung) was published in the Proceedings of the British Academy in 2007. He is currently carrying out projects evaluating the affirmative action programme in Northern Ireland, on the decline of traditional identities in Britain, on ethno-religious diversity and social cohesion, and is working with a team of European colleagues on a comparative study of ethnic minority education. In India he has worked with colleagues at the Centre for the Study of Developing Societies in Delhi on the National Election Studies and was an advisor to the five-nation study of the State of Democracy in South Asia.

Oliver Heath is Lecturer in Politics at Royal Holloway, University of London and was previously a British Academy Postdoctoral Research

Fellow at the University of Essex. His research interests include political stability, voting behaviour and party system change in 'second wave' democracies such as India, and political participation, electoral behaviour and civic engagement in Britain. He worked with Yogendra Yadav at the Centre for the Study of Developing Societies, Delhi, on the Indian election studies and has published articles on Indian and British politics in *Political Behavior*, *Electoral Studies*, the *European Journal of Political Research*, *Economic and Political Weekly* and *Seminar*.

Patricia Jeffery is Professor of Sociology in the University of Edinburgh. Her research interests revolve around aspects of gender politics, including seclusion and marriage arrangement, childbearing and family planning, education, and communal politics. Two current projects are 'Improving the Outcomes of Education for Pro-Poor Development: Breaking the Cycle of Deprivation' (funded by DfID) and 'Tracing Pharmaceuticals in South Asia: regulation, distribution and consumption' (funded by ESRC/DfID). Her recent publications include *Educational Regimes in Contemporary India* (with Radhika Chopra, 2005); *Confronting Saffron Demography: Religion, fertility and women's status in India* (with Roger Jeffery, 2006); and *Degrees without Freedom? Education, masculinities and unemployment in North India* (with Craig Jeffrey and Roger Jeffery, 2008). She has been a member of the Social Science Research Council (New York) and of the American Council of Learned Societies Joint Committee on South Asia. She is currently on the British Academy South Asia Panel.

Roger Jeffery is Professor of Sociology of South Asia in the University of Edinburgh. His research in South Asia since 2000 has included projects on household strategies, schooling regimes and social exclusion in Western UP, demographic change in north India, improving the outcomes of education and tracing pharmaceuticals in South Asia. His recent publications include *The Politics of Health in India* (1988/2009); *Branching Out: Joint forest management in four Indian states* (with Nandini Sundar and Neil Thin, 2001); and *Social and Political Change in Uttar Pradesh: European perspectives* (co-edited, with Jens Lerche, 2003). He is interim Chair of the European Association of South Asian Studies.

Vijay Joshi is a Fellow of St John's College, Oxford and an Emeritus Fellow of Merton College, Oxford. His research interests cover international economics, development economics and Indian economics. His publications on India include three major books: *India's Economic Reforms,*

1991–2001 (co-authored with Ian Little, 1996), *India—Macroeconomics and political economy, 1964–1991* (co-authored with Ian Little, 1994), and *India—The future of economic reform* (co-edited with Robert Cassen, 1995). His previous career has included stints as Economic Adviser to the Ministry of Finance, Government of India, and Special Adviser to the Governor, Reserve Bank of India.

James Manor is the Emeka Anyaoku Professor of Commonwealth Studies in the School of Advanced Study, University of London. He has previously taught at Yale, Harvard and Leicester Universities and at the Institute of Development Studies, University of Sussex. He is the former V. K. R. V. Rao Professor at the Institute for Social and Economic Change in Bangalore, and the former Director of the Institute of Commonwealth Studies, University of London. His most recent book on India (co-authored with E. Raghavan, 2009) is *Broadening and Deepening Democracy: Political innovation in Karnataka*.

Lucia Michelutti is Lecturer at the School of Interdisciplinary Area Studies, University of Oxford and was previously an ESRC Postdoctoral Research Fellow at the London School of Economics. She has worked extensively on local politics, caste, race, religion and democracy in northern India, and more recently in Venezuela. Her monograph *The Vernacularisation of Democracy* (2008) looks at the dynamics of the culture of popular democratic politics in contemporary India. She is currently investigating new forms of revolutionary politics in Latin America and looking at how anti-capitalist discourses have regained power in contemporary times across the globe.

Divya Vaid is an Associate Fellow at *Lokniti*: Programme for Comparative Democracy at the Centre for the Study of Developing Societies, Delhi. Divya's research interests include social stratification, class mobility, educational inequality and political participation. She is currently examining the electoral participation of minority communities in India, in particular the *Adivasis*. Divya was previously a Postdoctoral Associate at the Center for Research on Inequalities and the Life Course, Department of Sociology, Yale University. In her postdoctoral work she used national-level data to analyse trends in educational inequalities by caste, class and gender in India over birth-cohorts. In her D.Phil. (Oxford University, 2007) she explored the patterns and trends of intergenerational class mobility in India. Her dissertation also focused on the relation between social class and caste, and analysed their differing impacts on mobility opportunities.

Yogendra Yadav is a Professor at the Centre for the Study of Developing Societies (CSDS), Delhi, India. His research interests include democratic theory, election studies, survey research, modern Indian political thought and Indian socialism. He is the Founder Convener of the Lokniti Network, and was involved in designing and coordinating the National Election Studies from 1996 to 2004, the largest ever series of academic surveys of the Indian electorate. He is currently the editor of *Samayik Varta*, a monthly journal published in Hindi. He was an advisor to the National Council of Educational Research and Training and was also a member of the Expert Group appointed by the government of India to examine the structure and functioning of an Equal Opportunity Commission.

Preface

We must begin by expressing our thanks to the British Academy for funding and hosting the symposium (in October 2006) out of which the present volume emerged. Our original conference involved papers on the demography, politics and society of contemporary India, but it became clear to us that a major lacuna was the absence of a parallel review of the economy, which has of course been one of the driving forces behind change in modern India. We were therefore delighted when Vijay Joshi and Dipankar Gupta agreed to contribute chapters under very considerable time pressure. Their contributions have been invaluable. James Manor also made some trenchant comments at the symposium, and we were very grateful to him for taking up the challenge of turning these into a concluding chapter for the volume.

We must also thank all our other contributors who patiently listened to our editorial suggestions and (in some cases) went through a considerable number of drafts. In particular, given the inter-disciplinary nature of the volume, we tried to encourage our contributors to make the papers accessible to a non-specialist and broader audience who would not necessarily be familiar with many terms and concepts that Indianists take for granted. We are most grateful for their good-humour and understanding.

We would also wish to thank the many, normally unseen and unheard, assistants who have made our task so much easier. We would like to thank Jane Greig (who organised Anthony Heath's diary so that he actually had time to work on the volume), Sundas Ali (who turned our haphazard references into a consistent bibliography), Colin Baldwin our copyeditor, and the staff at the British Academy.

In the course of editing the chapters and discussing them with the authors, we have learned a great deal ourselves about change and diversity in modern India, and we hope that this has not been a purely selfish exercise but also one that many readers will find enlightening.

Oxford, March 2009
Anthony Heath
Roger Jeffery

1

Incongruities, Ironies and Achievements: India's Tryst with Modernity

ROGER JEFFERY & ANTHONY HEATH

NO-ONE DOUBTS THAT the transformations in Indian society, economy and polity have gathered speed since the early 1990s, and that they are now sufficiently important that Indian modernities—in their economic, political and social aspects—are of central interest to understanding the contemporary world. But agreement over significance is not the same as agreement over diagnosis or prognosis. The interactions among the spheres of economy, society and politics in India provide a potential minefield for those wishing to avoid the stereotypes that dominate public discussion and hinder engagement with a reality that is much more complex. Old clichés—such as 'India is the largest democracy in the world' and that India proves that democracy is compatible with widespread poverty, illiteracy and the lack of a genuine national language—have recently been joined by new ones. The most prominent of these hail India's 'shining' future as it emerges as a global economic powerhouse, and claim that India is now 'poised' to make great leaps forward. But, as Vijay Joshi asks in his chapter in this volume, should we believe 'the media hype that India has now achieved "take-off" into super-fast, self-fulfilling growth that will rapidly abolish poverty, make the country a global economic power, and return it to the position it occupied in the world economy three centuries ago'? Or will India become (or remain) 'a two-tier economy, with all the attendant dangers'? We are presented with images of a vibrant middle class, of sophisticated IT personnel, able to roam the globe in pursuit of pay and status; yet they come from a society where substantial numbers—almost half the population in some states—have had insufficient schooling to be able to read more than very simple texts (See Dyson's chapter in this volume.)

On the basis of new research in different intellectual traditions, this book considers some of the underlying processes that make possible such

Proceedings of the British Academy **159**, 1–18.

contrasting images in the different spheres of demography, economy, social stratification and mobility, and politics. We look both at the national picture, drawing on large-scale authoritative quantitative data that enable us to chart trends over time, and at the micro-level, exploring contemporary processes 'on the ground'. Because of the complex interplay between demographic, economic, social and political change we have invited contributions from all these disciplines. From these analyses we hope to provide a statistical over-view of the transformations underway in Indian society, but also to suggest what these changes mean for ordinary people in their daily lives. Thus, while Dyson, Joshi, Vaid, Heath and Yadav give us sophisticated quantitative treatments of India's changing demography, economy, stratification and party systems respectively, the Jefferys, Gupta, Hasan, Michelutti and Banerjee go behind the statistics in different ways to explore the processes and pressures 'from below' that may be driving the macro processes.

This juxtaposition of macro and micro levels of analysis, of quantitative and qualitative methodologies, does not lend itself to neat conclusions. Instead it often raises new puzzles and challenges. But as James Manor suggests in his concluding chapter, 'India—the most complex society and polity on earth—defies tidy summation, and so must any collection of sophisticated studies of it. The question to ask about such a collection is not whether it can be neatly synthesised (it cannot be), but whether it comes close to capturing the diversity of India.' We hope that the different perspectives offered by the varied papers in this volume will bring that diversity into focus.

Uneven modernisation?

Not surprisingly, India has long been the object of attention for those features of its social structure that appear to make it 'traditional'. Following Edward Said (Said 1978) and others, Ron Inden (1990) and more recently Nick Dirks (2001) have argued that India has been characterised more often in terms of how it differs from the West (assumed to be 'normal') than in its own terms. British colonial scholarship saw India as Hindu, and irredeemably religious in an other-worldly sense (see also Weber (1920/1958), who saw the underlying ethos of the caste system as a major hindrance to an indigenous development of capitalism). Since Independence, sociologists and anthropologists have tended to reinforce this representation rather than undermine it, by focusing on the village, caste and religion rather than factories, offices, towns and scientific institutions. India is still predominantly 'rural' (even allowing for misleading census definitions on this score), but it is clearly not enough to look at villages without also seeing the mass media, advertising, political links, religious reform movements and social networks—almost all 'urban' and in some senses 'modern'—that bind the rural and the urban together.

But what does it mean to be modern in contemporary India? Modernisation theories, of course, have their problems, and Indian authors —like other contemporary writers on social change in India—have taken contrasting positions on what modernity might mean for Indian society. Indian experiences of modernity have often been made to appear 'defective, blocked, still in transition, fundamentally "other"—and therefore beyond the scope of modernization theory—or schizoid—split between different arenas of experience, modern at work and pre-modern at home (following Singer 1972)' (Osella and Osella 2006: 570). The classic early contribution of Suzanne and Lloyd Rudolph spawned vigorous discussions of the 'modernity of Indian tradition'—with specific reference to the transformations of caste relationships (Rudolph and Rudolph 1967). Whilst one solution has been to claim that there are 'multiple modernities' (see, e.g. Eisenstadt 2000: 23–4), there have been few convincing empirical accounts of what these might be.

Dipankar Gupta has characterised the most common response by the Indian middle classes to any questioning of an Indian modernity: to stress India's material progress (how many cars, how much electricity consumed) or to draw attention to the moral decay of Western modernity (how many 'love' marriages, how much divorce, how little familial support for the elderly) (Gupta 2001: 12–13). Gupta's understanding of a universal modernity against which much of Indian life can be tried—and largely fail—rests on a combination of Parsons (achievement rather than ascription, and the adherence to universalistic norms), Rawls on intersubjectivity, and the ideals of liberal democracy. Satish Deshpande, on the other hand, has criticised such accounts and representations of modernity in India for defining modernity teleologically (Deshpande 2004).

In attempting to avoid these pitfalls, some writers have focused instead on how modernity is understood as an everyday term by social actors in India. T. K. Oommen, for example, sees modernity as a banner of particular social groups in their responses to contemporary discontents. He argues that movements against religious and caste elites in India preceded class-based movements, and have largely been incomplete, thus leaving issues of equality and identity as yet unresolved (Oommen 2004). As Craig Jeffrey and others also argue, drawing on Mosse (2003),

> recent accounts of educated un/under-employment in the global south point to the key importance of notions of 'modernity' and 'tradition' in young men's cultural styles. At almost the precise moment when scholars have come to critique concepts such as modern/traditional, urban/rural, developed/undeveloped as frameworks for academic thought, young people in situations of economic threat are often using these very categories to reflect on experiences, express aspirations, and signal social differences. (Jeffrey, Jeffery, and Jeffery 2008: 15)

Satish Deshpande cites a slogan painted on the back of a Delhi bus in 1996: his translation reads 'They should realize that we too are modern' (with '*modern*' being the word used in the original Hindi) and he notes the claim's earlier appearance in a TV advertisement (Deshpande 1999: 33). Similarly, the ethnographic research of Caroline and Filippo Osella has contrasted informants' narratives (produced by migrants from Kerala to the Gulf) that talk about what 'the modern' means to them, with classic modernisation analyses (Osella and Osella 2006). The Osellas argue that 'informants' life-stories suggest a different framework for analysis, pointing towards modernity as a singular—unified and global—phenomenon which is multi-centric and locally nuanced' (p. 570 see also Sivaramakrishnan and Agrawal 2003).

In respect of some key structural terms, however, India is becoming 'modern' in fairly standard ways, as Tim Dyson shows in this volume. Demographically speaking, and acknowledging considerable regional variations, this means mortality and fertility rates that are rapidly approaching the levels of industrial and post-industrial societies. In world-historical terms, these shifts are dramatic: within two generations since Independence, life expectancies at birth have risen from 27 to over 60, and the total fertility rate of Indian women has dropped from 5.9 to 3.5 (Dyson, this volume). In principle, these shifts offer the prospect of what is sometimes known as a 'demographic dividend': a period when the entry of a 'boom generation' into working age provides an opportunity to unleash an economic growth spurt, provided the right kinds of policies are in place to ensure that the extra workers are productively employed (Bloom, Canning, and Sevilla 2003).

As Dyson also shows, however, these shifts towards 'modern' family patterns have been very uneven geographically, with considerably higher life expectancy and smaller family sizes in south India than in much of the north. This in turn could have major political and social implications.

In 2001, the population of the big states of the Indo-Gangetic plain—Punjab, Haryana, Rajasthan, Uttar Pradesh (UP), Bihar, Madhya Pradesh (MP) and Jharkhand—constituted 411 out of India's 1,027 million (40 per cent) and the four southern states—Kerala, Karnataka, Tamil Nadu and Andhra Pradesh—constituted 233 million or 23 per cent. But they are growing at very different rates, about 2 per cent per year in the north and 1 per cent in the south. Within twenty years, differences in growth rates of this scale might well tilt the demographic balance further towards states that are poorer and seen as more 'backward' than those of the rest of the country. Migration between states—whether short-term, seasonal, or for longer periods—is unlikely to make a major contribution to rebalancing, despite the absence of any formal barriers to movement.

The seat-shares of different states in the Lok Sabha (the Indian lower House of Parliament) were set by the population distribution of 1971 and have been frozen since then. But this solution will become increasingly untenable. In the foreseeable future, the demographic weight of the country will continue to lie in these north Indian states, whose politics are increasingly different from those of the south, west and east, as we discuss later.

There are also other major regional demographic differences, in particular with respect to sex ratios and what they may tell us about differences in the ways men and women are valued in different parts of India. For a long time India has been one of those unusual countries with a surplus of males. In the late nineteenth century, in British and Princely India, female infanticide was said to be practised among particular dominant landed castes, but strong governmental action seemed to have stamped out the practice before 1900. Nonetheless, in many parts of northern India, the sex ratio at birth has remained more masculine than in most other parts of the world. Furthermore, age-specific mortality rates have suggested that girls were more vulnerable to childhood illnesses than boys, leading to juvenile sex ratios (females per 1,000 males under the age of 10) well below parity. The arrival of new technologies in the 1970s (amniocentesis using ultrasound) made it possible to ascertain the sex of the foetus from about thirteen weeks, and concerns about misuse of these technologies led to legislation banning pre-natal foetal sex determination.

Despite these moves, by the 2001 Census sex ratios for children aged 6 or less were 819 girls per 1,000 boys in Haryana and 798 in Punjab, compared to 960 in Kerala and 942 in Tamil Nadu. Some authors see a 'diagonal divide' across the country, with the south and east showing few differences in the life-chances of boys and girls, and as a result, having sex ratios for juveniles that are fairly 'normal' (Bhat and Zavier 2007). Others suggest that the 'divide' is breaking down, as sex ratios in southern states (such as Tamil Nadu) move towards those of northern states, and outside the 'normal' range (Srinivasan and Bedi 2009). Not only in Punjab, Haryana, UP and Rajasthan is it possible to see the results of attempts to discover the sex of the baby *in utero*, to manipulate the sex ratio at birth by aborting females among couples who already have a daughter, and then, through relative neglect, if nothing more active is involved, allowing more girls to die in childhood. In the demographic sphere too, then, what is often seen as a 'modern' social trait—planning small family sizes in order to invest in the quality of child-rearing—is inflected in India (as in China) by a continuing preference for boys, predicated on the costs of the dowry that must accompany a new bride and continue to be given well into her married life, and on the old-age support and residence norms that prioritise the links between a man and his parents over those of a woman and hers. We cannot represent what is happening anywhere in India as a simple process of demographic modernisation.

The economy is often seen as the major motor of modernisation. In the second half of India's post-independence career to date, growth has increased dramatically as a consequence of economic reform, which has unshackled the economy from the grip of controls and exposed it to international competition. As Joshi shows in his chapter, however, there are still several impediments to sustained rapid growth. Moreover, Joshi argues that the *quality* of India's growth is flawed. It has been relatively 'jobless' and, as a consequence, India risks becoming a two-tier economy. Growing wealth in the upper tier, and continuing deprivation in the lower tier, is a potentially explosive combination. The most daunting challenge that India faces, therefore, is the employment problem, the reverse side of the demographic dividend.

As Dyson shows, India's working-age population is growing rapidly. There will be a huge addition—of about 200 million people—to the 15–64 age-groups between 2005 and 2020. This figure is a good approximation to the likely increase in the labour force over the period (on the plausible assumption that an increase in the participation rate of women will be offset by more young people staying on in education). But, as Joshi argues, the employment picture for these people is dismal. Between 1995 and 2005, total employment (organised plus unorganised) just about kept pace with labour-force growth, but in the organised sector, employment is utterly stagnant. Jobs are being produced only in the informal, unorganised sector. Many of these are purely notional jobs of low quality.

A crucial reason for the exacerbation of the employment problem is that the transfer of labour from agriculture to industry has barely happened in India. This is reflected in the very modest increase from 1965 to 2005 in the share of industry and manufacturing in national output—in sharp contrast to other fast-growing economies in east Asia, where this share more than doubled. East Asian industrial expansion was rapid but, crucially, it was also powered by the growth of the manufactured exports sector, employing large numbers of people. India, by contrast, appears to be trying to skip the stage of labour-intensive industrialisation; as Vaid and Heath argue in their chapter, India shows an incongruous occupational structure, with a substantial 'salariat' coexisting with a huge agricultural sector and a relatively modest industrial working class.

India's recent industrial growth has been capital- and skill-intensive. Many of India's most dynamic industrial companies and sectors create few jobs. True, the services sector, now 51 per cent of GDP, has grown fast but its growth has also been 'jobless', which suggests that it has been skilled-labour-intensive. An example is the information technology (IT) sector. This has achieved international success, but it cannot provide the answer to India's employment problem: as Joshi shows in his chapter the output of the IT sector is merely 2.5 per cent of GDP. The sector currently employs only around one million people; by 2015, it may employ three million. But by then India's labour force will have grown by around sixty-five million and (as Dyson shows) much of the rise will occur in 'backward' states. The IT sector cannot answer the employment needs of millions of poorly educated people in rural and small-town north and east India. Nor do its values show signs of spreading to major parts of exporting enterprises, in the small-scale sector. As Gupta's chapter in this volume shows, even where external pressures for 'ethical' sourcing have been determinedly pushed forward, the effects on employment conditions have been very limited.

The story that Joshi tells, then, is one of lopsided growth and uneven modernisation. India's economy has highly modern elements coexisting with a huge and much less modernised agricultural sector. 'Modern' societies are also, as Daniel Lerner put it many years ago, 'mobile' societies (Lerner 1962, 1968) in which ascriptive factors such as caste, ethnicity, religion or social background play a decreasing role in determining one's life chances, thus delivering a degree of equality of opportunity. Yet, until Vaid and Heath's chapter in this volume, there has been very little research systematically exploring the effect, if any, of increasing modernisation and development on patterns of social mobility and inequality in the country.

Vaid and Heath distinguish a variety of ways in which modernisation might operate in the Indian context and might lead to increased equality of opportunity and social mobility. Economic reform and marketisation might be expected to eliminate discrimination, whether on gender, caste or class lines, since discrimination essentially means hiring a less productive worker from a favoured category (e.g. upper-caste men) in preference to a more productive worker from a disfavoured set (e.g. lower-caste women). Competition should mean that inefficient firms will be driven out by efficient ones, and hence firms will either have to eliminate discrimination against disfavoured groups or face the consequences of inefficient recruitment practices, and risk being driven out of business (or being unable to expand). Competitive market pressures can therefore be expected to be associated with greater equality of opportunity and this implies that the greatest improvements over time in equality of opportunity would be in those sectors most exposed to competitive market forces. This in turn suggests that trends towards increasing equality of opportunity might be most visible in the urbanised and more 'modern' sectors of the economy.

Another possibility (again discussed by Max Weber) is that the gradual extension of formal bureaucracies with formalised recruitment and promotion practices is the main driver of equality of opportunity. This suggests that it is the kinds of recruitment practice that employers use that are crucial, and that formal impersonal and transparent systems (typical of the German or British civil service in Weber's day, for example), will tend to be most associated with equality of opportunity. We might therefore expect rather little change in equality of opportunity over time in India since (as Joshi demonstrates), India's growth and modernisation have not been accompanied by any major expansion of the formal economy. We would not expect any decline in inequality of opportunity in the informal sector since (as Gupta's chapter reminds us) small businesses run on informal lines might continue to use informal recruitment practices, hiring workers on the basis of personal ties and word of mouth.

Vaid and Heath do indeed show considerably more 'openness' in the non-agricultural than in the agricultural sector of the economy. Their evidence also suggests that elements of Indian society have been relatively 'modern' for some considerable time. They argue, for example, contrary to expectations, that throughout the period since Independence father's *class* rather than his *caste* has been the stronger determining factor for access to salaried class destinations. But they find only the merest hints of increasing openness over time. In this respect, then, they provide very little support for any claim that India is 'modernising' (as a process) in this sphere.

Western writers dealing with equality of opportunity have largely focused on the role of social class background. The key debates have been about how far social class origins continue to influence educational and occupational attainment. In the Indian context, however, caste and caste-oriented educational and public-sector employment reservations have been the major focus of policy, though many scholars and activists have argued that class should have been the focus instead. Whatever the merits of the argument, though, Independent India has seen the implementation of reservation first for the Scheduled Castes (ex-Untouchables, now often known as *Dalits*, or oppressed) and Scheduled Tribes (sometimes known as *Adivasis* or original inhabitants). Later, reservations were added for Other Backward Classes (OBCs) (where the C literally stands for classes but in practice refers to castes). Overall, then, this provides another reason why we might not expect that class-based inequalities of opportunity in India will move towards 'modern' patterns, since the policy focus has been elsewhere.

The sphere of politics

As Joshi argues in this volume, 'There is no doubt that a consistent economic package can be designed which would maintain rapid growth, create employment and eliminate poverty. But in order to deliver it India's political class will have to walk successfully the tightrope of implementing reform while balancing diverse interests and managing the compulsions of mass politics.'

How far can we put flesh on the bones of the frequently reiterated claim that India is 'the largest democracy in the world'? If voting is the test, the figures speak for themselves: high and stable turnout, spread across age-groups and social classes in ways that other democracies would love to match; non-violent transfers of power on a regular basis after national and state-level elections, with only one occasion when the electoral process was delayed (the Emergency of June 1975 to March 1977, when many democratic rights were suspended). As Mukulika Banerjee says in this volume, 'elections are the most sacrosanct, secular, universal, public rite of modern India' and the Election Commission of India is, on this basis, credited with organising the largest event in the world, with

800,000 polling stations and an electorate of over 650 million for general elections. The Election Commission marshals a gigantic task force for each country-wide general election: nearly five million polling personnel and civil police forces. This huge election machinery is deemed to be on deputation to the Election Commission and is subject to its control, superintendence and discipline during the election period, for around eight weeks.

But the efficiency and honesty (in comparison to many other countries) with which the elections are organised sits oddly with Indians' own understandings of the increasingly corrupt and dishonest people elected by these processes. In contrast to many other spheres of Indian social life, the realm of politics is one where those previously regarded as lowly outsiders have forced their way in to take dominant positions. What Yogendra Yadav, Christophe Jaffrelot and others have denoted the 'second democratic upsurge' (after the transformations following Independence) took place in the 1980s and 1990s (Jaffrelot 2003; Yadav 2000). In the heyday of Congress dominance, lower caste groups were often represented by members of the higher castes, or were granted little more than token roles themselves. Since the early 1980s, however, members of these castes—often poorly educated, with agricultural or poor urban backgrounds—have developed their own political parties and gained power themselves in many states. Zoya Hasan's paper in this volume contextualises some of the arguments that accompanied legislative reform in two moments when this transformation became salient: Mandal 1 (in 1990) and Mandal 2 (from 2006).[1] Members of many 'forward castes' now see public service as irredeemably undermined by inefficiency, and the realm of politics as irretrievably corrupted by muscle power and criminality, associated with those from 'below the salt'. Outsiders—Dalits, OBCs, farmers, criminals—are epitomised by the example of Lalu Prasad Yadav, who (despite a criminal record that disqualified him from continuing as Chief Minister of the state of Bihar, a post he held from 1990–7), was Railways Minister in the Central Government from 2004–9. In UP, the dominant political actors since 1990 are Mulayam Singh Yadav (an OBC) and Mayavati (a Dalit woman). Mulayam Singh heads a party, the *Samajwadi* Party (Socialist Party, or SP), widely known to be the party of the Yadavs: Lucia Michelutti's paper in this volume shows in detail what it means to be a Yadav in one of the heartland UP areas controlled by the caste.

[1] Named after B. P. Mandal, the chair of a commission on OBCs that reported in 1980, but whose recommendations are still being raked over, nearly thirty years on.

Mayavati, elected Chief Minister of UP in 2007 with an almost unprecedented absolute majority in the State Assembly for her *Bahujan Samaj* Party (Majority People's Party, or BSP) has crafted a coalition of social support behind the unquestionable leadership of Dalits—especially those from the largest UP caste, the Chamars.

These upsurges in lower caste political empowerment have not been replicated to the same degree elsewhere in India, however, as Oliver Heath and Yogendra Yadav show in this volume. In MP and Rajasthan, coalitions led by the right-wing Hindu party, the *Bharatiya Janata* Party (Indian People's Party, or BJP) have exchanged rule with the cross-caste Congress Party. Since 1977, West Bengal has remained under the dominance of a coalition led by the Communist Party of India (Marxist) (CPM) that in terms of the social origins of its leadership, remains determinedly *bhadralok*, or middle-class intellectual (see Banerjee, this volume). West Bengal is the only state where political party membership is relatively widespread, fairly permanent, and enforced by strong intra-party discipline: elsewhere, with the partial exception of Kerala and Tamil Nadu, party membership is unstable, and almost irrelevant between elections. Regional dimensions also remain highly germane to voting patterns. In south India (Karnataka, Andhra, Tamil Nadu and Kerala) and, to a lesser extent, Maharashtra and Gujarat in western India, manifestos of efficient government have had much more electoral salience. But, in different ways, the BJP and other right-wing parties have also managed to make political inroads by playing up the significance of communal divisions—Muslims and Christians alike have been targeted (symbolically, but increasingly also physically) as being, in some senses, anti-national.

Adivasis remain largely outside the political mainstream, but caste barriers in the political sphere are being gradually undermined. The same cannot be said for exclusion on the basis of religion—especially for Muslims (see Sachar 2006). To some extent, this results from the conscious policies of what are known as the 'family' of the Hindu Right, those political parties (centrally, the BJP), social movements and pressure groups associated with the *Rashtriya Swayamsevak Sangh* (RSS or National Volunteer Corps). Whilst these have been visible in Indian politics since the 1920s, their significance has grown dramatically since the mid 1970s. The Hindu Right was part of the opposition coalition that emerged after Indira Gandhi's 'Emergency' to win the 1977 elections but which collapsed within two years. For a while it appeared that the Hindu Right was more severely hurt by this collapse than the other parties. By the mid-1980s, however, it re-emerged as the BJP, a forceful proponent of *Hindutva* (an attempt to fuse 'being Hindu' with 'being Indian'). Its allies, the *Vishwa Hindu Parishad* (VHP) and their associated women's and youth organisations, spearheaded a campaign to remove the Babari Masjid (a sixteenth-century mosque in Ayodhya), claiming that it was built over the birthplace of the Hindu god Ram. Their supporters demolished the mosque in 1992 and anti-Muslim riots flared around India.[2] A coalition led by the BJP was in power in UP from 1997–2002, and its leader was the Indian Prime Minister from 1998–2004 in a coalition government.

During the 1980s and 1990s, the Hindu Right echoed allegations repeatedly made in Hindu nationalist discourse since the early twentieth century that Muslims constitute a threat to the 'Hindu community' (P. K. Datta 1999). Hindu nationalist claims have focused *inter alia* on purported Muslim expansionism through invasions, forced conversions, and the abduction of Hindu women, and have characterised Muslim men as militant, sexually predatory, and a danger to India's integrity (Bacchetta 1994; Gupta 2002: 222–320; Jaffrelot 1996; Pandey 1990). This discourse also portrays Indian Muslims as potential traitors, with Pakistan (or occasionally, Bangladesh) as countries that can call on their 'natural' loyalty (Gupta and Sharma 1996; Jaffrelot 1996: 338 ff.). At the level of electoral success, the BJP has rarely managed to persuade a majority of voters to support them: but in a Westminster-style, first-past-the-post system, they need little more than one-third of the votes to gain power. At the level of taken-for-granted suspicions of Muslim untrustworthiness and potential threat, however, many more Indians have been persuaded by the anti-Muslim propaganda. Muslims find it hard to buy or rent property in 'Hindu' areas; and they are massively under-represented in senior positions in Government and in the private sector (Hasan, this volume). Muslims are often perceived as being somehow responsible for bombings or attacks (such as those in Mumbai in December 2008) that have been caused by (or are blamed on) terrorists of one hue or another who are also Muslim—even when many miles away from an event, and despite their vehement condemnation of those carrying them out.

[2] On the Ayodhya affair and the communalisation of politics in contemporary India, see Basu and Kohli (1998); Jaffrelot (1996); Jeffery and Basu (1998); Ludden (1996). The Ayodhya affair became prominent in late 1990, and was used by the Hindu Right to mobilise support when it feared the possible effects of the Mandal Report (see Zoya Hasan's paper in this volume) might undermine its position.

The publication of the Sachar Committee report in late 2006 marked a watershed in discussions of the position of Muslims in contemporary India. Sachar reported that Muslims in contemporary India are, on the whole, worse off than OBCs: for instance, in regard to levels of poverty, living conditions, access to secure and well-paid employment and achievements in formal education (Sachar 2006: 237). On some indicators and in some states (particularly the large Muslim-minority states of West Bengal, Bihar, UP and Assam) 'the situation [of Muslims] is particularly grave' (Sachar 2006: 237). The detailed tables in the Appendices to the Report show that on some educational indicators—such as proportions of the population completing at least Middle School (8th grade)—levels for Muslims in UP and West Bengal are now well below those for Dalits and Adivasis. Elsewhere in north India, Muslims are still somewhat better placed on these indicators than Dalits and Adivasis, but the differentials are shrinking fast (Sachar 2006: 297–8). On economic indicators in different parts of the country, Muslims also appear to be on average poorer than other sections of the population, and their relative position is generally worsening through time (see John and Mutatkar 2005: 1341; Sachar 2006: 158–60; and Shariff 1995). In addition, the report draws attention to many misconceptions in the public understanding of aspects of Muslim everyday life in India, for example by noting the relatively small proportion of Muslim children who rely wholly on *madrasahs* for their formal education.

In more general terms, and often showing continuities with the Congress governments of 1937,[3] the state and its various institutions have displayed 'banal Hinduism' (akin to the 'banal nationalism' identified in Billig 1995). Despite claims to secularism, made most prominently by Congress politicians, public institutions—such as schools, hospitals, offices and factories—have embodied a Hindu character in taken-for-granted ways: school assemblies, the temples and shrines attached to many public buildings, the celebration of festivals, all these have been introduced on the assumption that the pupils, staff, patients, employees etc. are Hindu. This is not surprising, given that even on the most restricted of definitions (i.e. excluding Dalits and Adivasis from the

[3] This has been argued persuasively by Gould (2002) who shows that Congressmen engaged with Hindu nationalism in the 1930s and 1940s for both strategic and cultural reasons. Two good examples are their espousal of Hindi rather than Urdu, which was interpreted as being a coded support for a 'Hindu Raj'; and their introduction of Hindu prayers into the government schools, under the cloak of Gandhian 'basic schools'.

'Hindu' group) about half of all Indians would count themselves as Hindu. But the implication is that 'Others' are not fully entitled to state benefits and facilities—an assumption that lies in part, for example, behind how Muslim, Dalit and Adivasi women are treated when they try to access Government medical facilities (Jeffery, Jeffery, and Rao 2007: see also Jeffery and Jeffery in this volume).

The patterns of social exclusion thus generated are not single-variable based, of course. The everyday and institutionalised communalism of the local state interacts with everyday and institutionalised sexism, so that state services have been delivered in ways which seriously disadvantaged all women, but especially poor women from the Scheduled Tribes and minority communities: what has been called 'gendered, institutionalized communalism' (Jeffery and Jeffery 2006: 95). As men have competed over the allocation of public resources, their own women as well as those from 'Other' groups tended to be excluded. As Heath and Yadav argue in this volume, then, the decline of Congress dominance has not led to the 'individualistic, cleavageless politics that has evolved in the West', rather

> the decline of the initial 'national' electoral foundation established at the onset of mass democracy has made way to social cleavages that perhaps bear more similarity to the Lipset–Rokkan model than they did earlier. Whether these cleavages persist in the future remains to be seen. Economic and social development may gradually weaken their hold, as they did in the West, but the current extent of poverty and inequality that exists throughout much of India suggests that this may still be some way off.

Reform and the Indian economy, society & politics, 1990 to 2010

Bringing OBCs and Dalits into the political fold, while leaving them (and Muslims) largely marginal to the economic benefits of economic growth, raises issues of how far individuals from different social categories and cultural markers can claim citizenship rights and make positive contributions as Indians. But concentrating on the realm of politics, and of democracy in particular, draws attention away from concerns about how the state—in its enabling and providing as well as in its exclusionary and punitive roles—differentiates amongst its citizens. Recent ethnographic work on the Indian state challenges the idea that theorising around the 'master concept' of the state is the sole or best route to more sophisticated understandings of its nature in contemporary India (Khilnani 1997). In the collection edited by Fuller and Bénéï, for example, several writers explore '. . . what the state variously means and does for people in India today' (Fuller and Harriss 2000: 10) through such diverse and routine manifestations of state activity on the ground as *anganwadi* (crèche) workers, land registry officers, District Commissioners' offices and health extension and hospital workers (Corbridge *et al.* 2005; Gupta 1993). Seeing the state as constituted from dispersed sites of activity not only enables ethnographic study of the state but also challenges any notion of the state as a unified actor; the state becomes visible rather as a range of actors and activities in pursuit of different and often conflicting ends. Above all, everyday perspectives on the state break down any easy dichotomies between 'state' and 'citizens' or 'civil society'. As Osella and Osella comment, 'the state is composed of people, and . . . analytical models which start from dualistic categories are bound to posit distance and overlook the quotidian intimacy of the state' (Osella and Osella 2000: 157). We need models that 'acknowledge networks of patronage, personalized relationships and shared cultural practices that link the state differentially to the people it is supposed to serve' (Jeffery and Jeffery 2006: 97).

Unfortunately, the everyday workings of local state institutions have not been given much attention in accounts of the Indian state.[4] General discussions of the operations of lower-level state functionaries (extension workers, health workers and teachers, for example) are either managerial in emphasis or concerned mainly with their role in factional and party politics and the class biases exposed in their patterns of work. More recent ethnographic literature on the Indian state tried to remedy this lack, and raises the issue of the nature of the distinction for individual Government workers between their roles as public servants on the one hand and as private individuals 'concerned with their position in their own social world' (Fuller and Harriss 2000: 13) on the other. Akhil Gupta uses the collapse of this distinction in practice to question more generally the adequacy for India of the Western-derived dichotomy between state and civil society. Whilst Gupta does not detail the substantive private interests pursued by the government employees amongst his informants, such phenomena lend themselves easily to explorations of corruption (Gupta 1993). Previous explanations of corruption in India—that it was

[4] See, e.g. Vanaik (1990). Of more general political discussions, Kohli (1987) is unusual in taking seriously the developmental activities of the Indian states; but he too is primarily concerned with their regional, caste and class dimensions and virtually ignores community and gender.

a by-product of the excessive controls and licences that restricted private enterprise and empowered government functionaries—seem no longer to apply, given the rolling back of such controls since 1990. Despite these reforms, however, the chimera of an efficient, transparent bureaucracy remains tantalisingly out of sight (Editorial 2009).

In the 1990s and 2000s, this multifaceted and somewhat incoherent state has been challenged in two very different ways. From one side, under promptings from neo-liberal advocates of the appropriate role to be played by the public sector, it has been under pressure to downsize, to abdicate responsibility for economic activities, and to reduce its interventions into market processes. Reform packages (such as that funded by the World Bank in UP, entitled the 'Uttar Pradesh Fiscal Reform and Public Sector Restructuring Loan/Credit'), have been designed to:

> strengthen the long-term process of reorienting government towards its core functions and reducing its role in the economy, improving civil service efficiency and strengthening fiscal management and financial accountability. (World Bank 2000: 4)

On the other hand, the World Bank, along with other donors, such as DFID, USAID and the European Union, has encouraged a deepening of government involvement in social welfare schemes—presumably working to a theory that places these as part of the 'core functions' of the state. Since the mid-1990s, but with more political support since the United Progressive Alliance Government (a coalition led by Congress) came to power nationally in 2004, several programmes have been designed to strengthen the welfare state—ironically, at just the same time that other processes have tended to undermine the possibilities that Government programmes might make a serious dent in patterns of poverty and social exclusion. The earliest of these projects targeted primary schooling. Known as the District Primary Education Programme, it focused on states where large numbers of children (especially, girls) were out of school, or failing to complete 5 years of schooling. In 2000, reflecting in part global programmes attempting to achieve Education for All, the Indian programme was renamed *Sarva Shiksha Abhiyan* (Complete Education Programme). International donors have contributed ideas and support, but most of the funding has come from the central Government. New school buildings have been erected, old ones refurbished, new teaching materials have been supplied, and states have been supported to employ extra teachers—but only on contracts with markedly inferior rights to those of existing teachers.

More recent programmes have attempted to contribute to reductions in child poverty and to raise school registrations, through (among other things) enhanced school meals programmes in every state; a National Rural Health Mission (NRHM); and (perhaps the most ambitious of all) the National Rural Employment Guarantee Scheme (NREGS). Amongst the many projects associated with the NRHM are incentives to encourage all pregnant women (some twenty-five million each year) to give birth in hospitals or other medical institutions, most of which are in the public sphere (see Jeffery and Jeffery in this volume). The NREGS also involves huge numbers: thirty-five million households provided with employment for some part of the year, to a total of 1,397 million person-days, 31 per cent for Dalits, and 24 per cent to Adivasis, nearly half being work for women ([http://nrega.nic.in/], accessed 3 February 2009). Like many other employment guarantee schemes, most of its benefits tend to go to those at the bottom of the economic hierarchy, since others are unwilling to do the hard physical labour required for enrolment in the scheme. But the programme has further goals: to increase transparency in government programmes (following from the success of right to information campaigns, especially those developed in Rajasthan) and to encourage bank deposits and other mechanisms to reduce corruption and to give the poor a stake in the banking system (Drèze and Khera 2008).

In other words, in the spheres of education, health and social welfare, the Government of India is attempting to extend its reach and deepen its relationships with its citizens. Yet, at the same time, its commitments to those citizens in terms of economic ties are under ideological and budgetary attack (see Joshi, this volume). These somewhat contradictory processes shed further light on the intractability and centrality of the state for Indian society.

The state in India has many attractions for powerful social groups. At the most basic level, the state provides subsidies to agricultural inputs, such as power, fertilisers and credit, which would prove costly in political terms were any party to propose to remove them. The state offers some opportunities for stable jobs on good financial and other terms—because most public sector employees still have status and job security. Many public sector jobs also offer the chance to earn rents or 'over-income', by exploiting opportunities to take bribes, or misappropriating public resources. Since so few jobs are being created by the particular form of economic growth that has characterised the Indian economy since the early 1990s, those in the public sector are heavily competed for, and may be as often allocated for political reasons, or in response to corrupt practices, as on the basis of merit. The press often report how many thousands have appeared for the examinations that are the start of a process—often lasting a year or more—that will lead to the appointment of fewer than one hundred posts. Even in the IT business, 25,000 jobs in Infosys can attract one and a half million applicants, offering them a less-than-2 per cent chance of success (Giridharadas 2006). In the public sector, the stakes may be higher. In a cause célèbre in UP, nearly 18,000 appointments to the state police forces were annulled by the new Chief Minister, Mayawati, in September 2007, on the grounds that they were political appointments (often from the same caste as the previous Chief Minister, Mulayam Singh Yadav) (Press Trust of India 2007). Thus, even though the state has not been the main provider of employment prospects, the imagined opportunities it offers still feed the political disputes that dominate media debates and everyday discussion.

Conclusion

This brings us full circle from the start of this introduction: the divergent trajectories of those with economic, social or cultural capital, compared with those with only transient and unreliable political clout—between the members of what Partha Chatterjee calls civil and political society (Chatterjee 2001). In their very different ways, all the contributions to this book grapple with these issues. In combination, the insights they render—whether into social mobility, how elections are organised, or how it feels to be marginalised from central social institutions—go a long way in challenging simple stereotypes and unhelpful dichotomies. Zoya Hasan's paper in this volume reminds us that these understandings are not of merely academic significance: they may have policy relevance, to find 'different and new means to bridge disparities and deepen social equality' and to help India avoid the bitter and violent struggles that have characterised much change in these directions elsewhere in the world—and in some parts of India as well. As James Manor suggests, Indian social change has seen many 'incongruities—painful ironies amid remarkable achievements' including the gradualism (in polity, society and economy) that has long characterised transformations in Indian society. We hope this volume will make a further contribution to the endeavour to make sense of India's tryst with modernity.

2

Growing Regional Variation: Demographic Change and its Implications

TIM DYSON

Summary. India has seen considerable demographic change during recent decades—with major falls in death rates and declines in fertility. Until quite recently, however, the country's rate of population growth remained fairly stable. Differences in the timing of demographic change—especially in relation to fertility decline—mean that population growth rate differentials between the country's major regions are actually rather larger now than they generally were in the past. Against this backcloth, and partly with respect to the future, this chapter examines recent demographic change in India and its major states. The subjects covered include mortality, fertility and population growth, as well as trends in age structure and urbanisation. The chapter considers some of the principal factors that have conditioned these changes and discusses some of their socio-economic, political and other implications.

Introduction

INDIA'S POPULATION IN OCTOBER 2006 was probably in the vicinity of 1,150 million.[1] This population, one sixth of humankind, is growing at

[1] This figure makes some allowance for under-enumeration in the 2001 census and subsequent population growth. The Symposium at the British Academy was held in October 2006. Therefore, unless otherwise stated, that is the reference date used in this paper. It should be stressed that all of the numbers cited here are approximate. My concern is not in discussing what are usually relatively small differences between different estimates, but rather in giving a reasonably

Proceedings of the British Academy **159**, 19–46.

approximately 1.6 per cent per year—implying a current net annual addition of around 17–18 million people. The census in 2011 will almost certainly provide a population total that is close to 1.2 billion. The country's crude birth and death rates are probably around 24 and 8 per thousand respectively. However, the birth rate is falling at an appreciable rate because of declining fertility, while the death rate is falling more slowly. In the recent past, therefore, the country entered a period in which its rate of population growth will continue to decline. Even so, demographic projections suggest strongly that by 2025 the population will be around 1.4 billion, and that by mid-century it may be around 1.6 billion. The population projections of the United Nations indicate that around the year 2030 India may overtake China to become the most populous country in the world.[2]

With this as background, the purpose of this paper is to provide a picture of demographic and related change in contemporary India—one that also takes some account of the country's great diversity. Since demographic changes tend to occur relatively slowly, the picture must sometimes be assembled with reference to information stretching back over several decades. Given the size of the subject, some degree of selectivity is inevitable. Both causes and consequences of population change will be addressed.

The paper has four parts. The first reviews demographic trends at the national level. Then, due to the country's size and diversity, the second does the same at the regional level, i.e. for the major states. The third part of the paper discusses some of the likely consequences of current population trends. The paper's final part summarises the main conclusions and comments on recent work that has tried to explain demographic change.

National trends

Contemporary demographic change in India must be seen within the context of the country's overall demographic transition (see Table 2.1). During the first half of the twentieth century both the birth and the death

---

reliable picture of the general situation. For a more detailed examination of the causes and consequences of demographic change in India, see Dyson, Cassen and Visaria (2004).

[2] The UN medium variant projection for India yields figures for 2025 and 2030 respectively of 1,395 and 1,449 million; the corresponding figures for China (excluding Hong Kong and the Macao Special Administrative Region) are 1,441 and 1,446 million (see United Nations 2005).

Table 2.1. Summary demographic estimates for India 1901–2001.

Period/ Year	Population (millions)	Increment per decade (millions)	Average annual growth rate (%)	Crude death rate (per 1,000)	Crude birth rate (per 1,000)	Life expectancy at birth (years)		Total fertility rate (TFR) (births per woman)	Per cent urban
						Male	Female		
(i)	(ii)	(iii)	(iv)	(v)	(vi)	(vii)	(viii)	(ix)	(x)
1901	238	—	—	—	—	—	—	—	10.8
1951	361	25	0.83	37.2	45.6	27.4	27.8	5.86	17.3
1961	439	78	1.96	25.9	45.5	36.8	36.6	6.11	18.0
1971	548	109	2.22	21.3	43.5	44.0	43.0	6.50	19.9
1981	683	135	2.20	16.0	38.0	50.0	49.0	5.40	23.3
1991	846	163	2.14	13.6	35.0	55.5	56.0	4.60	25.7
2001	1,029	183	1.94	9.3	28.2	60.8	62.3	3.50	27.8

Notes: Except for columns (ii) and (x), all the figures shown pertain to periods. For the first period (i.e. 1901–51) the figures given are averages of estimates for the five intercensal decades.

Sources: All the numbers are derived from census data. The principal source of the mortality and fertility estimates is Bhat (1989), but for further details see Dyson, Cassen and Visaria (2004: chapters 2, 5 and 6).

rate were high, and the population increased by an average of about twenty-five million people per decade. Between the two world wars there was a limited decline in the death rate. This resulted largely from a reduction in crisis mortality (some of it associated with famines) and modest gains that were made in some places against certain infectious and parasitic diseases, such as cholera, plague and malaria.

The years between about 1946 and 1952 saw a *very* sharp fall in the death rate—something that has generally been missed by demographers.[3] It is possible that during this short period life expectation in India increased at a rate of almost two years per year. This was a time of rapid mortality improvement in many countries (Dyson and Murphy 1991). Of course, the second World War had ended, Independence came in 1947, international trade expanded, and health measures that might otherwise have been introduced during 1939–45 were implemented. The birth rate, however, remained high throughout the 1950s. Consequently the annual rate of population growth during the 1951–61 intercensal decade reached almost 2 per cent—a figure around which census data suggest it remained up to and including 1991–2001 (Table 2.1).

There were further, sizeable rises in life expectancy during the last four decades of the twentieth century. The figures in Table 2.1 indicate that, measured in years, the increment in life expectancy from decade to decade declined only slightly during 1961–2001. The average increase between the two most recent intercensal decades was about 5.8 years. The main impression, therefore, is one of considerable *momentum* in the overall process of mortality improvement. The factors that have underpinned this sustained advance were, and remain, many and complex. However, the following considerations are important.

India has experienced major reductions in mortality from most infectious and parasitic diseases, often as a result of specific interventions. For example, from the late 1940s through to the early 1960s there was great success in the control of malaria—primarily through spraying with DDT. Before the late 1940s there were probably tens of millions of malaria cases in the country each year, and several hundred thousand associated deaths. However, it is thought that by 1965 the number of active cases of malaria had fallen to around 100,000 and that there were virtually no deaths

[3] For example, Visaria and Visaria (1982: 507) attribute the abrupt fall in the registered crude death rate to a deterioration in registration coverage. However, for research that suggests that the fall in the death rate in the subcontinent at this time was real see, for example, Frederiksen (1968*a*, 1968*b*) and Dyson (1989).

(Akhtar and Learmonth 1985). In recent decades the percentage contribution of malaria to total deaths appears to have increased by a factor of four or five. Nevertheless, in the 1990s the disease seems to have been responsible for less than 2 per cent of deaths in rural India. The malaria problem facing the country today is both difficult and complex, but this should not obscure the fact that it is very much reduced compared to earlier times (Visaria 2004*a*). The eradication of smallpox represents another significant gain resulting from a specific intervention. In the 1950s there were about 64,000 smallpox deaths in the country each year, but the last recorded case occurred in Assam in 1975 (Banthia and Dyson 1999). At different times, there have been major falls in mortality from diseases such as dysentery, cholera, leishmaniasis, leprosy, measles, and tetanus (Visaria 2004*a*).

Another factor contributing especially to the decline in child mortality has been the spread of immunisation—from levels that were negligible before the launch of the Expanded Programme of Immunization in 1978. By 2005, however, it is estimated that of children aged 1, about 59 per cent were immunised against polio and had received DPT3, and a similar proportion were immunised against measles (UNICEF 2006).[4] The decline in child mortality has also benefited from the decline in the birth rate during recent decades—the reason being that fertility decline has involved reductions in higher parity births to older women, which tend to have sharply elevated risks of death. The period 1961–2001 also saw a considerable expansion of health facilities and significant improvements in sanitation and water supply. Estimates suggest, for example, that in 1997 around 90 per cent of the urban population had access to potable drinking water, and that about half had access to some modern form of sanitation. Of course, these figures reveal huge room for improvement, but the point is that they represent significant gains compared to earlier times (Vira and Vira 2004). Two more associated changes worth mentioning in relation to the sustained mortality gains of recent decades are rises in education and the increasing secularisation of attitudes towards sickness and disease.[5] For example, children born to parents with little or no education tend to experience appreciably higher death rates than those born

[4] The DPT3 figure relates to one-year-old children having received three doses of diphtheria, pertussis (i.e. whooping cough) and tetanus vaccine. These numbers should be regarded with caution, but they are suggestive of the scale of the change.

[5] In a study of the increasing use of western medical facilities by people in rural south India, Caldwell, Reddy and Caldwell (1983: 204) state that 'declining mortality has been part of a profound social revolution, and even a theological one in terms of moving ever more areas of behaviour into the secular domain'.

to parents with higher levels of education. In this context the literacy rate for people aged seven years and above in India rose from 28 to 65 per cent between the 1961 and 2001 censuses, with some slight acceleration during the 1990s. Also, although a large gender gap persists—the 2001 literacy figures for males and females were 76 and 54 per cent respectively—the most recent intercensal decade saw a perceptible reduction in its size (Kingdon *et al.* 2004).

Table 2.1 shows that while the differential at the national level has generally been very small, female life expectation has tended to slightly exceed that of males. It seems that in India as a whole, it was only around 1951–81 that average male life expectancy marginally exceeded that of females (Bhat 1989). It is notable too that during 1961–2001 the momentum of mortality improvement, as measured by the average increment in life expectancy per decade, has been greater for females. The average male increment has not only been smaller, but it has also decreased in size from decade to decade. The result is that female life expectancy today probably exceeds that of males by two or three years.

Of course, in general one would anticipate a still larger female mortality advantage in a population where overall life expectation is probably now about 65 years. However, that female life expectancy exceeds that of males by a significant margin is noteworthy. It is not clear why females are currently doing so much better in this respect. It may be that as non-communicable diseases have become more prominent in the overall health and mortality profile—they now account for a clear majority of all deaths—so the modest innate mortality advantage that females have has greater opportunity to show through. In addition, male mortality at later adult ages (e.g. over 30) is proving especially resistant to decline—a fact that may reflect the operation of behavioural factors like greater alcohol and tobacco consumption among men (Visaria 2004*a*). Levels of HIV/AIDS infection are also a little higher for men, although it should be stressed that the overall HIV prevalence rate is very low. Thus in 2005–6 blood specimens were collected from a nationally representative sample of 103,000 adults. The test results indicated an HIV prevalence rate for the country of just 0.28 per cent—the figures being 0.36 and 0.22 per cent for men and women respectively (Ministry of Health and Family Welfare 2007).[6] Another, more important, factor that may help to explain the

[6] These figures, based on testing the general population, are appreciably lower than previous estimates that were derived from the testing of women attending antenatal clinics (e.g. see National AIDS Control Organization 2006).

improved health and mortality prospects of Indian females is fertility decline. The fact that, compared to say the 1960s, women are now giving birth to significantly fewer children, especially at later reproductive ages, has probably worked to improve their health status.[7] That said, the level and trend of the maternal mortality rate (i.e. maternal deaths per 100,000 live births) is difficult to estimate with any reliability. However, there is no doubt that the country's current maternal mortality rate is high by international standards—probably in the range 400–600 (Bhat, Navaneetham and Rajan 1995; IIPS and ORC Macro 2000).

Turning to fertility, Table 2.1 shows that there was a sizeable interval between the fall in the death rate and the start of the fall in the birth rate. In the 1960s women were still having an average of around six live births each. Indeed, it is likely that fertility rose somewhat during the 1950s and 1960s due to various modernisation effects, including reductions in widowhood consequent upon mortality decline.[8] A fall in the birth rate at the national level is only readily apparent in the 1970s. The age of women at marriage has risen from roughly 15 years in 1951 to over 20 years for women marrying today—an upward trend that almost certainly continues, and which has undoubtedly played a major part in the reduction of fertility among women aged 15–19 (Das and Dey 1998; Visaria 2004*b*). But the chief reason for the fertility decline from the 1970s onwards has been a very significant rise in the use of modern methods of birth control—especially female sterilisation. The proportion of married women aged 15–49 who are estimated to be currently using modern contraceptive methods is around 47 per cent (UNICEF 2006: 131). And female sterilisation accounts for roughly 80 per cent of this use (Visaria 2004*b*). These developments largely explain why the total fertility rate (TFR) in India today is probably in the region of 2.8 births per woman.

There is a growing consensus among demographers that mortality decline is the primary, remote cause of the fertility transition (see Ní Bhrolcháin and Dyson 2007). Ultimately, the reduction in fertility from high to low levels in any population constitutes a response by people to an earlier, continuous and major fall in mortality. The decline in the death rate in India not only resulted in an increase in the size of the national

[7] In the 1970s female death rates were higher than male death rates at ages below about 40. However recent data suggest that at ages 30–40 female death rates are now below those of males (Visaria 2004*a*: 42).

[8] Other possible contributory factors to the rise in fertility include increases in coital frequency due to declines in traditional restrictions on sexual intercourse and, perhaps, changes in patterns of breastfeeding.

population, but through the large falls in infant and child mortality that were involved, it also led to a corresponding expansion of average household size. Many factors have played a *facilitatory* role in the adjustment process that fertility decline represents. There have been major changes in attitudes towards family and sexual matters, influenced for example by the media (IIPS and ORC Macro 2000: 165–7). The country's family planning programme has helped to legitimise the idea of birth control and service the rise in demand for modern contraception that has occurred. In India, as elsewhere, there is much cross-sectional survey evidence showing that more educated women are more likely to contracept (and marry later). However, the fact that fertility decline is an adjustment process that almost certainly will occur across the board is reflected in the fact that almost two-thirds of recent fertility decline has happened among women with little or no education (see Bhat 2002*a*; McNay, Arokiasamy and Cassen 2003). On the present view, the uneducated (and poor) are just as capable of controlling their fertility, although for various reasons it takes them somewhat longer to do so.[9]

According to the census, the level of urbanisation in India rose from 17 to around 28 per cent during 1951–2001 (Table 2.1). Comparing 1981–91 and 1991–2001 the annual growth rate of the urban population fell from about 3.1 to 2.7 per cent. These figures are suggestive of a country with a low level and a fairly slow pace of urbanisation. That said, a strong case can be made that many areas that are currently classed as 'rural' actually have urban characteristics and should be reclassified.[10] Nevertheless, looking at the process of urbanisation as a whole, it was mortality decline after 1947 that really enabled sustained urban natural increase for the first time. Between 1951 and 2001 the size of the urban population grew from around 62 to about 285 million. In recent decades most urban growth has resulted from natural increase of the urban population. During 1991–2001, for example, estimates suggest that the natural increase of the urban population accounted for roughly 55 per cent of urban growth,

[9] Here education is regarded as a conditioning rather than a causal mechanism. And in very different—and extremely unlikely—circumstances it would be possible to conceive of education facilitating a rise in fertility back to high levels (see Dyson 2001*a*).

[10] Whether a place is classed as urban is influenced by political considerations. An area can become urban simply by being declared a municipal area. However, inhabitants of urban areas often face higher levels of taxation, and this can lead to resistance to reclassification. Some Indian villages have populations of several tens of thousands. In 1991 a total of 13,376 villages had populations of 5000 or more (indeed one had a population of over 100,000). Together these villages contained 113 million people, and were they to have been treated as 'urban' then the country's level of urbanisation would have been raised from 26 to 39 per cent (Visaria 2000).

rural to urban migration and reclassification together accounting for the remainder. India's urban hierarchy is becoming increasingly complex. Whereas in 1951 there were only five cities with a population of one million or more, by 1991 the number had risen to twenty-four, and the 2001 census recorded thirty-five such major urban units (Dyson and Visaria 2004).

Urbanisation is another process that in recent times has facilitated reductions in both fertility and mortality. It is clear that living arrangements in urban areas can exert particular pressures on households that have high fertility (for example, in terms of space). And urban areas can offer economies of scale in providing both health and family planning services. Also, the urban population is generally better provided with water, sanitation, educational facilities etc.—although, of course, there is massive intra-urban variation. While recent figures are unavailable, it is likely that life expectation in urban areas today is about six years higher than the figure for rural areas, and the level of total fertility in the urban sector is probably roughly one birth lower than that holding in rural India (see Registrar General, India 1999; IIPS and ORC Macro 2000: 83–90).

Census data show that rural to urban migration constitutes a modest proportion of all migration. For example, the 1991 census results indicated that about 21 per cent of all migrants were rural to urban migrants, a figure that rises to only 33 per cent if interstate moves are considered. That said, these figures have increased in recent censuses i.e. there are signs that migration is becoming somewhat more urban-orientated. In virtually all types of flow, the great majority of migrants are women. And in most cases they are moving for reasons of marriage. This is particularly true for moves over shorter distances, which constitute the vast majority of moves (Dyson and Visaria 2004). Interestingly, there appears to have been a decline in rates of interstate migration. It has been suggested that this may reflect the rising affirmation of cultural and political identities in different parts of the country (e.g. making schooling for children more difficult to obtain for interstate migrants) and an increase in socio-economic inequalities within states (Kundu and Gupta 2000). However, it may also reflect the rise in the number of larger cities—since this means that it is easier to move to a major urban unit without crossing into another state. Another notable recent change is the evidence of a decline in circulatory migration. This is significant because it points to the increasing phenomenon of commuting, facilitated by improvements in transport. In this context it is also relevant that for many potential rural out-migrants, the living conditions that they would experience in urban areas may be worse than those in rural areas.

In concluding this discussion of demographic change at the national level, four further points are worth making in relation to the information in Table 2.1. First, of course, fertility decline is bringing about a major change in the age structure of India's population. Thus in censuses up to and including that of 1981, with some variation, about 40 per cent of the population was aged 0–14. However, this figure fell to about 37 per cent in 1991 and 35 per cent in 2001 (Registrar General, India 2006). Really for the first time, the 2001 census clearly enumerated a smaller number of people at ages 0–4 than at 5–9 (age groups which constituted 10.7 and 12.5 per cent of the population respectively). Moreover, there was only a modest increase in the size of the population aged 0–4 between the 1991 and 2001 censuses—from about 102 to around 110 million. Related to this, the proportion of the population in the main working age range is rising. For example, the percentage aged 15–44 increased from 43 to 51 between 1981 and 2001 (see Dyson 2004; Registrar General 2006). A second point is that, while they are difficult to interpret—not least because of likely changes in census coverage level—census data suggest that there has been little change in the ratio of males to females in the overall population (i.e. at all ages combined) since 1971. At very young ages, however, between 1991 and 2001 there was a sharp increase in masculinity. Thus the sex ratio (m/f) at ages 0–6 rose from 1.058 to 1.078. There are good reasons to think that this reflects an increase in sex-selective abortion, especially in some northern areas. Thirdly, while the country's rate of population growth has declined slightly in recent decades, the size of the absolute increment in population has generally increased (see Table 2.1). In fact, it may be that the level of census coverage improved in 2001 (compared to 1991) and that this helps to explain why the addition indicated for the 1991–2001 intercensal decade rose to 183 million (Dyson 2001*b*). The increment during 2001–11 will probably be a little smaller than this figure, but it will be larger than occurred in most previous decades. Finally, a particular feature of Table 2.1 that is worth underscoring is the reduction in mortality. By the start of the present century, life expectancy had more than doubled compared to the situation in 1947. And, as noted, there is still considerable momentum to this upward trend. Arguably this represents the most important improvement to living conditions in contemporary India.

Regional trends

Analysis of census and other material shows that there has been a long-standing regional pattern of demographic variation in India—stretching back at least to the nineteenth century (Dyson 1984). Key elements of this regional pattern have been (i) generally higher levels of mortality and fertility in the north of the country compared to the south, and (ii) a significant quantum of excess female mortality in the north that has not been much evident in the south (much of this excess mortality pertains to young children). States in the east are harder to classify, but in general their demographic characteristics have more in common with those of states in the south. As will be seen, the basic regional pattern of demographic variation outlined above persists to a considerable degree, although in places it has been modified and overlain by the effects of more recent socio-economic developments. The basic north–south contrast is thought to reflect variation in kinship patterns. Variation in agrarian ecology in the distant past between the north and the south may also have some ultimate underlying relevance.[11] It has long been recognised that traditional patterns of kinship and marriage in the north were—and to a considerable extent still are—highly patriarchal. For example, daughters needed a dowry at marriage, and the marriages that were made were exceedingly restrictive as regards the degree of autonomy that they allowed young women. In contrast, in the south the institution of dowry was largely absent until recent times, and adult women tended to experience a somewhat higher degree of social status and personal freedom (e.g. see Karve 1953; Dyson and Moore 1983).

With this as background, Table 2.2 presents basic data from the 2001 census and accompanying demographic estimates derived from India's Sample Registration System (SRS) for each of the major states. The SRS estimates of life expectation and total fertility are thought to be reasonably reliable for most states. Table 2.3 gives additional measures relevant to fertility and mortality. The literacy rates from the census are perhaps of special note—given the previous comments concerning the role that education can have in facilitating both mortality and fertility decline. Notice, in particular, the very low levels of female literacy shown for the four main northern states of Rajasthan, Uttar Pradesh (UP), Bihar and Madhya Pradesh (MP). Most of the remaining figures in Table 2.3 come from data collected in state-level surveys conducted as part of India's National Family Health Survey (NFHS) round of 1998–9; again, the figures are thought to be fairly trustworthy, at least in general terms. Although the numbers in both of the tables are approximate, it is important

[11] For centuries, the north was associated with plough (i.e. male) agriculture, and the south was associated with rice-based agricultural systems which place greater value on the labour of women.

Table 2.2. Regional demographic variation—summary measures for the major states of India 1991–2001.

Region/state	Population 2001 (millions)	Growth rate (%) 1991–2001	Sex ratio 2001 (m/f)	Life expectancy at birth, 1996–2001 (years) m	f	f–m	TFR 1996–2001 (births per woman)	Per cent urban 2001	Urban growth rate (%) 1991–2001
(i)	(ii)	(iii)	(iv)	(v)	(vi)	(vii)	(viii)	(ix)	(x)
South									
Kerala	31.8	0.90	0.945	71.2	76.1	4.9	1.80	26.0	0.7
Tamil Nadu	62.1	1.06	1.014	64.1	66.8	2.7	1.96	43.9	3.6
Andhra Pradesh	75.7	1.30	1.023	61.7	64.2	2.5	2.34	27.1	1.4
Karnataka	52.7	1.59	1.038	61.4	65.3	3.9	2.41	34.0	2.5
Maharashtra	96.7	2.04	1.084	64.8	67.4	2.6	2.63	42.4	2.9
North									
Gujarat	50.6	2.03	1.086	62.3	64.3	2.0	2.93	37.4	2.8
Rajasthan	56.5	2.49	1.085	60.5	61.7	1.2	4.13	23.4	2.7
Uttar Pradesh*	174.5	2.27	1.109	59.8	58.9	−0.9	4.73	21.0	2.8
Bihar*	109.8	2.40	1.080	62.7	60.9	−1.8	4.28	13.4	2.6
Madhya Pradesh*	81.2	2.04	1.067	56.1	56.1	0.0	3.93	25.0	2.8
Punjab	24.3	1.80	1.145	67.3	69.6	2.3	2.64	34.0	3.2
Haryana	21.1	2.47	1.161	64.0	65.6	1.6	3.31	29.0	4.1
East									
West Bengal	80.2	1.64	1.071	62.9	64.7	1.8	2.44	28.0	1.8
Orissa	36.7	1.48	1.029	58.2	58.3	0.1	2.89	15.0	2.6
Assam	26.6	1.73	1.073	57.5	58.2	0.7	3.16	12.7	3.1
All-India	1,026.6	1.94	1.072	61.5	63.1	1.6	3.21	27.8	2.7

Notes: As noted in the text, the estimates of life expectancy and total fertility are based on data from the Sample Registration System.
* Figures relate to the former territorial jurisdiction, i.e. that holding before 2001.
Principal sources: Registrar General, India (1998, 1999); Dyson (2004).

to emphasise that where alternative estimates exist they generally show a similar regional pattern.[12] Notice that in both tables the states have been divided into subgroups within the north and the south. The classification of states between regions is inevitably rather crude. For example, the adjacent states of Gujarat and Maharashtra in western India have been allocated to the north and the south respectively, although their demographic features tend to be similar. Note too that for UP, MP and Bihar the figures shown relate to their former territorial jurisdictions (i.e. those that held before the creation from them, respectively, of Uttaranchal, Chhattisgarh and Jharkhand, late in the year 2000). A final point to underline, by way of introduction, is that at the time of the 2001 census the combined population of the four major northern states was 422 million i.e. about 41 per cent of the country's total population.

Table 2.2 shows that, in general, the southern states are experiencing appreciably slower rates of demographic growth than those in the north (see column (iii)). At the extremes, during 1991–2001 the average annual growth rates of Kerala and Tamil Nadu were both around 1 per cent, whereas the rates were well above 2 per cent in Rajasthan, UP and Bihar. Moreover, comparing the 1981–91 and 1991–2001 intercensal decades, most of the northern states experienced either little change or an increase in their rate of growth. However, all of the southern and eastern states experienced a significant decline in their population growth rate (Dyson 2001*b*).

Life expectancy at birth is generally somewhat higher in the southern than the northern states, although with respect to this measure the situation of the eastern states (West Bengal aside) is perhaps closer to those in the north (see columns (v) and (vi)). Within the south, Kerala is in a different league with a life expectancy of well over 70 years; in the north, Punjab is in the vanguard too. Both these states have been leaders in mortality reduction for several decades. Other states that have done relatively well in improving their overall level of mortality are Tamil Nadu and Maharashtra in the south, and Haryana and to a lesser extent Gujarat in the north.

While the SRS generally provides fairly reliable estimates of life expectation, the quality of the system does vary both over time and between states. Therefore it is more difficult to make detailed comments regarding recent changes in trend at the state-level. However, there is little doubt

[12] This applies, for example, to measures of fertility and mortality where independent estimates are available from the census, the NFHS and the Sample Registration System.

that life expectation is continuing to rise in every state. Comparing estimates based on SRS data for 1981–5 and 1996–2001 indicates a national gain of about 6.8 years.[13] The increments for both Kerala and Punjab over this period were respectively 5.2 and 5.4 years—consistent with the idea that increases become harder to achieve at higher levels of life expectancy. More interesting is the fact that the two largest increments indicated are for UP and Bihar—9.3 and 8.9 years respectively. Thus while mortality remains relatively high in these two very populous northern states, and related to this their levels of education are exceptionally low, both states do seem to have made significant progress. Table 2.3 underlines that there are large differences in immunisation coverage between the northern and southern states, a fact which holds out some prospect for a narrowing of mortality differentials in the future.

Today mortality is probably improving faster for females in all states. However, the estimates in Table 2.2 reflect the fact that in the past females experienced a large disadvantage in life expectancy throughout much of the north (a consequence of the particularly patriarchal institutional structures). For example, while the figures must be regarded with caution, sex-specific estimates of life expectation for 1970–5 based on the SRS imply that males outlived females on average by 2.2, 3.4 and 4.9 years respectively in Punjab, Haryana and UP (see Registrar General, India 1999). Table 2.2 shows that while life expectation in the period 1996–2001 was significantly higher for females in each of the southern states (especially Kerala), elsewhere the picture was more mixed. Moreover in UP and Bihar it could still be the case that male life expectancy slightly exceeds that of females.

There is no doubt that sex differences in mortality underpin much of the variation in population sex ratios that is shown in Table 2.2 (see column (iv)). In most of the southern states in 2001 there was rough equality in the numbers of males and females. The particular predominance of females in Kerala may partly reflect sex-selective out-migration to the Gulf. However, in the northern states—and especially Punjab and Haryana—population sex ratios are remarkably masculine. Comparison of the figures for the 1981 and 2001 censuses shows little change in sex composition for most states. But in Punjab, Haryana, Maharashtra and Gujarat the populations became more male in composition. And comparing census data for 1991 and 2001 reveals sizeable increases in the

[13] The sources of the comparisons referred to here are for 1981–5 Registrar General, India (1999) and for 1996–2001 Dyson (2004).

masculinity of the child (i.e. under-7) population in these four states, especially the first two (Dyson 2001*b*). There is little doubt that this reflects the increased practice of sex-selective abortion—making the sex ratio at birth, and therefore the child population, much more masculine than its 'natural' level of around 1.06 (e.g. see Das Gupta and Bhat 1999). In this context the state-level measures of son preference in Table 2.3 suggest, in general, an appreciably higher level of preference for sons in the north than in the south. While the indices should be interpreted with care, it is noticeable that Punjab and Haryana do not have exceptionally high measures compared to other northern states. Overall there are strong grounds to believe that the practice of sex-selective abortion will continue to spread in India, and that child sex ratios at the next census in 2011 will evince signs of the practice for other states, including possibly some in the south.[14] That said, looking further into the future, there is reason to believe that the degree of son preference will fall with general socio-economic changes that might be subsumed under the term 'modernisation' (e.g. rising levels of education and urbanisation). Indeed, the relative socio-economic advancement of Punjab and Haryana may help to explain why the levels of son preference indicated for these states in Table 2.3 are not exceptionally high. In addition, public policies in India are trying to foster an equal valuation of boys and girls among prospective parents. Therefore the rise in the sex ratio at birth may chiefly reflect a rise in access to the technologies that can determine the sex of a foetus. And at some point in the future the upward trend in the sex ratio at birth may well be reversed by a decline in the preference for sons (see Chung and Das Gupta 2007).

Turning to fertility, Table 2.2 shows that a strong regional gradient persists. Again, the precise figures should be regarded with care. But the SRS-based total fertility rate (TFR) estimates shown in column (viii) suggest strongly that the major southern states are either currently at, or are fast approaching, a figure of two live births per woman. Indeed, in Kerala and Tamil Nadu the TFR is probably below two births. Notice that the level of fertility is also relatively low in the more socio-economically developed northern states of Punjab, Haryana and Gujarat. However, in

[14] In fact, district-level child sex ratios for the 2001 census are strongly suggestive of the practice in north-eastern Rajasthan and western areas of UP, and to a lesser extent some parts of Bihar. Data from the 2001 census show little sign of an abnormal deficit of young girls throughout most of India's south and east. However child sex ratios from the last four censuses reveal, first for Salem district in Tamil Nadu, and then for districts that adjoin it, an emerging and spreading deficit of young girls. Initially this may have been the result of female infanticide and differential neglect, but more recently it may well reflect increasing resort to sex-selective abortion.

Table 2.3. Regional variation in selected population characteristics around the year 2000.

Region/ state	Age at marriage (years)		Literacy rate		Index of son preference	Current use of modern birth control	Women sterilised	Median age at sterilisation	Years between first and last birth	Child immunisation	Adults with HIV
	m	f	m	f		%	%	(years)		%	%
(i)	(ii)	(iii)	(iv)	(v)	(vi)	(vii)	(viii)	(ix)	(x)	(xi)	(xii)
South											
Kerala	27.9	21.5	94.2	87.9	14.6	56.1	48.5	26.4	6.8	79.7	0.74
Tamil Nadu	26.6	20.9	82.3	64.6	9.6	50.3	45.2	25.3	8.1	88.8	0.72
Andhra Pradesh	23.9	18.3	70.9	51.2	19.8	58.9	52.7	23.6	9.3	58.7	1.16
Karnataka	26.7	20.1	76.3	57.5	13.0	56.5	51.5	24.2	9.1	60.0	0.93
Maharashtra	25.3	19.8	86.3	67.5	27.1	59.9	48.5	25.0	8.4	78.4	1.27
North											
Gujarat	24.4	20.2	76.5	55.6	33.2	53.3	43.0	26.5	8.1	53.0	0.26
Rajasthan	22.3	18.3	76.5	44.3	47.5	38.1	30.8	27.0	11.2	17.3	0.16
Uttar Pradesh*	23.3	19.0	70.9	43.9	53.3	22.0	14.9	28.3	13.4	21.2	0.11
Bihar*	23.8	18.8	62.2	35.2	47.9	22.4	19.2	27.7	12.9	11.0	0.20
Madhya Pradesh*	23.5	18.9	77.0	51.0	42.5	42.6	35.7	26.4	11.3	22.4	0.29
Punjab	25.7	22.1	75.6	63.6	29.1	53.8	29.3	27.1	7.6	72.1	0.29
Haryana	24.6	19.8	79.3	56.3	37.5	53.2	38.7	26.5	9.0	62.7	0.29
East											
West Bengal	26.2	19.6	77.6	60.2	20.7	47.3	32.0	25.1	9.6	43.8	0.24
Orissa	26.6	21.2	76.0	51.0	37.6	40.3	33.9	26.3	9.9	43.7	0.19
Assam	27.8	21.7	71.3	54.6	38.2	26.6	15.7	26.7	11.6	17.0	0.19
All-India	24.9	19.7	75.6	54.0	33.2	42.8	34.2	25.7	9.9	42.0	0.50

Notes: The data underlying the measures in columns (ii), (iii) and (vi) to (ix) relate to 1998–9 and were collected by the second National Family Health Survey (NFHS-2), mostly from reports of currently married women aged 15–49. The literacy rates in columns (iv) and (v) are from the 2001 census. The NFHS-2 measures are: columns (ii) and (iii) singulate mean ages at marriage; column (vi) percentage of women wanting more sons than daughters; column (vii) percentage of women currently using modern contraception (including sterilisation, but excluding traditional methods); column (viii) percentage of women sterilised; column (ix) median age at sterilisation—this pertains to the age of currently married, sterilised women and wives of sterilised men at the time of sterilisation; column (x) the difference between the median age at first and last birth for women with at least one birth; column (xi) children aged 12–23 months immunised for BCG, measles, DPT (three doses) and polio; and column (xii) estimated percentage of adults aged 15–49 infected with HIV—these figures are given here because they are the only estimates available for all the major states, although they are probably overestimates (see above, n. 6).

* Figures relate to the former territorial jurisdiction i.e. that holding before 2001.

Principal sources: Registrar General, India (2006); IIPS and ORC Macro (2000); National AIDS Control Organization (2000).

each of the four populous and poorly educated northern states—i.e. Rajasthan, UP, MP and Bihar—the TFR during 1996–2001 was around four births. On the basis of the figures in Table 2.2, it is fair to say that in 1996–2001 there was a difference in total fertility of roughly two live births between the north and the south of India. The current differential will not be too much smaller than this.

Table 2.3 sheds light on the proximate factors that underpin these fertility differences. Women, and men, in the four main northern states marry at younger ages compared to their counterparts elsewhere in the country.[15] However, the most important differences relate to current use of modern methods of contraception. Contraceptive use rates are still exceptionally low in Bihar and UP, although they are somewhat higher in Rajasthan and MP. In the southern states, however, and in Gujarat, Punjab and Haryana, more than half of all currently married women are using modern methods of birth control. The statistics in columns (vii) and (viii) underscore the degree to which female sterilisation constitutes the main method in every state. Only in a few places are other means of birth control employed to a significant degree (e.g. the pill in West Bengal, and the IUD and condom in Punjab and Haryana) and then only in a secondary role. It is evident too that many women are undergoing sterilisation while they are still quite young. In general, the data in Table 2.3 suggest that childbearing patterns in India are moving towards a situation in which women get married while they are still relatively young, have two children in the space of perhaps eight years (e.g. see Kerala, Tamil Nadu, Gujarat and Punjab) and then get sterilised. The extent to which female sterilisation has come to dominate contraceptive use, even among women in their mid-twenties, is something that was not generally foreseen.

Research on district level data suggests that fertility decline began in coastal areas of southern India in the 1960s, and that it then moved inland and north, eventually extending throughout most of the Deccan peninsular. The onset of the decline in the north of the country started a little later, in the 1970s, in parts of Punjab, Haryana and Himachal Pradesh. The spread of the phenomenon has generally been somewhat slower in the north (see Bhat 1998; Guilmoto 2000; Guilmoto and Rajan 2001*a*, 2001*b*). Areas that were the last to experience fertility decline

[15] The later marriage ages for men, and larger age gaps between men and women at marriage, indicated in Table 2.3 for the southern and eastern states, at least partly reflect preferred forms of marriage between close kin—e.g. for a man, marriage to an elder sister's daughter (see Wilson and Dyson 1992).

included much of Rajasthan and MP, and much of the Ganges basin comprising large tracts in Bihar and UP. Fertility decline also came late to Assam.

At the start of the present century it is likely that falls in total fertility are bottoming-out in much of southern India, and in other locations where fertility is already comparatively low. State-level SRS data show this clearly for both Tamil Nadu and Kerala. Thus in the latter state the TFR has fluctuated around 1.8 births since 1990. In contrast, today the TFR is falling relatively swiftly in those states where the overall level of fertility is still comparatively high. It is differences in the timing of fertility decline that mainly account for the differences in population growth rates between India's states today (Table 2.2). Essentially, most of the northern states are a couple of decades behind the south in terms of their stage in the fertility transition. Analysis suggests that, once started, there has not been much difference in the speed of the decline in fertility between states in the country's north and south, although it is likely that fertility started to fall from a somewhat lower level in the south (see Bhat 2002*b*).

In general, levels of urbanisation are somewhat higher in southern India, compared to the north and the east. The figure shown for Kerala in Table 2.2 is surprisingly low, but this may well reflect the fact that settlement patterns in the state are diffuse, and many locations there that are classed as rural could well be classified as urban. Prior to the 2001 census Tamil Nadu made special efforts to address this issue through reclassification, and as a result the level of urbanisation rose sharply from 34.2 per cent in 1991 to 42.4 per cent in 2001—making it the country's most urban major state. The figures on the level of urbanisation shown in Table 2.2 are influenced by the existence of two especially dynamic urban systems. The first is in western India. Its main foci are Ahmedabad and Mumbai, but it stretches north to south throughout much of western Gujarat and Maharashtra. The second major and fast expanding urban system is that centred on Delhi in the north; its existence helps to explain the higher levels of urbanisation shown for both Punjab and Haryana.[16] With about 16 per cent of West Bengal's population, Kolkata accounts for the relatively high level of urbanisation shown for that state in Table 2.2. In 2001 the populations of Greater Mumbai, Kolkata and Delhi were respectively 16.4, 13.2 and 12.8 million, but the population of Kolkata is growing at a

[16] Delhi is a separate administrative unit and is not covered by the state-level figures shown in Table 2.2.

slower rate and it seems likely that Delhi will soon overtake it in terms of size (Chapman and Pathak 2000; Dyson and Visaria 2004). The next most populous urban areas in 2001 were Chennai (6.4 m), Bangalore (5.7m), and Hyderabad (5.5m), all in the south. Note the appreciably lower levels of urbanisation of the major northern states, and Orissa and Assam in the east (Table 2.2).

During the twentieth century the broad pattern of interstate migration was dominated by net movement of people out of Uttar Pradesh and Bihar, and this remains the case today. With their relatively high levels of urbanisation and expanding economies, Maharashtra and Gujarat experience net inflows from virtually all the other states. The scale of the net movement from UP to Maharashtra is particularly striking. The expanding urban system around Delhi, embracing much of both Punjab and Haryana, is the second major area of attraction for migrants.

Taken together the various demographic trends outlined above are leading to other important changes. At the risk of some simplification they can be summarised in terms of variation between the country's north and south. Thus due to fertility decline, the populations of southern states are not only growing more slowly, they are also appreciably older in terms of their age composition. For example, in 2001 about 38 per cent of the population of both Bihar and UP were aged under 15, compared to only about 26 per cent in Kerala and Tamil Nadu. The urban areas of all states are experiencing considerable growth (Table 2.2). Rates of urban population growth are somewhat greater in the north—where such growth results from both urban natural increase and net rural to urban migration. However, as rates of natural increase—including urban natural increase—decline in the south, so urban population growth results increasingly from net rural to urban migration (and reclassification). Indeed, projections suggest that the rural areas of southern states will experience only modest increases in population in the future, since rural rates of natural increase will be low and it is likely that net rural to urban migration will continue (Dyson and Visaria 2004). It has also been suggested that there may be higher rates of interstate migration from the main northern states towards states in the south, analogous to what already occurs with respect to movement from UP to Maharashtra. Such migration could result partly from the much greater demographic growth experienced in the big northern states, and from greater employment opportunities in the south arising both from the region's more developed urban sector and gaps in the rural labour market (Bhat 2001).

A final observation in this section is that the estimates in Table 2.3 suggest that levels of HIV prevalence are significantly higher in the southern states compared to those in the north. As elsewhere in the world, other things being equal there tends to be a positive relationship between the level of urbanisation and the level of infection with HIV (Dyson 2003). Although the figures for states are crude and should be interpreted with great caution, it is noteworthy that Maharashtra is especially badly affected. In the past Mumbai was the main entry point for epidemics of plague (in 1896) and influenza (in 1918), and there are strong indications that the city has also served as an important point of entry with respect to HIV.

Implications

Several different kinds of related demographic change have been touched on here and it is impossible to discuss all of their implications. Some of the changes involve increases in population scale and density. Others pertain to a particular parameter, for example the decline in fertility. The discussion has also raised issues of compositional change, for example relating to alterations in the age and rural/urban structure of the population. Yet another consequence of the different rates of population growth between major states is that the regional composition of India's population is changing.

Demographic changes such as these can go unremarked. They may not be evident over short periods of time. And in many ways they influence other variables remotely. That is, their effects are filtered through and modified by the particular social, economic, and other circumstances that prevail—a fact that may obscure their operation. Nevertheless although these changes are relatively slow, they are cumulative and they are often fundamental. Over the long run their consequences can be profound and largely inescapable.

The populous states of northern India—Rajasthan, MP, and, still more, Bihar and UP—are both growing slowly economically and fast demographically (Cassen 2002).[17] In contrast, most of the southern states—and Punjab, Haryana and Gujarat—are generally experiencing

[17] That these are generalisations should be underscored. Rajasthan's recent economic growth, for example, has been relatively fast, and there are considerable differences in growth performance between western and eastern districts within UP.

faster economic growth and appreciable declines in their rates of demographic growth. Moreover, levels of education and per capita income are generally appreciably higher in this second group of states. Looking at the period 2001–26, the populations of the first group of poor northern states are projected to rise by roughly 50 per cent. In contrast, the populations of most of the remaining states, predominantly in what has been referred to here as the south, will increase by only 20–30 per cent. Therefore the consequences of demographic growth that face different parts of the country vary greatly in terms of their magnitude and their context.

To give an idea of what the implications may be over a broad range of socio-economic subjects, the conclusions of a recent study of the country's prospects during 2001–26 are worth noting (Dyson, Cassen and Visaria 2004). The conclusions of the study were inevitably influenced by the scale of the demographic growth that is occurring, and the broad division of experience between states summarised in the previous paragraph. On the subject of education, for example, the attainment of universal primary schooling is likely to be much harder in the populous northern states—where existing levels of educational provision are low, and the size of the school-age population is still rising. In contrast, in most other states, including those in the south, not only is educational coverage already significantly higher, but the size of the school-age population is falling already (Kingdon *et al.* 2004). Turning to the prospects for employment, although the national rate of population growth is declining, the growth rate of the population of working ages is yet to peak. The ability of the country's agricultural sector to raise its absorptive capacity is debatable. And public sector downsizing means that the government's role as a provider of employment may decrease further. Although the Indian economy has recently grown at about 8 or 9 per cent per year, not much of this growth has been in sectors of the economy that are labour intensive. Therefore demographic growth represents a significant challenge in terms of employment creation (McNay, Unni and Cassen 2004).

As noted, most population growth is occurring at adult ages, and the absolute size of the population aged 0–14 in the country as a whole will almost certainly be appreciably smaller in 2026 than it is today. These demographic changes mean that there will be a reduction in the country's age dependency ratio, and they hold out the possibility that reductions in the school-age population will lead to advances in the quality of basic education that is provided, and that the level of savings in the economy may increase. It may also be the case that the improvement in health that increases in life expectancy reflect will lead to gains in labour productivity (Acharya, Cassen and McNay 2004). Research suggests that, working mainly through changes in age structure, such a 'demographic bonus' made a significant contribution to East Asia's spectacular economic growth of recent decades (see Williamson 2001; Bloom and Canning 2001). However, the prospect for such a bonus is limited in the main northern states, since they will experience only modest declines in their age dependency ratios in the next couple of decades. And even for the other states that are demographically more advanced, it is not certain that changes in age structure will produce higher rates of economic growth. What actually happens will depend, among other things, on political decisions and institutional structures. The East Asian experience suggests strongly that to capitalise fully on the demographic bonus requires investment in education. One area from which the resources for such investment might come are the huge and highly inefficient subsidies provided by states for transport, electricity and water. In a context of populist politics, however, reductions in these subsidies are very difficult to bring about.

The continuing increase in India's population means that there is an inevitable and sustained rise in the demand for basic food, such as cereals. The scale of the rise is such that even if the country were not committed to a rough degree of self-sufficiency in food production, it is unlikely to be met mainly through imports. Rather, the required increase must come largely from an increase in food crop yields. There are reasons to believe that the yields of most basic food crops can be raised at a sufficient rate to match the expected growth in demand (a majority of which results from demographic growth). However, this in turn has many implications. For example, it will almost certainly involve a very considerable rise in the application of synthetic nitrogen fertilisers—something that is currently happening regularly, year after year. It also means that there will have to be more efficient use of water resources (Hanchate and Dyson 2004).

The size of the country's population, its improved economic growth performance, and future growth in both these spheres, will certainly have many consequences for the environment. But in the present context there is perhaps no more important subject than water. India's overall demographic growth, and urban population growth within it, are both key influences on the increasing demand/need for water. Food and agricultural production currently accounts for about 80 per cent of the country's water use. And growth in urban water demand—with respect to both industry and residential use—has a significant demographic dimension as well. Severe water shortages, not all of them seasonal, are already common in many parts of the country. In both villages and towns there is conflict between users, a phenomenon that may increase. While there are certainly inefficiencies in the water supply system (including wasteful subsidies and leakage) and large inequalities in levels of consumption between the poor and the better off, it is also the case that if one is concerned with ensuring that everyone gets a basic minimum supply—say of 100 litres per day—then population and urban growth are clearly making the task appreciably harder. This would be true if the supply of water were to remain constant. But a large proportion of India's towns lack sewage disposal, and most are experiencing rising volumes of human and municipal waste—consequent in part upon rapid rates of urban growth. Accordingly, pollution is said to have a major adverse effect on both the quality and the quantity of useable water supplies; and the situation is worsening rather than getting better (Vira, Iyer and Cassen 2004).

Demographic changes are also having major repercussions in the political and administrative realms. For example, other things being equal one might hypothesise that over the long run a large increase in population scale will lead to an increasingly differentiated administrative hierarchy—due to what McNicoll (1984) has termed increasing 'administrative over-extension'.

At the time of the 1971 census India was divided into 356 administrative districts. In 2001 the number had risen to 593. The 2001 census enumerated 9.6 million people in the single district of Medinipur (in West Bengal). This is more people than there are, for example, in either Sweden or Switzerland. And it seems unlikely that this can remain a single district for long. Relatedly, several of India's 'Union Territories' have been made into states—Arunachal Pradesh and Goa, for example. It is also significant that the recently created states of Uttaranchal, Chhattisgarh and Jharkhand were all carved out of very populous states. States with extremely large numbers of people pose special challenges in terms of administration. They are also more likely to contain ethnic minorities of sufficient size to justify—or bring about—the creation of a new political unit (Dyson 2001*b*). In this context it is also notable that the three recently formed new states each have large tribal populations.

Another relevant political consideration is that since 1977 the number of seats in the Indian Parliament has been fixed on the basis of the 1971 census results. The idea at that time was not to penalise states for lowering their birth rates and hence their rates of population growth. It was originally intended that this 'freeze' on political representation would be reviewed and probably lifted in 2001. Instead, however, the freeze has been extended. The increasing disparity between the numbers of people in different states and their number of elected representatives is a potential source of friction. Together with differentials between states in their contribution to central government finances, it has underlain tensions between states. Those who have argued that India might break up as a country have been proved wrong. However, there are reasons to believe that demographic growth has been a force behind the decentralisation of governance.

A final implication of demographic change that will be touched on briefly here relates to the position of women in society. In just a few decades the demographic basis of many women's lives has altered a lot. Until the 1970s the life of an average woman was dominated by the concerns of childbearing and child care. This had always been so. But in the 1950s and 1960s it was probably accentuated by mortality decline which, among other things, increased child survivorship and may well have contributed to a rise in fertility. Of course, it remains the case that especially in much of north India many women's lives are preoccupied with the having and rearing of a large number of children. That said, especially in the south, but increasingly elsewhere too, conditions are moving towards a situation in which women have their last child while they are still in their twenties (Table 2.3). Therefore the childbearing and childrearing phases of life are being reduced greatly—a fact that is augmented because women are living appreciably longer. It is important to stress that these changes still have a long way to play out, but they appear to be inexorable. It has been argued that contemporary economic changes in much of the country are empowering women relative to men (see Rishyasringa 2000). With other developments, such as increases in the level of female education, it seems likely that these demographic changes will eventually contribute to a modification of gender roles. There are already tentative signs from census data that in urban areas of southern India, a small but increasing proportion of adult women are deciding to delay marriage substantially or not to get married at all. A life that does not revolve around getting married and having children will probably become increasingly acceptable in the next few decades (Visaria 2004*b*).

Summary and discussion

In summary, it is likely that by the middle of this century India will contain about 50 per cent more people than it did at the start. The level of mortality is improving, although it should be clear that major inequalities and health problems remain. In particular, there is an emerging 'double burden' of disease—where chronic diseases (e.g. cancers, circulatory ailments, hypertension, diabetes, etc.) coexist alongside infectious and parasitic diseases and other health problems that are strongly linked to poor living conditions (e.g. tuberculosis, malaria, diarrhoeal disease, anaemia, etc.). The phenomenon of excess female mortality is diminishing fast. Female life expectancy probably exceeds that of males by a significant margin. Son preference may be declining due to socio-economic changes like increased education and urbanisation. However, the phenomenon remains strong in much of the country, and the mortality of females prior to birth—i.e. through sex-selective abortion—is considerable and may well continue to spread as access to the relevant technology increases. Fertility is falling everywhere, mostly brought about by the widespread adoption of female sterilisation. India has recently entered a period in which its rate of population growth can be expected to decline steadily. Most growth is occurring at adult ages; the size of the population aged under 15 years will decline.

Census data give the impression of a country with a low level and a slow pace of urbanisation. This may be somewhat misleading, however, since some rural areas have characteristics that could well be regarded as urban. Nevertheless, the rate of growth of the urban population is appreciable, since it is fuelled both by urban natural increase and net rural to urban migration. Levels of fertility and mortality are appreciably lower in the urban sector compared to rural areas.

The broad division of the country between the north and the south has been a major theme here. In general, the southern states—plus Gujarat, Punjab, Haryana and West Bengal—are significantly more advanced in terms of their demographic characteristics. The north/south differential may amount to a timing difference of roughly two decades in relation to fertility and growth rate decline. The challenge of having to meet the basic needs of a young and growing population is being faced mainly by the big northern states; and within them the greatest challenge lies in Bihar and UP. In these states, especially, demographic growth will make it much harder to reduce the number of people living in poverty. In the south of the country, in contrast, mortality and fertility levels are lower, and rates of population growth are now much lower too. Tamil Nadu has been almost as much a leader in these developments as has Kerala. In the south of India more of the (slower) demographic growth that is occurring is ending up in the proportionately larger urban sector—either as a result of urban natural increase or rural to urban migration.

During the next few decades it is possible that some southern states will experience falls in the size of their rural populations.

A matter that remains is that of explaining contemporary demographic change, especially with regard to fertility and child mortality. The prominence of the issue has been heightened somewhat by recent econometric work which—often using much the same data (e.g. district level census information for 1981 and 1991)—comes to quite different conclusions. For example, Drèze and Murthi (2001) emphasise the importance of factors reflecting women's agency (e.g. female literacy) in influencing fertility and child mortality, while P. Bhattacharya (2006) has recently downplayed such variables in favour of those reflecting economic development (e.g. the availability of roads). There is little doubt that both social and economic factors can play a role in facilitating reductions in fertility and child mortality, and the sureness of the conclusions that are reached is sometimes unconvincing. However, leaving aside the short timescales used in such work (which is not far from being cross-sectional), limitations of the data used in relation to what they are claimed to represent, the fact that data on certain variables (e.g. marriage patterns) are normally unavailable, and, of course, the problem of confounding, such analyses invariably find a strong and highly significant effect for 'region'. Consistently, fertility and child mortality are found to be strongly affected by location—i.e. higher in the north and lower in the south—after controlling for the other variables used. While region is something that cannot be influenced by policy, it is regrettable that it is then so little discussed.

Standing back, it is clear that fundamental demographic change in India began with the onset of mortality decline, sometime in the first half of the twentieth century. And, ultimately, fertility decline is a lagged adjustment to this. To put the matter differently, mortality decline is the remote cause of fertility decline. Other things being equal, fertility might be expected to fall earlier in locations where mortality declined earlier. Other considerations—e.g. relating to education, economic development, institutional structures, and the extent of patriarchy—may promote or retard the process of adjustment, but they are not the ultimate cause of the fertility transition that is taking place. For various reasons we do not have a detailed spatial picture of how mortality decline has occurred. However, it seems to have started throughout much of the south, and a few parts of the north (e.g. Punjab, Himachal Pradesh) where, with a lag, fertility also started to fall relatively early. It seems too that sustained mortality decline came relatively late to the heartland of the Ganges basin.

Fortunately, with respect to fertility decline the work especially of Guilmoto and Rajan (2001*a*, 2001*b*) has provided us with a detailed picture of its spread—it appears largely through a process of diffusion. A striking feature of their results is the leading role played by coastal populations on both the country's eastern and western sides. It seems that fertility declined first in the south, at least partly because there was early permeation of new patterns of behaviour, and from both sides (i.e. east and west). And something analogous may well have happened with respect to mortality. In respect of many things, coastal regions have long been porous to outside influences, in contrast to the central, northern core (Sopher 1980). While many factors have influenced demographic change in India, a concentration on factors with little attention to the role of location has been unfortunate. That said, in the not-too-distant future, fertility will be relatively low everywhere, irrespective of all development variables, and region.

Lastly, the paper has also touched briefly on some of the consequences and implications of these various demographic trends—e.g. in relation to education, employment, the macro-economy, agriculture, the urban environment, water, and politics and administration. In this context, it is worth remarking on the speed and often unexpected nature of much that has occurred—perhaps especially, although not only, where new technologies have been introduced. That women in their twenties and early thirties would use sterilisation so much for their fertility control was largely unforeseen (e.g. see Nortman 1978). The growth in commuting seems to have been mostly unanticipated, and is a subject that remains under-researched. The speed and extent to which sex-selective abortion has spread was not generally acknowledged, and the future reach of this phenomenon may still take us unawares. For good reason, nutritional problems in India are usually thought of in terms of under-nutrition. But in the country's fast expanding urban sector about a quarter of all women now are either overweight or obese—another important development that was unanticipated and has happened very quickly (IIPS and ORC Macro 2000: 243–7). It has also been intimated here that in some parts of the country the lives that women lead may become increasingly independent with respect to those of men, in ways that are not currently anticipated. So with respect to demographic change and its consequences there is a lot that may take us by surprise.

3

Costly Absences, Coercive Presences: Health Care in Rural North India

PATRICIA JEFFERY AND ROGER JEFFERY

Summary. India's economy has been transformed since the early 1990s by a globalisation/liberalisation project that can seem to be in conflict with social goals, such as the reduction of the enduringly high levels of mortality and morbidity in states such as Uttar Pradesh (UP). Focusing on aspects of reproductive and child health (obstetric care, family planning and polio eradication), this paper examines the access of villagers in Bijnor district western UP to health care in the early 2000s. With respect to obstetric care, villagers are faced with moribund state provision and resort to private medical care to deal with obstetric emergencies. By contrast, 'vertical programmes' (such as family planning and polio eradication) are high-profile at the village level. People who resist such interventions in their lives may face coercion from low-level health workers, themselves answerable to a system that sets them achievement targets. People's experiences of the state's health-care provision remain coloured by the compulsions of programmes targeting single issues rather than health care in general. Despite recent health sector innovations (particularly the National Rural Health Mission), the state health-care system remains marginal in most villagers' curative health-care options and the market plays an increasingly dominant role. Either way, from the viewpoint of the village, the costly absences and coercive presences that characterise the public sector undermine the legitimacy of state-provided health care.

Proceedings of the British Academy **159**, 47–71.

Introduction

SINCE THE EARLY 1990s, the Government of India has set considerable store on its ranking on the Human Development Index and after the UN Millennium Declaration of 2000, India's social progress has been monitored (internationally and in the English-language press in India) in terms of whether the Millennium Development Goals (MDGs) are likely to be met by 2015. In relation to health, the MDGs include the resolve to tackle maternal mortality, child mortality and communicable diseases. Moreover, according to the World Bank's flagship publication on globalisation, *Globalization, growth and poverty* (Dollar and Collier 2001), successful globalisation depends not only on industrial or commercial factors, but also on good health and health-care provision, along with education, as essential preconditions (Deaton 2004: 6–7). Since 1990, India's economy has been transformed in terms of a globalisation/liberalisation project: in this chapter we ask whether there is a potential contradiction as these projects play themselves out in contemporary India.

On the one hand, the public sector's role is to be reduced, in order (*inter alia*) to overcome the known weaknesses of public provision in some sectors, reduce budget deficits, and allow private enterprise to flourish. Yet the state's role in providing health services has continued to be acknowledged, for instance by Manmohan Singh before he became Prime Minister (Singh 2002). For the large north Indian States—including UP—this circle has not been squared. Since 1991, health services reform schemes have failed to maintain, let alone improve, standards of care available at public health facilities. Some morbidity and mortality indicators suggest that general health conditions are still improving, but only slowly and incompletely. At least in UP, most people, especially the rural poor, find accessing health care highly unsatisfactory. We illustrate this by focusing on aspects of reproductive and child health—obstetric care, family planning and polio eradication—although many of our points apply to health in general. We are drawing on over twenty years of research in rural Bijnor district, in western UP, particularly in the adjacent villages of Dharmnagri (a Hindu and Scheduled Caste village) and Jhakri (a Muslim village), about 5 km from Bijnor town.[1]

[1] Our research in Bijnor district was funded in 1982–3 and 1985 by Economic and Social Research Council (G00230027 and G00232238) and Hayter Fund, in 1990–1 by Overseas Development Administration and Rockefeller Foundation, in 2000–2 by Economic and Social Research Council (with Craig Jeffrey, R000238495), Ford Foundation and Royal Geographical

Liberalisation, health status and health care in India

Health status does not just reflect government programmes in the health sector, of course. The wider context—especially employment and poverty profiles, nutritional status, literacy and education—impact crucially on mortality and morbidity, although not always directly. The effects of the liberalisation project on poverty profiles during the 1990s have been hotly contested, with some commentators seeing continuing—if uneven—evidence of declines in poverty, and others using different data (e.g. on nutrition) to suggest that poverty levels remain stubbornly high (see for example Datt and Ravallion 2002; Deaton 2003; Müller and Patel 2004; Patnaik 2007). Poverty and ill-health are not always directly linked: yet illness is the most common proximate cause of households falling into poverty (Krishna 2006) and the poor are more vulnerable to disease and accidental injury. Here, though, we focus on the narrower issues of health and illness, and the effects of government and private health services.

Mortality indicators continued to decline (especially those related to infant and child mortality) (Datt and Ravallion 2002; Deaton 2003; Müller and Patel 2004). Overall, for instance, the infant mortality rate (IMR) declined at approximately two points per year throughout the 1990s.[2] But regional and social class inequalities seem to have stagnated, or (particularly in the case of regional inequalities) may have increased (Datt and Ravallion 2002; see also Deaton 2003 and Dyson, this volume). Women in the poorer Indian states have shown the smallest improvements in life expectancies and literacy rates (Abbasi 1999: 1133). Taking UP, we can see how halting any improvements have been. Maternal mortality ratios (MMR) have declined slowly from in the region of 700 to 750 around 1990 (Bhat 2002) to 517 (95 per cent confidence interval

Society, and in 2002–5 by Wellcome Trust (GR067231). None of these bears any responsibility for what we have written here. We also thank the people of our study villages in Bijnor; and our research assistants over the years, Swaleha Begum, Zarin Rais, the late Radha Rani Sharma, Chhaya Sharma, Shaila Rais, and Manjula Sharma. We are grateful to participants at the British Academy workshop, and especially to Anthony Heath, for comments on our paper. Our village data include household censuses, maternity histories for all ever-married women, in-depth focus on about forty key informant couples throughout the period, and discussions ranging over birth accounts, health care, etc. Named individuals have pseudonyms and the quotations are our own translations from detailed notes taken at the time. For more on our earlier research on childbearing in Dharmnagri and Jhakri, see P. Jeffery *et al.* 1989.

[2] The IMR is the number of deaths of infants before their first birthday per 1,000 live births.

461–573) in 2001–3 (Registrar-General India 2006).[3] Routine antenatal care is provided only to those who come to government facilities on their own initiative and comprises weighing, tetanus injections (to prevent neonatal tetanus) and administration of iron and folic acid (to combat anaemia). According to the National Family Health Surveys (NFHS), the percentage of children in UP aged 6–35 months who were anaemic *rose* from 73.8 per cent in 1998–9 (NFHS-2) to 85.1 per cent in 2005–6 (NFHS-3); and the proportion of pregnant women who were anaemic also *rose* from 45.8 per cent to 51.6 per cent (IIPS and Macro International 2007). In UP, about 26 per cent of pregnant women made three antenatal visits, but only about 8 per cent of all pregnant women received iron and folic acid for six months before their most recent delivery, according to NFHS-3. Contraceptive prevalence rates in UP remain lower than the all-India average, especially in the rural areas: they have increased from 20.8 per cent in 1998–9 (NFHS-2) to 29.3 in 2005–6 (NFHS-3) (IIPS and Macro International 2007).[4]

Children are still dying at relatively high rates in UP. Since the early 1990s, mortality rates for children who have reached the age of one month have dropped considerably, but perinatal and neonatal mortality rates have declined very slowly: the UP neonatal mortality rate was 48 in 2005–6 (NFHS-3) (IIPS and Macro International 2007), having been 60 in 1992–3 (NFHS-1) (Griffiths *et al.* 2001: 607).[5] Much more change is visible at the higher ages: in UP post-neonatal infant mortality has dropped from 40 (Griffiths *et al.* 2001: 607) to 25 (IIPS and Macro International 2007: 185), and the overall IMR has thereby dropped from 100 to 73. In UP the child (1–5) mortality rate has dropped from 46 (NFHS-1) to 26 (NFHS-3) (IIPS 1995; IIPS and Macro International 2007). Of course, these averages hide considerable variations, but comparative figures for UP are hard to come by. Nationally, a child in the 'Lowest standard of living' quintile was more than 2.5 times as likely to die before age 5 than a child in the 'High standard of living' category in

[3] The maternal mortality ratio (MMR) is the number of women who died while pregnant, during childbirth or within six weeks after delivery, per 100,000 births. Since we were dealing with a small population in Dharmnagri and Jhakri it is inappropriate to calculate MMRs for these villages. With respect to infant and child mortality, contraceptive prevalence and child immunisations, our estimates for Dharmnagri and Jhakri are in line with the UP figures.

[4] Contraceptive prevalence rate is the percentage of currently married women aged 15–49 practising 'modern' contraception.

[5] The child mortality rate is the number of children aged from 12 months to age 5 who die in a year, per 1,000 live births; and the neonatal mortality rate is the number of deaths during the first twenty-eight completed days of life per 1,000 live births, in the relevant year.

the ten years prior to NFHS-2 (1988–97) (IIPS and ORC Macro 2000: 183; see also Labonte *et al.* 2005: 23–4); the figures from NFHS-3 suggest that differentials have increased, since the rates for the poorest are now three times those of children in the wealthiest quintile (IIPS and Macro International 2007: 182). Government services do not provide routine monitoring of small children and there is little outreach from facilities. Nationally, Rapid Household Surveys indicate a significant *fall* in full immunisations from 54.2 per cent in 1998–9 to 48.2 per cent in 2002–3; the UP figures indicate a decline from 43.7 per cent to 29.8 per cent (Planning Commission 2005*b*: 105).[6]

Most commentators agree that there are still large parts of India with poor overall health status and major health inequalities where public sector health services are incapable of making a substantial contribution to ameliorating the situation (Reddy and Sivaramakrishnan 2006). A World Bank spokesman told the British Medical Journal that 'Fundamentally, the bank's view is that "the institutional base for health services is weak," non-governmental organisations are underutilised, and finally, but perhaps most significantly, the private sector is "gigantic," virtually completely unregulated, and offers "some of the best and the worst care seen anywhere"' (Abbasi 1999). The Indian Planning Commission's judgement in 2005 is also telling:

> Inadequate progress on the health and family welfare front is a matter of grave concern. Unless prompt and decisive steps are taken, the Plan targets on IMR and MMR will not be met and the MDG targets too will almost certainly be missed. Unlike the case of primary education, where a well-designed intervention in the form of SSA [*Sarva Shiksha Abhiyan*, or the 'Education for All' programme] exists, there is no real blue-print for the development of the primary health sector. There is need to initiate a fresh approach in this area that can be initiated within the Tenth Plan period even if it can be fully operationalized only in the Eleventh Plan period. (Planning Commission 2005*a*: 10)

These concerns are even more intense in UP, one of the so-called 'Empowered Action Group' (EAG) States, a category created in 2001 to include those states where progress towards population stabilisation had been slowest. In about 70 per cent of UP's government primary health centres, fewer than 40 per cent of the 'critical' inputs and infrastructure (e.g. refrigerators, essential medicines) were present when a survey was carried out in 1999 (Planning Commission 2002*b*: Vol. 2, 86–7). In 2003,

[6] Full immunisation means protection against measles, tuberculosis, polio, and DPT (diphtheria, pertussis [whooping cough] and tetanus).

a survey based on unannounced visits and spot checks found that government health service doctors were more likely to be absent in UP (at 52 per cent) than almost anywhere else in India (average absence rate 44 per cent); absence rates for other health workers were, at 40 per cent, around the all-India average (Devarajan and Shah 2004: 910).

After the Montagu–Chelmsford reforms of 1919, most health expenditures were decentralised to the States. Central government has only limited powers with respect to health, and since 1947 has used them mostly to fund single-issue targeted programmes (family planning, eradication or control of specific diseases). Nevertheless, the UP state's ability to finance its health-care sector has been adversely affected by budgetary cuts imposed through World Bank loans in the 1990s and early 2000s, for instance, through restructuring programmes that limit the total size of public sector employment. At the same time, proponents of liberalisation have championed the market as a better means of providing curative health services (for more on this see P. Jeffery and R. Jeffery 2008).

Nevertheless, it is not simply a matter of 'rolling back the state'. The World Bank has increased its support to some public sector health activities—especially in child health. Since the mid-1980s the World Bank has been the largest single donor, often with co-funders (e.g. with the EU for reproductive and child health projects in the 1990s) and population and reproductive health remain very important to the World Bank. With USAID and UNICEF, it has also supported child nutrition programmes and disease control programmes such as tuberculosis, leprosy, malaria, HIV/AIDS, and cataract blindness, as well as several State Health System Projects designed to strengthen the referral system. The World Bank pioneered a 'sector-wide approach' which entailed more active donor involvement in programme design, including decentralisation, increased use of NGOs, and the so-called 'target-free approach' in reproductive health services. In the mid-1990s external assistance to family planning dropped, as did support for primary health programmes, whilst user charges were promoted and increased private sector involvement was encouraged where publicly provided health care was seen to be particularly deficient (Gupta and Gumber 2002: 28, 43–4).

The United Progressive Alliance government elected in 2004 also instigated a massive new public health services investment programme in 2005 under the National Rural Health Mission (NRHM). Going against a general trend of health sector cuts, the NRHM pledged to improve health-care provisions in rural India, particularly with respect to maternal and child health. The goal was to increase public expenditures on health from 'a paltry 1% of the GDP' to a promised '2–3% . . . before the end of the 12th Plan (2012)' (Ministry of Health and Family Welfare 2005: 59, 61). Co-funding has been sought from donors (including USAID) but the problems faced by NRHM are considerable: preliminary assessments in 2007 suggested that no states in India will achieve goals related to MMR by 2010 and only six to seven states will achieve the IMR and Total Fertility Rate (TFR) goals. Within NRHM, the *Janani Suraksha Yojana* (JSY, or Motherhood Protection Programme), aims to reduce maternal mortality by encouraging women—through financial incentives—to give birth in institutions assisted by skilled birth attendants (Ministry of Health and Family Welfare 2006). Yet spending the earmarked funds is progressing very slowly: the actual amount spent on child health in the first half of 2006–7 ranged between 0 and 15 per cent of planned expenditure at the state level and a meagre 2 per cent of planned expenditure at the national level (USAID 2007).

It is too early, of course, to ascertain the impact of NRHM in UP. It is clear, however, that public provision of health services has been receiving steadily declining shares of public sector resources over the longer term. Between 1980–1 and 1998–9, public expenditure on health as a share of total government expenditure fell in UP from 5.9 per cent to 4.1 per cent (Planning Commission 2002*a*). Over the country as a whole, public expenditures on health declined from 3.12 per cent of total government expenditure in 1992–3 to 2.99 per cent in 2003–4. State government health expenditures dropped from 4.96 per cent to 4.12 per cent of their total expenditures over this period, and the small rise in the share of Central government expenditures (from 1.31 per cent to 1.69 per cent) was inadequate to make up the shortfall (Planning Commission 2005*b*: 75).

'Only when the boat has started sinking'

The government dispensary in Dharmnagri is the locally visible face of declining state investment in health services.[7] Even in the early 1980s, its buildings were dilapidated but their fabric has deteriorated since then, and several are unused or used as staff residences rather than their designated purpose. Over the years, several doctors posted there have lived in Bijnor town rather than in their quarters; the ANM (Auxiliary Nurse-Midwife)

[7] We retain the local usage dispensary here, although the facility became an Additional PHC (Primary Health Centre) in the 1990s.

moved to Bijnor in the 1990s. Scarcely legible advertisements about TB, polio eradication and family planning dot the mildew-encrusted walls. Dense weeds (mainly marijuana) between the buildings add to the desolation. Plumbing is non-existent, despite readily accessible ground water. Electricity supplies are erratic and the dispensary has no back-up facilities, no autoclaves for sterilising equipment and no means of ensuring a cold chain for vaccines (cf. Drèze and Sen 2002: 201 ff.).

From our home on the dispensary compound in 1982–3, we were well placed to see how the conversational styles and body language of staff posted there constantly underlined their superiority over uneducated village women. They would chide women publicly for their inadequate mothering and poor hygiene practices, they would ignore patients rather than disengage from chatting with their colleagues (and us), they would talk patients down rather than listen to their narratives. Our own observations, then, endorse villagers' critiques of government services: of rude staff inattentive to their duties, even in an emergency; and filthy and unkempt premises because cleaning staff are no more diligent than their medical superiors. Villagers say government employees have no incentive to be polite, competent or hard-working, because they are paid even if they see no patients or if patients are dissatisfied. Patients also cannot expect free medicines: government staff are said to sell them to enhance their own incomes.[8] In Dharmnagri and Jhakri, women who did not seek antenatal care generally attribute this to a combination of their own work schedules, and the likelihood that government staff are absent from the dispensary at the times specified for antenatal clinics. Similarly, routine child immunisations must be actively sought and villagers complain about staff absenteeism and the frequent unavailability of the relevant vaccines. As one man put it, 'anyone who cares for their patient [ailing relative] will not take them to the government hospital'.[9]

Even in the early 1980s, indeed, patients from Dharmnagri and Jhakri often obtained advice and treatment from private practitioners (known as *doctor*, irrespective of qualifications) or government staff working illegally in a private capacity. In the interim, the numbers of private practitioners have increased, in both Bijnor town and its rural hinterland. Few rural practitioners provide any inpatient care, but by the early 2000s there were upwards of thirty private nursing homes in Bijnor town offering

[8] Such allegations have been widely reported in donor reports as well as the press. For example, see Kozel and Parker 2002.

[9] These findings are similar to those reported for elsewhere in India in R. Jeffery *et al.* 2007.

inpatient care, and numerous independent diagnostic facilities (such as ultrasound centres) and chambers where private practitioners offer outpatient care. By the early 2000s, villagers were seeking little curative care—whether for chronic or acute medical problems—from government health services. Most women who experienced problems during pregnancy resorted to urban private practitioners. Sick children are generally taken to private practitioners. Few parents, though, prioritise preventive interventions and there is little market incentive for private practitioners to provide immunisation or engage in other public health activities.

In terms of the *social* quality of care, doctors running private nursing homes and their employees—nurses, compounders (pharmacists), sweepers and so forth—are said to speak courteously and gently to all their patients, and to pay attention immediately if patients need something.[10] But villagers are not well-placed to evaluate the *medical* quality of care provided by private practitioners and nursing homes. For instance, no rural private practitioners have inpatient facilities capable of providing safe emergency obstetric care, whilst most Bijnor nursing homes offering obstetric services lack facilities crucial for dealing with emergencies (such as blood, oxygen, a resident anaesthetist and neonatal resuscitation equipment or incubators), and they are by no means unusual in that (P. Jeffery and R. Jeffery 2008; see also Jesani 2003: 214).

Villagers, though, emphasise the serious financial implications of seeking health care from private facilities. Fees paid to private practitioners and the costs of medicines are higher and more variable than in state facilities (see also Chakraborty 2002: table 10.9; Mishra 2005: 74), although villagers consider them more predictable and less subject to extortion than in government facilities. According to villagers talking about nursing home deliveries in the early 2000s, caesarean sections cost in the region of Rs15,000–16,000 for the operation alone, whilst episiotomies or forceps deliveries cost some Rs4000 or so. Add to this the opportunity costs of income lost by patients' attendants and their costs of travelling back and forth to town and of meals for them and their hospitalised relatives. Few village households, even the relatively better-off, have enough ready cash to fund even a brief hospital stay. All payments are out-of-pocket and meeting medical expenses without jeopardising household wellbeing is difficult, if not impossible. Villagers do not have any health insurance. Formal bank loans take time to arrange, and

[10] Villagers are often cynical about such user-friendly treatment which they see as a vital element in running a successful business (for more on this see P. Jeffery and R. Jeffery 2008).

require collateral (usually land), so they are unavailable to the poorest villagers. Moneylenders or pawnbrokers in Bijnor town lend quickly, but generally demand some valuables as surety and charge much higher rates of interest (in 2004, Rs10 per Rs100 borrowed, per month). In practice, kinfolk and neighbours are the major source of loans, usually but not always interest free. Generally, the poorest villagers cannot source enough cash from their equally poor relatives and must seek small sums from several sources: kin, employer, moneylender, sale of land, livestock or jewellery etc. Budgeting like this is typical of the kind of lives encompassed in the term *jugār kī zindagī* (an improvised life, a 'make-do-and-mend' life). One woman commented, 'there are many ways for the poor to die'—from lack of medical treatment or from the debts incurred by having it—whilst another insisted:

> Poor people don't have enough money to feed themselves completely, so from where would we be able to show ourselves to a *doctor*? . . . No, *bhenna* (sister), if a poor person gets food to eat that is a big thing. . . . The entire matter is one of money. Whoever has money will fulfil their *shauq* (desires). And whoever doesn't have money will kill their *shauq* [so that they no longer even want something]. The entire matter is one of money. (Authors' fieldnotes, 24 February 2003)

Thus, whilst private urban nursing home facilities are more available than in the 1980s, few villagers can readily afford to avail themselves of these new opportunities. Taking a labouring woman to a clinic is no easy or obvious decision. As one woman put it, 'without *taklīf* (distress, trouble), who would go to hospital?' In the early 2000s, in the course of up-dating our maternity history records for Dharmnagri and Jhakri, we heard several long accounts of labours that had began at home and ended in hospital, almost all private nursing homes: fifty-four out of the 620 deliveries between 1993 and 2002 (just two in the Bijnor government women's hospital), compared with four out of the 449 deliveries to the women of the two villages in 1973–82. Indeed, there might have been more institutional deliveries had not several women delivered on the buffalo or bullock cart taking them to Bijnor town. Whilst institutional deliveries have become more common since the 1970s, though, they are by no means normalised and almost all the women's accounts indicated that the decision had been taken only after lengthy discussion.

One woman's waters broke before her contractions had begun. She had several injections given at home to start the labour, but the baby was still not born after several days. Two private medical practitioners called to the house from a neighbouring village said she needed to go to hospital. Her stillborn baby was born *en route*—whereupon the mother was brought back home: 'Since the baby had been born on the way itself, what need was there for the hospital?' Another of her babies was born in the house of her husband's sister in nearby Begawala: a medical practitioner in Begawala had said that she would need a 'big operation' (caesarean section), and the *dāī* (traditional birth attendant) had said the same. This would have entailed going to a facility in Bijnor town. But she refused to go and said that if the baby was to be born, it would be born without operation:

> Since there was no money, I had to refuse to have an operation. It costs a lot of money to have an operation. There is a *doctor* in Begawala and that was why I went there, but thanks to Allah I also did not need to have the *doctor*. At 12 at night, the pains started and at that time there was no *doctor*, so they [her in-laws] called a *dāī*, and then the baby was born at 2.30. At that time my own life was in great danger—the *dāī* herself had said that the baby would only be born with an operation. (Authors' fieldnotes, 17 February 2003)

Another woman reported a difficult labour during which she had twelve labour accelerating injections given by a Begawala practitioner called to her house. For another delivery, she was taken to a clinic in Bijnor where she had a 'bottle' (intravenous drip) for a while, before being brought home again for the delivery. When we expressed surprise at both these accounts she said:

> Children are born in the village inside houses. Women are not taken to the town. Only when the boat has started sinking [i.e. at the very last moment] do they run off to town. (Authors' fieldnotes, 19 February 2003)

The tragic case of Razia from Jhakri encapsulates both the lack of care available in the village from the government facilities and the financial constraints on seeking obstetric care from private facilities. Razia had died in the Bijnor government women's hospital a few weeks before Patricia arrived in Bijnor in the autumn of 2002. Her case was undoubtedly extreme, but women in Jhakri repeatedly returned to it to illustrate general points they wanted to make while discussing their own hospital deliveries or health-care issues in general.

Rashid was a poor Muslim Sheikh, whose marriage to Razia in 1982 was one of several that we attended shortly after our first arrival in the area. By 2002 Razia had nine living children, the oldest a lad training to be a tailor who limped as a result of polio and the youngest a toddler of about 2. Rashid's father had little land and had not divided it amongst his sons, so Rashid plied a cycle rickshaw in Bijnor town and took on various kinds of irregular employment. Rashid struggled to keep his family fed and clad: one woman explained, 'He is poor. Only when he comes home in the evening do they cook the food. He brings the vegetables home and they get cooked [meaning his meagre earnings do not permit food to be bought in advance].' When Razia went into labour in late August 2002, the ANM had already gone home to Bijnor, whilst Sabra—the village *dāī,* who had been trained by the ANM—was visiting her brothers in another village.[11] Had Sabra been there, she would probably have recommended that Razia be taken to hospital, for Sabra has a reputation for caution. It seemed that Razia's baby was transverse, although this was not appreciated until the baby's arm appeared in the middle of the second night of labour. Eventually, Razia was helped onto a tractor-trolley requisitioned from a neighbour and taken to the government hospital in Bijnor. She and the baby both died shortly after arrival.

Jhakri women alleged the following: that Razia was asked on arrival at the hospital how many children she had; that she was slapped on the face when she told the truth and chided for producing still more; that her feet and legs then became 'cold' (a sure sign that she was about to die); and that the doctor administered an injection that poisoned her, as was evident from the blueness of her body when it was returned to Jhakri for the funeral the next morning. The truth-value of these commentaries is less important than what they convey about perceptions of the treatment that can be expected at the government hospital. Their narratives do not so much present 'what happened' as aim to allocate responsibility for the tragedy. There were nuanced differences in interpretations of the decision-making that took place in Razia's home. Several women said Razia should have been taken to hospital much sooner and that the *dāī* had been suggesting this for some time before Razia's in-laws agreed. Others, though, emphasised that Rashid and his family were not culpable—the delay was due to Rashid's poverty and his inability to raise sufficient cash for a private hospital delivery. Some women argued that Rashid had been at fault in taking Razia to the government hospital rather then a private nursing home. Others commented he had done so only because he was anxious about meeting the costs of a private delivery. Some said that he had been reluctant to go around the village cap-in-hand requesting loans to cover the expenses until it was too late. But women's voices were in unison about the government hospital. One young woman asserted that the

[11] For more about Sabra, see P. Jeffery and R. Jeffery 1996: 259–73.

biggest mistake was taking Razia to the government hospital: 'They don't even talk properly to patients there. If they had taken her to a private place that would have been good'; and her mother amplified the point:

> When they took her to the government hospital, the doctor was very angry and said that they had only just brought her now, and she shouted and swore at them a lot. Her pains increased even more and the doctor was sometimes telling them to get a *parchā* (prescription), sometimes this, sometimes that for her. Then when she looked at her [Razia] a long time later, the life was 'leaving her feet'. She died and the baby was not even born. (Authors' fieldnotes, 17 January 2003)

Women were not surprised to hear that Razia had been rudely questioned about her children, and then slapped and chided by the hospital staff: that was simply par for the course.[12] Even the notion that medical staff deliberately administered a poisonous injection was (for them) an entirely plausible interpretation. Far-fetched as it might seem, this view reflects the low estimation and legitimacy of government medical services, which are thought to be riddled with woeful faults, like government services in general.

Limiting fertility and eradicating polio

Both before and after economic liberalisation, the government health sector has retained a high profile in the rural areas in relation to 'vertical programmes', focused top-down programmes aimed at dealing with particular health issues (such as smallpox eradication). These often entail substantial financial inputs from the Centre which the states are then required to manage. Some programmes have received substantial funding from overseas donors too, and most can be characterised as being responsive to agendas generated in international arenas rather than at the Indian grassroots.[13] Some vertical programmes—e.g. malaria control, smallpox eradication—have operated through designated staff who work only on the programme, whilst others have entailed the periodic deployment of

[12] Indeed, two World Bank authors note, '*Voices of the Poor* and other surveys point to the helplessness that poor people feel before providers—nurses hitting mothers during childbirth, doctors refusing to treat patients of a lower caste (Koenig *et al.* 2000; Narayan and Pettesch 2002)' (cited in Devarajan and Shah 2004: 913). See also R. Jeffery *et al.* 2007.

[13] We cannot pursue the political implications of these international linkages here.

general health staff and even of people outwith the health service (such as teachers) for short-term intensive work.

Vertical programmes as they have developed in practice share several organisational features that have similar implications at the local level. Vertical programmes generally reflect a view—whether at national or international level—that there is a major threat that must be dealt with urgently and not marginalised within the health sector's general activities. Vertical programmes are typified by military metaphors and a sense of crisis, with documents peppered with the vocabulary of 'campaigns', 'camps', 'weapons', 'enemy', 'targets' and so forth. The fixation on the perceived problem usually results in some diversion of staff time and resources away from other pressing problems in the provision of comprehensive primary health care (whether curative care or public health measures). Staff may receive incentives for meeting the 'targets' they are set—and punishments may be meted out to those who fail. Unsurprisingly, staff often engage in various tactics—deceiving people about the purpose of the intervention, pressurising them to comply—in their efforts to avoid punishment. Bhattacharya notes this for the smallpox eradication programme that came to a climax in the mid-1970s: staff being instructed to use force if necessary, systems of active surveillance and aggressive searches for defaulters, deployment of police and paramilitary forces, inspection tours including foreign officials, and incentives to locals to report suspected smallpox cases (S. Bhattacharya 2006: 124, 201, 213, 226). Similarly, in his account of smallpox eradication, Greenough underlines the compulsions that affected government staff and their tendency to underplay the coercion that they themselves exercised over their target populations, with the result that coercion was normalised and could feed seamlessly into other campaigns (Greenough 1995*b*). In the face of such determination, the responses of target populations were diverse, with some sectors seemingly accepting willingly what is being pressed upon them and others offering resistance (S. Bhattacharya 2006: 230 ff.). Often, people's refusal to accept 'what is good for them' and for the body politic as a whole could delegitimise their entitlements to health care and even result in allegations that they were being wilfully anti-national. Often, too, those who refuse to comply are blamed for limitations and failures that are endemic to the programme itself. Not uncommonly, then, the tactics employed in vertical programmes undermine the legitimacy of the state health services, at least for some people. In some measure, all these points are exemplified in the family planning and the polio eradication programmes.

Family planning

The Indian family planning programme began in 1956, and initially focused primarily on responding to couples seeking contraception. Gradually, it became more proactive. 'Camps' (mobile operating facilities) were established and government health staff were expected to round up potential 'cases' for sterilisation operations. From the early days, 'acceptors' were rewarded, famously with transistor radios in the 1960s and 1970s and subsequently with cash incentives. By the early 1970s, international donors and government personnel became concerned that the demographic impact of the programme had been less than expected and the programme was given more funds and greater political support (Vicziany 1983). Particularly in north India, the programme took a markedly coercive turn during the political Emergency (1975–7), after health workers and other government employees were disciplined if they failed to meet their sterilisation 'targets' (Gwatkin 1979).[14] There was unparalleled public debate—as well as widespread distrust of government health workers.

More or less problematically for all women in rural Bijnor, the family planning programme has been the most conspicuous aspect of government health services for several decades and it has been an enduring presence throughout our work in Bijnor. Our first research in Bijnor district (in 1982) focused on childbearing. Although many villagers were puzzled by our interest in matters both shameful (and embarrassing to talk about) and 'natural' (and not contentious), they generally engaged with our questioning. Given the then recent controversies over the sterilisation drive associated with the Emergency, however, we initially avoided direct questioning about contraception. Indeed, we were closely watched for signs that we intended to 'motivate' couples to accept sterilisation. Unwittingly, we had taken decisions that seemed to ally ourselves with the family planning programme: our jeep was identical to those used by the health and family planning staff, and our residence on the Dharmnagri dispensary compound had last been used for sterilisation operations during the Emergency. Throughout the early stages of our research, villagers constructed us in the light of their images of other outsiders who made appearances in their villages, especially government staff intent on

[14] Tarlo 2003 provides a general account of the Emergency in Delhi. For more on contraception and the family programme in rural Bijnor, see P. Jeffery *et al.* 1989: 200 ff.; R. Jeffery and P. Jeffery 1997; P. Jeffery and R. Jeffery 2006: 39–42, 108–16; P. Jeffery *et al.* 2008.

motivating them to adopt family planning. Many people feared that we would send whatever we were writing *ūpar* ('above', meaning officialdom outwith the village), and would bring down some nameless retribution on them. As one man from Jhakri put it: 'Villagers know that people come saying things one way and then something bad happens which villagers can't control or take any revenge for' (Authors' fieldnotes, 19 March 1982). Suspicions took time to dispel and we had to back-pedal from issues of contraception and family planning.

Fortuitously, some three months into our fieldwork, we became involved in the admission of Rajballa to hospital for an emergency caesarean operation (ironically, she was sterilised with her own and her husband's consent at the same time) (P. Jeffery *et al.* 1989: 114–18). This episode enabled us to position ourselves more convincingly on the side of villagers. People relaxed and many volunteered commentaries on the family planning programme, revealing widespread anxieties that encapsulated assumptions about the state and its employees. We began hearing about outrages that had occurred in the locality during the Emergency: for instance, bus-loads of men from other villages were taken to Bijnor town and compulsorily sterilised. Conversations with village women often focused on complaints about the quality of service they obtained from government staff. Some people claimed that maternity patients in government facilities would be pressurised into being sterilised.[15] There were allegations that the ANM would provide routine antenatal care only if a pregnant woman promised to be sterilised immediately after the birth. Women commented that the ANM was solicitous and energetic in her attentions whilst motivating a woman for sterilisation, but utterly disinterested thereafter—even if the woman had health problems related to the sterilisation itself—because of the imperative to motivate other women. Some people regarded the services offered at the dispensary as mere sweeteners to persuade people to become sterilisation 'cases'. Several health workers whom we interviewed in 1982 during a survey in the district admitted to telling unwilling 'cases' that the laparoscopic sterilisation operation was merely an injection to prevent conception for five years.[16] The preoccupation with sterilisation was widespread within the

[15] In Bijnor, this is no longer a live issue, perhaps because so few women give birth in government facilities, but pressure was still being applied elsewhere in India in the 1990s (see, e.g. Van Hollen 1998, 2003).

[16] In the early years of the sterilisation programme, vasectomy predominated because female sterilisation required major surgery and anaesthesia. With the backlash against the excesses of the Emergency and the development of new surgical techniques—especially using the

government health service—as witness the occasion in 1991 when we accompanied a Muslim woman to consult an ophthalmologist about an ulcerated cornea: the first questions he asked were how many children she had and whether she had had the 'operation' (P. Jeffery and R. Jeffery 1996: 66).

Government staff were given greater incentives to motivate people for sterilisation than to accept IUCD (intra-uterine contraceptive devices), oral contraceptives or condoms. Villagers often alleged that sterilisation was the only method of family limitation mentioned by government staff and were surprised when we told them about other methods. Until the mid-1990s, formal family planning targets were imposed on government health staff by their superiors. During the Emergency, threats of salary docking were used. At other periods, staff who failed to motivate enough 'cases' might face humiliation before colleagues at monthly monitoring meetings, whilst those who motivated enough 'cases' received cash bonuses. Viewed from this angle, the pressures health staff exercised over villagers are more comprehensible (though not more forgivable).

In the early 1980s, infant and child mortality rates in rural Bijnor were still persistently high and many people objected to the finality of sterilisation. Since then, however, several aspects of this situation have changed. Infant and child mortality rates have declined markedly and many people are more confident that their children will live. In Dharmnagri and Jhakri, babies born in the 1970s had about a one-in-four chance of dying before age 5, whereas of those born in the early 1990s about one in eight died before age 5. Further, popular resistance and donor opposition to the target-driven family planning programme resulted in a shift away from pressuring staff and towards offering a 'cafeteria' of options, such as pills and IUCDs, at government facilities. Although the Indian family planning programme has adopted a so-called target-free approach, motivating family planning 'cases' is still crucial in the ANM's work, and various benefits (such as house-plots) may be available only to people who can produce sterilisation certificates. As the ANM posted at the Dharmnagri dispensary put it:

> I cannot say that it is completely like having *targets*. There is certainly this much, that we are told to make people in our *kshetr* (field of operation) ready

laparoscope—female sterilisation has predominated from the early 1980s onwards. The laparoscope is a small periscope (known locally as *dūrbīn*) that enables the operation to be conducted under local anaesthetic and entails only one stitch on the woman's abdomen—hence the local terms *dūrbīn-wālā* or *ek-tānkā-wālā* (one-stitch) operation.

> to accept *nasbandī*. We have to report how many *nasbandīs* (sterilisations) have been done. We have to explain to the villagers, but we cannot exercise *zabardastī* (force) over them. . . . If I say too much to villagers, they will say, 'What, are you feeding the children? Are you giving things to them?' I get to hear such things. . . . So it is like *targets*, but we are not told how many *nasbandīs* we should get done. (Authors' fieldnotes, 5 November 2004)

By the early 2000s, substantial numbers of women in Dharmnagri were practising some kind of modern contraception (including sterilisation) or were planning to do so. Most took for granted that their children would survive and argued that the costs of feeding and trying to educate children militated against large families. By far the most popular form of contraception was female sterilisation, in part a reflection of its historical priority within the family planning programme and in part because of perceptions that hormonal pills and IUCDs have adverse effects on women's health. By 2005, about 30 per cent of married women in Dharmnagri under the age of 40 had been sterilised. Most others expected that they would be sterilised in due course (cf. Dyson, this volume).

Villagers' initial characterisation of us as family planning workers had worried many women in Dharmnagri, but the anxieties were much more intense in Jhakri. In the early 1980s, whilst many Muslim women lamented their repeated childbearing and often asked us about family planning, we were frequently met with hostility and suspicion, and with allegations that we must surely have come to their village only because of sterilisation. In the early 2000s, high fertility remains problematic for Muslim women, but so too does family planning. The current ANM posted in Dharmnagri seems to have worked hard to establish good relationships in Jhakri and several women reported visiting her in order to obtain family planning advice (pills, injections, IUCD), as well as to obtain antenatal tetanus injections, and advice on menstrual problems—but contraceptive usage is still low compared with Dharmnagri. Most Muslim villagers view sterilisation (in particular) as contrary to Islam.[17] Many also see Muslims as having been particular targets of family planning workers (although the poor of other communities were also targeted) and there is considerable resentment that Muslims were being pressured to adopt a technique they believed went against their religion. Some even suggest that the government wishes to eradicate Muslims. For

[17] See P. Jeffery *et al.* 2008 for a discussion of the difficulties in reaching a definitive account of 'Islamic' views about family planning and of the reasons behind Muslim resistance to family planning.

Muslims, moreover, high-caste Hindu domination of health-care provision, government and private alike, is compounded by the widespread espousal by health staff of taken-for-granted myths about Muslims' anti-national attempts to out-breed Hindus (what we have called elsewhere 'saffron demography': see P. Jeffery and R. Jeffery 2006: 1–23, 94–9 & 108–16).

'Pulse' polio

Polio vaccination was part of the Expanded Programme of Immunisation (EPI) established in 1978. Around 90 per cent coverage had been achieved by the late 1980s. At that point, the programme was largely based on surveillance and containment of outbreaks by immunising those who had been in contact with reported cases. With international commitments to eradicate polio worldwide by 2000, however, the programme in India shifted into higher gear in 1995 and became a mass campaign. In order to overcome the difficulties of maintaining the cold chain and ensuring complete coverage, funding levels were increased and more funders contributed to the programme (including WHO, UNICEF, DANIDA, DfID, Rotary International, US-based Centers for Disease Control); the World Bank has also provided substantial loans to India ($226 million since 2000) (World Bank 2000, 2003).

Polio spreads particularly easily in dense populations with poor sanitation facilities—such as UP and Bihar, the two remaining pockets of polio in India. Unlike smallpox, people can carry the polio virus sub-clinically (maybe 100 or 200 people for every one case of paralysis), so its presence in a population is not readily detected. Thus, to ensure that populations are protected, all newborns entering the population must be covered in the programme. The polio eradication programme in India uses live oral poliovirus vaccine (OPV) and children must be given the drops several times each year (hence the term 'pulse' polio). In north India, the so-called *do būnd zindagī kī* (two drops of life) are supposed to be administered to all small children (initially those under 3, later all those under 5).[18]

Mass campaigns are liable to reduce staff inputs into other aspects of curative and public health work, unless donors and governments ensure that this does not happen (Taylor *et al.* 1997). We have already noted high

[18] The decision to use OPV rather than the more expensive inactivated poliovirus vaccine (IPV) administered by injection is controversial. See Arita *et al.* 2006; Paul 2006.

levels of health staff absenteeism. Additionally, the 'pulse' polio rounds deploy health staff, along with schoolteachers and members of local Rotary Associations and Lions Clubs etc. for intensive work over several days each time. One study, using data for north India from the NFHS 1 and 2, suggests 'little evidence to support synergy between polio campaign and non-polio EPI vaccinations' (Bonu *et al.* 2003: 1807). Another, which collected data in India in 1997–8, argued that no negative effects of the pulse polio programme could be identified, but that not all the possible positive synergies had been realised (Arora *et al.* 1999, cited in Loevinsohn *et al.* 2002). The WHO itself remains cautiously non-committal in its review of the world-wide data (Aylward *et al.* 2003). Critics within India remain unconvinced:

> The campaign mode of the PPI [Pulse Polio Initiative] program has also had an adverse effect on the routine immunization program . . . though systematic surveys have not been carried out by any responsible agency to authenticate this information. Pediatricians are reporting re-emergence of some of the vaccine-preventable diseases, such as tuberculous meningitis and diphtheria, that had almost disappeared in the past decade. (Sathyamala *et al.* 2005: 377)

The premium on meeting targets has further implications for how the programme is organised. If villagers experience government curative health care as a costly absence, the pulse polio programme presents a rather different face: intensive surveillance, energetic persuasion and sometimes coercive tactics in the face of resistance.

During our research in Dharmnagri and Jhakri in 2002–5, the pulse polio programme was in full swing. Staff at the Dharmnagri dispensary, along with the *anganwadī* (crèche, literally 'courtyard') worker from Dharmnagri and Sabra, the trained *dāī* from Jhakri, made regular 'rounds' in both villages administering polio drops to all children under age 5. The process of updating our maternity history data from the two villages often generated lengthy discussions about the programme. People commented—not always negatively—on the frequency of the *polio kā chakkar* (polio rounds) and the virtual invasion of both villages for several days each round by the pulse polio teams. Many said that the pulse polio rounds were practically the only time that health staff appear in the village. Villagers were sometimes unclear about how the drops differed in their effects from injections (such as DPT). Several women had heard of children being given the drops or some injections and still succumbing to 'polio'.[19] Yet in other

[19] This might be because of misdiagnosis of a child's fever and paralysis, because the parents misunderstood the purpose of earlier injections or drops, because the polio vaccines were not

cases, families with children who had polio made every effort to ensure that their other children would have the drops. One busy mother in Jhakri told us, laughing as she did so, how her 3-year old daughter would command an older child to carry her younger sister to obtain polio drops for them both the moment she heard the whistle announcing the start of the day's work.

The doctor posted at the Dharmnagri dispensary commented that many people—Hindu and Muslim alike—initially refused to allow their children to be given the polio drops. Some, he said, became violently argumentative, but the resistance has declined and the overall response was good. Nevertheless, he and the ANM resorted to various tactics to increase the coverage of polio drops:

> Now just a few days back, my own ANM, began saying, 'Dr Saheb, those people are not giving their children the polio medicine.' So I told her to say that this was not polio medicine but medicine for *khasrā* (measles). She should first give the measles injection and then give the drops but tell the people that the drops were not for polio but for *khasrā*, which is spreading a lot these days. . . . I want polio to be finished off by whatever means. When we do our work, we have to tell lies somewhere or other. (Authors' fieldnotes, 20 November 2003)

The ANM also commented on the problems that she still faces almost twenty years after she was first posted in Dharmnagri:

> Earlier no one even asked me to sit down—on seeing me, they'd close their doors. One of the people who went with me was beaten with a stick and I myself was sworn at. . . . Now, after a great deal of explaining, people have begun getting the injections and the polio medicine given to their children. But even now, it's not being done completely. Earlier, I used to frighten people a great deal and tell them lies and then get them to take the polio drops. Sometimes I would take the name of the DM [District Magistrate]. Sometimes I'd say that the police would arrest them. . . . With great difficulty and with telling lies, only after that do I give injections to 1–2 children. Everyone should have a *penalty*, that if you don't have the injection given to your children or don't let them drink the polio medicine, then you will not get a ration card, you will not get any help from the government, your children will not be admitted to school. . . . I have to tell lies in order to keep my work moving along. And even after doing all that, some child or other will remain [who has not had the drops]. (Authors' fieldnotes, 5 November 2004)

The lengthiest and most critical (or at least questioning) commentaries came from the Muslim village of Jhakri, where some women were

---

effective due to poor cold chain maintenance, or because of vaccine-associated paralytic polio (VAPP). See Arita *et al.* 2006; John 2006; Sathyamala *et al.* 2005.

worried about the effects of the drops and did not readily allow their children to have them. Several sought our assurance that the drops would not harm their children. Many women reported being told that the polio drops would make their children infertile or impotent and that their 'line' would die out. Some said that they allowed the drops to be administered only because they were compelled to do so.[20] Anisa, for instance, said she initially hid her daughter when the polio drops were being given: 'An old woman told me that children become useless after taking the medicine. They will not have any *phal* ("fruits", meaning children). That's why I got frightened.' But now the child was being given the drops 'because they force the children to take them. But I am still refusing and I am still frightened about what will happen to my children if they cannot have their own children in future.'

The Jhakri *pradhān* (head of village council) was involved in the pulse polio programme and he said that many women believed their sons would become *nā-mard* (impotent). When we asked if men also said this, he scoffed that 'men don't have spare time from their own *kām-dhandā* (activities)—only women say such *ūltī* (upside-down) things'. Several women in Jhakri, too, were disdainful about village women in general, that they did not understand the necessity of having the polio drops, that rumours 'just emerge from women's bellies', that 'women themselves create these things—they have nothing else to do and when several women are sitting together they just make up things', or 'some women have the habit of telling lies in order to make fun of people'. One commented:

> Some time earlier this idea spread that by making the children drink this medicine, boys will not be able to have children—they will have had *nasbandī*—and the government is doing this *jān būjh-kar* (intentionally). That's why women are not giving the drops to drink. But women here are very wrong thinking. [. . .] I don't know who started this rumour about the drops, but it has spread everywhere. (Authors' fieldnotes, 18 February 2003)

Sabra, the trained *dāī* in Jhakri, has placed placards proclaiming *do būnd zindagī kī* (two drops of life) prominently on the walls of her small house. She knows all the families where there are small children and can inform the polio team if they have missed anyone out. She commented that there used to be a great deal of smallpox but it was eradicated. And now the government is giving the polio drops because it does not want polio to remain either, 'but people fear the drops and hide their children

[20] We had several similar conversations in Qaziwala, a predominantly Muslim village nearby, when we were conducting research there in 2000–2 with Craig Jeffrey.

because they think that this medicine is to stop children being born, that it is to finish off their *nasl* (family line). We asked if people in the village believe her when she tries to persuade them this is incorrect: 'No, they don't believe me. They think I'm getting something from the government for stopping children being born, that I'm doing damage to the village people in order to build up my income.' Her daughter said that women often let their children have the drops only because they fear the 'big people' who come to the village to back up the team and that

> people in the village don't understand that the government wants to put a complete end to this illness, in the same way as *mātā* (smallpox). Even if one child remains who has not taken the medicine, then it could spread the illness to other children. But villagers do not understand this matter. (Authors' fieldnotes, 20 January 2003)

One young woman—also not opposed to the drops—told us how the polio team will catch a child and compel it to have the drops by opening its mouth and forcing the medicine in. When we asked if the team did not explain what the drops were for before doing this, she replied:

> The government is doing this for our benefit, but some women don't understand this. . . . The *doctornī* (female 'doctor', meaning the ANM) does explain the benefits. But even so, the village women don't understand, and *majbūr ho ke, zabardastī dawā pilānī partī hai* (having been compelled, she has to force the children to drink the medicine). (Authors' fieldnotes, 5 February 2003)

As Greenough notes, immunisation programmes are never just about immunisation, and a 'logic of resistance' reflects wider issues, such as the fears of minorities about the agendas of the majority (Greenough 1995*b*: 633). His comments are germane for the family planning and pulse polio programme alike. Most Muslim parents in rural Bijnor and north India more generally have accepted polio drops (if only after energetic persuasion). Yet resistance to pulse polio has been regarded as a particularly Muslim phenomenon, as witness the deployment of high-profile Muslims such as film star Shahrukh Khan to publicise and endorse the programme. The urgency of the polio eradication programme has been associated with coercion that government staff (and others drawn into the pulse polio programme) regard as essential if their task is to be completed. Yet a history of resistance being met with coercion results in a 'residue of resentment' that feeds into people's responses to other government health campaigns (Greenough 1995*b*: 643; see also Nichter 1995: 618). A belief that polio drops render children infertile is of a piece with how many Muslims read the state's other dealings with them, and especially their interpretations of the family planning programme and its associated coercive tactics.

Reported polio cases in India have declined from 4,791 in 1994 to 135 in 2004 (of which 82 were in UP and 40 in Bihar), and just 66 in 2005.[21] But there were setbacks in 2001–2 and again in 2006 (when over 500 cases were reported), which commentators attribute to the use of live vaccine that tends be associated with periodicity in outbreaks (e.g. John 2006). Yet this does not amount to the *eradication* of polio and some critics consider control rather than eradication to be a more realistic goal (Arita *et al.* 2006; Paul 2006). Nevertheless, the pockets of resistance to the programme—rather than system failures—are widely blamed for the continuing presence of polio in India well after 2000.

Concluding reflections

Whilst the UP government was not providing a comprehensive welfare state even before 1991, the costly absences in state health-care provision in rural UP have been exacerbated by the World Bank agenda for reducing state expenditures and opening spaces for private health providers to flourish in a context lacking in viable health insurance schemes or other forms of financing. The coercive presences are also part of international agendas, endorsed by urban middle classes—in India as well as those in the West who support foreign aid to health and family planning—paranoid about population pressures and major epidemics. The population control and immunisation programmes have always relied heavily on foreign financing. Paul Greenough calls this the creation of the 'immunizing state' (Greenough 1995*a*: 606). Moreover, many critics of vertical programmes—such as the family planning and polio eradication programmes—have also argued that they divert staff effort away from broader reproductive health and public health activities (see e.g. Qadeer 1998; Sathyamala *et al.* 2005: 377). Certainly, apart from the family planning and polio eradication programmes, villagers see little outreach from the government health services.

Nevertheless, more funding is being put into improving physical services and providing more staff. It is too soon to pass judgement on the *Janani Suraksha Yojana* (JSY, Motherhood Protection Programme), yet

[21] Several commentators, however, argue that a shift to a less inclusive definition for 'acute flaccid paralysis' means that the reported decline in polio may be exaggerated (e.g. Paul 2006).

early indications suggest that it, too, is failing to live up to its promise. For one, there is widespread evidence that the equipment and personnel that could guarantee safe institutional deliveries and an adequate referral system for emergency obstetric care (EmOC) are simply not in place, especially in states such as UP (IIPS 2005). Second, it is not a rights-based programme staffed by workers characterised by a service orientation. Numerous accounts (as yet anecdotal) suggest that government staff routinely behave in a manner that would discourage women from seeking institutional deliveries: aside from the familiar brusqueness and inattentiveness, reports suggest (*inter alia*) that staff sometimes insist on taking a substantial cut from the 'incentive' as payment for services rendered, that the incentive is given some months in arrears, or that women are compelled to remain longer in the institution than they wish before being given the incentive money (with all the ancillary costs of transport and food that are associated with hospital-based care) (CHSJ 2007: 109–17). Even apparently benign developments, then, can contain coercive elements in practice. Moreover, the functioning of UP's public sector health care is jeopardised by the tipping of the balance heavily in favour of the huge private sector. It is hard to see how initiatives such as JSY and NRHM more generally can recuperate a state-funded system whose legitimacy has been so seriously compromised—indeed this may be behind the problems faced by the NRHM in spending the funds allocated to it.

It is from this perspective that we can appreciate Bijnor villagers' dissatisfaction with government health services—with their absence, but also with the punitive and coercive aspects of their presence. Time and again, villagers asserted that the state *should* provide health-care services for the populace in general, and do so in a just, efficient and humanitarian manner, but that it fails to live up to these ideals (see also Hansen 2000; Lieten 2003). And, whilst virtually everyone complains and poor villagers are all vulnerable to the vagaries of the government health facilities, we can also note the marked communal dimension to this scenario. Put another way, the state's legitimacy has been undercut not only by the failures of the *state-as-provider* but by the coercive dimensions of the *state-as-regulator*. Few villagers believe they can alter the state's functioning at the local level, but this does not silence their criticisms.

4

Economic Resurgence, Lopsided Reform and Jobless Growth

VIJAY JOSHI

Summary. In the second half of India's post-independence career, growth has increased dramatically as a consequence of economic reform, which has unshackled the economy from the iron grip of controls and exposed it to international competition. However, there are still a number of impediments to rapid growth being sustained. Moreover, the quality of India's growth is flawed. It has been relatively 'jobless' and as a consequence India risks becoming a two-tier economy, with all the attendant dangers. There is no doubt that a consistent economic package can be designed which would promote rapid growth, create employment and eliminate poverty. But in order to deliver it India's political class will have to walk successfully the tightrope of implementing reform while balancing diverse interests and managing the compulsions of mass politics.

Introduction

IN 2007, INDIA COMPLETED SIXTY YEARS of independence from British rule. The country's political and social achievements during this period have been remarkable and impressive. To the amazement of many, this vast and complex country has managed to protect national unity, introduce and preserve democracy, and dilute traditional caste hierarchies.[1] But, for the first thirty years, economic performance was very disappointing. The growth rate of national income was only about 3.5 per cent a year

[1] Winston Churchill would have been amazed. He said in 1931: 'India is a geographical term. It is no more a united nation than the Equator.'

Proceedings of the British Academy **159**, 73–106. © The British Academy 2010.

(little more than 1 per cent per head). Since then, there has been a marked improvement. In the last thirty years, growth has averaged 6 per cent a year (about 4 per cent per head). Even so, poverty continues on a massive scale. Around a third of India's 1.1 billion people live in conditions of acute poverty; and around a third of the world's poor live in India.[2]

India's paramount goal for the future must surely be to achieve widely shared prosperity without sacrificing democracy and civil liberties. Direct redistribution of income can at best play a supportive role in achieving rising living standards for the poor. What is needed is sustained growth of national income of around 10 per cent a year for the next two or three decades. It is also essential, if the poor are to benefit, that the growth should be labour-demanding. This requirement has so far been conspicuous by its absence.

India's recent fast growth was facilitated by economic reforms that were initiated in the 1980s and radically intensified in the 1990s. These involved principally liberalisation of controls on trade, private industry and finance. But the reforms were also partial and unbalanced. Privatisation was attempted without success; fiscal consolidation was not completed; large deficiencies were left in infrastructure provision; employment protection legislation was left untouched; and agriculture and the social services were relatively neglected. As a result, growth, though rapid, was less rapid than it could have been, and it was also not 'inclusive' enough.

The Ancien Regime

Why did India fail to achieve rapid, participatory growth for three decades after independence? The basic answer is that Indian policymakers acted with a mistaken conception of the role of the state. The state was extremely energetic in areas that were outside its competence. Detailed regulation of economic activity created massive inefficiencies and stifled entrepreneurial drive. At the same time, the state neglected to attend to areas where it should have been active. In particular, it failed to ensure that poor people could gain access to primary health care and education. As a result, they were deprived of some of the elementary

[2] The poverty ratio was 27.5 per cent in 2004, using the official Indian poverty line. It was 34 per cent using the international 'dollar-a-day' measure of poverty.

constituents of the good life and denied the opportunity to enhance their principal income-earning asset, namely themselves.

In accounting for India's slow growth, I begin by noting that for thirty years from 1950 to 1980, India's growth did not budge from its slow pace despite a doubling of saving and investment rates. Low productivity of investment was clearly the main reason for this miserable performance. Low productivity in turn was the product of three features of economic policy: inappropriate and excessive state intervention in markets; the dominant role of the public sector; and neglect of critical social sectors.

The origins of dirigiste policies lay in the doctrines of collectivism and socialism, characterised by distrust of business, contempt for the price mechanism, and hostility to international trade that had a special resonance in many post-colonial societies. It was taken for granted that extensive government intervention and controls were necessary to subdue or supplant the market. In India, a further twist was given by the 'heavy industry' strategy, based on Soviet planning models, that was adopted in the mid-1950s and used to justify the physical allocation of investment. Once controls were established, the dynamic of rent-seeking took over and they grew like topsy to the point where no economic activity, unless of very small scale, could be legally pursued without obtaining dozens of permits and licences from different departments of government.[3] Controls permeated every aspect of business decision-making including investment, output-mix, pricing, credit, employment, entry and exit. Especially harmful were the controls on foreign trade and investment that stemmed from the belief in 'self-reliance'. Their consequence was that India became a backwater, isolated from the benefits of international division of labour and diffusion of technology.

Another aspect of the command and control strategy was the dominant role accorded to the public sector. The domain of the public sector extended well beyond the traditional utilities and included large swathes of manufacturing industry, many consumer goods and even hotels. Public sector enterprises were expected to be highly profitable and to serve as a spearhead of investment. The reality was different. Returns in most public sector firms were abysmally low. Many of them not only made losses but became 'sick', a polite Indian word for bankrupt, and imposed a large fiscal burden. In retrospect, this is not surprising. Experience all over the world indicates that the agency problem is far more severe in public than

[3] For an authoritative analysis, see Bhagwati and Desai (1970). See also Bhagwati (1993).

in private sectors.[4] Public sector managers are faced with many conflicting objectives, many constraints on their freedom to manage and, equally, no serious penalties for inefficient performance. There is an insoluble problem in reconciling managerial autonomy and public accountability. Some countries achieve a better compromise than others. India was among the worst.

The neglect of the social sectors is the third critical element in the explanation of India's stagnation. India's performance in the fields of primary health and basic education was inadequate, indeed shameful and shocking. These goods are both direct constituents of human welfare and major requisites of economic progress. It is now almost a cliché that the phenomenal success of the East Asian economies has been based on solid achievements in these areas, in addition to their outward-oriented trade policies. Of course, part of the reason for India's poor comparative performance is that it started from a lower base than the East Asian economies (other than China). Another reason is low growth itself and the consequent shortage of resources. But these are by no means a full explanation as some Indian states like Kerala made tremendous strides in these areas and achieved social standards equivalent to those in East Asia. Other states like Bihar and Uttar Pradesh failed miserably. There is little doubt that in these successes and failures, government attention and policy or lack of it played a crucial role. (See Drèze and Sen 1995.)

In sum, India's poor development was largely caused by misdirected state activity. India did not enjoy socialism but 'exclusive bourgeois socialism', a condition in which growth was strangled by controls and its benefits were largely channelled to a small minority of the population, often in the name of poverty-redressal.

Growth and poverty reduction since 1980

Reformist ideas began to make headway in India in the late 1970s and gathered steam in the 1980s. By this time, the contrast between East Asian success and Indian failure was becoming hard to ignore. The first sign of change was that government policy became more business-friendly. There was also some liberalisation of a piecemeal variety, in particular deregu-

[4] The agency problem concerns the difficulty faced by the principal, who employs the agent, in ensuring that the agent acts in the principal's interests. In this instance, the principals are the citizens of India and public sector managers are their agents.

lation of industrial licensing in some sectors and conversion of import quotas to tariffs. India was so far inside the efficiency frontier that even these minor changes, together with fiscal expansion, led to an acceleration of growth to nearly 6 per cent a year in the 1980s. This rise in growth, which occurred before the major reforms of the 1990s, has led some commentators to denigrate the importance of the latter. In my view, this is wholly wrong. Firstly, a contributory cause of fast growth in the 1980s was expansionary fiscal policy and foreign borrowing. The scale of these was manifestly unsustainable and resulted in a full-blown macroeconomic crisis at the end of the decade.[5] Secondly, reform in the 1980s was very shallow. There was little in the way of introducing genuine competition, domestic or international. Without the more sweeping reform undertaken after 1991, the growth acceleration would have fizzled out.

The crisis of 1991 provided the occasion for a more decisive change of strategy. As part of the stabilisation programme, India borrowed from the IMF and no loans would have been forthcoming without the promise of structural adjustment. Meanwhile, the world had changed. Communism had collapsed in the Soviet Union and Eastern Europe and with it collapsed the respectability of India's earlier strategy. One way or another, the ground was sufficiently prepared to use the crisis as an occasion for embarking on a transformation of the Indian economy. A programme of reform, more radical than anything attempted in the previous decade, was initiated in July 1991 by the minority Congress government headed by Narasimha Rao, with Manmohan Singh, a distinguished economist–civil servant, as Finance Minister.

Have the reforms been successful? One way of making a judgement is to consider the economic outcomes. Another way is to ask whether there has been progress in creating the new system that is the target of Indian reform. This is a competitive market economy with mainly private ownership, but with government intervention to deliver macroeconomic stability, correct market failures, and create a safety net for the poorest people.[6] I use a mixture of these two approaches below.

[5] The causes of the crisis of 1991 are examined in chaps. 7 and 8 of Joshi and Little (1994).

[6] Obviously, this model is not explicit or closely specified and has to be inferred from attempted changes in the direction of policy. At the level of ideas, it has plenty of controversial fringes, for example with regard to the desirable extent of privatisation. Moreover, reformers may prefer for political reasons to leave it undefined. Nevertheless, for a critic, comparison of the actuality of the policy framework against an end or target, even if imperfectly specified, is surely the appropriate course.

There has been a vigorous academic debate attempting to locate precisely the point of inflection when growth began to accelerate. This controversy is not particularly interesting because India's annual output data are not accurate enough to reach reliable conclusions. (See Bosworth, Collins and Virmani 2007.) But it is indisputably evident that the rate of growth began to increase some time in the second half of the 1970s, increased further in the following two decades and appears to have increased yet again after 2003.[7] In the account that follows, I adopt 1980 as the year of inflection, as that is good enough for my purposes.

Tables 4.1 to 4.4 summarise the salient features of the growth acceleration. Table 4.1 shows that until 1980, growth was slow, around 3.5 per cent a year, despite a significant rise in domestic saving and investment. After 1980, however, a similar rise in investment led to a pronounced increase in the growth rate. Evidently, the productivity of investment rose.

Table 4.1. Investment and growth.

	1950–60	1960–70	1970–80	1980–2005	2005–8
Investment (% GDP)	11.2	14.7	17.6	23.5	34.7
GDP growth (% p.a.)	3.2	3.9	2.9	5.8	9.2

Source: Reserve Bank of India (2007)

The following three tables decompose the growth acceleration from 1960–80 to 1980–2005 in a more analytic fashion. Table 4.2 shows growth in output, employment and output per worker in the two periods.

Table 4.2. Output and employment growth 1960–2005 (annual % rate of change).

	Output	Employment	Output/Worker
1960–80	3.4	2.2	1.3
1980–2005	5.8	1.9	3.8

Source: Bosworth, Collins and Virmani (2007).

[7] The causes and timing of India's growth acceleration are discussed in chap. 13 of Joshi and Little (1994), de Long (2003), Rodrik and Subramanian (2005), Panagariya (2008), Srinivasan (2005) and Virmani (2004).

Table 4.3 shows the contributions made to growth in output per worker by capital, land, education and 'total factor productivity' (TFP), which is economists' jargon for efficiency of resource use. This decomposition is based on the standard Solow–Denison methodology.

Table 4.4 decomposes growth in output per worker differently from Table 4.3 to show how much of it can be accounted for by weighted sectoral growth (the weights being the share of each sector in total output) on the one hand and shifts of resources between sectors on the other hand.

Tables 4.2–4.4 highlight some distinctive features of India's recent growth. Firstly, although the acceleration in growth of output and output per worker is shared by all the three broad sectors of the economy, it is most pronounced in services. This contrasts with the experience of China and the rest of East Asia where industry (led by exports) was the leading sector. Secondly, in the first period, growth was nearly all due to increases

Table 4.3. Sources of economic growth, 1960–2005 (annual % rate of change).

	Output/worker	Contribution of:			
		Capital	Land	Education	TFP
Whole economy					
1960–80	1.3	1.0	−0.2	0.2	0.2
1980–4	3.8	1.4	0.0	0.4	2.0
Agriculture					
1960–80	0.1	0.2	−0.2	0.1	−0.1
1980–4	1.7	0.4	−0.1	0.3	1.1
Industry (manufacturing)					
1960–80	1.6 (2.0)	1.8 (1.5)	—	0.3 (0.3)	−0.4 (0.2)
1980–4	3.0 (4.0)	1.6 (2.1)	—	0.3 (0.4)	1.1 (1.5)
Services					
1960–80	2.0	1.1	—	0.5	0.4
1980–4	3.8	0.7	—	0.4	2.7

Source: Bosworth, Collins and Virmani (2007).

Table 4.4. Growth of output per worker 1960–2005 (annual % rate of change).

	Whole economy (1)	Weighted sectoral growth (2)	Reallocation effects (1)–(2)
1960–80	1.3	0.9	0.4
1980–4	3.7	2.8	1.0

Source: Bosworth, Collins and Virmani (2007).

in factor supply with only a negligible contribution from TFP; the acceleration in the second period was, however, mainly driven by TFP growth. Thirdly, overall growth in both periods can largely be explained by intra-sectoral growth rather than by resource reallocation between sectors. This is important because value-added per worker is five to seven times higher in industry and services than in agriculture. Thus, unlike China and the rest of East Asia, India has not exploited the huge potential gain in shifting labour out of farming.

The touchstone of successful economic performance is poverty reduction. Table 4.5 shows official estimates of the population below an officially defined poverty line.[8]

Table 4.5. Population below the official poverty line.

Year	Poverty (%)	Number (millions)
1973–4	54.9	321
1977–8	51.3	329
1983	44.5	323
1993–4	36.0	320
2004–5	27.8	303

Source: Planning Commission (2002*a*); Planning Commission (2007).

The improvement since the late 1970s is evident: the incidence of poverty has fallen by 23 percentage points.[9] The absolute number of poor people has also recently started to fall. But there are still 300 million people below the poverty line; and, as Table 4.6 shows, India is still far behind successful East Asian economies in health and education outcomes.[10] The inclusiveness of the Indian growth process thus leaves a lot to be desired. (See also Jeffery and Jeffery in this volume.)

While the poverty ratio has fallen in the post-reform period, inequality has increased in various dimensions. The Gini coefficient of household consumption expenditure at the national level went up from 29.7 in 1994 to 36.8 in 2004. Urban–rural disparities have increased: since 1993 the rise in per capita consumption expenditure has been twice as great in urban

[8] The poverty line is defined in India as the minimum subsistence income that can support the consumption of 2,400 calories per person in rural areas and 2,100 calories in urban areas.

[9] Indian poverty estimates are a minefield of conceptual and measurement issues. See Deaton and Kozel (2005).

[10] Many other examples of India's low human development could be given. For example, according to the Planning Commission some 40–50 per cent of children in India are undernourished. See Planning Commission (2007).

Table 4.6. Social indicators: India, China, South Korea.

	Life expectancy (at birth)		Infant mortality (per 1000 births)		Adult literacy rate	
	1960	2005	1960	2005	1960	2002
India	44	64	165	56	28	65
China	47	72	150	23	n.a.	86
Rep. of Korea	54	78	85	5	71	98

Source: World Bank (2007).

areas as in rural areas. Such changes are not uncommon in the early stages of rapid growth. More politically salient is the rise in regional inequality. The Gini coefficient of state per capita incomes has risen from 21 in 1980 to 29 in 2001. The richer states have grown much faster than the poorer states; consequently, the gap in per capita income between the former and the latter has widened significantly. (For example, the ratio of per capita income in Punjab, the richest state, and Bihar, the poorest state, was 3.4 in 1970 and 4.5 in 2004. See Purfield (2006).)

Macroeconomic Balance[11]

Macroeconomic stability is a public good whose provision ranks with law and order as a necessary condition for advancing social welfare. It can be defined as keeping inflation low, avoiding serious recessions in economic activity, mitigating the adverse consequences of economic shocks and maintaining a sustainable fiscal and balance of payments position. Stability is a constituent of welfare in its own right but evidence shows that it is also a requisite of rapid long-run growth.

India was macroeconomically stable in the slow growth period. Ironically, the acceleration of growth in the 1980s was accompanied by an alarming decline in fiscal prudence, which was mainly responsible for the crisis at the end of the decade.[12] This crisis was resolved quickly, and in an orthodox manner, by fiscal retrenchment, devaluation and an IMF loan. Since then, macroeconomic performance has been very satisfactory (see Table 4.7). Growth continued at the rate of around 6 per cent a year

[11] India's macroeconomic policies are discussed in depth in Joshi and Little (1994), chap. 2 of Joshi and Little (1996) and chap. 3 of Acharya (2006).

[12] The political economy of the corrosion of fiscal rectitude is discussed in Joshi and Little (1994), pp. 68–72.

Table 4.7. Macroeconomic indicators.

	1960–80	1980–90	1990–2000	2000–5	2005–8
GDP growth (% p.a.)	3.4	5.8	5.7	6.0	9.2
Inflation (wholesale prices) (% p.a.)	7.5	8.0	8.1	4.7	4.8
Fiscal deficit (% GDP)	5.3	9.0	7.7	9.0	6.4
Current account (% GDP)	−1.2	−2.3	−1.3	0.6	−1.1
		1980	1990	2005	2008
Public sector domestic debt (% GDP)		26	41	80	76

Source: Reserve Bank of India (2007).

attained in the 1980s, but much more sustainably, since the balance of payments was stronger. From 2003, growth has speeded up further to 8.7 per cent a year (9.2 per cent in 2005–8) on the back of buoyant private saving and investment.[13] There have been no disastrous cyclical slowdowns in overall activity: annual growth of national income has not fallen below 4 per cent in any year since 1993. Inflation has been low by developing-country standards and has come down to less than 5 per cent a year after 2000. External deficits have been moderate. Indeed, from 2001–4, India experienced current account surpluses. Capital inflows have also surged, so India has accumulated a large stock of foreign exchange reserves, currently about $300 billion, providing more than a year's import cover. The fiscal deficit, however, has remained high. Despite some decline in the past three years, it is still in the region of 6 per cent of GDP (8 per cent of GDP if 'off-budget' subsidies are included).

This is not the place for a blow-by-blow account of macroeconomic events. I shall focus instead on one major macroeconomic success and one major macroeconomic failure. The success concerns India's monetary and balance-of-payments policies, which were instrumental not only in keeping inflation low but, more remarkably, in avoiding the currency and financial crises that have afflicted many developing countries since 1990. The failure concerns the inadequacy of fiscal consolidation.

[13] It is probable that recent super-fast growth was also, in part, the result of the exceptionally benign world economic conditions from 2002–7. These came to an end with the implosion of the US housing boom in 2007 and the ensuing 'credit crunch' that rapidly spread elsewhere. Indian growth will, for a time, be adversely affected.

Monetary and balance-of-payments policies

Open economy macroeconomic policy is subject to a trilemma, closely related to what economists call the 'impossible trinity', which can be stated as follows. Of the three desirable goals, interest-rate autonomy, exchange-rate targeting, and free capital mobility, a government can achieve any two but not all three. One alternative is to go for exchange rate targeting and free capital mobility, but that involves giving up the freedom to set home interest rates independently of foreign interest rates. The second alternative is to retain interest-rate autonomy, along with free capital mobility, and to let the exchange rate float. That is now the policy in many advanced countries. India chose the third alternative. This is to give up on free capital mobility, which makes it feasible to combine interest-rate autonomy and exchange-rate targeting.

Maintaining some focused capital controls was a wise choice.[14] They enabled India to use monetary policy for stabilising cyclical fluctuations, while simultaneously maintaining the exchange rate at a competitive level, without being swept off course by volatile capital flows. In particular, India did not suffer contagion from the East Asian crisis of 1997, despite the fact that some of its traditional 'fundamentals', such as fiscal deficits and inflation, were in worse shape than those of the East Asian countries. The reason India escaped is that it had very little short-term external debt in relation to foreign exchange reserves, as a consequence of controlling inflows of 'hot money'.[15]

Of course, as India's economy matures, making the capital account convertible may eventually be the appropriate course. This is a contentious issue but the important point to note here is that the Indian version of economic reform was not mindlessly wedded to laissez-faire.

The Fiscal Problem and Fiscal Reform

India's fiscal problem has a 'macro' and a 'micro' dimension. The 'macro' part relates to reducing the size of the fiscal deficit, which is excessive. The 'micro' part concerns (i) moving towards a more efficient structure of taxes and subsidies and (ii) changing the composition of government expenditure away from fruitless subsidies and towards spending on infrastructure

[14] India's capital controls are not pervasive. They are focused on short-term debt-creating capital movements. Foreign direct investment and portfolio equity flows face few restrictions.

[15] On India's response to the 'macroeconomic trilemma', see Joshi (2003), Joshi and Sanyal (2004), and Joshi (2008).

and the social sectors. The macro and the micro aspects have to be pursued together. This difficult transition is as yet far from complete.

As a result of the profligacy of the preceding decade, India entered the 1990s in dire need of fiscal adjustment. Fiscal stabilisation was reasonably successful in the first half of the 1990s but it was undone in the second half and remained unsatisfactory until 2003.[16] In 2003, a Fiscal Responsibility Act was passed by Parliament which decreed that the Central Government should balance its revenue budget and bring the fiscal deficit down to 3 per cent of GDP within five years. The timetable has been roughly adhered to, so far. Equally important, several state governments have passed their own similar Acts. Table 4.7 shows considerable improvement in the fiscal position in 2005–8. But this should not be taken at face value. Firstly, the official deficit figure understates the true deficit because it excludes various 'off-budget' government subsidies, especially those on oil and oil-related products. Secondly, the improvement in the deficit reflects the influence of a cyclical boom in tax revenues, which may not last; and thirdly, the future fiscal outlook is darker than it appears because of the probable large increases in government expenditure to implement the award of the Sixth Pay Commission and to compensate banks for the loan forgiveness extended to farmers in the budget of 2008. It would thus be rash to conclude that the fiscal problem has gone away. Reducing the combined central and state governments' true revenue deficit to zero will require a further fiscal adjustment of around 3 per cent of GDP in a normal year.

Resolving the fiscal problem is easy on paper but difficult politically. Desirable measures include increasing tax coverage,[17] restraining government employment and pay,[18] reducing interest payments by using privatisation proceeds to retire public debt,[19] and most important, restructuring public expenditure by cutting back on dysfunctional subsidies.

The explicit subsidies mainly go to food, fuel and fertilisers and constitute around 2.5 per cent of GDP.[20] Fertiliser subsidies are partly subsidies

[16] For a rigorous treatment of fiscal sustainability in India, see chap. 2 of Joshi and Little (1996) and Buiter and Patel (2006).

[17] One reason why tax coverage is low is that the Centre cannot (constitutionally) tax agricultural income and the states do not want to, for fear of antagonising farm lobbies.

[18] Government departments are grossly overstaffed and rates of pay are relatively high. Implementation of the Sixth Pay Commission recommendations will worsen the situation.

[19] Public enterprises could be sold at prices considerably higher than the present value of their profits.

[20] Most but not all food and fertiliser subsidies are shown in the budget. Fuel subsidies are explicit but 'off-budget'.

to the fertiliser industry, and partly to farmers, very roughly half and half depending on the import price. There is no sound economic argument for special protection of fertiliser plants: there is only a short-run argument that otherwise probably half the industry would collapse. But the subsidy should certainly be reduced, and high cost plants closed down in a phased manner. There is also no good argument for subsidising fertilisers to the farmer. Prices should rise to import parity.[21] Farmers would not lose if output prices were freed at the same time. Fuel subsidies are available on a universal basis for kerosene, used only by the poor, but also for liquid petroleum gas, mainly consumed by higher income households, and to a smaller extent for gasoline and diesel. Fuel subsidies have risen sharply with the rise in the world price of oil. There is a lot of room for cutting back on fuel subsidies without affecting poverty, by restricting them to kerosene and targeting them at poor families. Food subsidies represent the difference between the procurement prices paid to farmers and the issue prices of the public distribution system (PDS). But it is widely acknowledged that the PDS is a very cost-ineffective way of relieving poverty. The food subsidy bill could be halved by abolishing universal entitlement and withdrawing ration cards from those with visible signs of affluence.[22] Government buffer stocks could still be operated to moderate fluctuations in food prices, purchases and sales being made through normal commercial channels.

The explicit subsidies are only the tip of an iceberg. We must also take account of the massive hidden subsidies which permeate the provision of goods by the state (leaving aside pure public goods where free state provision is the appropriate course). If prices should reflect the true costs and benefits of different products and activities, the Indian subsidy system is

[21] The conventional wisdom of the development establishment of the 1950s and 1960s was that agriculture should be encouraged by subsidising inputs. This was preferred to higher outputs which did nothing to encourage the new methods that were needed to raise yields. Whatever the merits of this argument at the time, input subsidies are now clearly counterproductive. Subsidised electricity causes over-pumping of tube wells. Cheap water results in its excessive use and unduly encourages water-demanding crops. Fertiliser subsidies result in a bias in favour of nitrogen relative to phosphates, while also discouraging organic fertilisers. Further, all these results of input subsidisation work in the direction of capital intensity, thereby tending to reduce employment.

[22] Better still would be the introduction of food stamps or electronic 'smart cards' which would enable the costly and wasteful administrative machinery of the PDS to be wound down. Of course, the targeting problem would remain. But the identification of families below the poverty line has now been done in most states. Smart cards could also be used to target other transfers, including the kerosene subsidy.

a blatant denial of this principle. It is inefficient and inequitable and leads to inappropriate usage and under-investment. A detailed estimate of subsidies has recently been made, counting as subsidy the difference between cost and what is actually recovered (see Ministry of Finance 2004, and Srivastava *et al.* 2003). The calculation distinguishes between subsidies on 'merit goods' (defined as those with significant positive externalities, e.g. primary health and primary education) and 'non-merit' goods. The subsidy on merit goods is about 6 per cent of GDP, that on non-merit goods a massive 8 per cent of GDP, a figure which is as large as the overall fiscal deficit. This includes not only the fertiliser subsidy but also the notorious subsidies on power, irrigation water and other agricultural inputs, many of which are the responsibility of state governments. None of these subsidies accrues significantly to the poor.[23]

Deep fiscal adjustment is critical for the success of India's reforms. By 'deep adjustment' I mean one that embraces both a reduction in the fiscal deficit *and* a change in the composition of public expenditure towards the social sectors and investment in infrastructure. The technical possibilities are enormous but so far progress is barely perceptible. It is obviously only the nature of the political system and its balance of forces that prevents India from achieving these ends. The future of reform will be endangered unless this deadlock is broken.

Structural Reform[24]

Structural economic reform clearly has to be given much of the credit for India's resurgence.[25] I now turn to a review of reform in the main areas.[26] Its progress has been uneven. There has been remarkable movement in

[23] Even so, eliminating the agricultural input subsidies should only be done as part of a policy package, as explained later in the text.

[24] Assessment of Indian reform was pioneered by Joshi and Little (1996) and their analysis remains highly relevant. Since then, there has been an extensive literature. A recent, excellent and comprehensive treatment can be found in Panagariya (2008). See also Ahluwalia (2002) and OECD (2007).

[25] Basu and Maertens (2007) emphasise the importance of the spread of banks in raising the growth rate via a rise in household savings. But it is notable that prior to 1980, the growth rate did not rise despite the spread of banks. (Population per bank branch fell from 88,000 in 1960 to 18,000 in 1980.) The growth rate increased after 1980 because there was reform across a broad front.

[26] There is one significant omission in this review. It does not assess present and future policy with regard to the environment, including climate change.

some areas but little or none in others. In the following analysis, I place greater emphasis on the half-empty cup of achievement than on the half-full. But I must preface that by saying that significant changes have indeed taken place, on a scale that would have been unthinkable during the ancien regime.

Trade

Economic theory postulates and experience confirms that trade openness is a necessary (though not a sufficient) condition of efficiency and growth. Before reform started, India was one of the most closed economies in the world. It was protected by very high tariffs, as well as import quotas and licensing. Trade reform has been gradual but firmly in a liberalising direction, especially as regards industrial goods and services.[27] In the 1980s, some quotas were converted into tariffs. In the 1990s, quotas were abolished on virtually all producers' goods and tariffs on them were also brought down. Finally, in 2001, this process was extended to consumer goods. India's peak tariff rate on non-agricultural goods now stands at 10 per cent, though with some major exceptions such as automobiles; and customs revenue as proportion of merchandise imports is around 5 per cent. Trade liberalisation has made a significant difference. Export growth has speeded up, and the exposure to international competition has significantly raised the technological level of Indian industry. Recent research shows that greater trade openness has also had a beneficial impact on poverty reduction (see Hasan *et al.* 2007). Agriculture, however, continues to be heavily protected (as in most other countries).

Domestic taxation

Before the reforms, India's tax system was a mess.[28] The revenue sharing of different taxes between the Centre and the states, as laid down in the Constitution, did not help. For example, the Centre was assigned all customs revenue but had to pass on the lion's share of personal taxes to the states. This created perverse incentives: not surprisingly, customs revenue as a proportion of GDP trebled in the twenty years before 1991 while personal income tax stagnated. This absurdity has now been ended by a

[27] For a critique of India's trade reforms see chap. 3 of Joshi and Little (1996) and Panagariya (2004).

[28] See chap. 5 of Acharya (2006) for an analytical history of Indian tax reform.

constitutional amendment that has made all central taxes subject to sharing.

Indirect tax revenue comes principally from customs revenue and excise and sales taxes. Customs duties have been reduced sharply in pursuit of trade liberalisation, so their yield as a proportion of GDP has more than halved since 1991. The rest of the indirect tax system was a maze of cascading excise and sales taxes. The consensus view among tax experts is that a uniform value-added tax (VAT) combined with a few selective excises on 'demerit' goods provides the right balance between efficiency, equity and administrative simplicity (see chapter 3 of Joshi and Little 1996). Significant advance has been made in this direction. Central excises and state sales taxes have been converted into central and state VATs respectively and services have been brought under the VAT net. But the integration of central and state VATs or, better still, a uniform nationwide goods and services tax, is yet to be achieved and will be necessary in order to produce a single market for the country.

Customs revenue has fallen while the change to a VAT has been revenue-neutral. The potentially large reduction in tax revenue has been averted by an improvement in the yield of direct taxes on individuals and companies. These used to be at punitive levels in the old days. Now, the rates are very reasonable with the result that compliance has improved.

Reform of the tax structure is thus on the right track. The same cannot be said about the pattern of government expenditure (see above).

Private industry

Most controls over production and investment by domestic industry have now gone and private enterprises can compete in nearly all industrial sectors (see chapter 5 of Joshi and Little 1996, and chapter 13 of Panagariya 2008). The reduction of controls and the exposure to greater domestic and international competition has made Indian industry much more efficient and enterprising. Indeed, the entrepreneurial response has been dramatic. India now has world-class companies in many sectors such as iron and steel, cement, automobiles, pharmaceuticals and information technology.

An important interference with the free working and efficiency of manufacturing industry is the reservation of many products for exclusive production by small firms. This stunts the natural growth of firms and impedes technical progress and exports. Exports of mass consumer goods such as shoes, toys and garments may require production in factories employing large numbers of people. There are many examples of this in China and East Asia generally. India has missed out on this huge opportunity. In the last few years, small-scale reservations have at last been drastically pruned, but the effects have yet to come through.

Inward foreign direct investment has also been substantially liberalised. There are now very few sectors where entry is capped or forbidden. The response has taken time to build up since there were many obstacles on the ground, though not on paper. Recently, gross inflows have gone up to around $15 billion a year but that is less than a quarter of what China receives. At the same time, several Indian companies, not content with domestic expansion, have been making high-profile foreign acquisitions.[29]

There is a large fly in the ointment, however. India's recent dynamic industrial growth has also been 'jobless', a matter of grave concern for the future (see below).

Finance

Before reform, India's financial system was heavily repressed. Reserve requirements captured more than 50 per cent of bank deposits for the government. Of the remainder that was potentially available for lending, banks had to direct 40 per cent to 'priority sectors' (principally agriculture and small-scale industry) at subsidised interest rates. Interest rates were administratively set. Most banks were nationalised and did not compete among themselves. Ironically, this highly interventionist regime was accompanied by lax regulation and supervision of the banks' financial health. The result was that by 1991, banks had so degenerated that they served neither the transactions needs of the community nor channelled savings into socially productive investments. A traditional and essential bankers' skill—how to make good loans—had perforce been forgotten. Non-performing assets were 25 per cent of bank advances and half of the banking system had negative net worth.

Many useful reforms have been made (see chapter 4 of Joshi and Little 1996, Hanson and Kathuria 1999 and Basu 2005). The banks have been rescued with an infusion of public capital, along with the application of normal accounting standards and systems of prudential regulation. Gross non-performing assets have come down to 5 per cent of bank advances. Interest rates have been substantially freed. Government capture of bank deposits has been much reduced. Most government paper is now

[29] Recent examples include the acquisition of Corus by Tata Steel and of Novelis by Hindalco.

sold by auction. The system of directed credit, however, is largely unreformed. Most rural credit institutions are bankrupt due to subsidised interest rates and abysmal servicing and repayment. A substantial proportion of subsidised rural credit is cornered by the rich. There is plenty of evidence that concessional credit is not a cost-effective method of poverty alleviation compared with other methods. There is no good case for interest rate subsidisation or periodic loan forgiveness, though there is one for banks specialising in agricultural lending on commercial lines to take the place of the existing maze of insolvent institutions.

With deregulation and entry of new private banks, there is more competition among banks than before. Even so, it is doubtful if autonomy and efficiency can be achieved without substantial privatisation.[30] There have also been important reforms in the non-bank sector. Micro-intervention by the government in the flotation and pricing of equity issues has been eliminated. A regulatory body has been set up to supervise primary and secondary markets in stocks and shares. As a result, trading and settlement procedures have improved greatly. India now has a booming equity market that people can enter without feeling they are going to be cheated. Perhaps the most important shortcoming that currently exists is underdeveloped debt markets, which hamper the financing of large investments required in infrastructure.[31]

Liberalisation of international capital movements has been cautious and justifiably so (see above).

Public sector enterprises[32]

Public sector reform is an area of darkness. There has been a great wave of privatisation in the world in the last twenty-five years in recognition of the inefficiency of public sector enterprises, a wave that has not yet broken on India's shores. The case for privatisation is of course particularly strong in the tradable goods sectors. These sectors can always be made

[30] Public ownership has damaged the management efficiency of Indian banks by bureaucratic and political interference in recruitment, appointments to senior managerial posts and allocation of credit. In theory, publicly owned banks could compete more vigorously with one another and with private banks, and the pressures of competition would bring managerial autonomy in their train. In practice, this is far-fetched. Given the inherited advantages of public-sector banks in terms of branch coverage and customer base, the competitive threat from private banks is too distant to matter, given the short political and bureaucratic time-horizons.

[31] Putting this right will require reform of insurance and pension institutions.

[32] See chap. 3 of OECD (2007).

subject to competition provided international trade is not restricted; and competition annuls one of the main arguments for public ownership, the prevention of monopolistic exploitation. In India, public sector enterprises are present in many tradable goods industries, especially in basic metals, heavy machinery, oil and fertilisers.

There are around 250 central government enterprises. With the exception of the oil industry, they make low returns and over 100 enterprises (out of 240) are currently making losses that amount to 0.3 per cent of GDP. Further losses of 0.6 per cent of GDP are made by state government enterprises, of which there are about 1,000. Hard budgeting is promised but is hard to deliver. Long drawn-out decay, involving a serious waste of resources is the likely outcome. Privatisation is an urgent need (along with complementary reforms in factor markets) but the Indian government is still stuck with the fetish of 51 per cent ownership. Efforts to commercialise the operations of public enterprises have met with only moderate success. Such little privatisation as there has been has taken the form of partial divestment (in most cases less than 25 per cent of equity). This has little to be said for it. If the government owns more than half the equity, the firm is legally a government firm and subject to all the rules, regulations and procedures connected with government ownership. In such a setting, autonomy is impossible to achieve. These asset sales may also be criticised from a public finance point of view. Here the relevant question is whether these sales are a good bargain for the government in terms of cash flow—in other words, whether any reduction in debt service will more than offset the loss of dividends. Why would an investor want to buy a minority stake in an enterprise whose dividend policy will be controlled by the government, and whose profitability will be determined by the government both directly and indirectly (and the government may have an interest in reducing its profitability in pursuit of some other aim)?[33]

Infrastructure

The desirability of privatisation is less straightforward in the case of infrastructure provision, which consists mainly of non-tradable goods and services. This is because there may be elements of 'natural monopoly' for technical reasons, in instances such as the electricity transmission grid

[33] I have seen no good empirical work in this area but there are obviously grounds for suspecting that the sales have been made at unfavourable prices.

or the railtrack network. Where monopoly is inevitable, so also is regulation, though it is debatable whether the regulated monopoly should be private or public. 'Best practice' now suggests that vertically integrated monopolies should be 'unbundled', and monopoly retained only where technically necessary, the rest being opened up to competition, with the whole structure subject to an independent regulator.

At the start of the reform process, India's physical infrastructure was in an abysmal state and there was also little understanding of how to rectify the situation. Infrastructure was thought of as a public sector preserve. Neither the resource constraint in the public sector nor its serious operational problems were properly appreciated. Over time, lessons have been learned. It is now understood that significant private sector participation is essential both to provide the necessary resources and to address problems of incentives and efficiency. (See Ahluwalia 1998, chapter 7 of OECD 2007 and chapters 17–19 of Panagariya 2008.) But the intrusion of private investment requires a regulatory structure that enables earning good returns and inspires confidence in the fairness of dispute-settlement. A necessary condition for the latter is that regulators should be genuinely independent.

Progress has taken place along these lines in some sectors, especially civil aviation and telecommunications, where private entry has produced spectacular results.[34] Prices have fallen and the quality of service has improved greatly. Road transport has also seen some improvement. A large highway development programme has been mounted on the basis of public–private partnerships.[35] The major problems that remain concern electricity, irrigation and rural roads.

Electric power is produced and distributed by the State Electricity Boards (SEBs) which make huge losses. They suffer from low tariffs and large transmission losses due to theft. Their poor financial health has been a major factor inhibiting private investment since they cannot be trusted to pay their bills. The landmark Electricity Act 2003 has attempted to introduce a new framework which requires each state to unbundle its SEB into transmission, generation and distribution companies, privatise if desired, allow competition and private sector entry in generation and distribution, and set up regulators to issue licences and set tariffs. There has been some success in attracting private investment but it is as yet quite

[34] Ownership of mobile telephones is currently rising at 9 million per month.

[35] The revenue model involves private investors receiving earnings from tolls, with a capital subsidy from the government to make projects financially remunerative.

limited and there is a long way to go. India's infrastructure remains a major constraint on growth prospects.

Factor markets

There are also a good many impediments in factor markets to the efficient use of productive resources. (See chapter 5 of Joshi and Little 1996 and chapter 13 of Panagariya 2008.) Unless these are removed, the benefits of introducing competition in product markets will be blunted. I shall mention the most obvious:

(i) *Labour law*. The Industrial Disputes Act makes dismissal even for clear misbehaviour, or indeed for any productive re-arrangement of labour, very difficult: an affected worker can appeal to government conciliation where the case is likely to linger for years. The Act requires companies to seek the permission of the government to retrench workers. For political reasons, this is seldom given. Companies often get round this by costly layoffs, voluntary redundancy schemes etc. Nevertheless, the introduction of the government into medium and large firms is an egregious absurdity which reduces the flexibility of the labour market and can only be to the detriment of the whole workforce which outnumbers those protected by twenty times or more. (See Besley and Burgess 2004.) The closure of a company, amounting to retrenchment of the whole labour force, is even more difficult, as will be seen below.

(ii) *Land use and sales*. Land use regulations are dysfunctional. A particularly pernicious piece of legislation was the Urban Land Ceiling and Regulation Act (ULCRA). Its avowed intention was 'to prevent concentration of urban land . . . speculation . . . and profiteering . . .'. ULCRA banned private holding of vacant land above certain low limits. Any excess holding could be bought cheaply by the state and used for socially desirable purposes such as low-cost housing. But the state could also exempt land from acquisition for public interest reasons or because 'it would cause hardship to the firm that owns it . . .'. One does not have to be very sophisticated to understand that ULCRA was a charter for corruption. Very little land was acquired by the state but the owner could not sell it to anyone else. Together with rent control, this resulted in Mumbai, a city of 20 million people of whom more than a million have virtually nowhere to live, having some of the highest land values in the world. The Central Government has now repealed ULCRA. But states also have a constitutional right to pass land laws. The scrapping of ULCRA only meant that states were not obliged to retain their own ceilings on urban land. Some states have abolished their ceilings but others, including Maharashtra, of which Mumbai is the capital, have not. The relevance of this freeze-up of the urban land market for industrial policy is that it is a major factor preventing the winding up of bankrupt firms, some of which have extensive surplus urban land which they cannot sell.

(iii) *Company law*. In India, bankrupt firms do not disappear. Company law, land law and labour laws act in vicious concert to create the Indian phenomenon of 'sick industries'—firms that are bankrupt but cannot be closed down. Creditors cannot sell the assets and labour is unpaid. The waste of assets that should be redeployed is considerable. The Sick Industries Act was enacted and the Board of Industrial and Financial Restructuring set up in 1985 to deal with this problem. But both have effectively perpetuated the situation by putting an excessive emphasis on rehabilitation of companies. The Companies Act needs to be changed (along with land and labour laws) to facilitate liquidation and closure. Workers' rights can be protected by making dues owed to them (including fairly generous redundancy payments) the senior-most debt. The Central Government did attempt to modify company law in 2002 and 2003 but the new legislation was struck down in the courts, so the old system continues to function. In any case, the attempted legislation would not have been much of an improvement. India urgently needs a modern bankruptcy code. (See OECD 2007.)

Flexibility in factor markets is the key to industrial restructuring. Movement in this area has been glacially slow.

Agriculture[36]

Agriculture accounts for nearly a quarter of GDP but it has not received much attention in the reform process so far and agricultural growth has declined in the last ten years. About 60 per cent of the labour force works in farming and related activities and 75 per cent of the poor live in rural areas. Agriculture should have been at the forefront of the reforms as there is a close connection between agricultural growth and poverty reduction.[37]

[36] See chaps. 3 and 6 of Joshi and Little (1996), Gulati (1998) and chap. 14 of Panagariya (2008).
[37] This statement is compatible with the view that a necessary condition of development in the long run is a significant shift of labour out of agriculture.

Agriculture has suffered as much from distortionary interventions as any other industry. Trade protection of industry resulted in implicit taxation of agriculture. This was partially offset by massive subsidisation of agricultural inputs, notably fertiliser, irrigation water, and electricity. The 'offset' has remained though industrial protection has declined. It has not only created a fiscal burden but has also been very inefficient, for example by encouraging inappropriate usage. Less widely known is the fact that there is also extensive state interference in domestic agricultural trade through controls on movement, storage and processing of produce. These are activities in which the private sector has a comparative advantage. Some encouraging signs can be discerned. Government monopoly of the conduit between farmers and wholesalers has been abolished. Farmers can now even sell directly to supermarkets, in principle. Contract farming has been legalised and Indian corporates are beginning to get directly involved in agriculture.[38] This bodes well also for stimulating the food processing industry, which is at present fairly primitive.

External and domestic liberalisation combined with elimination of subsidies is unquestionably a necessary condition for faster agricultural growth. It is not, however, sufficient since the supply response in agriculture will also depend on the strengthening of physical infrastructure. As agriculture is liberalised, private investment in producer services and repairs, transport and storage can be expected to respond. But there is also a crying need for public investment in irrigation, roads and power. Unfortunately, this has been on a declining trend in recent years. Supply response in agriculture will also depend on the spread of primary health and education in rural areas (dealt with below) and the re-ignition of technical progress. Technical progress in the shape of new seed varieties clearly played a central role in the dramatic reductions of poverty in East Asia (and parts of India) in the 1970s and 1980s. But in recent years, yield enhancement in India has been sluggish. 'After the Green Revolution but before the Bio-Technology Revolution, what?' is thus a critical question. There is a pressing need for increased public funding of agricultural research (particularly in new seed varieties of the major cereals where the returns cannot be captured by private investors) and of agricultural extension services.

The liberalisation scenario hides a distributional problem. Freeing up output and input prices will create hardship for two groups. Firstly, while

[38] For example, some corporate buyers are trying to provide the 'cold chain' from farm to processing plant. At present, there are enormous losses due to wastage.

most farmers will on balance benefit (since they can more than recoup the loss on the withdrawn subsidies from the gains on higher output prices), this will not be the case for self-sufficient farmers. For this reason some subsidies might have to be retained for the very small farmer. This is a case where targeting, by size of ownership and operational holdings, may be relatively easy. Secondly, poor consumers of food will suffer a loss of real income. Of course, the rise in the demand for labour will raise real wages and in any case the changes do not have to be brought in overnight. Nevertheless, the price rise would clearly be serious for the very poor in both urban and rural areas, especially those unable to work. Direct anti-poverty programmes will therefore have to deal with this. The important point to note here is that the savings from the elimination of input subsidies in agriculture would be in the region of 3–4 per cent of GDP, leaving plenty of room for both increased public investment and more generous funding of anti-poverty programmes.

The social sectors

One can expect the liberal reforms to reduce poverty as compared with the old policy regime. Growth should be faster and changes in product-mix and techniques of production should make it more labour-intensive. However, two potential by-products of deeper reform in future may have unfavourable effects, if no compensating action is taken. The first is that increasing industrial efficiency in the public sector may require wide-spread redundancy before the favourable effects on employment take effect. The second, already alluded to, is that freedom of agricultural trade, and elimination of agricultural input subsidies, would hurt poor consumers, and also subsistence farmers.

The public sector employees who would be made redundant are not poor. Also, many of them would quite quickly find new employment, as the demand for labour grew. Nevertheless, redundancy would result in hardship for some, if not well compensated. But since the potentially redundant are being paid full wages to produce little or nothing, the public sector can both make generous redundancy payments and save money.[39] Note that these 'copper handshakes' would be largely saved, so privatisation could be pushed ahead quite rapidly without fear of inflation. A rise in farm input and output prices is a more difficult problem.

[39] See Joshi and Little (1996) for an outline of a scheme of 'copper handshakes'.

The knee-jerk reaction would be to increase food subsidies via the PDS. But it is well-known that the PDS is a grossly inefficient instrument for reaching the poor. Public Employment Schemes can almost certainly be more effective instruments of poverty relief than food subsidies, provided the wage offered is low since the genuinely needy then target themselves. The National Rural Employment Guarantee scheme is noteworthy in this context. It aims to provide 100 days guaranteed work a year to every rural household in the country at the statutory minimum wage for agricultural workers in the relevant state.[40] Despite the usual problems of waste and leakage it does offer the potential of a safety net for the rural population. Direct targeted transfers are appropriate for the disabled, for the old and for widows. Many states have such schemes. The Central Government has also assumed a role in helping the states with direct transfers, by instituting the National Social Assistance Scheme. Though at present limited in their coverage, these transfers, unlike public employment schemes, should not be regarded as interim measures whose need will vanish with the success of labour-demanding growth policies, but as permanent features of a good society.

So far we have considered government action in the social sectors to cushion the adverse short-run distributional impact of liberalisation. In the longer run, it is more important to invest in primary education and primary health care. There is overwhelming evidence that these are critical components of the virtuous circle of growth and poverty reduction. Labour-intensive development, especially in manufactured exports, will be severely retarded if the workforce is illiterate, innumerate and of poor physique. Female education has an additional link with rapid growth through reduction in fertility. In these matters, India has lagged far behind East Asian countries. Half of all women and a quarter of all men in India are illiterate.[41] A third of the children of school-age do not complete primary school. The figures are considerably worse in backward states and in disadvantaged caste and income groups.

Another striking feature of Indian education is the low level of qualitative performance, despite a level of expenditure per pupil (relative to GDP per head) that is not out of line with other emerging countries. Teacher absenteeism is high in publicly funded education despite satisfactory

[40] Reportedly, nearly all the 21.2 million householders that applied in 2006–7 received work averaging forty-one days.

[41] Note, however, that the overall literacy rate is a slow-moving number since it includes people in older age groups. Literacy rates among the young are more encouraging.

salaries. Teacher incentives need to be improved by linking pay to performance. (See Pritchett and Murgai 2007.) Absenteeism appears to be a serious problem among primary health care workers as well. (See Jeffery and Jeffery in this volume.)

Overview

Have India's economic reforms been successful? The short answer is yes and no. There has been significant, even dramatic movement in some areas but it is equally clear that, as a whole, the reforms have been unbalanced and are as yet highly incomplete.

The most notable achievements have been with regard to liberalisation. Many unnecessary and counterproductive controls have been eradicated in international trade, private industry and the financial sector. The role of the price mechanism and of private initiative have been significantly increased. Even so, much remains to be done, particularly in integrating agriculture with the rest of the economy and in promoting a labour-demanding pattern of growth. Domestic factor markets are still heavily restricted by land, labour and company laws. These laws were enacted with good intentions but no understanding of the fact that protection of incumbent workers reduces the demand for labour, and thus by exclusion harms poor outsiders; nor that company laws which protect incumbent managements often preserve an inefficient use of assets. Public sector reform has gone approximately nowhere. In theory, the abysmally inefficient public enterprises could be transformed by the grant of greater autonomy and by competition with the private sector, without a change of ownership. In practice, given India's political and bureaucratic culture, this is little more than a pious hope. Privatisation is an urgent need, of course with appropriate regulatory safeguards where competition is impossible. Despite some partial divestment (driven largely by fiscal exigencies) and commercialisation of SEBs in some states, the government has mostly avoided the hard issues. Progress in fiscal restructuring has been thoroughly inadequate. There have been welcome moves towards creating a simpler and more efficient tax system but the more radical steps that would be required to carry this reform through to completion have not been taken. Moreover, the deep fiscal reform that is required to reduce the fiscal deficit while simultaneously increasing government expenditure on infrastructure and the social sectors remains elusive. Finally, there is a crying need for purposive state action in primary health and education. Huge shortfalls remain in their delivery. Making good will require imaginative solutions, far beyond throwing money at the problem.

The next point that needs emphasis, even though it is obvious, is that there are strong interdependencies between the various aspects of reform. Liberalisation of the product markets or privatisation of public enterprises will not yield their full benefit if factor markets remain clogged up. Nor will liberalisation produce its large beneficial effect on growth and employment if the labour force lacks education or if infrastructure provision is inadequate. The value of spreading education will be limited unless there is growing demand for labour. The government cannot make its contribution to correcting deficiencies in physical and social infrastructure without fiscal restructuring. Given these interconnections, it is clear that India's reform has been lopsided: some aspects of the process have moved reasonably fast but others not at all. As matters stand, if the reforms are stalled, there will remain enough inconsistencies and obstacles in the Indian economy to prevent it achieving its potential.

The big question is whether the 9 per cent growth rate of 2005–8 can be sustained, let alone increased.[42] In my judgement, preventing a regression to a lower growth rate of around 7 per cent will require not only the easing of infrastructural bottlenecks but also substantial fulfilment of the other reforms I have advocated in this paper.

The future: opportunities and threats

India's growth performance in the last three decades has been impressive. If we extrapolate present trends, India will have the world's third largest national income (after the US and China) within twenty-five years from now.[43] But will the current trends endure? Moreover, if India is to abolish poverty, it needs not only to grow fast but to have growth that is inclusive and employment-creating. What are the prospects for this outcome?

India faces some favourable opportunities as well as some major challenges. There are several factors favourable to rapid growth. The first is

[42] Nine per cent growth was the product, in part, of a booming world economy. The global environment promises to be harsher in the next few years.

[43] This would be so at both market and purchasing power parity (PPP) exchange rates. Currently India has the world's fourth highest national income at PPP exchange rates and the tenth highest at market exchange rates. See Maddison (2007) and Wilson and Purushothaman (2003). Needless to say, twenty-five years from now, India's per capita income will still be well behind the advanced countries.

labour supply. India is due to receive a 'demographic bonus': while quite a lot of the world is aging rapidly, India is getting younger. In Japan and in parts of Western Europe, the share of the population of working-age in total population is falling sharply, creating large problems for pensions and public finance. This is also due to happen in China, from around 2010. In India, however, the share will keep rising until 2040, or even beyond. This late demographic transition is potentially a huge opportunity for India. It will obviously increase the physical labour supply but it could also raise the rate of saving, which is usually strongly correlated with a rise in the population of working age. But there is an important proviso. These benefits will follow only if the increased labour force is productively employed (see below).

The supply of capital can also be expected to grow fast. The rate of saving has been rising rapidly and will rise further if the demographic potential is harnessed. In addition, plentiful foreign savings are likely to be available, given the opportunities for catch-up growth. The incentive to invest should be strong since India's institutions are supportive: there is a stable democracy with secure property rights and an independent judiciary.[44]

Though democracy is a long-run asset, it can of course impose short-run obstacles. It is clear that the era of Congress one-party dominance is now gone, to be succeeded by unstable coalitions that include a large number of small parties with regional support. Arguably, the economy could prosper even if coalition governments come and go. I think this is too optimistic. It is unlikely that weak central and state governments could carry out fiscal restructuring or undertake measures to solve the employment problem.[45] India's reforms have rightly been praised for their gradualist pace, which have made them compatible with democratic governance. The corresponding danger is that with weak governments, gradualism will degenerate into stasis. The combination of democracy and strong government is, however, easy to advocate but hard to achieve.

[44] Even so, many observers have noted a deterioration in the quality of Indian institutions over time. See Subramanian (2007).

[45] A very clear example of this is provided by the experience of the minority government in power at the Centre from 2004–9. Its survival was dependent on the parliamentary support of the Communist Party of India. This hamstrung its reform efforts.

The employment problem

Probably the most daunting challenge that India faces is the employment problem, which is the reverse side of the demographic bonus (see Joshi 2004.) Unless this is addressed, India risks political and social instability, and disruption of its economic advance in the bargain.

As noted above, India's labour force is growing rapidly. From 2005 until 2020, the population in the 0–15 age-group will remain practically unchanged. But there will be a huge addition of about 200 million people to the population in the 15–64 age group (see Table 4.8). This figure is a good approximation to the likely increase in the labour force over the period on the plausible assumption that an increase in the participation rate of women will be offset by more young people staying on in education. How will this large increase in the labour force find productive employment?

Table 4.8. Projected age distribution of the population (millions of persons).

Age range	2005	2020	Change
<15	368	373	5
(%)	(41.8)	(36.0)	
15–64	673	882	209
(%)	(50.7)	(55.0)	
65+	51	76	25
(%)	(7.5)	(8.9)	
Total	1094	1331	169
(%)	(100)	(100)	

Source: Planning Commission (2002*b*).

Unfortunately, the employment picture is dismal. In the last ten years, total employment (organised plus unorganised) has just about kept pace with labour-force growth. But this is misleading. In the organised sector, employment is utterly stagnant (see Table 4.9). Jobs are being produced only in the informal, unorganised sector. Many of these are purely notional jobs of low quality.[46] Unless large numbers of productive jobs are created, India will remain an economy in which a significant part of the population is excluded from the benefits of growth.

[46] Note that according to the National Sample Survey, twelve million persons were openly unemployed in 2004–5. Desai (2007) estimates that in the same year, about 150 million persons were in low-quality employment.

Table 4.9. Organised sector employment 1991–2005 (millions of persons).

	Public	Private	Total
1991	19.0	7.7	26.8
2000	19.4	8.6	28.0
2005	18.0	8.5	26.5

Source: Ministry of Finance (2008).

A crucial reason for the emergence of the employment problem is that the transfer of labour from agriculture to industry has barely happened in India. This is reflected in the very modest increase in the share of industry and manufacturing in national output in the last forty years. This is in sharp contrast to other fast-growing economies in East Asia (see Tables 4.10 and 4.11) in which this share more than doubled.

East Asian industrial expansion was rapid but, crucially, it was also labour-demanding, powered by rapid growth of labour-intensive manufactured exports, which employed large numbers of people. India, in contrast, appears to be trying to skip the stage of labour-intensive industrialisation.

Table 4.10. Structure of Output and Employment, 2004.

	Share in output (%)	Share in employment (%)
Agriculture	22	58
Industry	27	19
(manufacturing)	(17)	(12)
Services	51	23
	100	100

Source: OECD (2007) and Planning Commission (2008).

Table 4.11. Share of Industry (manufacturing industry) in output: India and East Asia (% of GDP)

	1960	1980	2005
India	19 (13)	24 (16)	27 (16)
China	32 (n.a.)	48 (40)	48 (34)
Korea	20 (13)	40 (28)	40 (28)
Malaysia	18 (8)	38 (21)	52 (31)
Thailand	18 (12)	29 (22)	44 (35)

Source: World Bank (2007).
Note: figures in brackets give the percentages for manufacturing industry.

India's industrial growth has been capital- and skill-intensive. Many of India's dynamic industrial companies and sectors create few jobs. What about services? The services sector, now 51 per cent of GDP, has grown fast but its growth too has been 'jobless', which suggests it has been skilled-labour-intensive. An example of this is the information technology (IT) sector, which has achieved worldwide recognition for its dynamism. But it cannot provide the answer to India's employment problem. The arithmetic is simple. The output of the IT sector is about 2.5 per cent of GDP. The sector employed one million people in 2005; by 2010, it may employ three million. But by 2010 India's labour force will have grown by around sixty-five million (and much of the rise will occur in backward states).[47] We must remember also that the expansion of the IT sector will be limited by the rate at which the supply of educated labour can be increased. Note that less than 10 per cent of India's relevant age-group receives college education. The IT sector does not answer the employment needs of millions of uneducated people. They require industrial blue-collar work, with most training received on the job. Of course, labour-intensive manufacturing is not a panacea. Thriving agriculture and services are also necessary for balanced growth. India's capital-intensive and skill-intensive industries and services can and should continue to grow fast, provided they are efficient and internationally competitive, as many of them now are. But India also needs expanding demand for low-skilled labour. The only plausible, quantitatively significant, potential source for this demand is labour-intensive exports. An export boom in labour-intensive manufactured and agro-industrial goods could provide extra employment and growth, if infrastructure shortages were overcome, because labour supply is elastic and tradable inputs could be imported as necessary.[48] The experience of East Asia suggests that profitable exports would boost incentives for companies to save and invest; extra savings would also come from the rising incomes of the new recruits to the industrial labour force. This would help to reinforce the virtuous circle of higher savings and investment that is supposed to accompany the demographic transition.

The policies required to make labour-demanding growth possible are easy to specify but politically difficult to implement. Small-scale industry reservations that remain must be phased out. Labour laws that hinder

[47] The employment problem and the problem of regional divergence interact. Unless the former is addressed, the latter will get even worse. (See also Dyson, this volume.)

[48] Construction and tourism are also potential sources of high labour demand.

employment must be reformed. (See chapter 4 of OECD 2007 and chapter 13 of Panagariya 2008.) Delivery of primary and secondary education must be enhanced. Tax breaks that encourage capital intensity should be eliminated. Direct foreign investment should be welcomed in labour-intensive industries. Power and transport facilities, essential for international competitiveness, must be drastically improved. Trade liberalisation must be extended and excessive exchange rate appreciation avoided. Chinese-style special export zones should be put in place.[49] And adjustment assistance should be devised to cushion any adverse short-term effects of the above policies. East Asian countries, including China, now face higher labour costs and are moving up the ladder of comparative advantage. That gives India the opportunity to kick-start an export boom, especially as the textile quotas of the Multi-Fibre Agreement were abolished in 2005. Without labour-demanding growth, India's 'demographic bonus' could have highly unpleasant consequences.[50]

Concluding remarks

In the second half of India's post-independence career, growth has increased dramatically as a consequence of economic reform, which has unshackled the economy from the iron grip of controls and exposed it to international competition. It is tempting to go along with the media hype that India has now achieved 'take-off' into super-fast, self-fulfilling growth that will rapidly abolish poverty, make the country a global economic power, and return it to the position it occupied in the world economy three centuries ago.[51] My assessment is less upbeat. This outcome is certainly possible but also far from certain. There are still many impediments to rapid growth being sustained.[52] Moreover, the quality of India's growth is flawed. It has been relatively 'jobless'; as a consequence, India

[49] Recent efforts to do so have unfortunately been marred by the lack of a system to provide fair compensation to poor rural households who are displaced.

[50] One warning sign is the spread of the Naxalite movement, which is active in a quarter of India's districts. Maoism may be dead in China but in India it is alive and kicking.

[51] In 1700, India's GDP was about a quarter of World GDP. See Maddison (2007).

[52] This is so especially in the poor, populous and backward states such as Bihar, Uttar Pradesh and Madhya Pradesh, which are also the states where population is still growing rapidly. About 60 per cent of the forecast 620 million increase in India's population between now and 2051 is expected to occur in these three states. For them, implementing economic reform is an urgent necessity.

risks becoming a two-tier economy, with all the attendant dangers. There is no doubt that a consistent economic package can be designed which would maintain rapid growth, create employment and eliminate poverty. But can it be delivered? India's political class will have to walk successfully the tightrope of implementing reform while balancing diverse interests and managing the compulsions of mass politics. This will be Indian democracy's supreme test.

Postscript, November 2008

This chapter was written in early 2008. It was known then that global economic conditions would deteriorate due to the financial turmoil in the advanced countries that began in the latter half of 2007. In the event, the deterioration has turned out to be much sharper than predicted by previous consensus forecasts. It has now become clear that the US, Europe and Japan will have negative growth for a year or two and possibly longer, despite countervailing monetary and fiscal policies. Moreover, the optimistic 'decoupling' hypothesis—that India would maintain its growth momentum despite recession in the advanced countries—has turned out to be wrong.

The adverse effect on India is already in evidence and will get worse. Two channels of transmission are involved, finance and trade. As regards finance, foreign lending to Indian companies has dried up; in addition, foreign portfolio equity investment has turned from inflow to outflow. These two items together constitute a turnaround of around $75 billion in 2008–9. Not surprisingly, the Indian corporate sector is facing an acute scarcity of credit.[53] Trade transmission is related to the fall in demand for visible and invisible (principally IT services) exports, which are now around 20 per cent of GDP and have been growing at 25 per cent a year. Export growth is now expected to collapse.

Since these trends became evident, the Reserve Bank of India has followed a looser monetary policy, like central banks elsewhere. This has taken the form of reductions in the bank rate and substantial injections of liquidity. Even so, a slowdown is inevitable. GDP growth will decline to about 7 per cent in 2008–9 and probably to around 6 per cent in 2009–10. The scope for aggressive fiscal expansion is limited, given India's

[53] Indian companies' access to the domestic capital market has also declined significantly, due to a 60 per cent drop in the stock market, itself triggered by the pullout of foreign funds.

pre-existing high fiscal deficit. There is a silver lining to the cloud, however. The world recession has reduced commodity (especially oil) prices.[54] This will help to bring down inflation and moderate the current account deficit. India is fortunate also in having a strong reserve position which, in combination with some currency depreciation, should make it possible to contain balance of payments pressures caused by declining exports and capital inflows.

Thus, the near-term prospect is for a marked slackening in the pace of growth. The odds are that the slowdown will be over in a couple of years. But it could last longer if there is a prolonged global slump. What about the long-run outlook, after India has come through the near-term turmoil? On that score, I see no reason to revise my conclusion. This is that India's long-term growth rate is around 7 per cent a year. Sustaining the 9 per cent growth achieved between 2003 and 2008 and making it 'inclusive' in its reach will require fulfilment of the reform agenda outlined in this paper.

[54] The first seven months of 2008 saw huge increases in commodity prices. In consequence, India's inflation rate rose to 12 per cent a year. The rise in oil prices threatened to explode the current account deficit since India imports 75 per cent of its oil consumption.

5

The Blind Side of Globalisation: Auditing Merchant Producers in India's Export Sector

DIPANKAR GUPTA

Summary. While the rise of India's IT sector has attracted wide-spread attention, it needs to be recognised that IT is far from typical of the sectors contributing to India's recent remarkable economic growth. Much of the growth has been in the small-scale and informal sectors of the economy, where 'merchant producers' who operate on the classic merchant logic of buying cheap (in their case cheap labour) and selling dear predominate. While the western companies that outsource to India are concerned about the damage potentially done to their reputations by the worst practices, such as the use of child labour, of these merchant producers, fieldwork suggests that western audit investigations may often be by-passed. True, child labour is now relatively rare but was probably rarely cost-effective anyway in export-oriented industries. But in many other ways, which have received less attention from western auditors than child labour, the workers employed by the large numbers of subcontractors in the small and informal sectors continue to work in insalubrious conditions. Small-scale enterprises certainly provide employment but the workers in these enterprises are underpaid, overworked and are denied a host of basic privileges that are commonly taken for granted in western democracies.

Proceedings of the British Academy **159**, 107–128.

Introduction

India's remarkable growth rate, around 9 per cent in 2004–7, has spread justifiable optimism among investors, both in India and abroad. The fact that India until recently was an accomplished economic non-performer, shackled by 'red' tape, has been nearly forgotten. That is just as well, but what should not be forgotten is that there are still millions, roughly 30 per cent of the country's population, who are below the poverty line, and that the most rapid employment and economic growth are taking place in the informal/unorganised economy. (For further details see the chapter by Vijay Joshi in this volume.) Here the style of operation is closer to that of sweatshops, and far away from the IT world with which India's economic boom is often equated.

India's impressive growth rate is often attributed to the impressive rise of the Information Technology Enabled Sector (ITES). The ITES comprises both down the line, straightforward Information Technology enterprises as well as Business Process Outsourcing (BPO) units. That the management of some of these enterprises has chosen to replace the term BPO by KPO, or Knowledge Process Outsourcing, has not essentially changed the job description of these organisations.

The ITES gains a lot of attention because India can now claim to be a knowledge-producing country and not just a producer of basic goods and cheap luxury items. That Silicon Valley in California is studded by illustrious software experts from India adds to the glamour of our competence in the high tech knowledge world. But this huge success abroad should not lead us to overlook the fact that at home the Indian ITES employees and experts are not really at the cutting edge of technology. As the National Association of Software and Services Companies (NASSCOM) has recently confessed, India's ITES sector is technologically way behind the developed world. It has a long way to go if it wants to catch up with standards elsewhere in the world. But, to do this it must both strengthen and diversify its 'verticals' and not be limited to banking, telecom and financial services.[1]

According to NASSCOM data the Indian IT sector is internationally attractive because it offers services at rates that are 40–50 per cent less than what it would cost to do the same job in the west. Three quarters of what the ITES earns is from exports as the domestic market for these

[1] NASSCOM is India's premier trade body and the voice of the software and services industry.

products is still very small (NASSCOM 2006). Though the ITES attracts about 40 per cent of foreign direct investment (FDI) to India, it only employs three million people (Ministry of Finance 2007: 147). It is important to keep these figures in mind since otherwise it is possible to be misled by the overall growth rate and not pay sufficient attention to the disaggregated picture.

The dizzying climb up the growth charts is accompanied by yet another anomaly: employment in the organised sector has remained more or less stagnant, perhaps even come down a little between 1988 and 2000. Moreover the actual numbers are relatively small: from only 10.78 million workers in registered factories in 1988 to 10.2 million in 2000 (Institute of Applied Manpower Research 2005: 174–5). When we think of a country of one billion, these figures appear so miniscule. Where then is the employment growth actually taking place? If the organised sector is stagnant, if there are only three million employees in ITES, and if the agricultural growth rate has stopped at around 2 per cent per annum, where then are people finding jobs?

The rise of small-scale industries

The fastest expansion, both in terms of employment and output, is taking place in the unorganised sector[2] and in Micro and Small Scale Industries (SSI).[3] The informal sector is largely family or household based, and small-scale units are those whose fixed assets in land and machinery are below Rs. 50 million. But as this excludes cost of equipment—moulds, dies, jigs, tools, storage costs, transformers, generator

[2] According to the definition given by the National Commission for Enterprises in the Unorganized Sector (2007), the 'unorganized sector consists of all unincorporated private enterprises owned by individuals or households engaged in the sale and production of goods and services operated on a proprietary or partnership basis with less than ten total workers' (2007: 2)
[3] Earlier the definition of the small-scale sector was based on two criteria: if they used power then they could not have more than 50 employees, or from 50 to 100 employees without power. In 1999 the definition was radically changed and small-scale industries now meant units with less than Rs. 10 million as fixed asset investment. But this exempted the cost of equipment such as tools, jigs, moulds and dies, research and development, generator sets, transformers, cable installation, cost of storage, even fire fighting equipments. The latest definition has raised the bar from Rs. 10 million to Rs. 50 million. A medium-scale industry can go up to as high as Rs. 100 million, and on the other hand a micro industry is one that has fixed investment in land and assets not exceeding Rs. 2.5 million (Office of the Development Commissioner, Ministry of Micro, Small and Medium Enterprises 2008: *vide* S.O. 1642 (E), 29.09.06).

sets and even fire extinguishers—there is enough scope to fudge the records and present the enterprise as a small-scale one. The advantages in being classified as small-scale are many, from easier interest rates (the most attractive) to slatted factory sheds which are let out at subsidised rates.

There is a great degree of overlap between unorganised and small-scale sectors because of the 'informalization' of labour (see National Commission for Enterprises in the Unorganized Sector 2007: 4). The way in which jobs are farmed out to unorganised/informal units, and the way in which informal labour is also disguised as contract labour makes the whole chain from Small Scale Industries to the Informal Sector quite hard to distinguish except for the copy book cases. This is the reason why, with the possible exception of ITES, what applies to the small-scale sector must be read with the likelihood that the informal sector too is embedded within it. As it is often difficult to distinguish one from the other, it is best to treat them as one.

The activities in these SSIs and unorganised units range from hand-loom to carpet weaving, to *bidi* rolling, to shelling nuts, to crafting jewellery and polishing precious and semi-precious stones. *Bidi*[4] rolling is now entirely a cottage industry, but it was not always that way. While the Industrial Disputes Act of 1947 mandated certain restrictions on industrial employers, it exempted cottage and village industries from its scope. This provided the major incentive for *bidi* rolling to creep into the unorganised sector (Holmstrom 1985: 133). It is for these reasons that the number of units set up in the unorganised sector has grown at a lively pace of 4 per cent per annum and their export earnings went up by 27.4 per cent in 2005–6 alone (Ministry of Finance 2006: 149; see also TATA Services Limited 2007: 62).

To get a feel of how significant the SSIs and the unorganised sector are in India today, it is instructive to note that the production of mill-made cloth (that is, cloth made in the organised sector) has remained stagnant at six billion square metres for the past thirty-five years or so. The total production of cloth however is now twenty-five billion square metres and the increase is entirely due to the contribution of the small-scale and informal sectors put together (Ministry of Finance 2007: 141). Power looms in the small-scale sector produce as much as 80 per cent of

[4] *Bidis* are small thin rolls of tobacco leaves held together with a fine thread. They come in conical shaped paper packages and are usually bought by the poor as they are much cheaper than industrial cigarettes, let alone cigars.

all fabrics manufactured today (Ministry of Finance 2006: S-25), and the export of ready-made garments, woollen clothes and knitwear accounts for almost a third of all exports from India (Office of the Economic Adviser, Department of Industrial Policy and Promotion 2005: 177). These export items are generally produced in the small-scale and informal sectors, but it is important to remember that the two are deeply implicated with each other in terms of the labour component. There is no ready official statistic on the extent of labour informalisation in small-, and even large-scale units, but the phenomenon is easily visible in the course of fieldwork.

Moreover, it is not just that the small-scale sector is growing fast, but the smaller the enterprise the more rapid its growth. It is this inverse correlation that is the most striking feature of contemporary India's economic profile. For example, non-agricultural units that hire less than ten people have grown by 110 per cent between 1980–2005, and by 35 per cent in the short period between 2000–5 (Planning Commission 2002*a,* TATA Services Limited 2007: 35; see also Heuze 1990: 75). Most of these enterprises almost certainly fall in the unorganised sector. Incidentally, the Industrial Disputes Act of 1947 kept units employing less than 10 workers, those making *khadi* (handspun cloth) and cottage industries out of its purview. So, the trend in the growth of the unorganised sector started well before the economy was liberalised in 1991, although the pace picked up with these reforms.

Further, most of these small-scale industries and unorganised sector units are not in the traditional industrial centres where there is perhaps greater visibility regarding working conditions, wages, hazardous waste, and so on. A majority of manufactories of this kind are in the backward states of India, such as in Bihar, Orissa, Madhya Pradesh, Rajasthan and Uttar Pradesh. Further, one finds that proportionately there are many more small manufactories in the poorer regions of a backward state than in its better-off districts. For example, the Uttar Pradesh Census tells us that there are a larger number of small manufactories in its eastern districts, although these areas are less urbanised than the western parts of the same state (see also Kundu and Sharma 2001: 92).

As these SSIs, and their cohorts, are located in forgettable places off the map, and as they prefer to shroud their skeletons from publicity, it is easy to overlook their huge contribution to India's burgeoning export trade. Though ITES is much talked about, it really does not contribute much in terms of employment: as we said earlier, only three million people. But in the SSI and unorganised sectors (including agriculture)[5] the numbers run into several hundred millions. Jhabvala and Subrahamaniya conclude that approximately 92.5 per cent of the Indian workforce is concentrated in the unorganised and small scale sectors (2000: 17–18, 30; see also National Commission for Enterprises in the Unorganized Sector 2007: 5).

Merchant producerism and cheap labour

The SSI and the unorganised sectors are, then, very closely related. But in addition a large number of organised sector industries are also closely linked to the unorganised and SSIs to which they outsource a range of goods and services that embellish the finished and labelled products they put out for sale. A single hosiery unit probably gets its fabric dyed elsewhere, or its embroidery done in a cottage-based unit where wages are low and hours long. Very often some of the best-known companies primarily check pieces that are made elsewhere to judge whether they match specifications and then stamp them with their brand names (see Ramaswamy 1990: 162).

This, in fact, is the way a large number of export-oriented industries profit. Their advantage is that they can produce goods and services at rates much lower than their international price. This is not just true of ITES services, as NASSCOM has sadly observed, but for other goods as well. If the export factor were taken away many units would be forced to struggle for survival. What they produce does not have a domestic market, or if it does, it is not big enough to sustain them. Even if we take an item as quotidian as cosmetics, the per capita consumption in India is just over US$ 0.68 per year. This compares poorly against even other Asian countries where the annual consumption of cosmetics per capita stands at US$ 36.5 (Phookan 2004). So the domestic market is clearly not up to the task of absorbing the quantities they produce.

As most of these SSIs are dependent on consumers outside India, their connection with international trade cannot be overlooked. Today, this link is known by the term 'globalization'. The reason why globalisa-

[5] The informal sector labour force includes agricultural workers as well, but excludes those who work in plantations, in corporate and cooperative farms.

tion says a little more than just international trade is because the growing presence of SSIs and the unorganised sectors is an outcome of liberalised economic regimes which are anti-trade unions and in favour of foreign investment and free market enterprise. Gone are the days when organised labour could threaten captains of industry. The advantage in dealing with labour in SSIs and in the unorganised sector is that there is hardly any scope for workers' representation in these units. Trade unions have been effectively de-fanged.

These unorganised industries make profits not so much by improving productivity through greater rationalisation of the means of production but by simply depending on cheap labour. In this sense these enterprises operate on the merchant logic of buying cheap and selling dear. The difference between a true merchant trader and the 'merchant producers' who operate India's small scale and micro-industries lies in the fact that, whereas the former makes profit from circulation of goods, the latter does it from employing cheap labour in the production process itself. It is important for our argument to introduce this neologism for it also effectively separates the small-scale sector entrepreneur in India today from traditional industrial capitalists. Upgrading skills or technologies of production are of hardly any consequence in these fast growing units of merchant producers in India. This is why it is appropriate to term the entrepreneurs of these manufactories as 'merchant producers' and the activity they pursue with such profit as 'merchant producerism'.

One would have generally expected merchant producerism to characterise early capitalism, or a society which is somewhat autarkic in its economic policy. But in the Indian case neither of these presuppositions hold. Merchant producers are in the forefront in the export sector and, as even government records suggest, employment growth too is taking place primarily in these units.

In the light of the prominence that merchant producers have attained in India it is advisable to stay with the concept of globalisation. Yet, globalisation does not deserve the favourable press it has received from many because it has done nothing to transform the ethos of merchant producers, who continue to thrive on cheap labour and see no point in upskilling their workforce. Holmstrom noticed this feature in the 1980s, well before globalisation became a household world (see Holmstrom 1985: 212). Twenty-five years of a liberalised economy and bouts of structural adjustment have not prompted the merchant producer to think and act differently.

Globalisation and social audits

But globalisation often comes with an uncomfortable baggage. As the dependence on exports increases significantly, these units must subscribe to certain international norms even if they can calmly flout the home-grown ones. It is not as if India lacked laws regarding pollution, minimum wages, child labour, overtime and contract labour. In some instances, such as child labour legislation, the Indian law is little different from what international bodies have come up with: in India the prohibition against child labour applies to those who are not yet 14 years old whereas in many western societies the bar is only one year older, at 15 years of age. But as long as the inspectors could be paid off these domestic regulations were only so much printed paper.

So, it is not as if globalisation introduced these laws. The difference that the presence of exporters makes is in the somewhat greater consistency in the enforcement of these norms. This is because exporters know that their consumers back home would be properly outraged if they ever got to know how the goods with which they gladly adorn themselves, and their homes, were produced in a far away land with child labour. What offends international companies the most is the presence of child labour in production centres to which they outsource their goods. Nothing else that they insist upon is treated with anywhere near the severity with which they treat the presence of children in units which work for them. There is good reason for this. A child labourer can easily be photographed by many of the anti-child labour NGOs and conscience-laden journalists. These images can be put in the press, and, what is worse, in cyberspace as well.

Damaging pictures and commentary in the internet are what these international companies worry about the most. Through this medium one can give a bad name to a target organisation with very low investment. Given what happened to Nike less than a decade ago and what Victoria's Secrets had to encounter in 2007, it is not surprising that international brands sourcing out of India (and, by extension, elsewhere in the poorer world) have good reason to stay clear of such adverse notice. This directly impacts their sales and that is obviously not good news. It neutralises the advantage they get from coming to underdeveloped regions scouring for suppliers.

Even so, there are ways by which exporters in SSIs and in the unorganised units try to get around the vigil of the international buyers. In what is to follow (based on extensive fieldwork as a consultant)[6] we will detail how suppliers, who are nearly always in the SSIs and unorganised enterprises, get around the auditing eye of western buyers. We shall also narrate, as we go along, how far foreign buying houses are willing to go to make their Indian suppliers adhere to international norms.

Practice has taught these production units in the informal sector how to dress things up, although in some cases, as we will see, they also try to get away by a convenient reading of the law. In other cases, the stratagems they resort to are so intricate and well thought out that under any other circumstance one might even stand up and applaud their ingenuity. But we should keep in mind one overriding factor, namely that almost all suppliers with whom foreign buyers contract for goods have an aureole of subcontractors around them. It is possible that there may be several hundreds of such production sites that serve a single large supplier. Some of these units may be very small, cottage-like, in fact. This is particularly true of the carpet sector as well as in the many finished garments and metal-good producing enterprises.

The other feature which is common is that, whenever auditors and third party monitors from the buying company turn up at the supplier's site, there is a rush of workers towards the rear exit gates. These are employees who are not on the rolls but are put to work for long hours and with poor compensation. On some occasions I came across instances where, for want of time, these fleeing workers hid behind boxes in the packing unit and, if pushed further, dived into bales of cotton to conceal themselves.

Additionally, any conscientious auditor would look around for records other than what is handed out by the management. The neatly printed sheets that record attendance, wages, increments, paid holidays, and so forth, are very often for external use only. The information that is really important in terms of running the unit is to be found in untidy registers or on scraps of paper bound together by twine or stapled. A trained auditor would look for them in unlikely places such as in the guard's kiosk or on the desks of production unit supervisors. When workers are asked about their wages and benefits the answers are often uniform and flat, as if they have been rehearsed.

[6] Fieldwork took the form of scores of visits to small-scale enterprises, as well as overseeing the audits of hundreds of such units for KPMG, spread throughout India, as well as in some areas of Pakistan and Bangladesh, in the course of 1998–2006.

On one occasion, I even came across something akin to a book of catechisms instructing employees how to answer certain questions. Women workers are nearly always in some trepidation when auditors come around to them. On shop floors where women are in large numbers it is nearly always male superintendents who oversee their work. Many women workers have confessed outside the factory gates, and sometimes within but outside the hearing range of these men, of the state of fear they work under in these enterprises. In such cases, it is not sexual abuse as much as gender abuse that these women complain of. These male superintendents are nearly always foul-mouthed and rude when they interact with the women workers under their charge. This indeed is another fairly common feature of merchant producers' units, but it gets less attention than child labour.

Child labour

Contrary to popular impressions it is not very difficult to get rid of child labour in most of the SSIs and their surrounding micro and informal units. In a dyeing facility, for example, there is very little scope for child labour and the same would hold for textile enterprises too. In the carpet industry, which has gained worldwide infamy for its employment of child labour, it should be noted that here too employing someone below the age of 14 is of no great advantage, particularly as transgressions on this score can be so unambiguously pointed out. Photographs and voice recordings can do incalculable damage to the offending enterprise leaving it with very little room for manoeuvre.

It is not as if the merchant producers welcomed child labour earlier, but they did not strain to keep children out of their supply chain. In the past these small-scale exporting units rarely bothered about child labour as local inspectors were never a problem. Experience taught them that if they could be pacified as a tribe on other matters of law, why not on child labour too? But when international buyers became strict about the employment of children most suppliers got rid of them from within their premises. This is the reason why I found so few child labourers in carpet units that were producing for export. I mention this because of the widespread belief that the carpet industry in India thrives on child labour because of the 'nimble fingers' factor.

Initially the international buyers did not quite know how to enforce the anti-child labour laws as there were a number of factors that were not quite easy to control. For example, if a child were spotted by an audit team within the premises of a unit, then the management could explain it away by saying that the child had merely come to deliver lunch or tea to his or her parents. In other cases, the explanation could well be that the child does not work for the organisation but is employed by a service provider, such as the person who runs the tea stall next to the unit or even a contractor hired to replace wires, or redo the plumbing or perhaps add another wing to the existing infrastructure of the factory. Should the merchant producer who owns such organisations be penalised because of what others have done?

This issue was overcome when a few major international buyers resolved that, no matter what, no child should be seen in the premises of an enterprise that is part of the supply chain from which a foreign buyer purchases goods. If lunch has to be delivered, then the child should wait by the gate of the factory. If a service provider is to be used, then it should be made explicit that under no circumstance can a child in their employ walk into the premises of the unit. This has removed many of the ambiguities regarding the enforcement of anti-child labour rules, making it easier for auditors to make their observations. This, however, does not mean that the buyers will act automatically on the auditor's reports. They could be swayed by other considerations to reduce the severity of their sentence against the offending supplier, but they do react, and that is important.

If one still comes across occasional cases of child labour in these export-oriented units, then it is primarily for the following reasons. First, the owner does not quite know in advance if his unit will come up next for scrutiny. As we mentioned earlier, a large exporting house generally works with tens of sub-suppliers. This is why it is difficult to sense where the auditor will strike next. Further, as the supplier and his agents are not quite convinced about the validity of anti-child labour legislation, they tend to get lax on this matter. They might take care to keep their main office clean of child labour but do not stretch themselves to make sure that it does not happen in some remote production site to which it has out-sourced some of its work.

To be sure seminars and training sessions against child labour are held by large suppliers. But even if we accept that there is a genuine motivation to keep child labour out, it is not physically possible to watch over numerous small production centres that are often miles away, sometimes even in a distant state. In such situations the merchant producer's resources are hugely extended to make sure that the supply chain is free from children. It is in these very small production sites where the living and work space is common that child labour is usually found. This is not so much because hiring a child is economically rewarding for anybody. When it happens it is usually because of the carelessness on the part of the person who has been subcontracted in this great chain of intermediaries. Even when a child is spotted in such units it is a rather isolated event. It is not as if an entire shop floor, or a village shed, is full of children with their little heads bowed over their work.

Before the Iowa Senator Tom Harkin started the move to penalise those who traded in goods made with child labour, the situation was somewhat different. Internationally, the anti-child labour message was never pursued consistently, which is why the Harkin initiative was so important. While the letter of Harkin's Child Labour Deterrence Bill of 1999 may not be widely known, his intervention led to a world-wide awareness of child labour. It took a while, but western buyers who kept up a dogged auditing presence forced their suppliers to take the issue of child labour seriously. Thousands of children vanished instantly from Bangladesh's textile units at about the time Tom Harkin's proposal was first mooted in 1992. It is another matter that nobody really knew where the children had gone, but they were practically non-existent in units set up for export.[7] Wherever they occur it is more probably because of the employer's oversight, laxity or cockiness rather than because employing children fattens the bottom line. The 'nimble fingers' rationale does not really work in terms of output and cost price. In my fieldwork I have not found any carpet supplier suffering monetarily because it does not employ child labour.

Once a child labourer is spotted by an auditor, alarm bells go off immediately. The erring merchant producer in whose supply chain the child was found is immediately put on the mat. The management of such an enterprise is asked to explain how this happened, and if their account is not convincing then there are only two options left to the agents of the foreign buyer. They can either literally close shop with the supplier, or let the export company off with a stern warning that, should this happen again, it would be curtains forever. The latter admonition may be accompanied by mild forms of compulsory social work. Either the child is sent to school and the company pays for the education, or the management is forced to adopt schools in the neighbourhood for a specified probation period and to upgrade their quality. In most cases the first time a child

[7] For further discussion of the sometimes perverse implications of enforcement activities see Browne *et al.* (2004) and Pierik and Houwerzijl (2006).

labourer is found does not mean the guillotine for the supplier. There is usually a second chance. It is this margin of indulgence that most exporters bank upon.

The penalties are not that severe for other transgressions. Child labour is a much more emotive issue with foreign buyers than poor working conditions. Most SSIs and their line of suppliers function in sweatshop like conditions. While the formal agreement between the foreign buyer and the local exporter also mentions factors such as working conditions, overtime wages, formal contracts, hours of work, and so on, these are not insisted upon as stringently as the issue of child labour is. In fact, this bifocal view goes to the very top. In 2000, the Clinton–Gore administration flagged off an important initiative against child labour by doubling the grants from US$ 45 million to US$ 92 million in one year. But in the complementary drive against sweatshops only US$ 3.0 million were allocated. It would appear that issues of working conditions, from wages onwards, have a vague socialist tint and hence do not deserve quite the same degree of emphasis.

Contract labour

After child labour, the issue of contract labour appears to concern western buyers the most when they outsource from India. An examination of this practice will indicate clearly how 'informalisation' of labour actually works in small-scale industries.

Contract labour has a bad name particularly because of the connotations this term has acquired in popular lore as well as in historical records. The situation today is rather different from what the image of the labour contractor invokes, yet it is this stereotype that leads foreign patrons of merchant producers to be watchful on this score. Apart from brick-kiln workers, who have nothing to do with exporting houses, contractors almost never go to the villages of labourers and compel them to work in distant sites by using a mixture of threat and monetary extortion. It is often believed, but wrongly so, by some of these buying houses and agencies, that contractors have a long arm and that they can exploit workers across generations.

However, even a cursory examination will tell us that popular constructions regarding the relationship between contractor and worker need to be abandoned. In almost every case, as far as I could tell from my fieldwork, the contractor–labourer relationship begins at the factory gates. As most of the workers in merchant producer units are migrants there is always a network in place before they actually walk up to the unit looking for a job. Migrant workers almost never just buy a railway ticket and head out, say from east Uttar Pradesh, to Mumbai, Surat, Vapi, Tirupur or Panipat. There is always a network of friends and relations (almost unfailingly from the same caste) that is not just a source of information but also provides what little hospitality is required before the migrant gets a job.

It is true that a large number of merchant producers prefer to hire workers who do not belong to the region, but it is not as if contract labourers are always migrants. Local contract workers and migrants work together and, to the best of my knowledge, there are no wage differentials between them. This, again, is contrary to many popular impressions regarding the vulnerability of migrant workers. The reason why migrant workers are preferred by SSI entrepreneurs and other merchant contractors is because, once hired, such a worker tends to be present on most working days. It is true that during certain months of the year they are gone for long periods of time, but that is known well in advance and the employer can make anticipatory alternative arrangements in good time. Local workers, on the other hand, are constantly pressured by the presence of relatives in the vicinity to attend various rituals and family functions, even the less significant ones. This seriously upsets the routine and tempo of work in a production unit as there is often no advance notice, or premonition, of absenteeism. In this sense, it is better to employ migrants and not locals, and most entrepreneurs are wise to this fact.

There are various kinds of contractors. Some are fairly big operators handling over a thousand workers while others can be really tiny, almost invisible entities. As most of the jobs that contractors handle require very low skills, if any at all, labourers on the roll can be shuffled from one unit to the other depending on the following two considerations. Very often the merchant producer does not want workers in his unit for more than six months at a stretch for fear that they would ask for benefits such as bonus and paid leave—not to mention Employees State Insurance (see also Holmstrom 1985: 165). This encourages the contractor who works for this merchant producer to juggle around his workers from unit to unit.

Second, as the demand for goods from foreign buyers fluctuates, often by the month, workers need to be laid off during the slack season and hired in a hurry when the orders come back in. As different units have different cycles of work, the contractor can take labourers out of one factory and reassign them to another. Only a large labour contractor can manage this as he serves many masters. Smaller ones are not able to offer this cushion; consequently those who work with them may be more vulnerable. They may have to stay jobless for weeks extending to months. This is why a worker who is linked to a large contractor is quite fortunate. This fact does not sit well with the stereotype of the contractor.

The question that arises in this connection is why do merchant producers need subcontractors? Again the answer is in many layers. The first is that they need a helping hand to hire and fire workers depending on *fluctuating orders* from western buyers. Second, most merchant producers believe, incorrectly though, that if the subcontractor mediates between them and the workers they can escape any responsibility regarding workers' wages, compensation, etc. In fact, the law says just the reverse. The merchant producer may hire a subcontractor but legally remains the principal employer and, therefore, is responsible all the way.

Yet, because merchant producers have an incorrect understanding of the law they can tell an auditor with a straight face that they have no idea of how much the workers are paid although he tries to influence the subcontractor to be generous towards them. Such a merchant producer would also candidly confess that none of the papers regarding employment of the contract workers are with him. In his view, the auditor should go to the subcontractor for this information for only he maintains the records of those who are in his direct employ. The number of those who are officially in the employment rolls of the company is always a very small minority. Those directly on the factory register include technically qualified personnel who see themselves as rungs above the ordinary worker. They are usually responsible for checking the machines, keeping them in running condition, maintaining stable heat and light conditions, and so on (see Holmstrom 1985: 83–4; Ramaswamy 1990: 162). In dyeing units the person who is chiefly responsible for mixing colours also enjoys a superior position.

The majority of the workforce is, however, either contract or casual workers. My experience leads me to contradict the findings of Deshpande, Sharma, Karan and Sarkar who believe that contract workers constitute just about one fifth of the labour force in small-scale units (Deshpande *et al.* 2004: 92). The reverse is probably truer. Over and above contract workers, SSI units also hire casual labourers. It is usually this category of employees that is sent packing through the rear exit gates when the auditors arrive. But the merchant producer shows no signs of panic when it comes to contract workers. If these casual workers were spotted by the audit team, then it would be hugely embarrassing as none of them would probably have even a formal work agreement with the merchant producer.

But this small-scale entrepreneur thinks differently when it comes to contract labour. This is because the merchant producer often, and quite genuinely, believes that on this score the formal responsibility lies with the subcontractor alone. This is why the merchant producer finds contract labour so attractive. According to his reasoning, the presence of the labour contractor shields him from any blame that may arise with regard to the employment of contract labourers. Though this is far from being legally correct, many SSI entrepreneurs insist on holding on to it and are not easily persuaded to re-examine their position on this matter.

We also need to recognise that there are several kinds of contractors. Not only are there independent contractors who function from the outside, but in many cases, probably in an equal number of instances, there are contractors who function almost entirely 'in house'. This again is a fact that was noticed well before globalisation was formally inaugurated in India (see Holmstrom 1985: 176; Ramaswamy 1990: 162). There are however a few additional details that need to be taken into account in order get a comprehensive picture of these in-house contractors and how they work. On most occasions, the in-house contractor is an old, loyal employee of the merchant producer. This person is considered to be trustworthy and acts as a kind of elevated superintendent. He is usually in charge of a handful of workers—rarely above twenty. That this senior employee is made a contractor by the merchant producer is because a misreading of the law is accompanied by an imperative arising out of the work place. The in-house contractor is usually the most skilled in a particular craft and can therefore act as a master to a handful of apprentices and junior workers.[8]

So this subcontractor's responsibility is really to oversee the work process. He does not keep any record, indeed, would not know the first thing about maintaining books of any kind. But then again he is a useful deflector should auditors ask too many questions. Almost none of these in-house contractors are required to keep any records by the management of the company they work for. All the necessary information regarding wages and attendance of those who are formally under these contractors is actually kept in the merchant producer's office. The subcontractor may hand out the wages and take receipts from the labourers, but the money comes from the merchant producer's office and the documents also return to the same place. But the SSI entrepreneur endeavours to keep this well

[8] I have found this phenomenon quite prevalent in brass and metal industries in Moradabad as well as in pottery units both in India (Khurja) and Bangladesh (Dhaka).

hidden. So while contract labourers are out in the open, records regarding their employment are under wraps.

As the merchant producer believes that a subcontractor can absorb all the blame, he often tries to pass off even those who are directly hired by his office as contract labourers. I have come across instances when a worker was quite puzzled when told that his employer believed him to be a contract worker. He was genuinely perplexed for as far as he knew not only was his salary paid to him by the management, but he was interviewed and hired directly by the same body, and not through a subcontractor. The merchant producer often succeeds with this ploy as the auditors rarely go down to actually interview the workers. Furthermore, if the management is asked why they should have so many contract workers, they sometimes remark quite innocently that this is the only way to curb workers' representation and trade unionism. They believe that all right-thinking people would easily agree on this point and therefore it does not need further finessing.

The absent present worker

The issue also gets quite intricate when merchant producers claim that they have no contract labourers at all, and that all the workers are direct company employees. I have met many contract labourers who would dearly like to be company employees for it gives them added status and also makes them eligible for bonuses. Naturally, when the foreign buying house is told that in this particular factory there are no contract labourers the merchant producers of that unit get additional approbation, possibly leading to additional orders. The officials of the foreign companies are pleased that they have not only succeeded in improving the welfare of the workers within their range but have also made a small entrepreneur think like a global player.

But things may not always be quite what they seem. The following illustration may help. It is possible that a factory does not hire a single labour contractor, either from outside or from within, and yet the workers in these units may not be secure employees. It is true that, if these workers were interviewed, they would also say that they are direct company recruits. When asked how they found out that there was a vacancy in the unit, the familiar answer nearly always is that their friends and contacts (the network) had informed them about it. In some cases they also say that they did the usual rounds at the factory gates where vacancies are often posted. It would appear then that all was well and that indeed the workers were hired properly by the book. The company records would also have formal agreements between the worker and the management. Details of increments, Provident Fund deductions, overtime hours, wages, and attendance are also easily available in the company's office. However, a closer inspection of these documents would probably reveal an alarming and unexpected anomaly: the attendance registers of such organisations usually show that a large number of workers have been on leave for months, sometimes for the whole year, and yet their names are on the record. How can this be possible?

The usual management response would be that these workers have gone home and that they have no sense of responsibility, for which reason they have not yet returned to work. Why then are they still on the records? Well, that is because the management is very caring and, should they come back, whenever, they would walk right back into their jobs. No arguments about that although perhaps still a bit unconvincing, but why?

And then the penny might drop. Could it be that these workers had not gone home but had been fired? But as the registers keep up the fiction of absenteeism this lie could well go undiscovered. Once this realisation comes to life, a few quick and pointed interviews with workers reveal that they are perpetually scared of being sacked and that this can happen any day. Sometimes they may be re-employed, but very often the relationship is terminated for good. In such a situation the worker would have probably been better off with a large contractor who could have found an alternative job somewhere else. So what seemed like a case of best practice turns out to be quite the opposite.

Overtime

A merchant producer who pays regulation overtime wages is, in all likelihood, waiting to be born. According to the law a worker must be compensated at *double* the hourly wage rate for putting in overtime. To begin with, it is surprising that most merchant producers are not aware of this aspect of the law. They often candidly mention that they are good employers for they pay their workers full *single* compensation, not knowing that legally the wages have to be double.

However, they may also craftily and deliberately try to doctor what can be officially accepted as the hourly wage. A large chunk of the daily wage is portioned away as deductions for house rent allowance, medical care, and for teas and snacks in the factory's premises. In this way the hourly wage rate is chiselled down and the overtime compensation is calculated from this lower base. Consequently the workers get well below even the 'single' wage rate as overtime.

Effluents

Leather, dyeing, textile and pottery units usually have a problem with effective effluent management. Leather and dyeing units are most responsible for pollution in terms of discharging effluents and in contaminating ground water reserves. In my experience, leather units in the North Arcot region have managed most effectively to abide by the law as far as effluent treatment is concerned. The Tamil Nadu government had made it mandatory that every leather processing company must have an Effluent Treatment Plant (ETP). Most small leather units were unable to afford these plants and closed down their operations. The big ones stayed on and got bigger, but even here they often have to pool their resources and use a single ETP.

In many dyeing units one finds ETPs, though it is not clear how systematically they are used. ETPs are not just expensive to buy and install, but are expensive in terms of their running costs as well. The real problem lies in certifying whether the water coming out of the ETP has actually been treated according to specifications. The government authorities are supposed to send inspectors over to do these checks, but as the merchant producers correctly point out, these officials rarely, if ever, come to their units.

So if the foreign buyer is finicky about getting the records right the management/owners of these units hire a private company to provide them with a pollution certificate. Failing proper government documentation this is the best that can be managed. Yet, as the company that is doing the pollution check is hired by the merchant producer there is every possibility that the verdict may not be completely authentic.

Cultural escape hatches

It is not uncommon for merchant producers to come up with a cultural explanation to explain why they have faltered on this or that legal requirement. When it comes to child labour the merchant producer may well say that, as the prevailing cultural norm in the area does not allow a woman to step outdoors, widows send their boys to work. To deny these children jobs would be tantamount to starving the family for the sake of some distant and impersonal law. Likewise, workers are not given permanent positions in the units because it is argued that they up and leave the moment they get a call from their homes. It is true that workers are still closely related to their village and to their kin and clan, but interviews with them show that if they are made permanent they would stay back and abide by the regulation leave they are entitled to. As they are anyway fired and rehired in order to duck or dodge laws that provide them with certain privileges, they are in any case accustomed to breaks in service.

To be sure, there are some categories of workers who actually prefer to remain on contract because their skills are much sought after. A master dyer, or tailor or the chief glass blower or a particularly skilled weaver will always have a ready employer waiting for his services. However, as is quite obvious, this can be true only in a very limited number of cases; yet merchant producers cite these examples to generalise for the whole.

A qualitative change takes place the moment a person is hired directly by the factory. Although the actual wage may not differ much, there is the bonus that makes a big difference, not just to the pay packet but also in terms of the loyalty to the merchant producer who employs them. I have found that once workers are made permanent they are willing to stay back even during harvesting months when their presence is urgently required at home. Also, contrary to what merchant producers allege, workers are more than willing to learn multiple tasks. Merchant producers argue that they must fire workers when orders change, say from pillow cases to curtains, because they are culturally unwilling to retool themselves. But there is no need to bring culture into any of this as the skills required to stitch pillow cases and curtains are not that different. It is the sewing machine that does it all with a change of a button, or the addition of a fixture. Second, if some retraining were involved, workers say that they would happily enter such a programme. Incidentally, in their own work biographies many of these labourers have performed different tasks in different units at different points of time.

On the issue of trade unions and representation the stock answer that the merchant producer comes up with is that the workers look upon him like a father and therefore they have no need for trade unions. These merchant producers try to convince their foreign buyers and their auditors that this tendency to look upon employers in a kinship-like relationship is a cultural given and cannot be easily changed. Consequently, they are benevolent towards their workers as they would be to their children and provide them with the best that they can afford. It is just too bad that like errant children so many workers do not realise how much is being done for them. It must also be said that I have never seen a foreign buyer insist on workers' representation. It is almost as if they too have been waiting to find a good old-fashioned cultural excuse to overlook trade unionism in those units with which they have business relations.

In the light of all this I cannot but take strong exception to the point of view that in small-scale industries the workers are less alienated and feel more at home. This too is a cultural fallacy that merchant producers like to slip in from time to time. According to this version workers are happy with small interactive groups and do not like working in large factories. There is no evidence for this and all the workers I met in merchant producer units have vehemently disagreed with this proposition.

Has globalisation made a difference?

Globalisation has undoubtedly made a quantitative difference, if not exactly a qualitative one. Merchant producers thrived before globalisation and continue to do so even today. The number of such units has grown tremendously in recent years after globalisation became the standard *mantra*. To be sure, there are some qualitative changes, such as in the observance of child labour norms and the manner in which contract labour is accounted for in merchant producer units. On the other hand a major feature of globalisation has been the de-emphasis on working-class representative bodies and trade unions. The SSIs and unorganised sectors that merchant producers typically preside over are well suited for this new environment. The Industrial Trade Disputes Act is now hardly ever applied as the unorganised sector employs over 92 per cent of the working population.

After the 1991 liberalisation reforms which freed India from a number of regulations, it was hoped that this would move the organised sector to higher levels of production and employment. Instead, the emphasis has shifted to merchant producers in small-scale industries and informal units where the conditions of production are far from salubrious. SSIs certainly provide employment but the workers in these enterprises are underpaid, overworked and are denied a host of basic privileges that are commonly taken for granted in western democracies. Further, as Deshpande, Sharma, Karan and Sarkar (2004) have noted, in spite of a rise in employment in the SSIs and in the informal sector there has been a fall in wages, particularly in exporting units. While employment went up in these enterprises by 3.36 per cent between 1990–7, wages in the same period fell by 0.8 per cent (Deshpande *et al.* 2004: 60).

So should we then return the verdict that globalisation has not lived up to its billing as the great energiser of economic growth? Or should we say that the jury is still out? When coming to a judgement on this matter it is important to consider the economy as a whole as well as the fate of those who are not exactly 'people like us'.

6

Unequal Opportunities: Class, Caste and Social Mobility[1]

DIVYA VAID AND ANTHONY HEATH

Summary. This chapter focuses on intergenerational class mobility, that is on the extent to which sons (and daughters) follow in their fathers' footsteps. We ask how 'open' India is and whether it is becoming more 'open' with greater equality of opportunity as it modernises. We find that overall there are rather low rates of intergenerational social mobility in India, although there has been a long-standing trend (which precedes the recent 'liberalisation' of the economy) towards the expansion of the professional and managerial classes, and a corresponding contraction in agriculture. This has generated increasing 'room at the top' and this in turn has generated a modest degree of net upward mobility. However, after making allowance for structural changes, we find that inequalities of opportunity remain very considerable, being much greater within the agricultural sector than they are in the more 'modern' non-farm sectors. Surprisingly, class-based inequalities of opportunity seem to be greater than those based on 'community' while reservation policies do not seem to have increased the chances of members of the Other Backward Classes (OBCs) or Scheduled Castes reaching the salariat.

[1] We thank the data unit at the Centre for the Study of Developing Societies (Delhi) for providing us access to their National Election Study dataset. This chapter is based on the doctoral dissertation of the first author (Oxford 2007). The empirical research in this chapter has been presented in various versions: at the British Academy Symposium (October 2006), and by the first author at ISA RC 28 conferences at UCLA and Montreal; at the Development Studies Association (Open University) and British Association of South Asian Studies (Birkbeck) conferences; and at Oxford, Harvard and Yale.

Proceedings of the British Academy **159**, 129–164. © The British Academy 2010.

India, at least with respect to occupational mobility, appears to constitute a paradoxical mix of traditional and modern features.

Introduction

THE PAST FEW DECADES have seen dynamic economic and social changes in India. This has led to increased debate about the growth of the Indian middle classes and rising social mobility opportunities in Indian society. In this changing environment it has also been claimed that the historic association between hereditary castes and occupations is eroding due to the processes associated with modernisation and the resultant urbanisation. As a result of modernisation it is expected that the importance of ascribed characteristics such as social class origins, gender and caste or *jati* (sub-caste) on individuals' opportunities to gain access to scarce resources such as professional or managerial jobs will decline (see Gist 1954; Karanth 1996; Panini 1996 among others).

However, despite the growing theoretical literature on increasing social mobility opportunities in India and the centrality of caste in this context, little empirical research, especially at the national level, has been conducted in this area (McMillan 2005; Kumar *et al.* 2002*a*,*b* are notable exceptions). Moreover, this limited research has focused primarily on analysing men's class mobility opportunities, while the mobility of women has largely been ignored. The present chapter aims to fill this research gap by describing the trends of social mobility in India, for both men and women, and by exploring how far these trends reflect patterns of modernisation. Following the classic treatments of social mobility in the sociological literature we focus on intergenerational class mobility, that is on the extent to which sons (and daughters) follow in their fathers' footsteps or vice versa move to a different position in the class structure. More generally we ask how much social class origins, caste or community, and gender affect one's chances of 'getting ahead' in contemporary Indian society and how this has changed over time. Is India becoming a more 'open' society with greater equality of opportunity as it modernises?[2]

[2] The notion of equality of opportunity is a notoriously slippery one. In the Western liberal tradition equality of opportunity initially referred to the absence of legal barriers preventing groups, such as Catholics in eighteenth-century Britain, from obtaining government employment. Sociologists have often used the term more broadly to include the absence of *de facto* as

For the purpose of this study we use the National Election Study of 2004 which has detailed information on caste and class background as well as on the current occupation of over 27,000 women and men. (This is the same study as that used by Oliver Heath and Yogendra Yadav in their chapter in this volume.) As Indian mobility research has seldom employed advanced quantitative techniques to explore change at the national level, this chapter also pioneers the use of appropriate quantitative methods to further our understanding of social change in India.

We use the standard sociological approaches to social mobility: we thus look at mobility both in the 'absolute' sense, as in the straightforward percentages moving between classes over the two generations, and also in the 'relative' sense. Absolute mobility rates can tell us how many people are upwardly mobile, downwardly mobile, or remain in the same positions as their fathers. Relative mobility, or social fluidity, refers to the relative chances of people from different social origins of getting to a particular destination and of avoiding other destinations. Whereas measures of absolute mobility are heavily influenced by structural changes such as an expansion of the professional classes and a decline in the size of the agricultural classes, measures of relative mobility rates are not affected by such structural changes. In effect they can tell us whether there has been any additional trend towards openness after allowing for the mobility that structural change would have engendered on its own. Measures of relative mobility, or social fluidity, are for this reason considered better indicators of the openness of a society or of the inequality of opportunity in a society, with lower rates of fluidity indicating a higher level of inequality of opportunity. This distinction is explained further below.

We limit our discussion to patterns of intergenerational mobility of men and women who are actually in *paid employment*. This may be considered problematic in the case of women's mobility analysis as, according to official sources, women have a rather low rate of employment in India. But due to space constraints we do not cover the alternative avenue of mobility open to women, namely mobility through marriage. (These issues of caste and of marital mobility have been covered both theoretically and empirically in Vaid 2007.)

---

well as *de jure* barriers; for example the abolition of school fees for secondary education was seen as part of a programme of ensuring equality of educational opportunity for working-class children in Britain. We use the term here in this broader way. However, it should not be taken as a technical usage but only as a way to convey in ordinary language the more technical concept of relative mobility.

We begin our analysis with a brief discussion of the modernisation hypothesis and its relevance for India. We next describe the structural changes that have taken place in Indian society and economy, especially with regard to the changing sectoral and occupational distributions of men and women. We then move on to use the National Election Study data from 2004 to explore patterns of absolute mobility and of relative mobility and to consider the relative importance of class and caste background on mobility chances. The final section provides a discussion of the implications for our understanding of the process of modernisation of India. Our data and methods are described in the Appendix.

Theoretical framework—the modernisation thesis

The modernisation thesis as developed in the West has been one of the dominant theories 'establishing the distinctive properties of industrial societies' with respect to their trends and patterns of social mobility (Erikson and Goldthorpe 2001: 344). With this theory in mind and to test its predictions we can highlight three distinct features of industrial societies when compared to pre-industrial ones. In sum:

1. Industrial societies are characterised by a changing occupational structure with first a decline in the proportion employed in agriculture and a shift of the workforce into the manual (industrial) working class, and second a decline in the size of the working class and an expansion of middle-class professional and managerial occupations as the society moves to a 'service economy' or post-industrial society.
2. Industrial societies are characterised by high absolute mobility rates, and a distinctive *pattern* of mobility, with more upward rather than downward mobility, reflecting the expansion in the number of higher-level positions.
3. They are also characterised by declining inequality of opportunity as measured by relative rates of mobility, 'in the sense that individuals of differing social origins compete on more equal terms to attain (or avoid) particular destinations' (ibid.).[3]

[3] In this chapter we are not concerned with the predictions and expectations of the modernisation thesis with regard to similarity or convergence in rates of mobility and fluidity across countries. For more on this see Featherman *et al.* 1975; Grusky and Hauser 1984; Erikson and Goldthorpe 1992 among others.

In empirically checking on these predictions, sociologists make a key distinction between absolute and relative rates of mobility. The first of these, i.e. high rates of absolute mobility, is brought about by structural changes associated with increasing industrialisation. According to modernisation theorists such as Treiman (1970) the influence of industrialisation on social stratification leads to various structural changes which include a decline in the number of people engaged in agriculture, a shift from manual to non-manual occupations, an increase in new occupations due to the developing technology which leads in turn to an increase in clerical and managerial positions to manage these 'complex production systems'. These structural changes lead to industrial societies becoming 'increasingly "middle class"' (Erikson and Goldthorpe 2001: 345). In the next section these aspects of structural change will be analysed with regard to India, especially to see what pattern these changes have taken and whether they replicate those found in the West.

In addition to the structural changes that modernisation brings about, the proponents of the modernisation theory (Kerr *et al.* 1960; Ganzeboom *et al.* 1989; Treiman 1970) also hypothesise that, with an increase in economic development over time, ascription (inherited characteristics such as caste, gender or class origins) will no longer be the main determining factor with regard to gaining access to advantaged class destinations; instead achievement (that is, merit-based criteria) will become a more significant factor. This in turn would lead to a weakening of the link between class origins and class destinations even if no structural changes were taking place. In other words, we expect to find increasing equality of opportunity *in addition to* increasing absolute mobility rates as a society modernises. We can think of this as a distinction between the structural drivers of increased absolute mobility rates and the processual drivers of meritocracy and equality of opportunity: 'merit' based criteria like educational qualifications will gain in salience as selection criteria for advantaged social class positions at the expense of more ascriptive or non-meritocratic factors. To measure this increasing equality of opportunity, or 'openness' of society, sociologists have developed statistical techniques that enable us to measure the extent of equality of chances after controlling for structural change.

Empirical evidence on changes in relative mobility, or equality of opportunity, as societies modernise is rather inconsistent. On the one hand Ganzeboom and his colleagues (1989) in their study of 149 countries (of which India was one) found support for the hypothesis of increasing equality of opportunity over time, while on the other hand researchers like Erikson and Goldthorpe (1987, 1992) in their study of a smaller number of Western countries have found no support for the modernisation hypothesis although their conclusions have been challenged by Breen (2004) using more recent data. Heath and Payne (2000) using British Election Study surveys from 1964–97 cover a longer time period than Goldthorpe *et al.* (1980) and they find some evidence of a change, particularly an increase in fluidity for men, but their results are not supported by Goldthorpe and Mills (2004: 207). Of course, one problem with this research on Western countries is that these countries were already highly industrialised and had already become quite meritocratic by the time that large-scale survey work began to be carried out. In India, however, we have an important example of a country undergoing the process of modernisation and so Indian survey research can tell us about a much earlier stage of economic development than can Western survey research.

Modernisation and India: research questions

Applying a Western theory to India requires adapting it to the specifics of the Indian situation. India provides an unusual test of modernisation theory due to its recent rapid economic development but without going through the same sequence of stages that Western countries experienced, or at least not to the same extent. Thus as we shall see in the next section, India has seen an expansion of professional and managerial occupations alongside a huge and persisting agricultural sector and without the precursor of a large-scale industrial working class. Nevertheless India has experienced changes in the overall occupational structure with 'increasing room at the top', i.e. an expansion of professional classes and a contraction in the agricultural sector. And hence we expect to find in India, exactly as in the West, increasing rates of absolute mobility and in particular of upward mobility into the professional and managerial classes (Kumar *et al.* 2002*a*).

It is less clear what we expect to find with respect to equality of opportunity. This is partly because theorists of modernisation have not been especially clear about the nature of the mechanisms involved. However we can distinguish several different possibilities, with rather different implications for India. Some accounts focus on the demand side, that is on the side of the employers. These accounts suggest that it is free-market competition that drives equality of opportunity. Neo-classical economics holds that discrimination, whether on gender, caste or class lines, is inefficient since discrimination essentially means hiring a less productive worker from a favoured group (e.g. an upper-caste man) in preference to a more productive worker from a disfavoured group (e.g. lower-caste women). But competition means that inefficient firms will be driven out by efficient ones, and hence firms will either have to eliminate discrimination against disfavoured groups or they will have to take the consequences of having inefficient recruitment practices and risk being driven out of business (or failing to expand). On this account, then, competitive market pressures can be expected to be associated with equality of opportunity. This further implies that we expect to see the greatest increases over time in equality of opportunity in those sectors that are most exposed to competitive market forces. This in turn suggests that trends towards increasing equality of opportunity might be most visible in the urbanised sectors of the economy and apply less to the agricultural sector (or at least to those elements where subsistence farming continues rather than large-scale 'agribusiness').

Another possibility that has been discussed (going back to Max Weber) is that it is the gradual extension of formal bureaucracies with formalised recruitment and promotion practices that is the main driver of equality of opportunity. This account suggests that it is the kinds of recruitment practice that employers use that is crucial, and that formal impersonal and transparent systems, typical of the German or British civil service in Weber's day for example, will tend to be most associated with equality of opportunity. We might therefore expect to find rather little change in equality of opportunity over time in India since, as the chapter in this volume by Joshi demonstrates, India's growth and modernisation has not been accompanied by any major expansion of the formal economy. On this account we would not expect to see any decline in inequality of opportunity in the informal sector since small businesses run on informal lines might continue to use informal recruitment practices, hiring workers on the basis of personal ties and word of mouth. At the opposite pole from meritocratic recruitment in formal bureaucracies comes the direct inheritance of property or of land tenure. This is another reason for expecting little change in the farm or informal business sectors.

Western writers, when they deal with equality of opportunity, have largely focused on the role of social-class background. The key debates have been about the extent to which social-class origins continue to influence educational and occupational attainment. In the Indian context however caste, and caste-oriented reservation, has been the major focus of policy although many scholars and activists have argued that class should in fact have been the focus rather than caste. (See the chapter by Zoya

Hasan in this volume.) Whatever the merits of the argument, the fact is that India has seen the implementation of reservation first for the Scheduled Castes and Scheduled Tribes and then for the OBCs (where the C literally stands for classes but in practice refers to castes). This provides another reason why we might not expect to see much reduction in class-based inequalities of opportunity since the policy focus has been elsewhere.

Turning from the demand to the supply side, an alternative kind of explanation for why modernisation might lead to increasing equality of opportunity has focused on equality of condition between the classes. That is to say, as societies have modernised, they have also tended to become more equal with respect to the distribution of wealth and income. This at any rate was the long-term picture up until the 1980s, although since the 1980s inequalities have increased substantially in a number of Western countries, most notably Britain and the USA, possibly because of globalisation or perhaps because of Thatcherite and Reaganite deregulation and tax cuts for the very rich.

There are a number of reasons why inequalities of condition might also affect inequalities of opportunity. First, the greater the economic resources that the advantaged classes have (relative to the disadvantaged), the easier it may be for them to secure advantages for their children, for example by paying for expensive private education. Second, if there are big gaps between the classes, then parents from the advantaged classes may strive harder to ensure that their children do not drop down the social ladder. In a more equal society, such as the Nordic ones like Sweden and Iceland where inequalities of condition are much smaller, parents may not be quite so worried about the prospect of their children experiencing downward mobility.

India as a developing society is marked by very considerable inequality of condition, with higher inequality than in many Western societies.[4] Furthermore, there has been rather little change in levels of inequality over recent decades, with some research finding an increase in economic inequality since the post-reform period (Dev and Ravi 2007; Deaton and Drèze 2002; see also the chapter by Vijay Joshi in this volume). If these supply-side arguments are correct, then we would expect to find that

[4] However, we should note that recent UNDP estimates suggest that income inequality in India is fairly similar to that in the United Kingdom (although the latter is one of the most unequal Western societies). We should also note that inequality in India is not nearly as great as that in many Latin American societies. See UNDP 2008.

inequalities of opportunity (as measured by relative mobility rates) are much larger than in the West and have shown little trend over time.

We explore these various possibilities in the remainder of this chapter, beginning with an analysis of the structural changes that have been occurring over recent decades.

Structural change and increasing room at the top

In this section we describe the changes in the industrial and occupational distribution of the Indian workforce in the past few decades. This brief summary allows us to build a picture of structural changes in India which will in turn determine the prospects for absolute mobility rates. There are two sources that are available. First we can use published research based on data from the National Sample Surveys (NSS) to look at the changing sectoral distribution of the labour force over time. And second we can employ birth cohort analysis of the National Election Surveys (NES) to look at the changing occupational distribution.

Sectoral distribution of the workforce[5]

As Vijay Joshi has explained in detail in his chapter in this volume, the widespread economic reforms introduced in the early 1990s in India, often referred to as the liberalisation period, were an extension of the reform process set in motion in the 1980s (Nayyar 2006). But despite the enthusiasm surrounding these reforms and the celebrated high rate of growth of the economy, their effect on employment generation was relatively small. As Joshi explains, this was because, firstly, most of the economic growth has been in sectors that do not require an extensive labour force but rather are skilled labour-intensive industries, like the IT software industry (see also Harriss-White 2003). Secondly, Joshi shows that agriculture continues to dominate in terms of its share of employment, while industry is relatively small—much smaller than in neighbouring countries such as China, Malaysia and Thailand—and indeed makes a much smaller contribution to output and employment.

[5] Women's workforce participation in India has been consistently under 30 per cent in the past three decades according to the NSS 1972–2000. For men, this rate has also been fairly consistent at around 52 per cent over the same time period. (See also Chadha and Sahu 2002; McNay *et al.* 2004.)

India is a country with a historically large proportion of its working population engaged in agriculture and allied activities. Much of the recent print media has highlighted India's booming economy, the increase in computer/IT jobs, and the expanding middle-class, all elements of a 'modernising' Indian economy. The picture on the ground is somewhat different. Observing the sectoral breakdown of employment (Figure 6.1), one notices the relatively large proportion of the Indian population that continues to be engaged in agriculture. Even though Figure 6.1, for all persons from the NSS for 1972–2000, quite clearly shows a decline in participation of the workforce in agriculture, the decline has not been very rapid. When these figures for men and women are disaggregated (see Chadha and Sahu 2002; Vaid 2007) it appears that for men there has been a more substantial decline in the proportion engaged in agriculture than has been the case for women. In 1999/2000 just over 50 per cent of employed men were engaged in agriculture, whereas for women the figure was still over 75 per cent.

Outside agriculture we observe that the proportion of Indian labour engaged in trade, manufacturing and services has risen quite considerably since the early 1970s. In the manufacturing and construction industry,

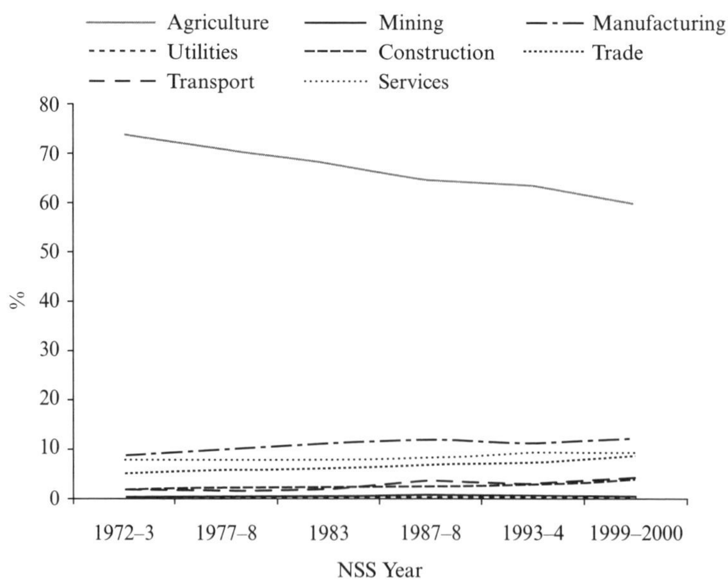

Figure 6.1. Industrial distribution of all persons, NSS 1972–2000.
Sources: Chadha and Sahu 2002: table 6; Visaria 1999: table 8; Sarvekshana (2001–2): Statement 12 and 13.

according to Gupta (1988) the proportion of women has increased, but these industries are largely in the informal sector with the concomitant poor wages and working conditions. (See also the chapter by Dipankar Gupta in this volume.) The service sector (made up of trade, commerce, transport and other services) too has had an increase in participation of women, though the growth in this sector has not been as high as in the West (Gupta 1988). And, even though the participation of women in the professions has increased slightly since the 1960s, they are concentrated in clerical work or as school teachers; jobs which according to Liddle are mostly performed 'under male supervision' (1988: 23; see also Deshpande & Deshpande 1999; Liddle & Joshi 1986). These figures seem to indicate that with modernisation and the creation of more mechanised and specialised jobs, men have gained more than women (Liddle 1988; Kishwar 1996). It has been suggested that women are increasingly engaged in agriculture, especially lower agricultural jobs, 'not because more work (is) available [in agriculture], but because of the non-availability of work in other sectors . . .' (Papola & Sharma 1999: 5).

Occupational change

We next study the class distributions of the respondents, both women and men, and their fathers by birth cohort using the NES data. (The data and methods including a detailed list of the occupations in each class are described in the Appendix.) While there are almost as many ways to measure social class as there are sociologists, the general principles are based on distinctions relating to property ownership and market situation (Marxists emphasise property ownership while Weberians emphasise market situation). We distinguish five broad classes (in general following the previous work of Kumar *et al.* 2002*a*) namely:

1. The **professional and administrative class or 'salariat'.** This includes higher professionals (e.g. doctors, state officials, managers), lower professionals (e.g. district level officials and administrators, supervisors) together with routine non-manual clerical workers (e.g. public sector employees, such as Class III (Clerical) and IV (peons etc.);
2. The **business class**. This includes both businesses with employees and petty businesses without employees;
3. The **farmer class.** This comprises large farm owners (greater than 5 acres of land) and small farmers (less than 5 acres of land) who work their own land, together with large tenant farmers;

4. The **manual class.** This includes skilled and semi-unskilled workers (not in agriculture) together with routine non-manual service workers such as waiters and maids;
5. **Lower agriculturalists** comprising agricultural labourers and non cultivators.

As pointed out by Kumar *et al.* (2002*a*) these classes should not be regarded as strictly hierarchical although the schema can be roughly ordered with the salariat at the top comprising the class whose members have formal contracts, regular salaries and better working conditions; and the semi and unskilled manual workers and the lower agriculturalists at the bottom, i.e. occupations with labour contracts and the worst working conditions. According to Kumar *et al.*, 'there is inevitably some degree of arbitrariness in the boundaries between these [. . .] classes', and that this is a problem 'which is intrinsic to large-scale survey research where we have only limited information about the detailed circumstances . . .' (2002*a*: 2984). We accept this but should nevertheless point out that this schema has been empirically and theoretically validated (Vaid 2007) against a range of outcomes associated with social class, such as housing and asset ownership. This validation exercise has established that the divisions between classes are indeed conceptually and empirically sound and this schema provides the best available tool to capture the extent and nature of inequality of opportunity in Indian society.

Ideally we would use a much more differentiated classification, distinguishing for example large businesses with employees from small businesses without employees, and Vaid has in fact used (and validated) a more detailed classification of this sort with the National Election Study data. However, for analysing trends over time we have to use these broader categories as otherwise our sample sizes for each period become far too small. We should also note that, although the principles we have used are similar to Western ones, the details are rather different reflecting the different contexts and institutional arrangements in India. Western writers for example would treat the clerical workers as a distinct, lower-level class. In the Indian context however, their job security and working conditions mean that they have more in common with other salaried workers than they do in the West.

In order to look at trends over time in occupational structure we break the overall 2004 sample down into separate five-year birth cohorts. One major problem with this approach is that life-cycle processes may well confuse the trends. That is to say, younger people may start work in lower-level positions and then, especially in the formal bureaucratic sector, may work their way up to higher-level positions over the course of their occupational career. Their occupations may thus be a product of over-time change in the structure of the labour market combined with life-cycle changes in their position within that structure. (How common such upward career trajectories are in the Indian informal or agricultural sectors could be debated.) However, this particular problem will be less acute if we focus on fathers' occupations, although there are other well-known difficulties when using father's class to explore changes over time in the occupational structure.[6] These patterns should therefore be regarded as provisional, although they are the best we can do in the absence of census data.

We begin by studying the class destinations of respondents, both women and men, and their father's class by birth cohort in Table 6.1. The table shows the same pattern of gradual decline in the agricultural sector that we saw in Figure 6.1 from the NSS. Thus if we combine the farmers and the lower agriculturalists together we see that nearly 70 per cent of the fathers of men born in 1945–9 came from these two classes, falling to around 60 per cent of the fathers of men born in 1970–4. As with the NSS

Table 6.1. Class distribution of respondents and fathers by birth cohort (row percentages).

	Salariat		Business		Farmer		Manual		Lower agric.	
	Father	Son/ daughter	Father	Son/ daughter	Father	Son/ daughter	Father	Son/ daughter	Father	Son/ daughter
Men										
1945–9	8.3	20.1	9.6	12.4	38.3	30.6	13.0	15.4	30.9	21.6
1950–4	8.8	17.2	9.6	15.2	36.3	27.6	16.4	19.2	28.8	20.9
1955–9	7.8	15.0	10.4	15.3	35.7	26.5	18.6	20.3	27.5	22.9
1960–4	9.1	15.7	9.3	15.0	36.9	26.5	16.0	19.0	28.7	23.8
1965–9	11.1	16.0	11.6	16.5	31.4	24.7	16.7	19.2	29.1	23.5
1970–4	12.2	15.1	11.6	17.1	32.4	24.8	17.1	21.0	26.8	21.9
Women										
1945–9	9.4	10.4	8.5	5.0	37.0	34.3	12.2	18.2	32.9	32.1
1950–4	8.6	11.7	9.2	6.5	36.1	29.4	16.8	18.7	29.4	33.7
1955–9	11.5	11.5	8.4	7.5	32.7	29.1	16.0	18.4	31.4	33.5
1960–4	11.8	13.6	8.7	6.6	31.8	25.7	15.1	18.4	32.6	35.7
1965–9	12.6	13.1	9.3	6.0	31.7	28.1	15.5	20.2	30.9	32.7
1970–4	12.4	13.4	10.0	6.8	33.0	28.4	15.7	19.5	28.9	31.8

Source: NES 2004.

[6] The difficulty is that fathers can only figure in the table if they have children and their probability of being represented will increase with the number of children they have, since it is children who are being sampled. In addition fathers have children when at widely differing ages, and hence we cannot equate the fathers of a particular birth cohort with precise historical periods.

data, the trend is a gradual one, although it should be noted that the NES estimates are consistently below those of the NSS. This may be because of response bias in the NES; for example lower agriculturalists may be less inclined to respond to surveys, leading to an undercount in the data. (It could also be due to differential fertility or mortality.)

Table 6.1 also shows corresponding increases in the size of the other three classes much as the NSS data showed gradual increases in the size of the non-agricultural sectors. There are increases over time in the size of the salariat, up from 8.3 per cent to 12.2 per cent among fathers (a 50 per cent increase), in the size of the business class, up from 9.6 per cent to 11.6 per cent (an increase of around 20 per cent), and an increase in the manual working class, up from 13.0 per cent to 17.1 per cent (an increase of just over 30 per cent). If we look at the data on sons (remembering to be cautious because of the possibility of life-cycle processes), we can see further expansions in the size of these three classes and corresponding continued declines in the size of the two agricultural classes. However, even for the youngest men we see that the two largest classes remain those of the farmers and the lower agriculturalists.

It is also useful to compare the occupational distribution of women (the daughters) with those of the men. As we can see, higher proportions of the women are in the two agricultural classes, particularly in the lower agriculturalist class. Conversely there are lower percentages in the other three classes, especially so in the business class. (More detailed analysis also shows that within these three classes women tend to occupy the lower levels; see Vaid 2007.)

We need to remember that these figures relate to women in paid employment. In the Indian context there is almost certainly a strong relationship between social position and women's paid employment: there will be much greater pressure on women in the agricultural sector to find employment whereas the wives of more affluent husbands in the salariat or in business may be more able to look after the home without taking up employment (Vaid 2007).

These trends thus demonstrate modest but continuing expansion of salaried, business and manual occupations and decline of farmers and agricultural workers, as was expected given the findings on sectoral change in the previous section. We also note that this is a different pattern from what is observed in the West where there has been a decline of manual occupations and a much larger expansion of professional and managerial occupations over the same period of time (Breen 2004). We do then see quite clearly a long-term and continuing evolution of the Indian occupational structure. Despite the 'job-less growth' of the formal sector, Indian occupational structure has not been static. As in the West we see gradually increasing 'room at the top' which will generate the same kind of net upward mobility that Western scholars have observed in their countries.

A further key feature of these trends is that they are both gradual and continuous. There is no sudden 'take-off' to modernisation corresponding to the economic liberalisation of the 1980s and subsequent decades. Indeed, there is no sign of any acceleration of the trends after 1980. Occupational change thus clearly precedes the liberalisation period. One way to look at this might be to say that the underlying trends are long-standing and have had little to do with economic liberalisation. In this sense, the job-less growth that Joshi reports is in fact entirely consistent with our evidence: the job-less growth character of the period after liberalisation is precisely why we fail to see any acceleration in the occupational changes.

It is also important to note that the current Indian occupational distribution still looks to be a distinctly 'non-Western' one, though equally it can hardly be characterised as 'traditional' either. What we see is an economy where agriculture is still dominant, at least with respect to employment although not of course with respect to output, where the manual class (which in the West has always been thought of as the numerically dominant class in an industrial society) is a relatively minor player, and where self-employment is still much more important than in the so-called modern economies of the West. And yet at the same time there is a relatively large and growing salariat composed of white collar, administrative and professional workers, more characteristic of a post-industrial service economy.

Trends in absolute mobility rates

The fact that there has been growing 'room at the top' in India and a gradually contracting agricultural sector means that we must inevitably see net upward mobility. This is required by the simple arithmetic of mobility tables: if the salariat has grown in size then sons will be more likely to be in the salariat than are their fathers, and if the salariat is regarded as being the highest class, then there must arithmetically be net upward mobility. However, the fact that these trends in occupational change have been gradual and extend over a long period, without any sudden 'take-off', suggests that we will see little in the way of trends over time towards increasing rates of upward mobility. Instead we expect to find some modest amounts of net upward mobility in all our birth cohorts.

First, however, before looking at trends over time we show a mobility table for the full NES dataset (without breaking it down into birth cohorts). This is shown in Table 6.2 for men and Table 6.3 for women. Essentially the mobility table is a cross-classification of respondent's class by his or her father's class. In Tables 6.2 and 6.3 we percentage the figures so that the total for all the cells in the cross-classification comes to 100 per cent. By summing the percentages down the main diagonal we can thus calculate the percentage who are intergenerationally stable. This comes to 69 per cent in the case of men and 75 per cent in the case of women. In other words 69 per cent of men and 75 per cent of women were in the same class as their fathers. Conversely of course we can say that 31 per cent of men exhibit intergenerational mobility compared with only 25 per cent of women. This is the opposite of what is seen in the West, where women are more likely to be mobile than are men. This suggests that in India men have been able to use the modest expansion in the occupational structure to their advantage, which supports our expectations discussed earlier. We should also note that these rates of mobility are a great deal lower than those found in the West, although once again this is unsurprising given the very large size of India's agricultural sector.

The off-diagonal cells in the table then show the percentage of the sample who were intergenerationally mobile. Those below the diagonal will be upwardly mobile (their own class being higher than their father's class), and those above the diagonal will be downwardly mobile. As we can see, overall around 20 per cent of men were upwardly mobile and 11

Table 6.2. The social mobility of men (percentages of total).

	Class of respondent					
Class of father	Salariat	Business	Farmers	Manual	Lower agriculture	N
Salariat	5.3	1.9	0.9	1.4	0.6	*1175*
Business	1.5	7.3	0.3	0.8	0.2	*1162*
Farmers	3.6	2.3	25.1	2.7	1.0	*4054*
Manual	2.6	1.8	0.5	11.2	1.4	*2044*
Lower agriculture	2.1	2.0	0.8	3.0	19.6	*3188*
N	*1761*	*1782*	*3201*	*2224*	*2655*	*11623*

Source: NES 2004.

Table 6.3. The social mobility of women (percentages of total).

	Class of respondent					
Class of father	Salariat	Business	Farmer	Manual	Lower agriculture	N
Salariat	5.5	0.9	1.2	1.1	1.0	*472*
Business	1.4	3.0	0.3	0.8	0.3	*282*
Farmers	1.8	0.7	26.7	2.1	1.5	*1614*
Manual	1.9	0.7	0.7	10.8	1.4	*757*
Lower agriculture	1.6	1.2	1.4	3.0	29.2	*1784*
N	*596*	*316*	*1482*	*879*	*1636*	*4909*

Source: NES 2004.

per cent downwardly mobile. In the case of women, upward mobility is rather lower at around 15 per cent with again about 10 per cent being downwardly mobile. This reflects the different occupational structures of course, with women tending to be in lower-level classes and thus exhibiting less upward mobility.

In sum, we conclude that India presents a picture of a very inter-generationally stable society for both women and men. But, despite this high intergenerational stability, the direction of mobility of women is the same as that of men, i.e. there is more upward than downward mobility. This is similar to the patterns seen in the West. (See for example various collections in Breen 2004 and Erikson & Goldthorpe 1992.) As in the West this surplus of upward over downward mobility has occurred due to changes in the occupational structure that have resulted in increasing 'room at the top'. But this surplus is not as high in India and is an indication of the slower rate of change in the occupational structure in India, especially the slow rate of expansion of the non-manual classes, and the slow rate of contraction of the agricultural classes.

Moving on from observing the overall pattern we next analyse trends in absolute mobility rates over birth cohorts. The total, upwards and downwards, mobility rates are graphed in Figures 6.2 and 6.3 (for men and women respectively).

These figures suggest that there has been decreasing upwards mobility and increasing downwards mobility across our birth cohorts. This sounds rather surprising but is almost certainly caused (either in whole or part) by the life-cycle processes that we mentioned earlier. In other words, the younger birth cohorts are at earlier stages of their career and have had less time to be upwardly mobile. We might therefore expect to find that the upwards mobility of the younger cohorts will later increase as they become older.

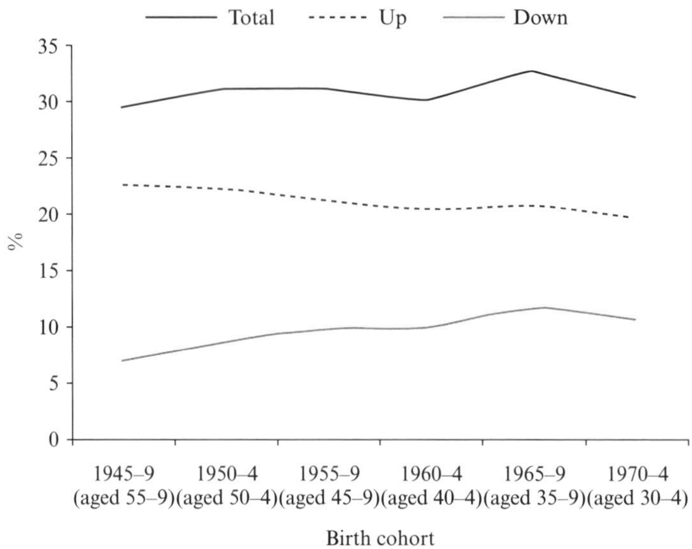

Figure 6.2. Intergenerational mobility rates for men, NES 2004.

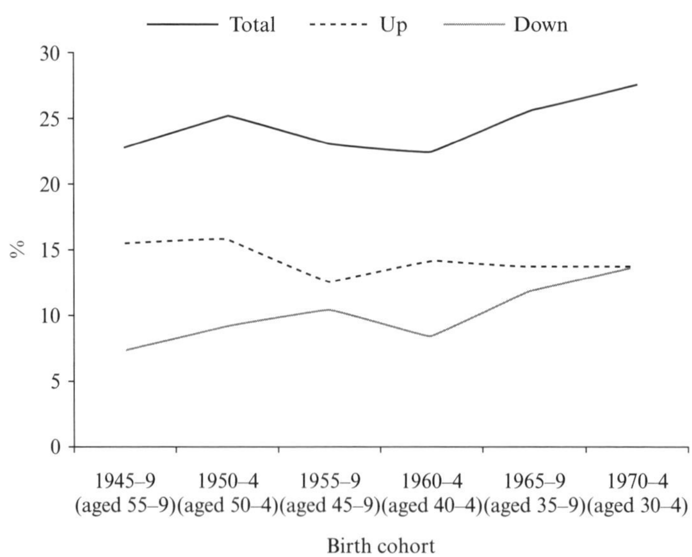

Figure 6.3. Intergenerational mobility rates for women, NES 2004.

It is probably safer, then, to focus on the trend in total mobility, and this shows very little change over time either for men or for women. (The fluctuations can largely be attributed to sampling variations.) The overall picture that emerges is one of continuity and of only slight change over the birth cohorts. This story is entirely consistent with the continuing but gradual structural change we observed in Figure 6.1 in our discussion of published NSS results and in Table 6.1 through the NES data. Had there been a sudden 'take-off' following the economic liberalisation of the 1980s, then we might have expected to see an increase in social mobility among the later cohorts. Instead, the patterns are very much what we would expect from the long-standing but gradual evolution of the Indian occupational structure with its slowly decreasing agricultural sector and its slowly increasing salariat.

Trends in inequality of opportunity

Next, in order to analyse whether there has been any change in the 'openness' or equality of opportunity in Indian society over time, we move on to explore patterns of relative rates of mobility. As we explained earlier, in contrast to absolute mobility, relative mobility is a measure of the 'openness' of a society after allowing for the extent of structural change. It is a measure that is not influenced by structural changes in the class distribution, such as the 'increasing room at the top' brought about by the decline in agriculture and increasing size of the salariat, in the way that absolute rates are. Hence they are preferred as indicators of the inequality of opportunity in society. Note that trends in relative mobility do not have to show the same pattern as those in absolute mobility that we saw in the previous section. The logic of the two different measures allows them to move in different directions. Equally, however, it is possible to have the same trends, or lack of trends, and indeed modernisation theory expects that both absolute and relative mobility will increase together over time. Whether they do or not is of course a matter for empirical investigation.

Odds ratios are the basic measures used by sociologists to study relative rates of mobility. These ratios show us the relative risks of someone from one origin 'making it' to a destination and avoiding another one (Heath & Payne 2000) in comparison with people from a different social origin. An odds ratio of 1 shows equal odds, which can be interpreted as complete equality of opportunity. If there is increasing equality of opportunity, therefore, in Indian society over time, we should expect to see the odds ratios moving gradually closer to 1.

In a mobility table like the one shown in Tables 6.2 and 6.3, there are many possible odds ratios that can be calculated (to be precise 100 in a five-by-five table such as these). However, as we noted earlier when we discussed modernisation theory, we might expect to see rather different trends within different sectors of the society. For example we might expect to see little trend towards equality of opportunity within the agricultural sector whereas in the more 'modern' urbanised sector a trend towards equality of opportunity might be most likely. We therefore begin by focusing on specific odds ratios. We look at the lower agriculturalist : farmer odds ratio, which will enable us to investigate whether there is any trend towards equality of opportunity within the farming sector (but not really expecting to find one for the reasons mentioned earlier). We also look at the manual worker : salariat odds ratio which is the one where we think some trend towards equality of opportunity is most likely. For comparison we also look at the farmer : salariat odds ratio in order to look at movement between sectors. The results are shown in Figure 6.4 for men and Figure 6.5 for women.[7]

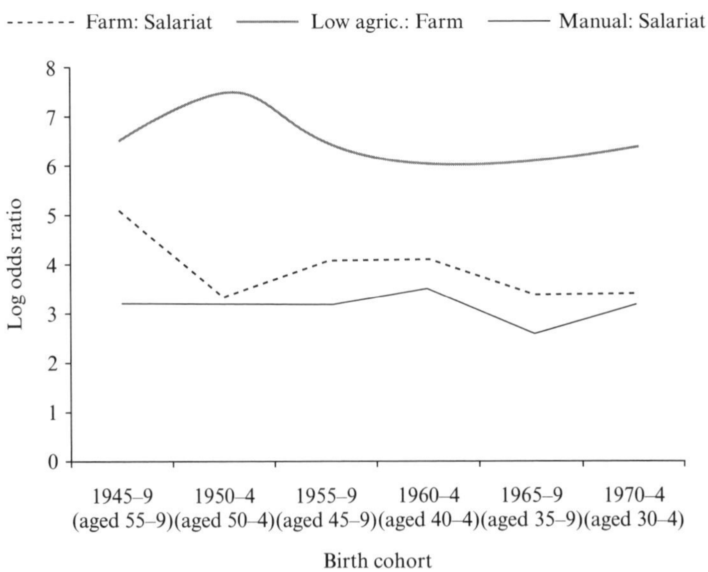

Figure 6.4. Symmetrical log odds ratios for men, NES 2004.

[7] Technically these are known as 'symmetrical' odds ratios. For technical reasons we report the log of these odds ratios, but the interpretation is essentially the same: the larger the log odds ratio, the greater the inequality of opportunity.

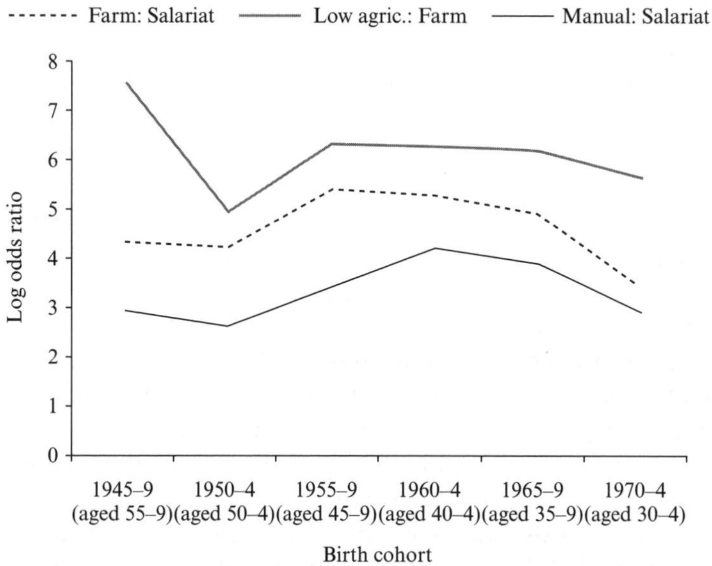

Figure 6.5. Symmetrical log odds ratios for women, NES 2004.

First of all, Figure 6.4 shows that inequality of opportunity is much greater in the farming sector than it is in the non-farm sector, with log odds ratios over 6 compared with log odds ratios of around 3 in the case of the manual : salariat odds ratio. This is of course exactly what we would expect in a society where farming positions are largely inherited while the salariat is exposed to more formal and open methods of recruitment. The farmer : salariat odds ratio is consistently higher than the manual : salariat ratio, suggesting that there are some sectoral barriers in addition to the class barriers. What is rather interesting however is that there is little sign of growing equality of opportunity in the case of any of the three odds ratios. The trends are rather bumpy, reflecting in part the small sample sizes involved and hence the large standard errors. There are hints of a downwards movement, but the picture is far from clear.

We see a very similar picture for women with much higher inequality of opportunity in the agricultural sector than in the non-farm one. Interestingly however, the farmer : salariat odds ratio is substantially higher for women than it is for men. This indicates that movement between farming and salariat jobs (and vice versa) is distinctly harder for women than it is for men. This may well be because, in a patriarchal rural society, men are more likely to receive from their families the investments needed to make a successful transition to the urban environment.

However, this is the only major difference that we observe between Figures 6.4 and 6.5. As with the picture for men in Figure 6.4, Figure 6.5 shows little sign of any increase in equality of opportunity for women. All three odds ratios remain stubbornly high.

A basic comparison of symmetrical odds ratios for India with those in Western countries shows the much higher 'stickiness' between Indian classes, and is a sign of higher levels of inequality of opportunity and of the closed nature of Indian society. (For discussions of odds ratios in some Western countries see Breen 2004; Erikson & Goldthorpe 1992; Heath & Payne 2000.)

So far we have focused simply on three illustrative odds ratios. We can also use loglinear modelling to test formally whether there has been any significant change in the odds ratios over time. The results are shown in Table 6.A1 and are discussed in the Appendix. Briefly the formal modelling shows that the model of 'constant social fluidity', which hypothesises no change in the odds ratios over time, fits the data for women rather well although it fits slightly less well for men. We also fitted the 'uniform difference' model which provides a useful summary measure of whether the odds ratios are changing over time. However, this did not provide a significant improvement in fit over the 'constant social fluidity' model. Overall we have to conclude that there has as yet been little in the way of any demonstrable increase in equality of opportunity in Indian society, either within the agricultural sector or even within the supposedly more 'modern' non-agricultural sector. That there has been no real change in the farming sector is not surprising; on theoretical grounds we had not expected to see much change in equality of opportunity here given the importance of inheritance of land and tenure. Nor had we expected to see much change within the informal economy, given the reliance here on self-employment and the use of informal ties for recruitment. It is however more surprising that access to the salariat has not become more open since this is the paradigm case where formal meritocratic recruitment methods might have been expected.

However, as Hasan explains in her chapter in this volume, unlike Western countries where policy debates have largely focused on class inequalities of opportunity, in the Indian context debates and policy initiatives have focused much more on caste, in particular with the extension of reservation policies within the public sector. It may then be that the impact of modernisation in India will be seen more with respect to caste background than with respect to class background. We turn to that in the next section.

Class and caste

Caste and class have often been taken to be closely associated but, as has been argued elsewhere (Vaid 2007), major theoretical and substantive advantages are to be gained by distinguishing them when analysing 'who gets ahead'. Empirical research (ibid.) based on this view has shown that caste and class are indeed associated in contemporary India but that there is no one-to-one relationship. It is therefore technically possible as well as theoretically interesting to compare their effects. In particular, given the prominence of the debates about reducing the disadvantages suffered by backward castes in India, in contrast to the Western focus on class inequalities, it makes sense to see whether there has been some decline over time in the importance of caste for access to advantaged social positions.

In a modernising society such as India, especially since the opening of the Indian economy and liberalisation, researchers like Panini (1996) believe that the influence of caste on class destination should decline over time.[8] Kolenda (2003) for example argues that modernisation may create 'differentiation within a caste' making castes more heterogeneous; she suggests that 'new identities may gradually outweigh caste identity' although she goes on to add that 'except among some urban elites, the caste social unit is too strong to allow a solidification of social classes across caste boundaries' (2003: 406).

If we do indeed find that the influence of caste has declined even if that of class origins has not with respect to gaining access to advantaged social positions, we may be able to conclude that the influence of modernisation is apparent in India. To analyse this aspect of modernisation we specifically look at access to salariat class destinations, as modernisation is expected to have an influence initially on occupations where 'direct' inheritance plays less of a role[9] and because it is a sector within which there has been the most policy innovation. While reservation policies apply of course only to public sector employment and not to the private sector, and thus apply only to a minority of salaried positions, reservation policies in higher education—which is a major stepping stone to salaried

[8] For an alternative view see Basile and Harriss-White (2000: 41) who in their study of village *Arni* do not find support for Panini's view.

[9] Basile and Harriss-White (2000: 178) have argued that caste networks are still important for 'recruitment' purposes in the informal sectors of the economy. Here we maintain that, though this might be the case for the informal sectors, we would expect there to be a declining influence of caste on the expanding professional sectors where 'merit' may have a greater role to play.

positions generally—might be expected to have wider impact on access to the salariat as a whole. We therefore look at changes across time (strictly speaking across birth cohorts) in the relative chances of men and women from different class and caste backgrounds gaining access to the salariat. For this exercise we use the same five-class classification that we have used previously in this chapter, together with an eight-fold classification of caste/community.

The classification of castes is a highly problematic and contentious matter. Four *varnas* make up the Hindu system of caste; these are the Brahmins (primarily priests, doctors and so on); Kshatriyas (warriors); Vaishyas (businessmen) and Shudras (lowest caste, mainly artisans and manual labourers).[10] The untouchables were those people who lay outside this caste system and in a sense formed a fifth category.[11] Each *varna* in turn can have thousands of sub-castes or *jatis*. As caste is a complex institution, and there is no pan-Indian consensus on the position of various *jatis* within the larger castes or *varnas*, it makes it particularly difficult to study *jatis* at the national level, and any generalisations may well be counter-productive. Instead, for the present study on changes in inequality of opportunity, we focus on communities that have been constitutionally recognised for preferential policies or 'reservations' aimed at encouraging the upward social mobility of these disadvantaged groups. These reservations guarantee the most 'backward' groups positions in government-run educational institutions, public sector employment and in the legislature (Galanter 1984). The main 'backward' groups for these policies are the Scheduled Castes (SCs, ex-untouchables), the Scheduled Tribes (STs, geographically and socially isolated communities) and the Other Backward Classes (OBCs, a collection of slightly less 'socially and educationally' deprived groups when compared to the SCs, but considered nonetheless 'backward' when compared to the 'forward' higher castes). Within the forward castes we distinguish peasant and non-peasant segments, since we anticipate that there might be significant differences between them in access to the salariat; and within the OBCs we distinguish between the

[10] According to Zwart (2000) 'varnas . . . are not actual groups. They form an ideological scheme, used by people as a handy gross classification of others' (Mandelbaum 1970: 13). For more on the differences and relations between *varna* and *jati* see Srinivas (1962). The 'operative term' for caste as Deshpande (2002) puts it is *jati* and not *varna*. Hence, in addition to the generic term caste, *jati* is the other term that will be used in this chapter while referring to sub-castes.

[11] The British moved to outlaw untouchability, and its practice has been constitutionally illegal in India since 1950. By necessity this is a sketchy view of caste; for a more exhaustive review refer to Srinivas (1996, 2003), Fuller (1996*a*), Dumont ([1966] 1980) to name a few.

higher and lower segments. We analyse the inequalities in opportunities faced by these groups and compare these to the other communities (especially Muslims). This enables us not only to separate the lower castes from the higher ones but it also allows us to study the mobility patterns across a broad range of communities. (See the Appendix for more details.) We are aware of the heterogeneity within each of these broad categories, but for a study of mobility and inequality at the national level, these broad generalisations are a useful tool to analyse major differences.

We use logistic regression to investigate access to salariat class destinations as this is the standard technique in sociology for analysing a dichotomous dependent variable. In the logistic regression we include class origins and the communities/castes as independent variables; with access to the salariat as the dependent variable. We use deviation contrasts (similar to Kumar *et al.* 2002*a*) to arrive at the parameter estimates which can be interpreted as fitted log odds ratios. In this regression 'deviation contrasts compare each group . . . to the un-weighted average of all groups' (Nichols 1997). Put another way, all parameters above 0 show that for the origin category in question there are more favourable odds than average of gaining access to the salariat and avoiding any other class; and anything below 0 shows less favourable odds (Kumar *et al.* 2002*a*). The parameter estimates shown in Tables 6.4 and 6.5 can be interpreted in the same way as the odds ratios in the previous section as measures of the extent of inequality of opportunity.

Looking first at the general patterns in the two tables we see that class inequalities of opportunity are substantially larger, across all birth cohorts, than the caste/community inequalities. Men or women from salariat origins have much the most favourable relative chances of gaining access to the salariat and of avoiding other destinations, while men and women from lower agricultural backgrounds have much the least favourable chances. In between come the business, farmer and manual categories, with people from farm backgrounds being rather more disadvantaged than those from manual backgrounds (reflecting the additional sectoral barriers described above), and those from business origins being perhaps slightly less disadvantaged.

We also see a clear gradient in the case of our eight caste/community categories but the range of parameter estimates is only half that for class. In other words, the gradient or hierarchy is not as steep. Unsurprisingly we see that the non-peasant forward castes are the most advantaged in the competition to reach the salariat. The peasant forward castes come next, albeit some way behind, and there is not a great deal of difference in the

Table 6.4. Logistic regression of access to the salariat by birth cohort, men (parameter estimates).

	Born 1945–9	Born 1950–4	Born 1955–9	Born 1960–4	Born 1965–9	Born 1970–4
Father's Class						
Salariat	1.8*	1.7*	1.5*	1.9*	1.6*	1.8*
	(0.3)	(0.2)	(0.2)	(0.2)	(0.2)	(0.1)
Business	−0.2	−0.5	−0.1	−0.5*	−0.3	−0.1
	(0.3)	(0.3)	(0.2)	(0.3)	(0.2)	(0.2)
Farmer	−0.6*	−0.4*	−0.3	−0.4*	−0.2	−0.4*
	(0.2)	(0.2)	(0.2)	(0.2)	(0.1)	(0.1)
Manual	−0.4	−0.5*	−0.5*	0.1	-0.3	−0.2
	(0.3)	(0.2)	(0.2)	(0.2)	(0.2)	(0.2)
Lower agric.	−0.6*	−0.3	−0.6*	−1.0*	−0.8*	−1.1*
	(0.2)	(0.2)	(0.2)	(0.2)	(0.2)	(0.2)
Caste						
Forward caste	0.5*	0.6*	0.6*	0.4*	0.5*	0.1
	(0.3)	(0.2)	(0.2)	(0.2)	(0.2)	(0.2)
Peasant forward caste	−0.4	0.4	−0.2	0.1	0.1	0.3
	(0.5)	(0.4)	(0.4)	(0.3)	(0.3)	(0.3)
OBC higher segment	−0.5	−0.5	−0.3	−0.3	−0.2	−0.0
	(0.3)	(0.3)	(0.3)	(0.2)	(0.2)	(0.2)
OBC lower segment	−0.1	0.1	0.4	−0.0	−0.5*	−0.4*
	(0.3)	(0.2)	(0.3)	(0.2)	(0.2)	(0.2)
Scheduled caste	0.0	−0.1	0.2	−0.6*	−0.2	−0.4
	(0.3)	(0.3)	(0.3)	(0.3)	(0.2)	(0.2)
Scheduled tribe	−0.1	−0.6	−0.4	0.2	−0.1	0.4*
	(0.3)	(0.3)	(0.3)	(0.2)	(0.2)	(0.2)
Muslim	−0.2	−0.1	−0.4	0.1	−0.0	−0.3
	(0.3)	(0.3)	(0.3)	(0.2)	(0.2)	(0.2)
Other minority	0.7*	0.2	0.0	0.1	0.4	0.4
	(0.3)	(0.4)	(0.4)	(0.3)	(0.3)	(0.3)
Constant	−1.3*	−1.6*	−1.7*	−1.7*	−1.8*	−1.7*
	(0.1)	(0.1)	(0.1)	(0.1)	(0.1)	(0.1)
N	*563*	*852*	*944*	*1291*	*1467*	*1565*
Chi sq.	66.6	91.4	74.8	163.1	159.3	178.5
	(11 df)	(11 df)	(11 df)	(11 df)	(11 df)	(11 df)

Source: NES 2004.

Notes: Standard Errors in parenthesis; * indicates that the parameter estimate is more than twice its standard error, and hence significant at the 5% level.

For presentational purposes we have calculated deviation contrasts (and their standard errors) for all groups rather than leaving one group as excluded. This means that the number of parameter estimates shown is not the same as the number of degrees of freedom.

Table 6.5. Logistic regression of access to the salariat by birth cohort, women (parameter estimates).

	Born 1945–9	Born 1950–4	Born 1955–9	Born 1960–4	Born 1965–9	Born 1970–4
Father's Class						
Salariat	1.7*	1.6*	2.1*	2.4*	2.3*	1.6*
	(0.5)	(0.4)	(0.3)	(0.3)	(0.3)	(0.2)
Business	1.3*	0.8	0.6	0.6	0.9*	−0.1
	(0.5)	(0.5)	(0.4)	(0.4)	(0.3)	(0.4)
Farmer	−1.0*	−0.6	−1.6*	−1.7*	−1.4*	−0.8*
	(0.4)	(0.4)	(0.4)	(0.4)	(0.3)	(0.3)
Manual	−0.1	0.4	0.1	−0.1	−0.9*	0.0
	(0.5)	(0.4)	(0.4)	(0.3)	(0.4)	(0.3)
Lower agric.	−2.0*	−2.2*	−1.2*	−1.3*	−0.9*	−0.8*
	(0.6)	(0.6)	(0.4)	(0.3)	(0.3)	(0.3)
Caste						
Forward caste	0.0	0.8*	0.6	0.4	0.1	0.6*
	(0.5)	(0.4)	(0.4)	(0.3)	(0.3)	(0.3)
Peasant forward caste	0.9	0.9	0.3	−0.2	0.3	−0.7
	(0.7)	(0.6)	(0.5)	(0.5)	(0.4)	(0.7)
OBC higher segment	−0.5	−1.0	−0.3	0.1	−0.8	−1.6*
	(1.0)	(0.7)	(0.7)	(0.4)	(0.5)	(0.7)
OBC lower segment	0.3	0.3	0.2	−1.3*	−0.1	-0.1
	(0.5)	(0.4)	(0.4)	(0.5)	(0.4)	(0.4)
Scheduled caste	−0.8	0.1	−0.6	−0.7	−1.3*	0.1
	(0.7)	(0.5)	(0.5)	(0.4)	(0.5)	(0.3)
Scheduled tribe	0.2	−0.5	−0.6	0.4	0.4	0.6
	(0.7)	(0.7)	(0.6)	(0.4)	(0.3)	(0.3)
Muslim	−0.9	−1.0	−0.6	0.0	−0.2	−0.9
	(1.0)	(1.0)	(0.7)	(0.5)	(0.5)	(0.6)
Other minority	0.8	0.4	1.0	1.2*	1.6*	2.0*
	(0.6)	(0.6)	(0.6)	(0.5)	(0.4)	(0.4)
Constant	−2.0*	−2.0*	−2.1*	−1.7*	−1.8*	−2.0*
	(0.3)	(0.3)	(0.1)	(0.2)	(0.2)	(0.2)
N	*267*	*348*	*435*	*520*	*659*	*689*
Chi sq.	39.3	54.8	80.5	125.2	143.3	113.6
	(11 df)	(11 df)	(11 df)	(11 df)	(11 df)	(11 df)

Source: NES 2004.
Notes: Standard Errors in parenthesis; * indicates that the parameter estimate is more than twice its standard error, and hence significant at the 5% level.

extent of disadvantage experienced by the other categories. Focusing primarily on the trend or change in the parameter estimates, some of the main highlights of the tables are as follows:

1. For both women and men the parameter estimates for class origin display 'trendless fluctuation'. For instance, the salariat origin

parameter estimates for men over the birth-cohorts are 1.8, 1.7, 1.5, 1.9, 1.6, and 1.8—ending up where they started. Similarly for men from lower agricultural origins the parameter has remained negative and significant in all but one birth-cohort and is the highest for the youngest birth-cohort (although for women this parameter seems to have declined quite gradually over birth-cohorts).

2. In terms of caste the parameter estimates for Forward Caste men remain positive and significant in all but the youngest birth-cohort. This might be an indication of the decline in the significance of caste on class destinations but as this birth-cohort has not reached 'occupational maturity' (and the picture might be confounded by the life-cycle processes discussed earlier), we cannot draw this conclusion with confidence. For women the parameter fluctuates trendlessly from one birth-cohort to another.
3. Another parameter that stands out is for the Lower OBC men in the youngest two birth-cohorts where it is negative and significant. Again, it may be too soon to conclude that a Lower OBC background has a negative effect on access to professional class destinations. But this could indicate that Lower OBC men are different from the forward or advanced sections of this caste category.
4. With regard to the Muslim community we see that none of the parameters is significant, although most are negative. This implies that coming from a Muslim community may reduce one's chances of gaining access to salariat destinations but that this disadvantage is much smaller than that faced by members of the Scheduled Castes.

We do not therefore see any clear trend in the influence of caste on access to the salariat in the logistic regression. A major result of this analysis, therefore, is that contrary to expectation father's class rather than caste has, over all birth-cohorts, been the stronger determining factor for access to salaried class destinations. In this respect India seems to have displayed a picture of quite a 'modern' society throughout the period since Independence. Furthermore this analysis suggests that the policy of reservations may not have benefited the SCs and STs as much as might have been hoped: despite these policies these groups seem to consistently lag behind the high castes in terms of access to professional class destinations, with little or no improvement in their relative position over time.

One caveat regarding our results needs to be mentioned: they are specific to a particular way of categorising caste and class. Thus, the comparison of the parameter estimates made here is specific to the particular measure and aggregation of caste and class used. If we used more detailed classifications, such as information on individual *jatis*, we might get a stronger result for that particular *jati*, though perhaps not for the others. However, having noted this, given the broad constitutionally recognised categorisations used here, we can conclude that class has long been an important influence on access to professional destinations and continues to remain so.

Discussion

In this chapter, following the classic treatments of social mobility in the sociological literature, we have focused on intergenerational class mobility, that is on the extent to which sons (and daughters) follow in their fathers' footsteps. We asked how 'open' India is and whether it is becoming more 'open' with greater equality of opportunity as it modernises. And we asked about the continuing importance of 'traditional' features of Indian society such as caste on occupational opportunities. Has the political emphasis on reducing the disabilities stemming from caste led to any diminution over time in the relation between caste and occupational attainment?

Some of our results are fairly unsurprising, given the stage of India's development, while others are more surprising and perhaps even paradoxical.

It is not at all surprising to find that India still has a rather 'traditional' occupational structure with a continuing huge agricultural sector. Nor is it surprising that the pace of change has been rather slow; India can be likened to a huge oil tanker that cannot quickly change direction unlike small Nordic countries (e.g. Iceland) that were able to transform themselves from a largely agricultural society to a postindustrial society in the course of a couple of generations. However, it is much more surprising that this slow evolution away from agriculture is evident throughout the period since independence, that it clearly predates the market liberalisation of the 1980s and of more recent reforms, and indeed that there has been no increase in the pace of occupational change since these reforms.

Given India's continuing huge agricultural sector, it is not at all surprising to find that overall there are rather low rates of intergenerational social mobility in India; and given the inequalities of condition that persist in Indian society, it is not at all surprising that inequalities of opportunity remain very considerable. We should not be surprised that both absolute and relative rates of mobility in India remain low by Western standards. Nor should we be surprised that inequalities of opportunity appear to be much greater within the agricultural sector than they are in the more 'modern' non-farm sectors. But it is more surprising that, even in the non-farm sectors, inequalities of opportunity are not declining over time. Modernisation may be leading to a larger salariat, but there is little sign that the salariat is becoming more open to people from other social backgrounds.

It is not surprising that there are gender inequalities in mobility chances, just as there are in the West, and that women are more likely to be found in the lower levels of each class. But it is more surprising that women have not yet come to predominate in the routine clerical and junior white-collar positions in the same way that they have done in the industrial and postindustrial societies of the West. It is also surprising that there has been no sign of younger generations of women catching up with men in the non-farm sectors.

Finally it is not surprising that both class and caste backgrounds are important in influencing who gets ahead. But the greater importance of class background, an importance that appears to be rather long-standing, is perhaps our most surprising finding. To be sure, more detailed analysis of individual *jatis* in place of our broad caste/community categorisation would lead to an increased measured importance of caste. But this still leaves the finding that the legal categories on which reservation policies are based are not as important as might have been expected for occupational attainment.

Overall, the findings of this chapter suggest that simple contrasts between tradition and modernity are not especially helpful for understanding contemporary India. Deshpande, while underlining the dominant influence of social anthropology rather than sociology on academic discourse in India, concludes that

> . . . most studies of modernisation in India located themselves in the world of tradition and looked out upon modernity from that vantage point . . . Indian social anthropology failed to cultivate intensively those methods (such as survey or quantitative techniques) and research areas (like industry, the media or the class structure) of sociology proper . . . This in turn affected the manner in which

> the discipline dealt with the question of modernisation, particularly since this question privileges generalisation from a macro-perspective, something which anthropology is neither theoretically inclined towards nor methodologically equipped for. (Deshpande 1999: 23)

The present research using a macro-perspective and quantitative research methods suggests that using a sociological framework does indeed underscore that 'tradition' is only one part of the Indian story, that traditional elements coexist alongside various modern aspects, and that Western models of modernity and modernisation are not necessarily useful concepts for understanding contemporary India.

Appendix 1: Data, variables and methods

Data

The 2004 National Election Study (NES) conducted by the Centre for the Study of Developing Societies (Delhi) is the primary data used in this research.[12] The study consists of a nationally representative, stratified random sample of over 27,000 respondents (approximately 14,700 men and 12,400 women) drawn from the electoral rolls and covering all twenty-eight states and four (of the seven) Union Territories. There was a high response rate of 77 per cent. For our analysis we include all respondents aged 18 and above.[13]

This dataset is especially useful for the present study as it includes detailed background information on both the respondent's and father's occupations (the NES does not collect information on mother's occupation, but this should not be a major issue as the proportion of women in employment in the mother's generation would have been quite small), and their caste and community affiliation. For this study any respondents who did not have information on their own and their father's occupation and on community background were dropped from the analysis on mobility and caste, leaving us with a sample of just under 10,000 (6861 men and 2981 women) respondents.

[12] For a discussion and history of NES practices and the methodology of the Election Studies especially the 2004 NES dataset see the special issue of the Economic and Political Weekly (18 Dec. 2004) which also discusses alternative research areas where NES datasets have been utilised.

[13] In contrast to Western studies where mobility is analysed for respondents usually aged 20–64 in the present research we set no upper age limit for the analysis. This is because given the large informal sector in India (Harriss-White 2003) there is no 'retirement' age for a majority of the working population, most of whom continue to work all their lives. Setting an upper age limit would not capture all these people and hence we include all respondents aged over 18 years. This decision might have implications for our results due to the possible effect of differential mortality, especially as mortality is not random with respect to class. But we maintain that in the Indian case the arguments for observing the whole sample and not just people up till the age of 64 seem stronger than the argument for having an upper age limit.

In addition to the NES data, we refer to secondary published data from the National Sample Surveys (NSS) for 1972–2000 for mapping change in employment participation over time. The NSS collects five-yearly national employment and unemployment information.

Class schema

Numerous class schemas have been employed in mobility analyses in both India and the West. As 'there are almost as many class schemas as there are sociologists' (Kumar *et al.* 2002*a*: 2983), in this chapter we use a schema which has, in its various versions, been used to specifically study national mobility patterns in India, albeit men's mobility patterns. This is the schema employed by Kumar *et al.* (2002*a*,*b*; see also McMillan 2005). It has recently been updated and validated by Vaid (2007) and used to study women's mobility alongside men's class mobility for the first time. Briefly, this schema aims to distinguish between discrete classes on the basis of employment relations, for example distinguishing between people who occupy salaried positions in bureaucratic organisations with regular 'service' contracts; the self-employed who are essentially independent; and wage labourers who supply their labour power in a 'wage-effort' bargain. (See Goldthorpe *et al.* 1980: 39. For more details on the conceptualisation, operationalisation and validation of this scheme, as well as more on the detailed occupations that make up each class, see Vaid 2007; and Kumar *et al.* 2002*a*). In its expanded form the updated class schema has eleven classes, which for the purpose of the present study are collapsed into five classes, in order to avoid small sample sizes.

The NES did not directly collect information on the nature of employment relations but coded occupations to a detailed list of just under 100 occupations. These have been coded to the five broad classes as follows:

1. **Salariat Class**: higher professionals, administrators and officials; elected officials (central/state level); managers; lower professionals, administrators and officials; elected officials (district level); technicians, supervisors; high grade routine non-manual employees, other administrators, Class IV (peons etc), sales executives, sales persons, shop assistants, traditional clerks, Class III (clerical).[14]
2. **Business class**: big business (with 7+ employees), medium business (3–7 employees), small business (1–2 employees or family workers); petty shopkeepers, rentiers.
3. **Farmer class**: farm owners with more than 5 acres of land; farm owners with 0–5 acres of land; tenant farmers (with 5+ acres of land).
4. **Manual class**: skilled manual workers; semi- and unskilled manual workers (not in agriculture); low grade routine non-manual employees—waiters, washer men, barbers, ayahs, other service etc.

[14] In this context Class III and IV here are the Indian government classifications for public sector employees.

5. **Lower agricultural class**: agricultural labourers and non-cultivators; small tenants (with 0–5 acres of land).

Caste

The 2004 NES has information on ninety castes and tribes, which were recoded into eight categories, referred to interchangeably as community or caste in this chapter. All Muslims, and other religious minorities that had information on their SC or OBC status, are excluded from the SC, OBC list, but included instead within their religious category. This enables us to treat caste as essentially Hindu, and compare these Hindu castes with the other community groups.[15] These ninety castes and tribes were coded into our eight-fold caste/community classification as follows:

1. **Non-peasant forward caste**: Brahmin, Bhumihar, Rajput, Kayasthas, Vaishya, Jain, Punjabi, Khatri, Sindhi, other upper caste.
2. **Peasant forward caste**: Jat, Reddy, Kamma, Nair, Marathas, Patel, Raju, Velama, Kapu, other peasant.
3. **OBC higher segment**: Gujjar, Yadav, Kurmi/Gowda, Lodh/Munuru Kapu, Koeri/Mudiraj, Vokkaliga/Kalinga, Lingayat/Thorpu Kapu, Gaderia/Koopula Velama, Kunbi, other peasant OBC.
4. **OBC lower segment**: Bunkar/Padmasali, Darzee/Meera, Thatihar, Lakhera/Boya, Badhai/Kamsali, Kumhar, Lohar/Kanchar, Sunar, Medara, other craftsmen, Kewat/Pallekari, Dhobi/Rajaka, Nai/Mangali, Teli/Gandla, Jogi/Dudekula, traders OBC, toddy tappers/Perika, landless labourers/Bhartraju, entertaining caste/Kalavanthulu, other service OBC.
5. **Scheduled castes**: Chamar/Jatav/Madigas, Balmiki/Bhangi, Pasi/Pano/Adi Andhra, Rajbanshis/Mala, Namasudras/Mahar/Malajangam, Dhobi/Relli, Dom/Sindhollu, nomadic, lowest SC, other SC.
6. **Scheduled tribes**: Mina/Sugali/Boro, Bhil/Yerukula/Karbi, Gond/Koya/Abor, Oraon/Konda Dhora/Miri, Kamars/Irular/Nega/Yanadi, Santhal/Paniyan/Mizo/Boya, Munda/Kuruba/Khasi/Savara, Andh/Malyali/Chakma/Jatapu, Naikda/Nayaka/Kuki/Chenchu, other STs.
7. **Muslims**: Ashraf, Mughal, Rajput Muslim, other upper caste(Muslim), peasants+traders, craftsmen+weavers, service Muslims, Muslim Dalit, other Muslim OBC, Muslim no caste.
8. **Other minorities**: Jat Sikh, Khatri Sikh, OBC Sikh, Sikh no caste, forward caste Christian, OBC Christian, Dalit Christian, Christian no caste, Buddhists, Dalit Buddhist, other minorities.

It is acknowledged that this categorisation may not be entirely accurate as, for example, some *jatis* are on the relevant list in some states but not in others. To ensure

[15] We are of course aware that castes have also been observed in other religions, but this issue is beyond the scope of the present chapter. For more on caste and other religions see Dumont ([1966] 1980), chapter 10; for a brief summary see Pingle (2003); for more on caste and Muslims in India see Ahmad (1973); Bhatty (1996); Fanselow (1996); for caste among Christians see Thalamangalam (1996).

some compatibility with the official lists the OBC, SC and ST names in the dataset were compared to the Scheduled Caste, Tribe and OBC lists available from the various caste commissions.[16]

Birth cohorts

To study the effects of modernisation and changes over time, a birth-cohort method is followed. A study involving over-time change would ideally require data collected using similar questions and sampling techniques over a period of time. In the absence of any such national level data for India, due especially to the exclusion of women and the inconsistency of procedures followed in the National Election Studies, the next best strategy is to use the cross-sectional data available and to divide the respondents in the data into 'birth cohorts' (Heath 1981: 81).

There are a few drawbacks of employing this procedure, namely, that the individuals in the same age group do not necessarily present a representative sample of all those born in those years due to deaths, selective migration and so on. Moreover, differential mortality may be an important issue given that mortality is not random with respect to class and older cohorts might be a selection of people who have been upwardly mobile, thus depressing the amount of downward mobility observed. Furthermore, those born in earlier cohorts will have spent longer in the labour market, hence many young people who might seem downwardly mobile now, may be quite successful later on in their lives (see also Heath & Payne 2000: 258; also Breen & Jonsson 1997 for issues of recall bias in reporting parental occupations especially for older birth-cohorts).

Despite these drawbacks the birth-cohort approach used here has been followed by others (see Erikson & Goldthorpe 1987; Heath & Payne 2000) and in the absence of requisite longitudinal or panel data it provides the best available indicator of the trends of mobility over time. The analysis presented here is similar to that of Erikson and Goldthorpe (1992) in as much as it deals with what are called 'quasi-cohorts' rather than true birth cohorts, 'that is, with the survivors of true cohorts, following on losses due to mortality and emigration, to whom immigrants will then be added' (p. 71).

Statistical methods

To explore patterns and trends in mobility, we employ both mobility tables and log-linear models and to study caste and modernisation we use logistic regression models.

As there are a number of independent odds ratios that can be calculated from one mobility table, we use loglinear analysis to test among other things, whether the complete sets of odds ratios are constant over time. As one of the research questions

[16] For more details see: the Ministry of Tribal affairs [http://tribal.nic.in/index1.html]; and the National Commission for Backward Classes (NCBC) [http://ncbc.nic.in/backward-classes/index.html] websites. As OBCs are listed by state, an effort was made to ensure that these national names were in the state lists.

is whether social fluidity has remained constant over time or whether fluidity has increased as would be expected under the modernisation thesis, these loglinear models are the appropriate way to test for increasing fluidity.

As the models we employ are fairly standard in social mobility research, we only briefly discuss their formulation and significance tests here (see Breen 2004, especially chapter 2; Vaid 2007 for more). In the first model called the complete independence (or perfect mobility) model: origins, destinations and birth-cohort are hypothesised to be independent of each other (for both women and men). The notation for this model is $\log_m = \lambda + \lambda_i^O + \lambda_j^D + \lambda_k^C$.[17] As this model of perfect mobility never usually fits any data we move on to the models of real interest, the CnSF and the Unidiff models. The Constant Social Fluidity model (CnSF) postulates an association between origins and destinations, but it is presumed to be constant over time; i.e. there are hypothesised to be identical relative rates of mobility for each birth cohort (see Erikson & Goldthorpe 1992). This model extends the complete independence model by adding three two-way interaction terms, OC, DC and OD:

$$\log_m = \lambda + \lambda_i^O + \lambda_j^D + \lambda_k^C + \lambda_{ik}^{OC} + \lambda_{jk}^{DC} + \lambda_{ij}^{OD}$$

Simply put, this model hypothesises that there has been no change over time in the OD association. If this model does not fit our data, we can conclude that there has been change over time in the association between class origins and class destinations, either towards or away from greater fluidity. But to determine specifically which direction change has taken, we fit the Unidiff model (Erikson & Goldthorpe 1992; Xie 1992). According to Erikson and Goldthorpe, under the Unidiff model 'all odds ratios expected under the model for different cohorts will differ uniformly (though not by a constant amount) in moving together either towards or away from independence' (1992: 92). The Unidiff model (reproduced here from Erikson and Goldthorpe 1992: fn. 24) extends the CnSF model.

$$\log F_{ijk} = \lambda + \lambda_i^O + \lambda_j^D + \lambda_k^C + \lambda_{ik}^{OC} + \lambda_{jk}^{DC} + \beta_k X_{ij}$$

In the equation, X_{ij} refers in this case to the pattern of association between origins and destinations for women or men and β_k is a 'table specific multiplier that raises or lowers the overall strength of all the odds ratios in a uniform manner' (Breen 2004: 34). If this model fits our data we observe the parameters which indicate whether the origin-destination association has become weaker over time, indicating increasing social fluidity, or it has remained constant.

In order to evaluate which of the loglinear models best fits the data we compare some summary statistics (for a discussion see Breen 2004: 25–27; Erikson & Goldthorpe 1992: especially chapters 3 and 7) such as the G^2 or likelihood ratio χ^2 statistic, the Index of Dissimilarity (Δ), the rG^2 and the Bayesian Information Criterion or *BIC*. The Index of Dissimilarity is the 'percentage of cases misclassified', i.e. the number of cases that are allocated to wrong cells by the model being studied

[17] Where O=origins, D=destinations and C=birth-cohort; (lambda) is a constant term in the models.

(Erikson & Goldthorpe 1992: 89); and the rG^2 shows 'how much of the total association between class of origin and class of destination' a model is able to account for (Erikson & Goldthorpe 1992: 88). The lower the Δ and the bic, and the higher the rG^2, the better the fit to the data provided by the model. The results are shown in Table 6.A1 and are discussed in the chapter.

Table 6.A1. Log linear models for social fluidity trends, men and women.

	G^2	d.f.	P	Δ	rG^2	bic
Men (N=6861)						
O, D, C	8141.3	136	0.000	47.3	—	6940.4
CnSF (OD)	112.4	80	0.010	3.3	98.6	−594.0
Unidiff	105.6	75	0.011	3.2	98.7	−556.9
Women (N=2981)						
O, D, C	3742.8	136	0.000	50.3	—	2654.8
CnSF (OD)	80.8	80	0.454	4.0	97.8	−559.2
Unidiff	73.8	75	0.517	3.5	98.0	−526.2

Notes: O=Origins; D=Destinations; C=Cohort; CnSF=Constant Social Fluidity Model (see text for details).

7

The Die is Cast(e): The Debate on Backward Caste/Class Quotas, 1990 and 2006[1]

ZOYA HASAN

Summary. Affirmative action has a long and controversial history in India. While reservations for the Scheduled Castes and Scheduled Tribes in higher education, government employment and the legislature have been an accepted feature ever since independence, reservations for the 'other backward classes' have been much more controversial. A central issue has been how to define the backward classes. Were they to be defined in terms of economic position or was caste to be the unit? The first attempt, by the Kalelkar Commission, was unsuccessful with many dissenting voices on the Commission, including the Chairman himself. Its recommendations were not accepted by the Congress government when it reported in 1955. Subsequently the Janata Dal-led government set up the second Backward Classes Commission in 1978 (the Mandal Commission) and while the following Congress government failed to implement its recommendations, the proposal to introduce reservation in government employment was accepted, amid considerable controversy, by V. P. Singh's non-congress coalition government in 1990 (Mandal I). Most recently, in 2006, the Congress-led UPA government has extended reservation for the other backward classes to higher education. But many issues still remain unresolved, in particular the position of the more affluent segments (the 'creamy layers'), the position of minorities and perhaps most fundamentally how to resolve other non-caste bases of social exclusion and disadvantage.

[1] The title of this chapter is a variation of the theme title of the *Little Magazine* issue on reservations (*Little Magazine*, Vol. VI, issues 4 & 5).

Proceedings of the British Academy **159**, 165–187.

Introduction

IN THE LAST FEW DECADES, the expansion of group-based preferential policies has dominated public debates in India. Even as affirmative action programmes worldwide have come under fire from people advocating group-blind policies, India has persisted with and even gone ahead to expand mandatory reservations and affirmative action, which are by any standards unprecedented in their scope and extent, and radical in their content. Both central and state governments have implemented, in varying degrees, policies for reservations that aim to increase opportunities for backward classes/castes in government employment and education. The access of these castes to public institutions was traditionally low. The government's position in 1950 was that only two categories—the Scheduled Castes (SCs) and the Scheduled Tribes (STs)—were entitled to reservations in education, public employment and the legislature. However in August 1990, Prime Minister V. P. Singh of the Janata Dal-led National Front government announced the implementation of reservations in central government jobs for the Other Backward Classes (OBCs) (we shall call this 'Mandal I'). Fifteen years later, in April 2006, the Congress-led United Progressive Alliance (UPA) government made moves to introduce reservations for the OBCs in institutions of higher and professional education ('Mandal II'). The Mandal Commission, which submitted its report in 1980, had recommended 27 per cent reservations in both the government and the education sector, but V. P. Singh did not extend it to educational institutions because he was apprehensive that it was likely to fuel even stronger protests, and could thus dissipate the likely political gains from implementing OBC reservations in government jobs.

Both decisions have been a major source of conflict. For any understanding of why this is so, it is important to separate Mandal I and Mandal II. Mandal I essentially acted as a catalyst to open up the political and bureaucratic system for sections of the OBCs. Mandal II sought to increase educational access and opportunities for disadvantaged groups at the point when the post-Independence consensus on the Nehruvian mixed economy model and the Congress social coalition of extremes (upper castes, SCs and minorities) had broken down. (See the chapter by Oliver Heath and Yogendra Yadav later in this volume for more details of these changes.)

This chapter focuses on the controversy generated by the UPA government's decision to extend reservations for OBCs in higher education. Two issues have dominated Indian policy debates regarding reservations for

OBCs. The first issue is whether caste is an indicator of disadvantage, especially in the case of OBCs. The key concern is whether OBCs should be identified on the basis of caste or on the basis of economic and occupational criteria. The second issue pertains to the conception of backwardness itself. Backwardness, as it was widely defined, excluded non-Hindus. Both issues assume a new importance in the context of the vast social and economic changes that have taken place in the country in the past two decades, which have important implications for social relations and which also raise further questions with regard to the fairness and relevance of reservation policies and their implications for excluded groups.

Mandal I: reservations in central government

The Constitution provided clear policies of reservations for Scheduled Castes but it did not do so in the same unambiguous terms for the backward castes, even though the OBCs as an official category gained currency during the Constituent Assembly debates in the late 1940s. After Independence the number of groups entitled to reservation was expanded to include the OBCs. When India became independent, Nehru gave them a new name—'other backward classes'—implying classes other than the untouchables and tribes.[2] The Constitution refers to 'backward classes' in Articles 15(4) and 16(4), under which the state is empowered to make special provision for any socially and educationally backward classes of citizens. But in its usage it was an all-encompassing category that would include the underprivileged and the marginalised castes: 'it was not a class category and it has been understood to mean certain castes' (Galanter 1984: 166).

Article 340 of the Constitution empowers the state to appoint a commission 'to investigate the condition of socially and educationally backward classes'. At the all-India level two such commissions have so far been appointed. In 1953, Kaka Kalelkar, an erstwhile disciple of Gandhi, was asked to head the first Backward Classes Commission with terms of reference to

- Determine the criteria to be adopted in considering whether any sections of the people in the territory of India (in addition to the

[2] Jawaharlal Nehru's inaugural speech in the Constituent Assembly on 13 Dec. 1946. *Constituent Assembly Debates* (*CAD*), Official Reports of, Lok Sabha Secretariat, Delhi, 1989, Vol. I: 59.

Scheduled Castes and Scheduled Tribes . . .) should be treated as socially and educationally backward classes; and, in accordance with such criteria, prepare a list of such classes setting out also their approximate number and their territorial distribution.

- Investigate the conditions of all such socially and educationally backward classes and the difficulties under which they labour, and make recommendations . . .

The Kalelkar Commission reported in 1955. The majority defined backward classes in terms of low social position in the traditional caste hierarchy, lack of general educational advancement among the major section of a caste or community, and inadequate representation in government services and in the fields of trade, commerce and industry (Yadav 1994). The Report then made two main recommendations. First the backward classes should benefit from a 70 per cent quota in technical education institutions. Second, quotas should be reserved for them in central and state administrations: 25 per cent of vacancies in Class I, 33.3 per cent in Class II, and 40 per cent in Class III and IV (Government of India 1955). There was however a dissenting, minority report and in his covering letter to the President the Chairman himself expressed doubts:

> It is only when the Report was being finalized that I started thinking anew and found that backwardness could be tackled on a basis or a number of bases other than caste. I only succeeded in raising the suspicion of a majority of my colleagues that I was trying to torpedo the recommendation of the Commission. This was another reason why I signed the Report without even a minute of dissent. (Quoted in Patil 1990: 2740)

The Congress government decided not to act on the report's recommendations with regard to central government jobs, but invited the state governments to go ahead and 'draw up their own lists of backward classes and fix their own quotas for reservations'. The rejection of reservations in the central government was only a partial setback for the OBCs, however, as several states had already granted them extensive reservations in government employment and educational institutions.

It was left to the Second Backward Classes Commission, constituted in 1978, during the Janata Party regime at the Centre, to examine the desirability or otherwise of making a provision for reservation for those backward classes that were not adequately represented in public services. The Commission's report marked a watershed in redefining the official discourse, which had from the time of Kalelkar's dissenting covering letter sought to emphasise economic backwardness as an important factor for decisions with regard to social and educational backwardness. Disregarding Kalelkar's approach, the Mandal Commission charted its approach on the lines adopted by State Commissions which had defined backwardness in caste terms rather than socio-economic terms. It recommended a reservation of 27 per cent for OBCs in central government jobs; this would be in addition to the 22.5 per cent posts for SCs and STs already reserved in all services and public sector undertakings (Government of India 1980).

When the Mandal Commission submitted its report in 1980, the Congress party was in power and it was unwilling to act on the report. Indira Gandhi did not do anything on the Mandal report. Neither did Rajiv Gandhi. He told his aides, 'It's a can of worms; I won't touch it.'[3] Thus it was only in 1990 when a non-Congress coalition government came to power that it proposed the implementation of the Mandal Commission recommendations. In this context, V. P. Singh's decision to implement reservations of government jobs had far-reaching implications in changing the balance of power between castes. It signified a major victory for the backward castes and the non-Congress parties advocating 'Mandalization' (a term coined to convey the upward mobility of the backward classes) of opportunity structures and politics.

The historic decision prompted widespread disturbances and violence in several parts of the country. Despite the violent protests the government went ahead and implemented the decision on 27 per cent reservation for OBCs in central government jobs. This was not done through legislation (as in the case of Mandal II in 2006) but through an executive order following a decision in the cabinet. As Arjun Singh was to say much later in April 2008 after the Supreme Court upheld 27 per cent reservations for OBCs in higher education, 'V. P. Singh's was a knee-jerk reaction'.[4] There was no build-up to it, there was no discussion with other political parties, and several of them criticised the government for acting hastily without consulting them. However, all of them extended support to reservations because none of them could afford to alienate the huge lower-caste constituency.

Social justice was the 'key legitimating concept in the political arguments over reservations in the Mandal debate' (Bajpai 2006: 329). The Mandal position held empowerment and participation of the backward castes in public institutions as critical for the creation of a more just

[3] Quoted in *The Indian Express*, 18 May 2006.

[4] Interview with Arjun Singh, *Outlook*, 22–8 April 2008.

society. The basic issue was with regard to the importance attached to historical discrimination as against current inequalities. V. P. Singh described his decision to implement the recommendations of the Mandal Commission as 'a momentous decision of social justice'.[5] For its proponents, reservations were not a means for economic well-being and improvement in material needs; they were a means to facilitate inclusion of OBCs in arenas of education and state power where they had been underrepresented. The central rationale of OBC reservations was therefore to break the upper-caste monopoly on government jobs and professions that remained unchanged after nearly half a century of democracy. The motivation of the project was quintessentially political—the point was that it would help to erode the hold of upper castes on public employment and thus enable OBCs to have a sense of participation in running the affairs of the country.[6]

Subsequently in 1991 the new Congress minority government led by Narasimha Rao proposed that 10 per cent of the vacancies in civil posts and services under the Government of India should be reserved for other economically backward sections of the people who were not covered by any of the existing schemes of reservation. This, however, was never implemented. In its judgment on the *Indira Sawhney vs. Union of India* case on the challenges to both the Singh and Rao government decisions, the Supreme Court in a majority decision upheld the 27 per cent reservation for socially and educationally backward classes (in effect the OBCs) but struck down the 10 per cent reservation for economically backward people. The main opinion, authored by Justice Jeevan Reddy, supported the argument that, in the context of contemporary Indian society, economic criteria alone cannot be the basis of backwardness, although this may be a consideration along with or in addition to social backwardness. In deciding the constitutionality of reservations for the OBCs, however, the court mandated that the government must make use of economic considerations in helping the truly backward, by which it meant that government must find ways to disqualify the more advantaged individuals in these classes. At the same time, in the same decision the court also forbade reservations for economically disadvantaged upper castes. In other

[5] V. P. Singh, Rajya Sabha Debates, 7 Aug. 1990. Speech cited in Bajpai (2006).

[6] Further political reasons for V. P. Singh's decision may have been to undercut both farmer politics and the emerging communal politics of the BJP. And one reason for acceptance of the decision may have been because the objections were overtaken by the politics of religion, which trumped the politics of caste for a while.

words, the court ruling suggested that to be a member of an OBC, it was not enough to be in a lower caste if one's father was a government minister or bureaucrat in the government, just as it was also not enough to simply be poor if one was of a high caste. It is worth quoting the court's judgment in the *Sawhney* case:[7]

> Over the years caste has become synonymous with class for the purpose of reservations. Government policy has relied on courts, which have given their imprimatur of approval to the conflation and substitution of caste and class. The deliberate use of the term classes rather than castes in the constitutional text has been interpreted by the court to mean general social groupings rather than economic classes.

Clearly, the judiciary has played an active role in imposing procedures for programme design and in striking a balance among the competing interests articulated in the constitutional blueprint and group interests in society. The Mandal I decision led to widespread protest and unrest but once the court approved the proposed changes, there was widespread public acceptance (Cunningham and Menon 1999).

The changing face of the Indian bureaucracy is in a large measure attributable to this elaborate regime of reservations. The OBCs had a negligible presence of about 2 per cent in government employment in 1990 when the Mandal recommendations were accepted. Even this small representation in employment was restricted to the lower rungs of government jobs. Upper castes constituted 37.6 per cent of the civil services (Goyal 1989: 429, 430). Even though the full impact of the Mandal initiative will be known only after twenty years, the recent data on social profiles of the 400-odd individuals who annually clear the civil service examination to join the IAS, IFS, IPS, and other services show that 'people who had no access to the civil services are coming in. The city-born and city-bred are busy chasing a plethora of new economy options while those born and schooled in district and small towns, often from the lower castes, are flocking to the IAS' (Puri 2007).

The radical change began after the implementation of OBC reservations in government jobs. The significant increase registered by the OBCs has been made possible entirely by the 27 per cent reservations for them. Their representation in the civil services has been boosted as many have made it to the general category also. By 2000, the SCs, STs, and OBCs together accounted for more than 55 per cent of the total recruitment in

[7] Indira Sawhney & Others vs Union of India AIR 1993 SC 477: 1992 Supp (3) SCC 217.

the union civil services. This marked a dramatic shift from the pattern that was prevailing until the early 1990s when 60 per cent of all Hindu officers belonged to the upper castes (Goyal 1989: 430).

Mandal II: reservations in higher education

In April 2006, Human Resource Development Minister Arjun Singh made an announcement that the central government was planning to extend reservations to OBCs in central educational institutions. It stirred a huge public debate even though it was not for the first time that the central government was considering reservation for backward castes. Supporters called the proposal a belated move to promote social justice and inclusion in upper-caste-dominated higher education, even as opponents warned that India's edge in the knowledge economy would dwindle, competitiveness erode and multinational companies move away.

The preceding discussion indicates that OBCs have been the subjects of preferential treatment previously because of under-representation in governmental structures. But this group, unlike the SCs or Muslims, is not a statistical minority; in fact the OBCs are a statistical majority as they constitute roughly 40–50 per cent of the population. Neither are they a minority in the sociological sense of lacking political and bureaucratic power as noted above. But they are under-represented in significant levels in higher and professional education.

Despite decades of preferential treatment in different forms, public life in India outside of politics is disproportionately dominated by upper castes. They continue to dominate public institutions, skilled professions, and the media, while the SCs, STs, OBCs and Muslims are way behind the upper castes in all spheres of public life and in higher and professional education specifically. The spread of higher education among deprived groups is generally low; the gaps across categories remain very large. It is these large differences in educational attainment and access that state intervention in the form of reservations seeks to address.

The forerunner to the 2006 political controversy was the decision of the Supreme Court in August 2005 which made it clear that it was impermissible to enforce reservations in private educational institutions which do not receive financial support from the state. This meant that educational opportunities in the private institutions would remain outside the purview of affirmative action policies of the state for disadvantaged groups. The 93rd amendment was thus necessitated by the Supreme

Court's judgment in the *Inamdar* case in 2005.[8] The seven-member bench went into all these issues, and noted that though the issue of reservation was not a central one in the *Pai Foundation* and *Islamic Academy* cases, it had to be taken into account, especially where minority institutions were involved.[9] The judges observed: '. . . [in the case of private institutions] neither the policy of reservation can be enforced by the state nor any quota of percentage of admissions can be carved out to be appropriated by the state'. One of the key issues considered by the court in these judgments was the right of minority institutions to run their colleges the way they want to.

The issue of access to higher education has always been an emotive one, especially in India where the barriers to entry in higher education are still very high. Higher education has grown enormously since Independence—from 25 to 348 universities and 700 to 17,625 colleges. About eight million students in India join undergraduate studies each year although this is only 8–9 per cent of the relevant age group between 20 and 24 years who are enrolled in these institutions, as against 50 per cent or more in some developed countries. With the changes in India over the past 25 years, especially the phenomenal economic growth of recent years, there has been an escalating demand for higher education, particularly professional and technical education, in engineering and medical colleges and management institutes. Elite institutions like the Indian Institutes of Technology (IITs), Indian Institutes of Management (IIMs) and medical colleges are in great demand from various sections, most notably the upwardly mobile middle classes, because these institutions provide heavily subsidised high-quality education which can fetch a good job anywhere in the world. The emergence of knowledge-based empowerment as a major source of income and privilege has further enhanced their significance as professional courses have become an even more important means for upward mobility (Ghosh 2006).

[8] *P.A. Inamdar & Ors. vs. State of Maharashtra*, 2005 AIR (SC) 3226.

[9] *WP No. 350 of 199—Islamic Academy of Education + 1 vs. State of Karnataka and Ors* (2003) 6 SCC 697. Reviewing the role of private higher education providers, an 11-member bench of the Supreme Court in the *Pai* judgment had ruled that fees charged by unaided institutions cannot be regulated but no capitation can be charged. This was once again challenged in the Supreme Court, which reiterated the concept of keeping fees imposed by private education providers within 'reasonable' limits. Consequent to *Islamic Academy*, some state Governments, notably Karnataka and Kerala, sought to tighten controls on the unaided private colleges, and enacted legislation to this effect. Their Acts were, however, struck down by the courts and, at the Education Ministers' conferences held in 2004 and early 2005, the state ministers asked the central government to enact legislation which would enable them to exercise the powers they wanted.

The national-level data from the 55th Round of the National Sample Survey Organisation (NSSO) (1999–2000) showed in stark terms the inequalities in access to higher education. Students from the middle classes and upper castes traditionally associated with more education—comprising roughly 20 per cent of the population—dominate higher education, compared to 9 per cent or less for all other categories. (For a discussion of unequal access, see Deshpande 2006.) The Hindu upper castes formed a little more than a third of the total urban population, but they accounted for two-thirds of professional and higher education—in other words, their share in higher education is twice their share in the population. The obvious consequence of the upper-caste over-representation is the under-representation of other groups.

The UPA government amended the Constitution in 2005 to permit reservations in aided and unaided educational institutions in favour of SCs, STs and OBCs, except in institutions run by minorities. After the passage of the 93rd Constitutional Amendment Act, which was essentially an enabling provision, the supporters of OBC quotas argued that it necessitated further legislation to ensure the implementation of affirmative action in institutions of higher education. Once the demand for reservations gathered momentum, the central government had to implement the provisions of Article 15 (5) in respect of all institutions and universities under its purview. Moreover, several states had either already made laws or were going to make laws to implement this provision. Treating this as an enabling legislation, the UPA government decided to introduce quotas for OBCs in publicly funded educational institutions, premier technology institutes, medical colleges, and central universities. The government was under considerable pressure from coalition partners and political parties which unanimously favoured an expeditious introduction of reservations in higher education for the OBCs.

The official argument in favour of reservations offered two principal justifications: first, extending quotas in higher education was the continuation of preferential treatment in public employment to the OBCs since 1994; and, second, it came up in 2006 mainly in the context of the legislation on private unaided institutions. The government's position was that it had already amended the Constitution; a new clause (5) had been added to Article 15 (which is a fundamental right); the constitutional amendment has been carried with near unanimity by Parliament; and there was an all-party consensus on the issue. Moreover, unlike the Mandal I decision, which was rushed through without adequate consultations, this legislation was the result of wide-ranging consultations with MPs from all political parties, and it had been routed through the cabinet and various government departments.

Acute dissatisfactions arising out of unequal representation in prestigious educational institutions and the historical disadvantage in education of certain groups are among the primary reasons for the institution of reservations in higher education. Therefore the principal justification was cast in terms of the need to enhance equality of opportunity for the weaker sections of society, especially under the new economy. Government reasoning regarded equality as a positive right which requires the state to minimise existing inequalities and to treat the underprivileged with special care as envisaged in the Constitution. Promotion of equality and elimination of inequality formed an essential part of the basic structure of the Constitution, and not providing reservations to SCs, STs and OBCs would be a violation of this basic structure. For the first time, the government put forward the basic structure doctrine in its affidavit to the Supreme Court: reservation is part of the basic structure of the Constitution and therefore the government had no option but to introduce reservations for the OBCs. Further, Clause (5) of Article 15 was inserted to enable the state to implement it.

Controversies and protests

The UPA government decided to introduce the Central Educational Institutions (Reservation in Admission) Bill 2006 to cover central universities, institutions of national importance set up by Parliament, and institutions directly or indirectly aided by the central government or linked to central universities or centrally created institutions. It excluded private unaided institutions and it excluded minority educational institutions. The Bill provoked a major agitation by doctors. The countrywide agitation was organised by a group which calls itself Youth for Equality (YFE). It started from the All India Institute of Medical Sciences (AIIMS) and included students from premier medical colleges and from the IITs and IIMs. Spearheaded by the doctors of AIIMS, the agitation originated in this institute, which remained its 'nodal point' throughout. A government-appointed committee headed by the University Grants Commission Chairman S. K. Thorat (to look into complaints from MPs and media reports on allegations of harassment of SC and ST students at AIIMS) noted in its report that the 'AIIMS became the venue of the protest primarily to paralyze healthcare for thousands of people and attract public attention against reservation. Paralyzing of the healthcare services including emergency services would put pressure on the government.'[10]

For nineteen days, doctors and medical students were on strike, bringing essential health services to a standstill. The main support came from the corporate sector, traders associations, chambers of commerce, industry lobbies, the Indian Medical Association, executives of information technology companies, residents welfare associations in many cities, business executives, and, above all, owners of private professional colleges.[11] As in the anti-Mandal agitation of 1990–1, the students engaged in mockery of lower castes by enacting casteist forms of protest such as the symbolic sweeping of streets, shoe-shining, and shouting slogans that lower castes are indeed fit only for menial jobs, while others are 'naturally' suited to respectable professions such as engineering and medicine.[12] The doctors called off their agitation after the court's directive that they resume work or face contempt.

The National Knowledge Commission (NKC) opposed OBC reservations and publicised its opposition through its majority (6 : 2) report in the media.[13] Two members of the NKC decided to quit in protest against OBC reservations. Despite the protests and media support for the agitation against OBC reservations, public sympathy was largely in favour of OBC quotas, except among the elites and the upper middle classes, who were clearly unhappy with the decision. The media coverage may have succeeded in making it a national and emotive issue but it does not seem to have made much difference to the strong pro-reservation position on this subject. Asked if they were in favour of reservations, 63 per cent of the respondents in the *Indian Express*–CNN–IBN poll expressed support for reservations and only 34 per cent were against them.[14] But it is impor-

[10] Report of the *Committee to Enquire into the Allegations of Differential Treatment of Scheduled Castes/Scheduled Tribes Students in AIIMS* (2007), p. 67.

[11] These colleges admit over 530,000 students and charge capitation fees upwards of Rs. 50 lakhs for admission to professional colleges, such as medical and engineering colleges.

[12] For instance, during the agitation, upper-caste student protestors blocked busy streets and started polishing shoes (imitating shoeshine boys) with placards that read: 'This is what we will be reduced to because of the reservation system.' Notice the implication: the occupation that they (the upper castes) would be reduced to was a 'Dalit occupation'. In other words, it is all right for Dalits to continue to do the menial jobs, but if upper castes have to descend to this low level, it is unacceptable. Needless to add, the belief that reservations would push the upper castes down to the menial jobs was only a presumption, not supported by any evidence.

[13] The National Knowledge Commission is a high-level advisory body to the Prime Minister set up with the objective of transforming India into a knowledge society.

[14] CNN–IBN poll conducted by A. G. Nielsen reported in *The Indian Express*, 25 July 2006.

tant to note that a larger majority of respondents—67 per cent—expressed a preference for economic criteria, irrespective of caste, for identification of beneficiaries.

Shifts in public debate

In the years since Mandal I, the political and economic landscape has changed almost completely. Market reforms have contributed to the breakdown of the Nehruvian consensus on a mixed economy and the Congress social coalition of upper castes, minorities, and SCs. (See further the chapter by Oliver Heath and Yogendra Yadav in this volume.) India's GDP has grown steadily over the past two decades, and during 2004–7 its annual growth has exceeded 8 per cent. The economy has witnessed an explosion of high finance, stock market, information technology, software exports, media, entertainment, and real-estate speculation. But the bulk of people have not gained significantly from the paradigm shift in economic policy. Economic boom and high growth have brought benefits to the top 20 per cent of the population, which has seen an unprecedented rise in income and job opportunities (Ghosh 2004).

The basic feature of the process of economic development has been exclusion—from control over assets, from benefits of growth, from education, and from income-generating opportunities. The imbalances and exclusions have led to the creation of two economies across the social and regional landscape of India. Government jobs were drying up, even as salaries in government continue to be modest in comparison to the astronomical pay packets in the private sector and the media. Consequently, the upper castes and middle classes have flocked to the booming managerial and executive jobs in the corporate sector, but they want subsidised high-quality education to provide them with the credentials for access to such jobs. Graduates from these institutions find immediate placement in the private sector; hence the increased stakes in elite institutions, which open up opportunities for high-salaried jobs as opposed to the civil service, which has lost its sheen for the upwardly mobile middle classes. These are the groups that took an active part in the anti-quota agitation. The agitators in 1990 were primarily from the lower-middle classes interested in government jobs, whereas in 2006 the protestors were principally interested in private-sector employment.

For the past two decades or so the politics around reservations for OBCs has centred on two dimensions. At one level it has been characterised by clashes between social and political forces that support and oppose reservations for OBCs in education and employment. Those who support quotas perceive reservation-based affirmative action as an instrument to uplift sections that have been oppressed for centuries and to lessen the dominance of upper castes. Those who oppose reservation look at the issue of upper-caste dominance differently. They claim that their dominance is solely due to merit, and that any attempt to undermine merit will result in the erosion of progress. This will hurt India's rise as an economic power and therefore the government would be well advised to allow market forces and merit to produce a twenty-first-century economy. The crux of the argument is that reservations militate against merit and allow degrees or qualifications to be awarded to people with less than deserving performance and aptitude. Such a system is inefficient as compared with openly competitive systems. These measures are unfair benefits given to particular caste groupings undeserving of such protection and hence pandering to vote-banks of politicians. A study by Satish Deshpande has noted however that:

> Merit in the Indian context refers to certification of competence, aptitude or knowledge acquired through examination of some kind . . . What matters is not how well one does in the exam but how much better one does than others taking the same exam. (Deshpande 2006: 2442–3)

Supporters argue that higher education inherently involves exclusion and 'merit' legitimises such exclusions. Unlocking the gates of higher education was necessary to dilute the upper-caste monopoly (Bidwai 2006).

In the past fifteen years, the Mandal initiative has helped to change the face of the polity; the grammar of entitlement has become part of the new language of politics, and all parties now accept the logic of quotas. The political class, including the BJP which brought down the V. P. Singh government for implementing the Mandal report and whose political base lies among upper-caste Hindus, seems to realise that a reversal of reservation policy is no longer possible. However, outside the political domain, the opposition to reservations amongst the intelligentsia, media, and civil society at large continues to be strong. The arguments in civil society were broadly of two types: arguments about institutions and arguments about caste disadvantage. The institutional argument mainly focused on the importance of merit for maintenance of institutional efficacy in the field of higher education. Merit and inclusion were interpreted as irreconcilable in the new post-economic reforms discourse (Mehta 2007).

On the issue of caste disadvantage, two sets of arguments came up. One argument recognised that caste is associated with inequalities and discrimination, and it is the responsibility of public policy to address these. But there were differences among those espousing this argument with regard to the efficacy of quotas for achieving these outcomes or whether alternative strategies could be devised for this. A second set of arguments highlighted the difference between SCs, who are poor and exploited, and the OBCs, who are powerful and do not deserve quotas—a point that had been emphasised by Rajiv Gandhi in his Lok Sabha speech. There is also the argument that the regime of reservations does not actually help the weaker sections among the deprived since the benefits are cornered by the affluent among them (this too was highlighted by Rajiv Gandhi). The OBCs were economically empowered through the democratic system in the 1960s and 1970s; they have economic and political power and are administratively empowered by reservations in government service and therefore do not require reservations in higher education as well. This line of reasoning was particularly strong among the upper-middle-class opponents of Mandal II and in regions which have had no tangible exposure to reservations in the education sector. Not surprisingly, in the four South Indian states as well as in Maharashtra and Gujarat, which have had a long experience with quotas, the opposition to OBC reservation was muted.

A third important feature of the civil society debate in Mandal II was the complete disengagement from the political process, as there was a pervasive feeling among the protestors that they were above the political process. The disdain towards the political class and Parliament encouraged the protestors to concentrate on the judiciary and the media, which they perceived as friendly towards their cause. This was evident from the tendency to arrogate powers to decide on the public policy of affirmative action rather than leave it to the state to decide. It also derives sustenance from the belief that excluded groups do not possess the intelligence or aptitude for higher education. This was palpable from the condescending attitude of the student leaders to the very policy of quotas: the state can address the problem of discrimination and disadvantage as long as state intervention through affirmative action did not reduce opportunities for them.

Mandal II sought to cut through the conceptual tangles that have besieged the issue of OBC reservations. The UPA government relied on previous court rulings which had clearly given their approval for the substitution of caste for class and to privilege caste over other identities. It was repeatedly argued that often caste is social class and if a group was backward socially it would be a backward class for the purposes of Article 16(4). While caste cannot be the sole criterion to determine the class of persons for whom reservation must be sought, caste can indeed be one of the factors (or even the primary factor) relevant in determining which sections of society in India require reservation in employment or in the reservation of seats in institutions of higher education. In other words, it is constitutionally justified to take caste as the social unit or class to be examined and tested for backwardness or its absence in terms of the criteria of social and educational backwardness devised by the government.

Political response

The decision on OBC quotas in higher education was part of a plan to demonstrate the backward-caste and social justice credentials of the Congress party. This party had traditionally supported the reservation principle, starting with Nehru, who pushed the constitutional amendment in 1951. However, the Congress leadership was ambivalent on the issue since Rajiv Gandhi questioned the scientific basis of OBC quotas in his Lok Sabha speech in September 1990 and argued for a comprehensive action plan for the disadvantaged groups. He had criticised the V. P. Singh government for thinking only 'around caste' and 'vested interests in particular castes'.[15] The 2006 move was an attempt to counterbalance the long-standing distrust of the backward castes towards the party, which was seen as generally an upper-caste-friendly party. Against this perception, the reservation gamble was a crucial element in the new strategy to wean the OBCs away from regional and state-based parties which have been the preferred choice of the backward-caste voters. Even though there was disagreement within the Congress with regard to the timing of the quota proposal (and more so with Arjun Singh for trying to take credit for it), the party leadership could hardly afford to vacillate or disown the issue. On the other hand, open support would alienate the upper castes. If, however, the Congress stuck firmly to its pro-reservation stand, it could hope to win some OBC support and offset the lower-caste advantage enjoyed by regional parties like the *Samajwadi* Party and the

[15] Rajiv Gandhi's speech on the Mandal Commission in the Lok Sabha, reproduced in *The Indian Express*, 9 June 2006.

Bahujan Samaj Party who claimed to be the champions of the disadvantaged in north India. The Congress general secretary stated:

> The issue isn't politics alone. At its core is social justice. We will not, I repeat, we will not recant on the quota issue. That is settled and the perceived silence of the prime minister and the Congress president must not be mistaken for ambivalence or confusion. Both are supportive of this policy.[16]

Propelled by the pressures and counter-pressures, the UPA government was keen to strike a fair balance between competing claims of the disadvantaged and the advantaged. The UPA chairperson Sonia Gandhi underscored the point that extension of OBC quotas to central educational institutions would go hand in hand with an increase in seats for general category students. This approach found approval in the Cabinet. One newspaper reported that the Union Cabinet meeting that cleared the bill on reservation for the OBCs 'witnessed the most serious and purposeful discussion so far in the life of the UPA Government'.[17] The advocates of quotas made a strong case for a total and complete changeover to the new reservation regime for the OBCs. A senior minister cited 'centuries of injustice' that had been the OBCs lot and argued that the Backward Classes were not asking for a 'backlog' compensation but were merely demanding correction of the injustice. The OBCs are demanding today their legitimate, long-delayed share in social privileges like centrally funded higher education. Some ministers drew the attention of the Cabinet to the Supreme Court pronouncements on the concept of 'creamy layer' (that is, the economically more affluent segment) and on the need to gradually phase out these strata from the reservation regime. However, the opinion was firmly in favour of retaining the creamy layer. The prime minister urged his colleagues 'not do anything that would destroy the country's "knowledge strength"'. The final decision reflected his three main concerns: (*a*) there should be no dilution in the existing seats and opportunities available in the 'non-reserved' categories; (*b*) the extension of the 27 per cent reservation for the OBCs should be staggered to ensure that the requisite infrastructure was in place; and (*c*) certain institutions of 'national/strategic' importance should be kept out of the reservation regime.[18]

The UPA government decided to increase the number of seats in the general category so that seats filled by 'open competition' do not shrink.

[16] As reported in *The Times of India*, 14 July 2006.
[17] *The Hindu*, 23 April 2006.
[18] Ibid.

Under this formula the number of unreserved seats would be increased in proportion to the 27 per cent to be reserved for the OBCs. However, the government's plan of accommodation through expansion rather than cutting into general category seats failed to halt the protest. The opponents remained unconvinced, indeed sceptical about the government move, which according to one critic 'exemplified the way government thinks of admissions: goodies be distributed to whoever they want, a mechanism for buying out different groups' (Mehta, 2007).

The Lok Sabha unanimously approved the legislation for reservations for OBCs in central educational institutions by a voice vote in December 2006. Cross-party support marked the Lok Sabha debate on the Bill as virtually every speaker lauded the UPA government's initiative to introduce reservations for OBCs in higher education, which they argued was long overdue. The support for the legislation cut across parties, barring the BJP's opposition to the provision on the exclusion of minority educational institutions. Inspired by key provisions in the Constitution, namely, Articles 46 and Article 15(5), the new legislation was a significant measure, as it was the first time that Parliament has through laws recognised reservation of seats in educational institutions for OBCs as a necessary measure to give effect to the constitutional provisions.

The most striking feature of the political response was the wide-ranging political support for Arjun Singh's proposal, in contrast to the more limited support for V. P. Singh's attempt to provide reservations for OBCs in government jobs: reservations in higher education garnered the support of all parties and MPs. In the first place, the Congress, which initiated Mandal II, had opposed Mandal I. The second noteworthy difference is that prior to this Act, reservations at the central level were the result of an executive decision implemented usually through an Office Memorandum; there was no statutory backing for these polices. This led to several court rulings interpreting constitutional provisions in a manner perceived to be against the interests of backward classes (Venkatesan 2006). As executive actions, the court found it easy to stay the operation of such an Official Memorandum in 1990. Mandal II, however, went through a much wider consultative and legislative process. Nevertheless, the court stayed the operation of this Act too. Thus, an active role of the judiciary is a strong feature of both episodes. In both cases the judiciary questioned procedures and methodologies for design and assumed the role of policy-making.

Judicial intervention

The court intervened in the middle of the Mandal II agitation, staying the law and declaring that the OBC reservation issue 'requires judicial review'. This put paid to Congress–UPA quota plans of rolling out OBC reservations in 2007. But significantly the court had not overturned reservations for OBCs. The petitioners in *Ashoka Thakur vs Union of India* claimed that the Act and the Amendment violated their fundamental right to equality. The Court's two-judge bench had issued an interim order on 29 March 2007 partly staying the law but as it involved substantial constitutional issues, the government sought the reference of the case to a Constitution Bench. This included Chief Justice K. G. Balakrishnan and Justices Arijit Pasayat, C. K. Thakker, R. V. Raveendran, and Dalveer Bhandari. The five-judge Bench heard marathon arguments for twenty-five days spread over three months from 7 August 2007 to November 2007. The basic issue was whether the 93rd amendment was unconstitutional and violative of the basic structure of the Constitution and whether it confers on the state unbridled power to make special provision for the OBCs. The five-judge Constitution Bench on 10 April 2008 upheld the Constitution (93rd Amendment) Act, 2005, under which the state had been empowered to make special provisions for socially and educationally backward classes in admission to educational institutions providing for 27 per cent quota for OBCs in IITs, IIMs and other central educational institutions. The court, while declaring that the creamy layer should be excluded from the quota, held that the Act does not violate the basic structure of the Constitution. It also said that reservations should not be in perpetuity but should be revised at periodic intervals.

The judgment was in keeping with the Supreme Court's long-standing interpretation of the constitutional provisions on equality, namely that the fundamental right to equality is compatible with schemes like reservations that confer benefits on disadvantaged groups. The Chief Justice pronounced that affirmative action, though 'apparently discriminatory, is calculated to produce equality on a broader basis'. He reasoned that a constitutional amendment which 'moderately abridges or alters the equality principle' but does not abrogate it would not violate the basic structure of the Constitution.[19] The government counsel justified the 'identification of socially and educationally backward classes on the basis

[19] Arguments in the Supreme Court and final verdict reported in *The Hindu*, 12 April 2008.

of caste in view of the societal structure of the country' while making submissions on the 27 per cent quotas in higher education for the OBCs.[20] As in Mandal I, the government counsel argued that caste should be construed as a unit leading to reservation. However, the Chief Justice, referring to the arguments made against the application of the creamy layer to educational institutions, stated that: 'They are excluded because unless this segment of caste is excluded from that caste group, there cannot be proper identification of the backward class. If the "creamy layer" principle is not applied, it could easily be said that all the castes that have been included among the SEBCs (Socially and Educationally Backward Classes) have been included exclusively on the basis of caste.'[21]

The die is cast(e)

Several important issues and concerns emerge from these controversies. From the beginning, reservations for backward castes have been haunted by questions regarding definition and identification, the relationship between caste and deprivation, its implications for the core commitment to SCs/STs, and the exclusion of minorities. A striking point with regard to the political and legislative history of affirmative action for backward castes is that caste remains the most important unit of identification in reservation policy, which in turn has intensified competition among the disadvantaged groups and caused resentment among those excluded from preferential treatment.

One issue that has been far from settled is the question of the relationship between caste and class and whether OBCs constitute a caste or class. By the time of Mandal II, caste and class had become almost inseparable—in fact, caste stands for class. The 2006 OBC quota law said that 'caste is the starting point for identification of socially and educationally backward classes'. Legal jurisprudence has accepted caste as a basis of classification, as is evident from the Mandal II judgment. Several court verdicts in favour of the equivalence of caste and class held that class included persons grouped on the basis of their castes. In line with the court's long-standing interpretation of the constitutional provisions on equality, the court ruling in *Thakur* reiterates that caste itself can be used as a criterion for identification.

[20] *The Hindu*, 11 Oct. 2007.
[21] *The Hindu*, 11 April 2008.

The internal differentiation and social heterogeneity among the OBCs suggests that the 'creamy layer' or the privileged within the OBCs must be excluded. However, governments have been wary of excluding the well-to-do sections from the ambit of reservations for fear of political repercussions. The OBC-dominated parties like *Rashtriya Janata Dal*, *Dravida Munnetra Kazhagam* (DMK) and the *Pattali Makkal Katchi* (PMK), which are key members of the UPA, were opposed to it. The National Commission for Backward Classes has periodically conducted social audits to determine the status of various castes, but has not excluded them (Raman 2007). The dominant castes such as Nadars and Yadavs continue to remain on the list. As a result, caste groups that benefited from past systems of quotas or which have disproportionate political/economic power continue to enjoy the benefits of reservations and keep the majority still deprived.

The principle behind the creamy layer exclusion is that if the starting points in most respects for various groups are equal, then there is little justification for giving them the benefits of reservation. To put it differently when it comes to the OBCs, caste alone cannot be a justification for treating them differently. The Court, recognising the multiple disadvantages that characterise Indian society, was demanding that government should provide justification for policies and balance different considerations. It felt that the exclusion of the creamy layer would imply that reservation was not based on caste alone but on other factors such as social and economic backwardness. Without excluding the creamy layer, the affluent among these castes would stand to benefit more from reservations in higher education and in effect get more benefits than the poor.

The supporters of OBC reservation on the other hand argue that the move to exclude the 'creamy layer' is misplaced and would negate the very purpose of reservation, which is not removing poverty but changing the social composition of higher education. Since the opportunities for higher education are generally availed by the privileged in every social group, only the creamy layer in every group is able to access higher education. 'By disqualifying those most likely to succeed in elite institutions, creamy layer exclusion undermines the very purpose of the proposed law' (Deshpande 2008). As a result, most of the seats reserved for the OBCs would remain unfilled. But the fact remains that group rights do not entitle all individuals in the group, which means there has to be some criterion for admitting specific members of the OBCs to educational institutions. Creamy-layer norms could be used to ensure that the more privileged are given last preference.

The third important issue pertains to the attitude towards affirmative action for minorities. If there was one group that needed special treatment in view of its educational backwardness and under-representation in government employment, it was Muslims. Affirmative action was above all needed to tackle their educational backwardness. The chairman of the National Commission made a strong plea for greater access for Muslims in the available higher educational institutions. He suggested the need to evolve 'a suitable mechanism' to ensure an equitable share of minorities in higher education. But there was no serious consideration of 'suitable mechanisms' for ensuring access for educationally backward Muslims to modern higher education. This was because backwardness is only recognised in relation to castes despite the fact that there are glaring disparities between Muslims and other groups in higher education. There is neither affirmative action nor adequate provisioning of schools and colleges in minority-concentration areas. Disadvantage is so defined as to exclude non-Hindus, although theoretically the OBC category includes backward classes from all religions. Given this definitional bias, it would be natural for such groups to see themselves as objects of structural discrimination (Parekh 2004: 441). Yet, there was no agreement on a suitable mechanism for doing this, despite a recommendation of the Parliamentary Standing Committee that a suitable mechanism to ensure access of minorities should be created.

These issues highlight the unresolved tensions in regard to reservations for OBCs. Throughout the evolution of this policy there has been little philosophical or constitutional consensus on preferential treatment for the OBCs. When reservations were introduced by the new state, the idea was to tear down the barriers to social exclusion and promote the participation of historically excluded and disadvantaged groups. Policies of affirmative action were viewed as instruments through which to offset the advantage enjoyed by some and to equalise opportunities for others. Moreover, they were seen as complementary to the commitment to an active welfare state that would ameliorate the conditions of the masses by providing an additional boost to the hitherto excluded and poor. It must be remembered that the liberalisation of the economy has resulted in widening inequalities and disparities between the rich and the poor and social conflicts have become more acute during the past decade of growth. In the context of the rising economic divide, reservations address only the most exclusionary aspects of one axis of inequality—caste-driven exclusions. Furthermore, reservations, though politically necessary and practically helpful, are not the main instrument for the construction of a more egalitarian society. For that far more foundational changes are required, such as a major redistribution of income and wealth-generating assets like land, better schooling and colleges, special training and skill development programmes, preferential treatment in the allocation of government licences and contracts, employment-generating policies, and so on. Once the need for foundational changes is recognised and taken forward, then there is certainly a strong case to be made for alternative, more sophisticated forms of affirmative action than reservations. It is now time to think about how to use different and new means to bridge disparities and deepen social equality so that the pursuit of equality and justice does not remain anchored in caste and caste alone.

8

The Rise of Caste Politics: Party System Change and Voter Realignment, 1962–2004

OLIVER HEATH AND YOGENDRA YADAV

Summary. Indian electoral politics can be divided into three main periods. First, up until about 1967 there was the period of Congress dominance with essentially an absence of major social cleavages in voting patterns and with a party system built on the foundation of a unifying opposition to British colonial rule. In the second period, the Congress-Opposition system from 1967, caste divisions strengthened appreciably with the Jan Sangh in particular showing a similar profile to the later BJP, while Congress became more reliant on Scheduled Caste and Muslim votes. The election following the state of emergency in 1977 marked a major reversal back to the earlier character but then in 1980 we see a revival of cleavage voting. A new phase of multiparty competition begins with 1989 and by 1991 it is clear that cleavages have strengthened markedly. This process reaches its peak in 1996 and then declines somewhat, although remaining at an historically high level.

The natural interpretation of these findings is that they reflect the electoral rise of parties like the BJP and BSP which have made specific appeals to distinct caste groupings. The emergence of the caste cleavage has tended to be stronger in socially divided states, particularly those that are beset by poverty. In this sense social conditions are now mirrored in patterns of political conflict to a much greater degree than was ever the case previously, and in this respect the Indian party system has become more representative of the society at large. However, it is important to recognise that parties themselves play a role in shaping, and reshaping, the nature of social

Proceedings of the British Academy **159**, 189–217. © The British Academy 2010.

identities. Parties can play a role in heightening the awareness of communal groupings (as in the post-Ayodhya election of 1996), or alternatively by forming cross-party alliances (as in 1977) they may blur social divisions.

Introduction

SINCE THE FIRST ELECTION in 1952 democracy has operated in India with only a brief intermission for the state of emergency which was declared by Indira Gandhi in 1975–7. For much of the period from independence until the emergency electoral politics was dominated by the Congress Party, which attracted support from a broad cross-section of Indian society. In social terms, India was like other developing societies with a highly stratified society, gross inequalities in wealth, occupation, privilege and poverty, but these were not mirrored in any major way in patterns of political conflict. Even today, Congress remains a major player—and in 2004 formed a minority government with support from a number of coalition partners—but, over the thirty years since the end of the emergency in 1977, it has been out of office for more years than it has been in office. The new parties that have come to the fore, such as the BJP (*Bharatiya Janata* Party: Indian People's party), have a much more distinctive social profile than Congress did, and political mobilisation along caste and religious lines has become a major source of political division.

This process of electoral realignment in India raises a number of interesting questions about the dynamics of party system change. To understand why a seemingly stable party system rapidly decomposes it is necessary to explore the bonds that link parties to their social constituencies and to analyse how the bonds change or become eroded in the light of particular political conjunctures (Roberts 2003: 43). In this respect the work of Lipset and Rokkan (1967) has been a highly influential starting point. Lipset and Rokkan argued that cleavages were frozen at the time of the establishment of mass democracy in Europe, and have remained more or less constant ever since, at least until the 1960s which was when their research was carried out. They identified four main lines of cleavage—centre/periphery, church/state, land/industry and owner/worker. Subsequently Clark and Lipset (1991) have in essence argued that these old cleavage structures have been thawing, with a general decline in the role of social cleavages and the emergence of a more individualistic, less group-oriented basis to political behaviour. This line of reasoning has been developed *inter alia* by Franklin and his colleagues (1992), Inglehart (1990), and Dalton (1984), amongst others who all posit that class and ideological divisions in Western Europe have decreased and valence issues based on the economy have increased.

However, since this theory (or rather theories) has been developed in the West, and has mainly been applied to mature advanced post-industrial democracies in Western Europe and North America, it is not clear how it should apply (if at all) to other socio-cultural and economic contexts (see Randall 2001 for an extended discussion). Indeed attempts to export the concept around the world to Africa (Bienen and Herbst 1996), Asia (Berry and Kiely 1993; Chibber and Petrocik 1990) and Latin America (Dix 1989) have, by and large, not received much empirical support—although exceptions can be found in Chile (Scully 1995) and Eastern Europe (Evans and Whitefield 1993). Moreover, there are a number of good reasons why it might not directly apply. For example, in India the critical period of party formation just before the transition to democracy was dominated by questions of national independence. The experience of colonisation and the struggle for independence thus provides a very different historical background to the development of the party system compared to Western Europe, and perhaps initially at least, this experience may have led to the development of a unifying electoral 'foundation', with Congress institutionalising the conflict with British imperialism. Thus social cleavages were subordinated or incorporated within a single 'national' basis of mobilisation (Randall 2001: 246). Congress (and perhaps parties of Independence in other post-colonial countries), then, was premised upon a very different kind of political conflict, between society and the colonial power. As the salience of this conflict declined over time, this unifying foundation of electoral politics in India may have 'crumbled', but rather than the individualistic, cleavageless politics that evolved in the West, we may now be witnessing the emergence of alternative cleavages representing internal social divisions based on region and caste.

Our aims in this chapter are to explore the relationship between India's social structure and its contemporary patterns of political behaviour and how this relates to theories of social cleavage alignment. We test, at the national level, these two main theses of initial freezing around a unifying national foundation of electoral politics and a subsequent crumbling of that foundation and its replacement by internal communal divisions. In doing so we examine change in the cleavage structure of party competition, and explore how different (or not) contemporary patterns of political conflict in India are from those of the past.

Data and methods

To explore the relationship between social structure and voting behaviour we use the series of national election surveys that have been conducted in India since 1967 by the Centre for the Study of Developing Societies (see Yadav 2004 for an overview). This data set is unique among developing societies. They are representative of the whole of India based on sophisticated methods of random sampling and face-to-face interviewing, and offer a precise account of the social characteristics and electoral behaviour of the adult population. We use the 1967, 1971, 1980, 1996, 1998, 1999 and 2004 all-India national election surveys. All the surveys were post-election surveys apart from 1980, which was a pre-election survey. We can use the recall data from the 1967 survey to tell us about voting in 1962, recall from the 1980 survey for vote in 1977, and recall from 1996 for vote in 1991. We use the vote intention data from the 1980 survey to tell us about voting in the 1980 election. Unfortunately we are missing data on the 1984 and 1989 elections, but otherwise we have almost complete coverage of Indian elections since 1962. This is not only the longest time series available in India, but is also comparable to the longest national election series available anywhere in the world.

Three caveats are however worth mentioning: first, our main focus in this chapter is on the All-India patterns. We recognise the complexity of state and local differences in cleavage structures and all three need to be looked at independently. This chapter provides a first, admittedly simplified, overview of the trends. Second, we focus on the emergence of a community cleavage based on caste and religion. Again, reality is more complex than that, and there are many other possible cleavages, such as region and language, country/city, owner/worker etc. that may be important, but the community division is the one that has been at the centre of recent debates and anxieties in India, and therefore is the one on which we focus. Third, we primarily focus on big aggregations of community, rather than individual *jatis*.

Indian elections since Independence

Before examining how the political salience of social cleavages has varied over time in the period covered by our surveys, it is helpful to first provide a brief overview of the political system in India (see Heath *et al.* 2005 for an extended discussion) and to highlight some of the major changes that have taken place in the structure of party competition since Independence. India has a parliamentary system based on the Westminster model. There are two houses of parliament, the *Lok Sabha* (lower house) and the *Rajya Sabha* (upper house). For elections to the lower house, which is the major legislative body, there are single-member constituencies and a first-past-the-post (single member plurality (SMP)) system exactly as in the UK. As with the UK, general elections are held every five years, or earlier if the *Lok Sabha* has been dissolved by the President. There is a total of 543 seats in the *Lok Sabha*. For elections to the upper house there is an indirect system. *Rajya Sabha* members are elected by each state *Vidhan Sabha* (legislative assembly) using the PR-STV system. Despite being based on the Westminster model, India deviates from the UK in two important ways. First it is a federal system, with substantial powers given to the state legislative assemblies. The *Vidhan Sabha*s are directly elected bodies set up to carry out the administration of the government in the twenty-eight States of India. Elections to the *Vidhan Sabha*s are carried out in the same manner as for the *Lok Sabha* elections, with the states and union territories divided into single-member constituencies and the SMP system used. The assemblies range in size, according to population. The largest *Vidhan Sabha* is for Uttar Pradesh, with 403 members; the smallest, Pondicherry, has thirty members. Second, India has a remarkable system of reservation in which some constituencies are reserved for candidates from the Scheduled Tribes or from the Scheduled Castes (see further below). This essentially was a system devised to secure representation for the 'depressed classes'. It was originally introduced as a temporary measure but has continued to this day.

Since the first elections in 1952 there have been some major changes that have taken place in the structure of party competition, which can be characterised in three broad stages (see Yadav 1996). First, from 1947 to 1967 there was a long period of dominance by the Congress Party. Congress, which was founded in 1885 and had had a long and distinguished record in the struggle for independence, dominated Indian politics up until 1967 and was in office for the whole of this period. Congress was a secular, catch-all party that drew its support from across the social spectrum (Kothari 1964). However, it would be wrong to think of Congress as equivalent to a contemporary European catch-all party. So while it drew support both from high and low caste Hindus and from Muslims, it did so not simply as an electoral strategy to maximise its share of the vote but also out of a positive commitment to national integration.

Following the period of Congress dominance, from 1967 to 1993 there was what can be termed the Congress-Opposition system. Congress remained the most prominent party at the national level but it was no longer straightforwardly dominant. Although it was a key player everywhere, at the state level it faced a range of different but often effective opposition parties. Under Indira Gandhi, Congress split and, after the state of emergency, the *Janata* Party (People's Party), a coalition of opposition parties, took office in 1977. In turn, the *Janata* Party split and Congress returned to power only to be defeated once more by a new coalition of the National Front/*Janata Dal* in 1989. Thirdly, from 1989 onwards India has seen a move towards a genuine competitive multiparty system (Heath 1999*a*), which can no longer be defined with reference to Congress. In particular we have seen the rise of the BJP, a Hindu nationalist party, which was in office from 1998 until 2004 either as a minority government or in coalition with regional parties, and the emergence of several Backward Caste parties, such as the SP (*Samajwadi* Party: Socialist Party), the RJD (*Rashtriya Janata Dal*: National People's Party), and the BSP (*Bahujan Samaj* Party: Majority People's Party).

The Congress dominant party period

The first election covered by our surveys was in 1962, when Nehru led Congress to a resounding victory in the polls, winning 45 per cent of the vote and 73 per cent of the seats, and entered his fourth term as prime minister. In 1952 and 1957 Congress had made much of its being the party of the freedom struggle, but in 1962 its campaign focused more on what it had done since (Guha 2007: 330). Its policies, it said, had increased agricultural and industrial production, enhanced education and life expectancy and promoted the unity of the country.

From Table 8.1 we can see that at the national level Congress won its support evenly from all social groups, getting 80 per cent of the upper caste vote as well as 81 per cent of the Muslim vote.[1] On the surface at least, it does appear as a party of national unity. Turning to the other parties, the most notable feature is that the BJS (*Bharatiya Jana Sangh*: Indian People's Alliance), the forerunner of the BJP, was given rather

[1] Although the survey over-represents the true level of support for the Congress party, there is no reason to suspect that this over-reporting is higher for any one group compared to another, and so the pattern of support should be unaffected.

Table 8.1. Community and vote in 1962 (row percentages).

	INC	BJS	Socialist	Communist	Other	*N*
Hindu upper	80	4	5	4	7	*305*
Hindu OBC	78	3	6	7	6	*418*
Scheduled Caste	82	1	3	5	9	*184*
Scheduled Tribe	(70)	(5)	(15)	(10)	—	*20*
Muslim	81	—	6	5	8	*108*
Other	76	1	3	2	18	*117*
All	79	2	5	5	9	*1152*

Source: NES 1967.
Note: recall data.

more support by the Hindu upper castes and much less support by the Muslims. In fact not a single Muslim reported having voted for the *Jana Sangh*. In this respect the BJS's profile of support mirrors that of the BJP thirty years later (as we shall see in tables below), and is skewed towards those at the top of the Hindu hierarchy.

At the aggregate level, then, the political salience of the caste–community cleavage is relatively weak, not withstanding the support given to the *Jana Sangh*. However, it would be wrong to assume that this meant caste was politically irrelevant. After Independence the Congress Party used 'traditional' structures such as the *jajmani* system and local factions (see e.g. Brass 1965) to mobilise its electorate. It transformed the patron–client relations between so-called 'dominant castes' and other castes into a vote bank through 'vertical mobilisation' (cf. Rudolph and Rudolph 1967: 36–64), and in doing so the Congress put together coalitions of upper and lower castes. Thus even during this period of relatively small variation between the social groups in terms of who they voted for, caste was still an important electoral anchor.

The Congress-Opposition period

The next election in our series is 1967, which marked the first serious setback to Congress dominance. Following Nehru's death in 1964, a prolonged succession crisis was brought to an end when Indira Gandhi, Nehru's daughter, was unexpectedly thrust into office in 1966. However, internal power struggles, successive droughts and a major war with Pakistan gave rise to grave concerns about the democratic and united future of India. 'The future of the country is dark for many reasons', wrote the *Hindustan Times*, 'all of them directly attributable to 19 years of Congress rule.'[2] In the face of a more united opposition Congress won 41 per cent of the vote in the general election and 54 per cent of the seats, down from 73 per cent of the seats in 1962. Its losses in the State Assembly elections were even greater, and eight out of the then sixteen states returned non-Congress governments. The 1967 general election thus heralds the start of a new era in which Congress for the first time faced serious opposition at both the state and the national level.

Tables 8.2 to 8.5 show that the pattern of electoral competition throughout this period was somewhat different from what had come before. In 1967 the emergence of parties to challenge Congress had made some impression on Congress's support base, with the Hindu upper castes (48 per cent) and OBCs (47 per cent) somewhat less likely to support Congress, and the Scheduled Castes (57 per cent) somewhat more likely. The *Jana Sangh* once again was very much more popular among the Hindu upper castes (15 per cent) than it was among the Muslims (2 per cent). The other parties did not have particularly distinctive profiles with respect to caste–community, and so we should be cautious about reading too much into minor differences, since the sample sizes involved are relatively small.

In 1971, for the first time, the elections for parliament were held separately from elections for assemblies, making national issues the central focus of the elections (Michelutti 2008). Mrs Gandhi's campaign was based on the populist slogan *garibi hatao* (abolish poverty), and Congress swept the polls, overwhelmingly defeating the breakaway Congress (O), which had defected over an internal power struggle for the nomination of President. However, despite this resounding victory, in which Congress was the dominant party in all social groups alike, we can see that its support was not entirely evenly drawn from across the different communities

Table 8.2. Community and vote in 1967 (row percentages).

	INC	BJS	Swatantra	Socialist	Communists	Other	*N*
Hindu upper	48	15	7	8	5	17	*543*
Hindu OBC	47	7	7	5	9	25	*630*
Scheduled Caste	57	5	4	8	8	18	*275*
Scheduled Tribe	(60)	(17)	(0)	(13)	(7)	(3)	*30*
Muslim	45	2	12	13	3	25	*168*
Other	59	4	5	2	1	29	*195*
All	50	8	7	7	6	22	*1841*

Source: NES 1967. Figures for the Scheduled Tribes are bracketed because of the small numbers involved (*N*=30).

[2] S. Mulgaokar, 'The Grimmest Situation in 19 Years', *Hindustan Times*, 3 Nov. 1966 (cited in Guha 2007: 414).

Table 8.3. Community and vote in 1971 (row percentages).

	INC	BJS	Socialist	Communist	Congress O	Swatantra	Regional	Other	*N*
Hindu Upper	65	6	3	4	6	4	2	9	*803*
Hindu OBC	53	7	4	6	8	5	7	11	*790*
Scheduled Caste	68	3	3	4	4	1	7	10	*443*
Scheduled Tribe	62	6	5	14	4	1	0	8	*178*
Muslim	75	0	0	11	1	0	2	12	*344*
Other	46	1	4	0	3	1	17	29	*121*
All	62	5	3	6	5	3	5	11	*2679*

Source: NES 1971.

(Table 8.3). Once again, it was somewhat less popular among the OBCs, where it obtained 53 per cent of the vote, than it was among the Scheduled Castes, where it obtained 68 per cent of the vote. Congress was also significantly more popular among the Muslims, where it obtained 75 per cent of the vote. These Congress sources of over- and under-representation must of course be matched by inverse patterns among other parties. However, given the dominance of Congress and the fragmentation of the opposition parties in 1971, it is hard to discern any clear patterns; many of the differences could plausibly be attributed to chance. Nonetheless a few patterns are statistically significant. Most notably we find that once again the *Jana Sangh* was significantly under-represented among Muslims. The Left Front was significantly over-represented both among Scheduled Tribes and among Muslims. The OBCs who were the group to abandon Congress in greatest number did not coalesce behind any one party in particular, but were somewhat more likely to support the breakaway Congress O and other minor parties.

These emerging patterns of caste–community mobilisation were disrupted by the elections to the sixth *Lok Sabha* in 1977, which took place in the immediate aftermath of the state of emergency. Following a series of corruption scandals against Congress, and widespread agitation against the government, a state of emergency was declared in June 1975. Opposition leaders and activists were arrested, censorship was imposed on the press and the fundamental rights of liberty were suspended. 'The regime gave unbridled power to officials and Congress politicians, who used it in an arbitrary, motivated and frequently violent manner' (Chatterjee 1997: 26–7).

However, in the face of growing international fears about the future of democracy in India, Indira Gandhi surprisingly called for fresh parliamentary elections to be held in 1977. Her opponents were released from jail, and the leaders from the *Jana Sangh*, the *Bharatiya Lok Dal* (Indian People's Party), the Socialist Party and Congress (O) hurriedly came together to contest the elections under a common banner of the *Janata* Party (Peoples Party). The elections were inevitably dominated by the emergency, particularly in north India where its effects had been felt most keenly. The veteran opposition leader Jayaprakash Narayan warned: 'if you vote for the Opposition you vote for Freedom. If you vote for the Congress you will vote for Dictatorship.'[3] In the event the *Janata* coali-

[3] *Illustrated Weekly of India*, 6 March 1977 (cited in Guha 2007: 523).

tion won an absolute majority, and decimated Congress support in the north of India, where Congress failed to win a seat in either Uttar Pradesh or Bihar, and won just one seat in Rajasthan and Madhya Pradesh. This election thus saw the first non-Congress government returned to power at the centre, with Morarji Desai taking over as Prime Minister.

The backlash against Congress was most evident among the two groups long considered to be its most loyal 'vote banks', and there was a substantial swing away from Congress among both the Scheduled Castes and the Muslims (see Table 8.4). Whereas in 1971 Scheduled Castes had been one of the groups most likely to support Congress, in 1977 they became less likely than the national average to do so—almost certainly because they had suffered particularly badly from Sanjay Gandhi's sterilisation programme. (See also the chapter by Jeffery and Jeffery in this volume.) Similarly, support for Congress among Muslims plummeted from 75 per cent in 1971 to 52 per cent in 1977, a drop of 23 percentage points. The upper castes (53 per cent) and OBCs (48 per cent) were more likely to support *Janata* than they were Congress (39 per cent and 40 per cent respectively). However, although significant, none of these differences between the social groups was particularly large, and caste-community does not appear to have played a particularly strong role in these elections, which were dominated by larger questions about democracy and authoritarianism.

Despite the massive '*Janata* wave' of 1977, which led some commentators to speak of a revolution, the coalition struggled to form a stable government, and was dogged by internal power struggles which eventually led to the formation's collapse and split. Fresh elections were called in 1980, and against a divided opposition Congress stormed back to power, winning 353 seats, one more than in the *garibi hatao* elections of 1971. As before, it did very well in the south, but this time in the north it

Table 8.4. Community and vote in 1977 (row percentages).

	INC	Janata	Communists	Regional	Other	*N*
Hindu upper	39	53	2	4	2	*1051*
Hindu OBC	40	48	4	6	2	*829*
Scheduled Caste	41	51	3	4	1	*507*
Scheduled Tribe	56	35	2	1	6	*100*
Muslim	52	37	2	3	6	*267*
Other	50	37	6	6	1	*127*
All	42	49	2	4	3	*2881*

Source: 1980 NES.
Note: recall data.

Table 8.5. Community and vote in 1980 (row percentages).

	INC	Socialist	Communists	Other	*N*
Hindu upper	53	35	4	8	*1045*
Hindu OBC	61	27	7	5	*807*
Scheduled Caste	67	22	6	5	*510*
Scheduled Tribe	78	6	11	5	*101*
Muslim	73	13	6	8	*275*
Other	52	26	13	9	*145*
All	60	27	6	7	*2883*

Source: 1980 NES.
Note: vote intention data.

benefited from the rival *Janata* factions splitting the anti-Congress vote. In the key state of Uttar Pradesh, for example, the Congress obtained 36 per cent of the vote, yet won 60 per cent of the parliamentary seats. One *Janata* faction got 23 per cent of the vote, the other 29 per cent; but between them they won just thirty-two seats in the state compared to Congress's fifty. However, despite this upturn in the polls Congress support remained relatively low among Hindu upper castes and OBCs in relation to the support it drew from the Scheduled Castes, Muslims and Scheduled Tribes (see Table 8.5). By contrast, the socialist parties (the *Janata* Party and *Janata* Party Secular) were more popular among the Hindu upper castes and the OBCs.

This period of the Congress-Opposition system thus witnessed a number of important changes in the social base of party support. As we have seen, traditionally Congress had drawn its support more or less equally from all social categories. However, the decline of Congress in the late 1960s and 1970s was marked in particular by the electoral realignment of the Hindu OBCs and upper castes, who became relatively less likely to support Congress and more likely to support one of the emerging parties. Frequent party splits and mergers among the opposition parties provided an obstacle to realignment, and so there is some volatility in terms of which party they supported. However, the key point is that during this period, regardless of who they voted for, they became much less likely to support Congress.

The period of multiparty competition

The factions of the earlier period and the splits of the middle period both probably had the same underlying cause—the distinct regional power bases of state politicians—and can be seen as two sides of the same coin.

In the third period these regional power bases have become institutionalised as enduring regional parties, leading to a shift from intraparty conflict and negotiation to interparty relations, and the emergence of a genuine multiparty system.

After a ten-year gap in the coverage of our surveys we rejoin the situation in 1991 (Table 8.6). By this time the structure of party competition had changed dramatically with the emergence of the BJP at the national level, and the BSP in India's largest state of Uttar Pradesh. Following the collapse of the National Front, which had formed a coalition government in 1989, the Congress returned to power in 1991, winning 37 per cent of the vote. However, the major development was the rise of the BJP and its ally *Shiv Sena* (Army of Shiva, named after the founder of the Maharata empire), who won 20 per cent of the votes and 120 seats. As might be expected, the BJP was much stronger among Hindus in general, and among upper caste Hindus in particular (30 per cent), than among Scheduled Castes (8 per cent) or Muslims (1 per cent). The BSP conversely was strong only really among Scheduled Castes, 5 per cent of whom gave their votes to the BSP nationally, although this was largely concentrated in the northern states, where they received 13 per cent of the Scheduled Caste votes. The OBCs, and to a certain extent the Muslims were both relatively more likely than the other communities to vote for one of the socialist parties.

These new pressures had a substantial impact on the Congress vote. In the north they lost votes from the upper castes to the BJP, and from the OBCs and Muslims to the Socialist *Janata* parties. Even though they remained relatively strong among the Scheduled Castes, they also lost some votes from this group to the BSP. The impact of these changes on the Congress's support base meant that on the surface at least it once again looked like a catch-all party, with support evenly drawn from all

Table 8.6. Community and vote in 1991 (row percentages).

	INC	BJP	Socialist	Communists	BSP	Other	*N*
Hindu upper	47	30	6	8	1	8	*1446*
Hindu OBC	42	16	14	7	1	20	*2103*
Scheduled Caste	53	8	5	17	5	12	*1124*
Scheduled Tribe	60	11	10	4	1	14	*558*
Muslim	54	1	19	10	1	15	*625*
Other	62	10	2	4	1	23	*225*
All	49	15	10	9	3	13	*6081*

Source: 1996 NES.
Note: recall data.

social groups. However, whereas in earlier times this was an outcome of an explicit policy of integration, now it was more the result of having each piece of its support base eaten into by one of the other major parties (see Heath and Yadav 1999).

These emerging patterns of electoral support were further consolidated in 1996, which witnessed the start of a period of electoral instability in India in which there were three general elections in little over three years as both BJP and Congress struggled to form an overall majority (Heath 2005). It also heralded the beginning of coalition politics as first the BJP and then the Congress attempted to form pre-election alliances with other smaller mainly regional parties. Following the demolition of the Ayodhya Mosque by Hindu militant activists in 1992, and the Hindu–Muslim riots that followed, leaving many dead, the elections that took place in 1996 were the most divided along community lines in India's history. From Table 8.7 we can see that the social bases of support for each of the major parties were remarkably lop-sided. The BJP was substantially more popular among the Hindu upper castes (41 per cent) than it was among any of the other social groups, with just 3 per cent of Muslims reporting to have voted for them. The socialist parties, such as the *Samajwadi* Party were substantially more popular among the OBCs (16 per cent) and Muslims (30 per cent) than they were among other groups, and the BSP was popular among the Scheduled Castes (14 per cent) but struggled to attract votes from anyone else. The support base of the Congress Party once again bears the imprint of this mobilisation, and is correspondingly weaker among those sections, leaving them most popular among the Scheduled Tribes. Thus, with the exception of the geographically dispersed Scheduled Tribes, each of the caste–community

Table 8.7. Community and vote in 1996 (row percentages).

	INC	BJP	BJP allies	Socialist	Communist	BSP	Other	*N*
Hindu upper	31	41	10	4	7	0	7	*2104*
Hindu OBC	24	25	6	16	7	3	21	*2698*
Scheduled Caste	36	15	1	6	13	14	15	*1570*
Scheduled Tribe	45	22	1	7	8	1	16	*751*
Muslim	38	3	1	30	12	1	15	*873*
Other	30	10	1	13	8	3	36	*262*
All	31	24	5	12	9	4	16	*8258*

Source: 1996 NES.

groups coalesced behind a different party, and this four-way split was much more pronounced in the north of India than it was elsewhere.

After the first BJP-led government collapsed (after thirteen days) a succession of United Front governments led the country. However, with the breakdown of the coalition fresh elections were called in 1998. Once again the BJP and allies were the largest combine at the polls, but were still some way short of an overall majority, and had to rely on support from a diverse band of assorted minor parties to achieve a majority. As Table 8.8 shows, the support base of the main parties once again followed fairly pronounced social divisions, although the BJP's attempt to broaden its appeal and attract both new voters and new alliance partners led to a slight toning down of its divisive *Hindutva* agenda (see Heath 1999*b*). The BJP retained its strong support from upper caste Hindus (38 per cent), as did its ally partners, although to a lesser degree. Once again Congress received most support from Scheduled Tribes (47 per cent), and rather weaker support from the upper castes (27 per cent) and OBCs (23 per cent). Meanwhile the Scheduled Castes continued to be the only major community that had any propensity to vote BSP.

The BJP coalition was besieged by internal power struggles, and when the AIADMK (*All India Anna Dravida Munnetra Kazhagam*: Dravidian Progress Federation) withdrew from the coalition fresh elections were held in 1999. Although the respective vote shares of the major parties did not change by much, the arithmetic of new alliance partnerships meant that the BJP was able to strengthen its grip on power and secure a workable majority. The broad pattern of support is similar to 1998 and 1996, with large social differences between the support base of the BJP, socialist parties and BSP, particularly in the north (see Table 8.9).

In the elections of 2004 the ruling BJP was widely tipped to win by a comfortable margin. However, despite record economic growth, their electoral campaign based on the slogan of 'India Shining' failed to find resonance among the large swathes of the population who still struggled to make ends meet, and the Congress returned to power with support from an extended network of alliance partners. As in previous years the Congress remained strong among the Scheduled Castes (39 per cent) and Muslims (49 per cent) and weaker among the upper castes (29 per cent) and the OBCs (30 per cent). The BJP was correspondingly stronger among the upper castes (42 per cent) and OBCs (30 per cent), although its social profile was somewhat less marked than in previous elections (see Table 8.9).

Table 8.8. Community and vote in 1998 (row percentages).

	INC	INC allies	BJP	BJP allies	Socialist	Communist	BSP	Other	*N*
Hindu upper	27	0	38	16	5	10	1	3	*1841*
Hindu OBC	23	5	28	14	16	5	2	7	*2707*
Scheduled Caste	32	3	14	8	13	11	12	7	*1250*
Scheduled Tribe	47	1	22	6	7	6	1	12	*635*
Muslim	38	12	5	2	28	9	1	4	*831*
Other	43	1	12	17	15	7	3	3	*212*
All	30	4	25	12	14	8	3	6	*7476*

Source: 1998 NES.

Table 8.9. Community and vote in 1999 (row percentages).

	INC	INC allies	BJP	BJP allies	Communist	Socialist	BSP	Other	*N*
Hindu upper	24	—	39	21	7	1	1	8	*2056*
Hindu OBC	28	7	21	24	5	5	2	9	*2833*
Scheduled Caste	36	5	12	13	11	1	12	10	*1493*
Scheduled Tribe	48	—	20	14	7	2	—	10	*629*
Muslim	47	11	4	9	11	8	2	9	*814*
Other	35	2	17	20	13	—	1	12	*304*
All	32	5	22	19	8	3	3	9	*8129*

Source: 1999 NES.

Table 8.10. Community and vote in 2004 (row percentages).

	INC	INC allies	BJP	BJP allies	LF	BSP	SP	Other	*N*
Hindu upper	29	5	42	9	5	1	1	8	*5860*
Hindu OBC	30	9	30	13	7	2	3	7	*6472*
Scheduled Caste	39	6	18	8	10	13	2	5	*3075*
Scheduled Tribe	31	3	22	17	7	0	0	19	*2946*
Muslim	49	14	9	3	7	2	8	10	*1979*
Other	39	3	18	20	6	2	0	12	*1419*
All	33	7	28	11	7	3	2	9	*21,751*

Source: 2004 NES.

The changing social bases of party support

The story since 1962, then, shows some continuity in the social bases of party support but some quite new developments. The most notable of the continuities were, first, Congress's strength among Muslims and its relative weakness among the Hindu upper castes and OBCs, particularly since the late 1960s and the onset of the Congress-Opposition system. Second, there are traces of continuity on the side of the Left Front, again with somewhat greater strength among the Muslims and lesser strength among the upper caste Hindus. Third, the *Janata Dal* parties and its socialist successors also have a tendency towards greater strength among the OBCs. It should be noted that these continuities are somewhat blurred in the post-emergency election of 1977 which seems to have disrupted traditional patterns of affiliation. However, there have also been marked discontinuities, first with 1977 and then with the rise of the BJP and BSP. The rise of these parties, which have tended to appeal to particular social groups rather than broad cross-sections of society, has led to a strengthening of the caste–community cleavage as a basis for electoral competition.

To get a clearer idea of the nature and magnitude of these changes over time it is useful to employ the statistical technique of odds ratios. This provides a measure of the relative support given by the different social groups to the parties. They have the statistical advantage that they are unaffected by the overall changes in the parties' shares of the vote, and as we saw in Table 8.1 there have been major changes in these shares. Odds ratios thus allow us to inspect the relative levels of support given a party independently of the changing overall levels of a party's popularity. There are many possible odds ratios that can be calculated from Tables

8.1 to 8.10, but in Table 8.11 we focus simply on support for Congress versus the other parties, and chart the changes over time in the relative strength of support given by the various social groups. An odds ratio of 1 indicates that the relative support for Congress is the same in the specific group as in the electorate as a whole, while values above 1 indicate that support is stronger for Congress and values below 1 indicate that support in that group is weaker than their overall level of support.[4]

Table 8.11 brings out very clearly both the continuities and the changes in the social bases of Congress support. Throughout the period Congress has tended to receive relatively greater support from the Scheduled Castes and Scheduled Tribes and from the Muslims, where the odds ratios are consistently greater than 1 (apart from Scheduled Castes in 1977 which we have already drawn attention to, and the Scheduled Tribes in 2004, which was probably a consequence of mobilisation around the new state boundaries which were drawn up in Tribal areas). Congress has also been consistently weaker among the Other Backward Castes throughout the period, where the odds ratios have tended to be less than 1, indicating that this group is less likely to support Congress than is the electorate as a whole. Congress support has also declined among the upper castes. Whereas in 1971 the upper castes were relatively more prone to support Congress than the overall electorate, this changed in 1977, after the state of emergency, and thereafter they remained somewhat less likely than the electorate as a whole to give their support to Congress.[5]

Table 8.11. Odds ratios of Congress vote, 1962–2004.

	1962	1967	1971	1977	1980	1991	1996	1998	1999	2004
Hindu upper	0.98	0.93	1.15	0.89	0.74	0.92	0.96	0.87	0.66	0.81
Hindu OBC	0.93	0.87	0.68	0.93	1.01	0.76	0.68	0.72	0.81	0.84
Scheduled Caste	1.28	1.32	1.29	0.94	1.32	1.19	1.21	1.11	1.17	1.28
Scheduled Tribe	0.67	1.49	1.01	1.75	2.38	1.56	1.80	2.04	1.99	0.91
Muslim	1.21	0.82	1.79	1.47	1.80	1.23	1.34	1.44	1.86	1.89
Other	0.89	1.43	0.52	1.40	0.73	1.72	0.92	1.73	1.10	1.29

Source: 1967, 1971, 1980, 1996, 1998, 1999 and 2004 NES.

[4] For example, Table 8.3 shows that 65 per cent of the upper castes in 1971 voted Congress whereas 35 per cent voted for other parties. This can be expressed as odds of 65:35 or 1.86:1. Let us compare this with the overall level of support for Congress in 1971. The bottom row of Table 8.2 shows that, overall, 62 per cent of the sample voted Congress while 38 per cent voted for other parties, giving odds of 62:38 or 1.63:1. We can express the upper caste odds as a ratio of the overall odds; in other words we can calculate 1.86:1/1.63:1. This reduces to 1.14:1.

[5] The 'others' are a rather heterogeneous grouping, and their numbers in the sample are rather small. We should not therefore perhaps place too much weight on the changes over time.

As we have pointed out, some of these figures are based on rather small sample sizes, and we have to be cautious in drawing strong conclusions. Some of the changes could be due solely to sampling variation rather than to changes in the real world. What we can do is use the technique of loglinear modelling to test whether the odds ratios have remained constant over time. We fit to the data a model which postulates that support for Congress varied from election to election and that support also varied from group to group. Crucially, however, we also postulate that the pattern of group support for Congress is the same in all elections. In other words, we postulate that the odds ratios had remained constant over time. We can then ask whether this model gives an acceptable fit to the data. For example, in the surveys taken together the odds ratio for the upper castes will average out at just under 1. What we want to know is whether the observed figures of 1.14, 0.89 and so on are values that could have occurred as a result of chance sampling variation around a 'true' figure of just under 1.

Our loglinear model tests whether the discrepancies between the actual odds ratios (as shown in Table 8.11) and the postulate that the odds ratios had remained constant at their average level could have occurred as a result of chance sampling variation. When we fit this loglinear model to the data, we find that the discrepancies between the actual odds ratios and the model's postulate of constant odds ratios gives a Chi square of 82.4 (with 15 degrees of freedom). This is a highly significant discrepancy and we therefore reject the null hypothesis that the odds ratios have remained constant over time. We conclude that there have been real changes in the relative strength of support given by the different groups to Congress. The loglinear model provides a global test of the full set of odds ratios. However, by inspecting the residuals we can check where the significant discrepancies between the model and the real world occurred. What we find, for example, is that the support given by the upper castes to Congress was significantly higher in 1971 than it was in later years, while that given by Scheduled Castes was significantly lower in 1977 than it was in the other years. The residuals of the Muslims, however, are relatively low for all the surveys. This shows that there has been very little variation over time in the level of support that they gave to Congress.[6]

[6] To check whether this trend of continuity over the period covered by our surveys is significant or not, we can test the differences between the observed and expected results with a log linear model. The model postulates that the odds ratios of Muslim support for Congress have remained constant over time. A rejection of this hypothesis would therefore mean that there have been real

We can carry out similar analyses for support for the other parties. Given the changing structure of party competition in India over the thirty years it is difficult to make sensible comparisons over time. However, one fairly stable feature of party competition has been the presence of the Communists who contested, either singly or in alliance, all of the elections covered by our surveys. We follow the same procedure as before. So, for example, in 1971 the odds ratio of 0.69 : 1 for the upper castes indicates that the upper caste Hindus were less likely than the nation as a whole to offer their support to the Communists. Table 8.12 shows that on the whole there has not been a great deal of variation over time in the level of support given to the Communists by each of the main social groups. Throughout the period the Communists have tended to receive relatively greater support from the Scheduled Castes and Muslims, where the odds ratios are consistently greater than 1, and relatively weaker support from the upper castes, where the odds ratios are consistently less than 1 (with the exception of 1998 which is probably a consequence of sampling error). There is some evidence that communist support may have declined somewhat among the OBCs. Whereas in the 1960s and 1970s the OBCs were relatively more prone to support the Communists than the overall electorate, this has not been the case in more recent elections during the era of multiparty competition, and they have since remained somewhat less likely than the electorate as a whole to give their support to Communists, as shown by odds ratios of slightly less than 1. However, the magnitude of these changes does not appear to be great, and could be the consequence of sampling variation.

Table 8.12. Odds ratios of Communist vote, 1962–2004.

	1962	1967	1971	1977	1980	1991	1996	1998	1999	2004
Hindu upper	0.69	0.77	0.68	0.71	0.63	0.87	0.81	1.27	0.98	0.75
Hindu OBC	1.36	1.52	0.98	1.22	1.22	0.76	0.75	0.66	0.69	0.99
Scheduled Caste	1.10	1.26	0.63	1.14	0.90	2.08	1.58	1.42	1.39	1.49
Scheduled Tribe	2.14	1.09	2.59	0.71	1.89	0.38	0.90	0.73	0.91	1.05
Muslim	0.92	0.47	1.97	0.80	1.02	1.17	1.40	1.19	1.30	1.04
Other	0.33	0.16	0.00	2.04	2.33	0.38	0.87	0.92	1.57	0.91

Source: 1967, 1971, 1980, 1996, 1998, 1999 and 2004 NES.

and significant changes in the voting behaviour of Muslims towards the Congress party. To measure these discrepancies we use a Chi square test. The result of this (1971–98) is 5.0 with three degrees of freedom. As this is not a significant result we must accept the null hypothesis that the odds ratios have remained constant over time. (Loglinear 1967–98; Chi square 16.6 with 4df. significant).

One other continuity in the Indian party system has been the presence of the socialist parties, who in their various different guises have also contested all of the elections covered by our surveys. Following the same procedure as before, we can see that the relative sources of support for the socialists have changed somewhat over time (see Table 8.13). In particular, during the early phases of electoral competition during the 1960s and 1970s when Congress was the dominant party, the upper castes were more likely to support the socialists than were the electorate as a whole, as shown by odds ratios consistently above 1. However, from the 1990s the upper castes have switched their allegiance to the BJP, and support for the socialists has been somewhat less than the national average. Parallel to this there has been a strengthening in the level of support among both the Hindu OBCs and the Muslims, with the Muslims in particular much more likely to support the socialists than the electorate as a whole (as shown by the very high odds ratios of 3.57 in 2004). Support among the Scheduled Castes has tended to be somewhat lower than the national average, and despite some minor fluctuation, this pattern of support does not appear to have varied much over time.

Lastly, one other useful comparison is that between *Jana Sangh* in the 1960s and 1970s and the BJP from the 1990s onwards (see Table 8.14). However, it is important to note that the small numbers involved in the early years means that there will be rather large sampling errors and any results for the *Jana Sangh* must be treated with caution. Nevertheless, Table 8.14 strongly suggests that the sources of the *Jana Sangh*'s relative strength were much the same as those of the BJP twenty-five years later. Thus the upper castes, and to a lesser extent the OBCs gave more support both to the *Jana Sangh* and the BJP than did the electorate as a whole (shown by odds ratios greater than 1). Conversely, the Scheduled Castes, Muslims and other groups consistently gave less support both to the *Jana Sangh* and to the BJP than did the overall electorate. The only deviant

Table 8.13. Odds ratios of Socialist vote, 1962–2004.

	1962	1967	1971	1977	1980	1991	1996	1998	1999	2004
Hindu upper	1.03	1.20	1.06	1.21	1.44	0.56	0.30	0.37	0.24	0.59
Hindu OBC	1.15	0.71	1.34	0.98	1.03	1.42	1.48	1.23	1.64	1.43
Scheduled Caste	0.53	1.21	0.81	1.12	0.76	0.47	0.49	0.98	0.35	0.74
Scheduled Tribe	3.39	2.04	1.49	0.57	0.17	0.98	0.60	0.44	0.50	0.03
Muslim	1.32	2.00	0.00	0.62	0.41	2.16	3.18	2.55	2.82	3.57
Other	0.50	0.21	1.37	0.62	0.96	0.21	1.13	1.10	0.10	0.06

Source: 1967, 1971, 1980, 1996, 1998, 1999 and 2004 NES.

Table 8.14. Odds ratios of *Jana Sangh*/BJP vote, 1962–2004.

	1962	1967	1971	1991	1996	1998	1999	2004
Hindu upper	1.47	1.96	1.34	2.29	2.21	1.87	2.19	1.90
Hindu OBC	1.38	0.78	1.43	1.04	1.04	1.18	0.95	1.12
Scheduled Caste	0.47	0.58	0.61	0.47	0.56	0.51	0.52	0.55
Scheduled Tribe	2.14	2.18	1.34	0.65	0.87	0.88	0.81	0.73
Muslim	0.00	0.20	0.00	0.06	0.10	0.17	0.15	0.26
Other	—	0.47	0.19	0.59	0.34	0.43	1.06	0.58

Source: 1967, 1971, 1980, 1996, 1998, 1999 and 2004 NES.

group were the Scheduled Tribes, but here we need to remember the very small numbers involved.

The *Jana Sangh*, therefore, although it was much less successful than the BJP overall, appealed to the same kinds of groups. In a sense it demonstrated the potential of these groups for a distinctive Hindu party. However, it required disillusion with Congress before that potential was turned into major support for the BJP. The other striking feature of Table 8.14 is the fact that the odds ratios are much more polarised between extreme values than any we have seen for Congress. For example, the odds ratios for the BJP among the upper castes were 2.21 in 1996, whereas the odds ratios among Muslims were just 0.10. This means that BJP support is much more socially distinctive than Congress support ever was.

The political salience of caste–community

These odds ratios show that the support bases of the three main parties have become more divided over time: Congress has become significantly less popular among the upper castes and OBCs, while the BJP is significantly more popular among upper castes, and the socialists are significantly more popular among the OBCs. There is thus evidence that the party system as a whole has become more structured along caste–community lines than it was previously. We can get an overall idea of the magnitude of these changes by examining measures of association between caste–community and vote choice at the party system level. There are a variety of different measures that one can use, but the method we consider here is the index of dissimilarity.[7] This provides a measure for

[7] Another measure that has been used to summarise the level of cleavage voting is kappa, which is the standard deviation of the log odds (see Hout *et al.* 1995). The correlation between the

the political salience of caste–community at the party system level (rather than the individual party level which we considered previously). The index of dissimilarity tells us how similar (or different) the voting patterns of the different communities are in relation to each other. It compares the observed distribution of the different communities' vote choice (that which we observe in the real world) to a hypothetical expected distribution that we would expect to see if all communities behaved in the same way (that is, if caste–community did not have any impact on vote choice at all). When the index is large then there are substantial differences between the communities in terms of their vote choice, and when the index is small there are only minor differences between them. The index of dissimilarity thus provides a summary indication of the salience of the caste–community cleavage in structuring vote choice in the electoral system as a whole. It ranges from 0 to 200, and is computed for each year.

Figure 8.1 plots the caste–community cleavage index over time and shows the extent to which electoral competition has been structured along caste–community lines since 1962. The index is at its lowest level in 1962, during the latter stages of the Congress Party dominance period. Although we unfortunately lack data before this time, we hypothesise that

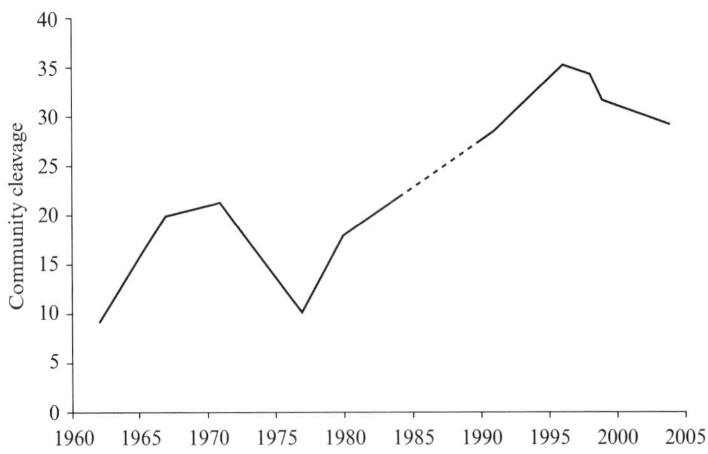

Figure 8.1. The strength of the caste–community cleavage, 1962–2004.

index of dissimilarity and kappa across states in 2004 is 0.81, so it does not make a great deal of difference which measure is employed since they both measure the phenomenon in more or less the same way. However, we prefer to use the index of dissimilarity since it takes into account the size of the community group, and deeply divided large groups therefore count more to the overall index than divided small groups.

the level of caste voting would have been at similar levels to 1962 in previous elections. The salience of caste is somewhat higher during the period of Congress-Opposition, from 1967 to 1980 (with the exception of the post emergency election of 1977 which disrupted traditional patterns of allegiance). However, there is a sharp increase in 1991 and the strength of the caste–community cleavage has been very much stronger in the third period of multiparty competition, peaking in 1996 and then tailing off somewhat but remaining at historically high levels.

This clearly shows that at the aggregate level of the party system, the caste–community cleavage has become increasingly important in determining vote choice. However, it should be emphasised that the salience of caste is not equally strong in all electoral contests in India, and is more important in some states than it is in others. By disaggregating the all-India patterns by region, we can see that the post 1980 increase in the salience of caste–community voting is very much greater in the north of India, the heartland of parties such as the BJP, BSP and SP, than it is in the other states, where the level of caste voting has not changed much since the Congress-Opposition period and the emergence of regional parties as a source of competition to Congress in the 1970s.

There is thus evidence of substantial variation over time in the level of caste voting, but also substantial variation between regions. One obvious factor for the increased politicisation of the caste–community cleavage over time is the emergence of new parties, particularly in the north of India,

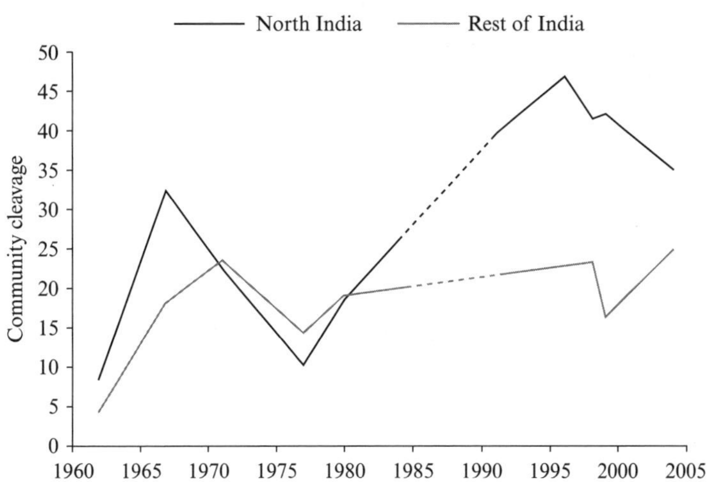

Figure 8.2. The strength of the caste–community cleavage by region, 1962–2004.

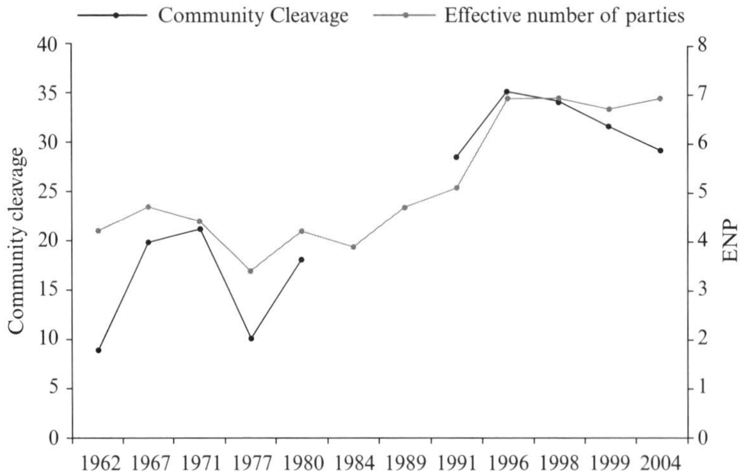

Figure 8.3. Community cleavage and the effective number of parties, 1962–2004.

which have explicitly sought to mobilise voters along caste–community lines, such as the BJP, BSP, SP and RJD. We can examine the impact of these changes in the party system by inspecting the association between party system format and the salience of caste–community cleavage.[8]

Figure 8.3 shows that the strength of the caste cleavage over time is strongly related to the number of effective parties in the party system. As the party system has fragmented and new parties have emerged the structure of political competition has become more closely aligned along caste–community divisions. The increased salience of community is thus related to the rise of new parties rather than the polarisation of existing parties.

Conclusion

The evidence shows rather clearly that at the beginning of our period, in 1962, cleavages nationally were at their weakest. To a certain extent this is still a reflection of the Independence movement, which formed a unifying

[8] To examine the impact of the party system format we use an index for the effective number of parties. This index is a way of summarising the number of major parties or 'effective parties' in the party system. Broadly speaking the number of effective parties is equivalent to the number of parties gaining over 10 per cent of the votes.

foundation for electoral mobilisation, over-riding internal social divisions. With the onset of the Congress-Opposition phase from 1967, caste divisions strengthened appreciably up until 1971, with the *Jana Sangh* in particular showing a similar profile to the later BJP, while Congress became more reliant on Scheduled Caste and Muslim votes. However, there was no steady trend upwards. 1977 marked a major reversal back to the earlier character. Partly this was because parties like the BJS, which had a distinct social base, merged into the larger formation of the *Janata*. Possibly also the state of emergency and ensuing wave of support for *Janata* overrode the social divisions within Indian society. The central political issue in 1977 was not a communal issue but one about authoritarianism and democracy, not rooted in any distinct social grouping.

We then see in 1980 a revival of cleavage voting, but not reaching the same level as 1971. Again, it is notable that there simply was no party in 1980 with a distinct social base like *Jana Sangh* had had. We lack data on 1984, but our suspicion is that it would also have been an election with few major social cleavages, possibly at similar levels to the other elections during this period. A new phase probably begins with 1989, on which unfortunately we again lack data. But in 1991 it is clear that cleavages have strengthened markedly and to much higher levels than in any of the previous cycles. This process reaches its peak in 1996 and then declines somewhat, although remaining at an historically high level. Again the natural interpretation of these findings is that they reflect the electoral rise of parties like the BJP and BSP which have made specific appeals to distinct social groups.

The emergence of these parties is clearly a consequence of the decline of Congress, which created the space for new parties to emerge and more internal cleavages based on caste and community to come to the fore. But at the same time, the pressures that led to the emergence of these parties may in turn have contributed to the decline of Congress. The reasons for this decline are complex, but it was in some sense also probably inevitable. The electoral significance of the initial national foundation of electoral politics had a limited shelf life. By 1962 more than half the electorate had come to political maturity after the struggle and sacrifice of the nationalist movement (Hardgrave and Kochanek 2008: 381), and the old conflict with British colonialism perhaps was not as relevant to them as it had been to their parents. Moreover, internal factions within Congress, based on regional, language and class identities, and on caste and religion, added to this problem by putting increasing strains on the Congress edifice.

The emergency of 1975–7 severely dented the legitimacy of Congress, particularly in the north, and the subsequent decline of Congress in the north paved the way for new parties to emerge. In this respect the emergency represents a turning point. And as Figure 8.2 clearly illustrates, since then there has been a sharp increase in the salience of caste as an electoral anchor in the north.

The emergence of the caste cleavage has tended to be stronger in socially-divided states, particularly those that are beset by poverty. In this sense social conditions are now mirrored in patterns of political conflict to a much greater degree than was ever the case previously, and in this respect the Indian party system has become more representative of the society at large. However, it would be wrong to think that the crumbling of the initial national electoral foundation constructed by Congress somehow organically revealed these internal social conflicts. The pattern is much more complicated than that. The figures for 1977 and 1980 suggest that a crucial element is the nature of the options offered by the parties to the electorate. Moreover, it is important to recognise that parties themselves play a role in shaping, and reshaping, the nature of social identities. Indeed, this is one reason why Mahatma Gandhi opposed reservation and separate electorates. Parties can play a role in heightening the awareness of communal groupings (as in the post-Ayodhya election of 1996), or alternatively by forming cross-party alliances (as in 1977) they may blur social divisions. The relationship between polarisation and party system format clearly highlights this.

The logic of the Indian electoral system may encourage parties to form alliances, both political and social, since no grouping on its own can be sufficient to win power. Our data show clearly the potential within Indian society, as in other societies, for parties to emerge with distinct social bases. In that respect differences between Indian and other democracies have been exaggerated. But the nature of the complex cleavage system in Indian society, based on religion, caste, region and language means that appeals to just one group will never be sufficient to gain political power. Also geography means that Muslims or Scheduled Castes for example are not concentrated in any one place, so no community can win power on its own. This imposes a constraint on how far parties can go in appealing to a single distinct group. The BSP for example has to be willing to work with other parties in coalition if it is to be more than a pressure group. This tension between social divisions and electoral constraints may also help to explain the cyclical nature of Indian politics.

These findings pose some fairly obvious challenges to the Lipset and Rokkan model of party-cleavage formation. On the one hand the caste–community cleavage itself is somewhat different from the sort of cleavages that Lipset and Rokkan emphasised. But to the extent that the model's cleavages do apply, their relative importance and sequencing, and implications for party formation, do not necessarily conform to the model's original expectations. Lipset and Rokkan (1967: 34) argue that, in Europe, 'the decisive sequence of party formation took place at the early stage of competitive politics, in some cases well before the extension of the franchise, in other cases on the very eve of the rush to mobilization of the finally enfranchised masses'. In contrast, in India (and other second wave democracies which underwent a much swifter transition to democracy) this initial mass mobilisation took place along explicitly political lines relating to regime change, rather than along internal social lines. Thus in India at the critical period of party formation prior to gaining political independence, social cleavages were subordinated or incorporated within a single 'national' basis of mobilisation (Randall 2001). The salience of this foundation was perhaps destined to decline over time, and as it did so the emergence of alternative cleavages representing internal social divisions based on first region (or centre–periphery) and then caste–community have come to the fore. Thus rather than the individualistic, cleavageless politics that has evolved in the West, the decline of the initial 'national' electoral foundation established at the onset of mass democracy has made way to social cleavages that perhaps bear more similarity to the Lipset–Rokkan model than they did earlier. Whether these cleavages persist in the future remains to be seen. Economic and social development may gradually weaken their hold, as they did in the West, but the current extent of poverty and inequality that exists throughout much of India suggests that this may still be some way off.

9

Understanding Popular Politics: Caste, Kinship and Factionalism among Yadavs in North India

LUCIA MICHELUTTI

Summary. This chapter explores the rise of caste politics and the dynamics of Indian popular politics in the 1990s in the state of Uttar Pradesh. By using the political ethnography of one of the most assertive and visible 'backward' castes in north India (the Yadavs) the chapter shows how the interrelation between *vernacular* socio-cultural idioms and structures (such as for example kinship structures, folk theories of descent, popular cults and local cosmologies) have been paramount in making 'democracy' part of the Indian political imagination and in informing the political upsurge of the common people and the shaping of political cleavages based on caste/community. The Yadavs of Mathura town represent an informative case study about processes of democratisation in India and provide fresh data on why certain groups are more apt to successfully exert their influence within the democratic political system, and why others are not, regardless of the fact that in many instances they have similar economic and political incentives and resources.

Introduction

DURING THE 1990s Indian democracy witnessed an upsurge in the political participation of lower castes/communities and the emergence of political leaders from humble social backgrounds who present themselves as promoters of social justice for underprivileged communities. Lower castes and

Proceedings of the British Academy **159**, 219–242.

communities have hence emerged as major vote banks in opposition to the 'forward castes' and gradually revolutionised the Indian political arena at all levels (Jaffrelot 2003; Jaffrelot and Kumar 2009; see Heath and Yadav in this volume). As a result, today in India, in contrast to much of the West, it is the historically disadvantaged groups who are more likely to vote than their well-educated and wealthy counterparts (Y. Yadav 1997: 180–8; also 2000). To quote Khilnani (1997: 17), 'the democratic idea has penetrated the Indian political imagination and has begun to corrode the authority of the social order and of a paternalistic state'. But crucially, 'democracy as a manner of seeing and acting upon the world' (ibid.) has also affected the ways Indians view themselves in society and how they relate to each other beyond electoral politics. 'Democracy' has hence taken social roots in Indian society (see Alam 2004), producing new social relations and values which have changed the political arena at all levels. I call this transformation 'the vernacularisation of democratic politics' (Michelutti 2008) a process of change by which Indian democracy becomes embedded in local socio-cultural practices, and in turn also transforms everyday life in often surprising ways. Thus I argue that the interrelations between *vernacular* socio-cultural idioms and structures (such as for example caste, kinship, religion, kingship, popular cults, local cosmologies and so on) and 'the political' have been paramount in making democracy part of the Indian political imagination and in informing the political upsurge of the common people and the shaping of political cleavages based on caste/community.

It follows that the entrance of 'the lower orders' into mass politics has been not merely a response to changes that took place in party politics, but rather is the result of ongoing transformations in the social and cultural structure of society which political parties then caught up with and reacted to and also contributed to reshape. Indeed, the rise of caste-based political parties (such as for example the *Bahujan Samaj* Party (Popular People's Party) and the *Samajwadi* (Socialist) Party in north India) and development of caste populism in the 1990s has been encouraged by a number of interlinked social processes. Here, I focus on the rise of caste politics by looking at the weakening of the legitimacy of caste hierarchy, the formation of ethnic-like castes and the role of caste culture (in particular kinship ideologies and structures) in shaping political behaviour and political socialisation. More specifically I use the political ethnography of one of the most assertive and politically powerful caste formations in contemporary India (the Yadavs) to illustrate the interrelations between society, culture and popular politics in a north Indian town (Mathura, Uttar Pradesh).

The Yadavs (also known by the name of Ahirs) were traditionally a low- to middle-ranking cluster of pastoral-peasant castes. Importantly, their political leaders (like Mulayam Singh Yadav in Uttar Pradesh and Laloo Prasad Yadav in Bihar) have acquired a pivotal role in mobilising lower caste groups and communities in north India. By exploring the political rise of the Yadavs through the prism of vernacularisation I will show how kinship ideologies and structures have significantly contributed to the internalisation of democracy in Yadavs' consciousness. In turn the internalisation of democracy has informed changes in the morphology of Yadav caste/community, in terms of who they vote for and how they become socialised into politics and how they perceive politics and political leaders.

Caste politics, the Other Backward Classes movement and the Yadavs

In the early 1960s, the Indian sociologist Srinivas wrote that 'Caste is so tacitly and so completely accepted by all, including those who are most vocal in condemning it, that it is everywhere the unit of social action' (1962: 41). After more than four decades the same comment could be applied to describe the life of ordinary citizens in the town of Mathura. If, on the one hand, internal divisions and separations within the caste are viewed by many as obsolete, as institutions from a 'backward past' and as synonymous with 'backwardness' and 'non-progress', caste dressed up as an ethnic community is considered legitimate and a 'secular' and 'democratic' category. And, indeed, it is a product of democracy. At first glance the post-independence nationalist elite's efforts to create an equal and casteless society look like miserable failures. But, as the ethnography of the Yadavs shows, the idea of equality (at least social if not economic) has made important inroads in popular consciousness and, paradoxically, it has been precisely the working towards equality and freedom through democratic means (particularly through voting) which has, and is, promoting the political use of caste and its social reinvention into quasi-ethnic communities. The shift from 'caste' to 'caste as ethnic group' has been described as the 'substantialisation of caste' (Dumont 1980: 226–7) or as 'the ethniciation of caste' (Barnett 1975: 158–9; see also, Fuller 1996: 22–5). The caste system, defined by hierarchical relations, is said to have changed its nature. As a result, castes are increasingly becoming 'horizontal', disconnected groups with their own distinct culture and way of life (Searle-Chatterjee and Sharma 1994: 19–20). This shift is reflected by the substitution of the term *jati*, which refers to caste, with the term *samaj*, which refers to community (Mayer 1996: 59).

In the 1990s the Yadavs entered the political arena as 'a *samaj*' mobilised by caste-based political parties (like the *Samajwadi* (Socialist) Party). The process of Yadav community formation has a long history. It is the product of a dialogue between Ahir/Yadav scholars, social activists, religious reformers, and politicians on the one hand, and on the other the colonial and post-colonial state. The politics of identity representation in colonial times and democratic politics in independent India provided ordinary Yadavs and their leaders with a stage on which the community's interests and demands could be successfully articulated. And it is precisely through participating in the democratic game 'as a caste/community' and by trying to get a share of state resources 'as a caste/community' that an all-India Yadav community has been created. Democracy provided members of the Ahir/Yadav community with the opportunity to decide who they were, how many they were and how they wished to be represented. In the late colonial period, Yadav caste associations were formed and took an active role in shaping how their community was to be represented in the democratic arena. Drawing on myths, oral epics, folk kinship theories, an ambiguous position in the caste system, colonial and post-colonial ethnography and classifications, Hindu nationalist narratives, and also sacred topographies and historical artefacts, a series of Ahir/Yadav community social workers, political activists and historians created a multivocal 'heritage' (cf. Turnbridge and Ashworth 1996: 1–19) which gave the idea of democracy a vernacular base.[1] The Yadav case, of course, is not unique.[2] However, the Yadavs have been particularly suc-

[1] 'Heritage is, by the original definition of the word, determined by the legatee . . .' (Turnbridge and Ashworth 1996: 6) and 'The resources from which heritage is assembled is a wide and varied mixture of past events, personalities, folk memories, mythologies, literary associations, surviving physical relics, together with places, whether sites, towns, landscapes with which they can be symbolically associated (ibid.: 7). I find the concept of heritage to describe Yadav ethno-historical imagination useful because it conveys what Yadav scholars and experts have chosen to inherit and pass on to the next generations as well as the plethora of resources they have chosen to use. Moreover it was precisely the word 'heritage' that Yadav scholars mostly used (when talking and writing in English) when they referred to their past.

[2] A number of socio-historical studies have explored the relation between specific caste communities and colonial classifications. For example Conlon's (1977) work on Saraswat Brahmans, Leonard's (1978) monograph on the development of the Kayastha caste community,

cessful in re-imagining themselves by linking their 'democratic' present to a 'democratic' and 'secular' past. Ahir/Yadavs did not only find themselves in particular historical circumstances which invited them to reshape their community but they also had at hand a repertoire of vernacular idioms and structures which helped them to make best use of the imaginative power of democracy (Khilnani 1997: 17). The result is a resourceful and flexible community ethno-history which binds contemporary Yadavs to their heroic and mythical past and to the democratic present.

At the core of the Yadav community lies a specific folk theory of descent according to which all Indian pastoral castes are descended from the Yadu Dynasty (hence the label Yadav), the dynasty to which the god Krishna (a cow-herder, and supposedly a Kshatriya) belonged. Thus, although the Yadavs are divided into different subdivisions which have different ritual ranks (Yaduvanshi, Goallavanshi, Nandavanshi, etc.), there is nonetheless a strong belief amongst them that all Yadavs belong to Krishna's line of descent, the Yadav subdivisions of today being the outcome of the fission of an original and undifferentiated group. In Yadav political rhetoric Krishna is also depicted as a democratic-socialist politician and as 'the first fighter for social justice'. Statements like 'we (Yadavs) are a caste of politicians' and 'we are the natural leaders of the oppressed' were commonly made to me to draw attention to local Yadav political activism in the town of Mathura. By the same token, the 'political qualities' of contemporary Yadavs were often traced back to the Yadav caste patron deity, the pan-Indian god Krishna. The use of ideologies of caste and descent and religious idioms in Yadav vernacular reinterpretations of democracy shows how the principal political actors in contemporary Indian politics are often not individual citizens but rather castes, tribes and communities (see, for comparison, Tambiah 1997; see also Heath and Yadav in this volume).

One of the foundations of this understanding of democracy based on caste categories is the policy of reservation for marginalised communities set up first by the colonial government and then adopted by post-colonial India. The Indian Constitution recognises a language of community entitlements based on policies of affirmative action. Accordingly, it established

Washbrook's (1975) study on caste organisation in South India and the recent work of N. Datta (1999) on the formation of Jat identity. For an ethnographical exploration of caste community formations and their relation to post-colonial classifications and politics see Hardgrave's (1969) study on the Nadars of Tamil Nadu and Molund (1988) on the Koris of Kanpur. For more recent studies on caste, class and politics in Uttar Pradesh see Ciotti (2006) and Jaoul (2007) and Jeffrey *et al.* (2008).

a policy of reservation which aimed to uplift the former untouchables (Scheduled Castes, SCs), the tribal groups (Scheduled Tribes, STs) and a less specified group of lower caste people (Other Backward Classes, OBCs) by reserving quotas in government jobs, education and in the legislative assemblies. This essentially was a system devised to secure representation for the disadvantaged communities and to redress the balance in what was thought to be an extremely hierarchical and unequal society. (See the chapter by Zoya Hasan in this volume.) Although it was originally introduced as a temporary measure, it still continues today and has become one of the bases of Indian popular politics. It follows that, for example, north Indian Yadavs have been constructing their political success by taking a leading role in the so-called Other Backward Classes movement (Rao 1979) in the 1960s and 1970s and then again in the 1990s and by portraying themselves as the leaders of the Backward Classes at the all-India level.

While the question of identifying the SCs and STs was settled before independence, the category 'other backward classes' was left to be defined, at least at the central level. In the early 1950s, the Kalelkar Commission made the first attempt to characterise 'backwardness' and in its report made it clear that caste was an important index of economic and social marginalisation. The central government rejected the recommendation by pointing out how the commission failed to apply other criteria such as income, education and literacy in determining backwardness. On the wave of the rejection, the Yadav caste associations began to lobby the government for the adoption of the caste criterion for determining the status of the OBCs. By the early 1960s, both the general secretary and the president of the All India Backward Classes Federation belonged to the Yadav community and had active roles in the All India Yadav Mahasabha (AIYM), a caste association which was founded in 1924 to promote Yadav interests at the all-India level. In the 1960s and 1970s, at its annual conferences the AIYM began to pass resolutions demanding the revival of the caste criteria and the implementation of the recommendations of the Backward Classes Commission (Rao 1979: 157). The Mahasabha condemned the central government for shelving the Backward Classes Commission's report and campaigned for the implementation of its recommendations and for the revival of the caste criterion for determining 'backwardness' (see Dhanagare 1968).

Meanwhile, in the following years numerous state commissions were formed to develop means to identify what 'backward' meant. Finally, in 1978, a new Backward Classes Commission, headed by B. P. Mandal

(Yadav by caste), was appointed. Its report identified 3,743 castes as 'backward' (over 52 per cent of the Indian population). This list was developed out of the last available data on caste, which was the 1931 Indian Census. With the 1941 Census, the British stopped using caste categories because it was thought that they contributed to the politicisation of caste. By the same token, the post-colonial government rejected caste tabulation in an attempt to deprive caste of its legitimacy. Constitution makers believed that in a democratic state caste demography had no place (see Dirks 2001: 280–83).

In the absence of reliable data, predictably, the search for 'backward' castes was not a straightforward process. The problems encountered by colonial census officers in defining caste as 'an all-over India' classificatory tool were to be experienced again by the members of the Backward Classes Commission. As in the 1920s, when British census officers were overwhelmed with claims from caste groups which attempted to be classified as 'Rajput', 'Kshatriya' or other higher status caste/*varna* titles, the Mandal commission was engulfed by petitions from communities which claimed to be 'backward' (Pinch 1996: 145). The Yadav caste associations successfully pursued such a path (see Yadav 1994). By the 1970s, the Yadavs of Uttar Pradesh had gradually introduced themselves to the political process at the local, state and national level. It was during the 1960s as followers of Charan Singh that the Yadavs entered the State Assembly of Uttar Pradesh (and also Bihar) in large numbers. Indeed, the rise of the OBCs is the rise of the Yadavs and the Kurmis (Jaffrelot 2000: 100). The number of Yadav MPs and Yadav MLAs steadily increased from the 1980s. Throughout the 1980s the implementation of the Mandal recommendations became one of the major focuses of the All India Yadav Mahasabha. The following are extracts from publications and speeches published and held in this period. The AIYM lobbied for the implementation of the recommendations 'in the name of Krishna'.

> Lord Krishna, holding the Goverdhan Giri took the stand of this people against injustice and proposed himself. In the Mahabharata, favouring justice, he rooted out the injustice done to the respectful people of this race. For the progress of the poor people of India below the poverty line, especially for the Backward, Scheduled Castes and Scheduled Tribes, show the way today![3]

[3] Jagadami Prasad Yadav, Member of Parliament, letter published in the AIYM, 49th Session Madras's Souvenir, 1983 (originally in English).

Krishna is represented as a social-democratic hero who combats injustice and social inequalities. The Yadav leaders, in the name of Krishna, 'the prophet of social justice', represent the Yadavs as the natural leaders of the OBCs. Krishna was the leader in *Dwapara Yuga* (the age of Dwapara), and the Yadavs, as his descendants, were supposed to lead the society in the *Kali Yuga* (the age of Kali) and fight the injustice and the exploitation of the backward classes by the forward classes (see Rao 1979: 214). This rhetoric, which would be further developed in the 1990s by Yadav politicians (see Michelutti 2008: chapter 6) was accompanied by an emphasis on the power of the Yadavs' numerical strength and the promotion of an all-India process of Yadavisation.

The following is an extract from the meeting held in 1983 in Madras, Tamil Nadu.

> 'All are our habitations. All are our relatives' is the ancient saying. Lord Krishna led us towards such a goal. This is because of various divisions that crept among us in the course of time. The dawn of the need for unity marked the dawn of our Mahasabha . . . at one time Yadav population was 56 crore. Now it is supposed to be 10 or 12 crore. As a result of subcaste subdivisions, it is not easy to determine the exact number of Yadavas. We should all unite and write Yadav after our names that will reduce the ambiguity which arises as a result of use of subcaste names.[4]

In 1990, the Janata Dal Prime Minister V. P. Singh implemented reservations for the OBCs. This provoked disapproval from all over the country. Young students belonging to high castes immolated themselves in a sign of protest. By the same token, Yadav leaders were jubilant. The Yadav caste publications of the period are full of articles which portray Yadav leaders as the saviours of the backward classes and B. P. Mandal (Yadav) as their messiah. The latter has become one of the legendary personalities of the Yadav community and he is glorified in the Yadav caste literature. The following is an example of such 'devotion': 'B. P. Mandal was a man with great foresight. He worked for the upliftment of the poor and oppressed. He was a great advocate of social justice. His greatest contribution to the cause of social justice is the Mandal commission report. He is rightly called the Messiah of Backwards.'[5]

[4] Flag-hoisting speech by Harmohan Singh, AIYM Convention, Madras 1983 (originally in English).

[5] Resolutions voted at the AIYM's Platinum Jubilee Session, Vaishali-New Delhi, 25 and 26 Dec. 1999.

In 1999, the AIYM resolved that the portrait of B. P. Mandal, the messiah of the backward classes, should be placed 'in the Central Hall of the Parliament without any further delay'. In the 1990s, the Mahasabha's OBC front led by socialist leaders such as Harmohan Singh Yadav regained power. Harmohan Singh Yadav is described in the words of a caste publication as 'a devoted social activist, a humanist with immeasurable warmth for the poor, the downtrodden and the oppressed. A firm believer in secularism, social justice and democratic values.'[6] In 2008, he was a member of the Rajya Sabha and an active member of the *Samajwadi* (Socialist) Party. In the 1980s and 1990s under his leadership the Mahasabha revived its local branches and began to focus more on issues of political representation and participation. This massive reorganisation and revival is historically parallel to the implementation of the policy of reservation for the OBCs. The meetings of the AIYM began to be held regularly and their venue shifted outside the Hindi belt. As of 2009, there are no comparable examples of caste associations in India that extend across state boundaries and include members of different cultural and linguistic backgrounds to the extent of the AIYM. In Uttar Pradesh, many of the active members of the Yadav caste associations belong to the *Samajwadi* (Socialist) Party which is the party that gives political voice to the local Yadavs in Uttar Pradesh. By 1998, the Yadavs occupied 23.6 per cent of parliamentary seats (Jaffrelot 2000: 99). In the last decade Yadavs and other 'lower castes' have made their votes even more effective thanks to their organisation, and the development of electoral majorities based on caste and community seems to matter more than at any time before (see Heath and Yadav in this volume).

Yadavs in Mathura town and their political involvement

Mathura lies in the Braj area which is well known as the place where Krishna was born and where he grew up. Yadavs inhabit three neighbourhoods in Mathura: Sathgara; Anta Para; and Ahir Para. My research over the last ten years has focused on the neighbourhood of Ahir Para. Ahir Para is part of Sadar Bazaar which lies on the outskirts of the old part of Mathura. It is worth noticing that, within Mathura, Sadar Bazaar is now

[6] AIYM Platinum Jubilee Year, Souvenir, 1924–1999 (1999).

considered a Yadav 'small town' and the presence of other communities is often downplayed. Sadar Bazaar/Ahir Para Yadavs traditionally belong to the Nandavanshi-Ahir subdivision. During British times, they immigrated to Mathura from the neighbouring districts of Mainpuri, Etah, Farrukhabad and Kannauj. At the time Mathura was an important army-training centre for Ahir soldiers. In addition, they were employed as bullock-cart and/or truck drivers. However, military service was not the only source of employment and income offered by the army structure. The civil and military population of the Cantonment demanded regular milk supplies. Consequently, Ahirs and Goallas from nearby districts migrated to Mathura and began to work in large numbers for the Cantonment dairy, or set up their own milk business.

After Independence, the shift of an important battalion caused a sudden fall in local demand for milk supplies. This together with the lack of grazing land, the reinforcement of rules implemented to regulate the commerce of milk, and the establishment of a public dairy, brought about important socio-economic changes in Ahir Para. Several milk vendors began to use the surplus milk to make sweets and set up *halwai* shops (sweet shops). They then began to invest their profits in other types of businesses such as transportation and small-scale construction industries. This economic transformation followed a recurrent pattern: a shift from cow-herding and milk-selling occupations to the transportation business (from bullock-cart to motor vehicle) and then into the construction business. A significant number of Yadavs in the Braj-Ahirwal area are involved in the real estate and building sectors. Since the 1970s, when the Mathura Oil Refinery opened, a substantial number of Ahir Para Yadavs have transported oil for the refinery on a contract basis. Those Yadavs who did not go down this path sought jobs in the army and the police, the other two traditional spheres of occupation for Ahir/Yadavs in northern India.

More recently, working for the government has become one of the more esteemed avenues of employment, especially amongst the new generations who benefit from caste reservation. In Ahir Para the number of people involved in the milk business is not very high and has decreased with the years. However parallel to these mainstream occupations there is also a realm of illegal activities: extortion; 'protection'; usury; and petty criminality. And they are widespread, even if difficult to assess in a systematic way. The Yadavs of Ahir Para are often described by outsiders as *goonda*s (strongmen). This unsavoury reputation is further linked to the political involvement and connections of a number of local Yadavs as fixers and brokers, and to their muscular culture (Michelutti forthcoming). Local Yadavs are extremely politicised. For a start three out of four ward representatives of Ahir Para/Sadar Bazaar area belong to the Yadav community. In almost all Ahir Para/Sadar Bazaar households, there is at least one person involved directly or indirectly with local politics or who has relatives who are ward representatives, village representatives or MLAs or MPs in nearby towns and villages. Similarly, a very high proportion of the local Yadavs personally know someone in politics, and on a regular basis they contact politicians in their constituency. Yadavs clearly have more political connections than other communities in Sadar Bazaar. Ahir Para/Sadar Bazaar Yadavs are not only very well connected 'politically', they are also highly active politically. Moreover, such political activism is not limited to a marginal elite group. Most local Yadavs vote; they are members of political parties, they actively participate during election campaigns and they love to talk about it. But why is it so? Why are Yadavs in Mathura so highly politicised and why are they more politicised than other local communities which have similar economic and political recourses and incentives?

Almost two years of participant observation in the neighbourhood taught me that 'factionalism' is one of the driving forces of local political socialisation and participation. Internal divisions had the indirect effect of introducing 'democracy' to the neighbourhood. Since the 1960s, the 'democratic' political socialisation of the majority of local Yadavs has been mainly carried out by the 'fever' of the municipality elections which is the arena where disputes between local factions are played out. Most Yadav males begin their political career or interest in politics at a very young age by helping their father, grandfather, uncle or cousin in their campaigns for the municipality elections. This active participation in the local political process also introduces them to the city and to district party politics. It is my suggestion, therefore, that the high political participation found amongst the Yadavs of Ahir Para partly has its roots in the political 'battles' provoked by the rivalries within the community. I will now provide ethnographic evidence of how factionalism enters the local political arena. Thereafter I will try to explain how endemic factionalism is also linked to a particular kinship structure which has been revitalised by electoral democratic politics.

Ideologies of descent, 'primordial factionalism' and local elections

To begin with I should emphasise that it has not been easy to live in the highly factionalised and violent world of the local Yadav community. In order to maintain an impartial position, and hence access to the different Yadav factions, during my fieldwork I lived in two different places. This choice matured after a couple of months of fieldwork and the realisation of the endemic factionalism and tensions present in the community. As noted earlier, Ahir Para is part of Sadar Bazaar which lies on the outskirts of the old part of Mathura. Sadar Bazaar is like a small town in itself and it is seen as Mathura Yadav 'urban territory'. It is composed of different *mohallas* (neighbourhoods) which are caste specific. During fieldwork I rented a house in the Sadar Bazaar locality from a non-Yadav landlord and a room in the centre of Ahir Para from a Yadav family. In the latter setting I had access to the social world of the 'Chaudhri Parivar', which represents one of the largest and politically powerful Yadav lineages of Sadar Bazaar; while in the former members of other Yadav factions, castes and religious communities felt comfortable to visit me. Moreover, these double living arrangements prevented me from being too closely associated with a particular Yadav faction and, to some extent, with the Yadav community in general.

In Ahir Para locality factions are more or less defined by kinship. Yadav kinship is strongly patrilineal. Local Yadavs are extremely conscious of their genealogy. In short, the largest kinship categories within the local Yadav community are the *vanshs* (lines of descent): the Yaduvanshi, the Nandavanshi and the Goallavanshi. Each *vansh* traces its origin to a heroic ancestor related to the mythology of Krishna. Progressing down towards smaller kinship units, the next unit after the *vansh* is the *got* (clan). After the *got* comes *parivar* (lineage and sub-lineage). Today, of all the segments mentioned the ones which play the largest role in defining the Yadav community are the clan and the lineage. The boundaries of the *vansh* categories are ill defined. Locally, when the concept of *vansh* is used to express rules of endogamy, it is usually understood as the concept of 'kindred of recognition' illustrated by Adrian Mayer (1960: 161). Accordingly, the boundaries of the *vansh* are subjectively perceived, and it is within its boundaries that marriage takes place. However, how fixed these boundaries are is very subjective and historically constructed (see Michelutti 2008: chapter 4).

Today an increasing number of people view their community as internally undifferentiated. Such ideas are accompanied by the popular assumption that contemporary Yadav subdivisions are the outcome of the fission of an original group: the descendants of Krishna; and that all the Yadav belong to a unique stock. It is to this vision that people refer when they claim to be Krishnavanshi-Yadavs. The emergence of the encompassing Krishnavanshi social category is an explicit sign of the decadence of 'traditional' Ahir endogamous kinship units. In contrast, the unit of exogamy, the *got*, and the localised portions of the clan, the *parivar* are still relevant. For the sake of the argument of this chapter I shall concentrate on the *parivar*. Generally, in fact, members of a faction are not individual households but minimal or maximal lineages (*parivar*). Locally the term *parivar* is used to talk about the localised segment of the clan (*got*) and about the group of agnates with whom individuals normally have direct contact. The 'Chaudhri Parivar' (the head family), the 'Dudh Parivar' (the milk family), the 'Phatak Parivar' (the level crossing family) and the 'Netaji Parivar' (the leader family) are the main 'families' of Ahir Para. However, they do not make up the entire Yadav population of Sadar Bazaar. There are many other small *parivars* which live in Ahir Para itself, or in the other *mohallas* of Sadar Bazaar.

During my fieldwork in 1998–2000, Ahir Para/Sadar Bazaar Yadavs were divided into two stable factions: the members of the Chaudhri Parivar and their allies, and the members of the Dudh and Netaji Parivars and their allies. The allied castes were composed of other Yadav clans and other castes which were linked with the main factions by patron-client relations. As will become clear in the following sections, the neat divide between the Chaudhri Parivar, Dudh Parivar and Netaji Parivar was determined by the battle for the pursuit of local power and for honour. Although active faction membership is confined to men, the women are not completely excluded. Women whose husbands belong to different factions are not supposed to talk to each other, even if they come from the same natal place.

Factions and their allies seek to promote their own interests and activities rather than those of their community as a whole. Among each faction, members have close interactions. They go to the same wrestling gymnasium and tea stalls. Members consult each other on matters related to business and marriage. In particular, it is during the process of marriage arrangement that cooperation and solidarity between members of the same faction become most visible. By custom, the most prominent men of a faction visit the family of the prospective bride 'to check' her background. Marriage arrangements thus rely on the approval of faction members. At the marriage ceremonies those who belong to hostile factions are not invited.

On a day-to-day basis, members of the different factions spend a great deal of time gossiping (*gap-sap*) about members of rival factions and making 'plans' to put them in a bad light. For example, two months after my arrival in Ahir Para my bicycle was stolen from in front of the house of the leader of the Chaudhri Parivar. Members of the Chaudhri Parivar immediately blamed the members of the Dudh and Netaji Parivars. They said the theft should warn me about the bad nature of the other two factions. They are thieves (*cor*), I was told. By the same token, members of the Dudh and Netaji Parivars told me that this episode should open my eyes to the 'bad' (*badmash*) and 'criminal' nature of the Chaudhri Parivar. According to them, nobody in Sadar Bazaar would have the courage to steal from the house of such a powerful man in broad daylight. In their opinion, only a member of the Chaudhri Parivar could have done it; 'to put us in a bad light'. The bicycle episode is one of many disputes which, most of the time, were created 'out of nothing' to maintain and feed hostilities and rivalries between the different factions. On many occasions these disputes sparked violent confrontations, which mainly took the form of *lathi* (bamboo sticks) fights between the young males.

Rivalry manifests itself not only between different factions but also within factions. Non-Yadav informants often told me that amongst Ahir Para/Sadar Bazaar Yadavs there was no recognised leader because every Yadav wants to be the chief. On several occasions local *Banias* (the merchant caste) made fun of their Yadav neighbours' endless rivalry. They said that each Yadav believes he is Mulayam Singh Yadav and wants to be the boss.[7] This internal competition is expressed daily by 'talking badly' about everyone who is perceived as a competitor. The atmosphere between the different factions in the neighbourhood was often incredibly tense, and violent confrontations between them regularly occurred during my fieldwork but they became more intense during election times.

Local municipality elections are the arena in which factionalism, personal issues and economic interest are fought over (Michelutti 2004). The pursuit of local power is driven by the urge to obtain a share of state resources. To be a municipality representative has its practical advantages.

[7] Dipankar Gupta describes how also amongst the Jats of western Uttar Pradesh, every Jat thinks of himself as a *chaudhry* (headman) (Gupta 1997: 154).

To each ward representative a certain budget is yearly assigned for the development of the local area. Allegedly, part of this money usually ends up directly in the representative's pocket. Furthermore, a ward representative has access to the state administrative machine, which provides access to government employment and to jobs or contracts. Each of the *parivars* struggle, therefore, to get one of their members elected to the *Nagar Palika* (municipality board). The ethnography of the municipal by-election for Ward 2, held on 18 April 1999, shows how local elections are used to sort out personal interests as well as questions of honour. Ward 2 includes a part of Ahir Para. This section of the neighbourhood is better known as Regimental Bazaar and it is under the Cantonment Board administration. There are a total of 870 registered voters in the ward. It is inhabited by Yadavs (300 votes), Dhobi (200 votes, who are members of the SCs), Valmiki (75 votes, who are also members of the SCs), Brahmans (50 votes), Brahman-Carpenters (50 votes), Muslims (100 votes), Christians (60 votes), and others (35 votes).

Arjun Yadav, an advocate and moneylender in his early forties and a member of the 'Dudh Parivar', was elected in 1992. At the time, he defeated Shiv Yadav, a member of the 'Chaudhri Parivar'. In 1998 he contested again and was beaten by seven votes by Shiv Yadav, who died six months later from a 'heart attack'. The 'Chaudhri Parivar' accused the 'Netaji Parivar' and the 'Dudh Parivar' of killing him. The stories behind the 'homicide' are highly contradictory. Needless to say, the atmosphere in Ahir Para became even more tense than usual.

When the by-election campaign was finally called on 27 March 1999, such acrimonies became even more explicit. Shiv Yadav's son, J. B. Yadav, contested against Arjun Yadav. Amongst the other candidates were G. S. Yadav and V. Yadav, both local young BJP activists who tried to create a third front. When the election campaign began all the residents got involved in it. The men of the different factions sat outside their houses with the voting list in their hand discussing in little groups. They had the air of planning a war and they looked as though they were really enjoying the 'election game'. Needless to say, all the candidates asked me to campaign for them. They were not only thinking that my support would have been of general benefit for them, but were also aiming to mobilise the Christian votes and 'who better than a Christian from Italy to do it?' Arjun Yadav said, 'you are the Sonia Gandhi of Sadar Bazaar'.

The election campaign was extremely important because each vote really mattered. The 'Chaudhri Parivar' was confident of being supported by all the Yadavs of their clan (*Jaweria*) and by the Dhobis. The Muslims and the Valmikis were regarded as 'Arjun' votes. In the evening, the candidates and their followers canvassed door to door. The 'Chaudhri Parivar' offered saris and fabric in exchange for votes, Vinob Singh, an uncle of the contestant, said 'we do not buy votes we just make presents'. However, Arjun Yadav bought the votes of the Valmikis and Muslims for two hundreds rupees a piece.[8] The battle for every last vote was a matter both of honour and interest. Out of 870 votes, only five persons did not go to vote because they were either in bad health or out of town. Such high turn-out reflects how seriously local people took the election. J. B. Yadav won by a margin of fifty-two votes.

The 'Chaudhri Parivar' organised a party to celebrate his victory. In the evening, the youngest men of the *parivar* walked through the streets of the bazaar screaming 'J. B. Yadav *zindabad* ('long live J. B. Yadav') and '*Jai Sri Krishna*' (hail the victory of Lord Krishna), while shooting in the air with their guns.[9] The death of J. B. Yadav's father was partly vindicated and the honour of the family re-established.

Winning an election, then, does not only mean gaining state resources. These are not the only fruits of politics. It is a question of honour as well. The passionate political participation during the municipality election campaign mirrors, after all, the intense feeling of competition and rivalry that exists between the different *parivars*. In Ahir Para, informants also explicitly said that rivalries within their community are endemic and do not only concern material resources. Rivalries are considered ancestral. Paradoxically, the same symbols of Krishna and the ancient democratic Yadavs, which are so often mentioned as symbols of a successful and united community, were also used locally as metaphors for expressing the 'primordial' origin of rivalries existing within the community. Various local tales try to explain this 'ancestral' phenomenon. Most of these tales have as a protagonist the god-ancestor Krishna and narrate how the Yadavs are the cause of the death of their ancestor and of the endemic rivalries within their community. Amongst these tales the most commonly known in Ahir Para is the one about the curse of *Durvasa Rishi* (sage). The tale goes like this:

> A group of Yadav children went to play nearby Durvasa Rishi. They covered their bellies with a metal plate (*tasla*) and asked the Rishi what he thought their

[8] Money was offered to the potential voters during the election campaign's door to door canvassing.

[9] Guns are very popular in the neighbourhood and usually every male adult possesses at least one gun or rifle.

> bellies were covered with. Very annoyed, the Rishi answered: 'whatever it is covering your bellies, that will be the cause of your destruction and endless battles among your people'. The children got scared and went back to the elders and told them about the incident. The elders said the words of the Rishi could not be untrue and ordered the children to destroy the metal plate. With the help of stones, the children broke it into pieces, and then into powder. In the end, only one small piece was left, and they dropped it in the Yamuna river. A fish then ate the metallic piece. When a fisherman opened the fish and found the small piece of iron, he kept it and used it as a spear to hunt animals. He went to the forest to hunt and, taking him for an animal, by mistake he shot the toe of Krishna, who died.

As Vinob Singh said: 'Yadavs will never stop fighting each other, we will never change'. Competition between different factions during the elections is, therefore, locally perceived as an old phenomenon. Equally during regional and national meetings of the Yadav caste associations it is acknowledged that Yadav internal rivalries are endemic and ancestral. Leaders tend to joke about this aspect of 'Yadav culture' and the audience usually responds by laughing. It almost appears that Yadavs are proud of their internal competitions and feud-like conflicts. For most it is further evidence that they are fighters and 'political animals': born to compete and rule. As A. P. Yadav said to me, politics after all, is about quarrels and fights and Yadavs are undoubtedly masters of that because they spend their life competing with their brothers. Undoubtedly internal divisions have had the indirect effect of introducing 'democracy' to the neighbourhood. Since the 1960s, most Ahir Para Yadavs have been introduced to politics at an early age by actively participating in the municipality elections.

A careful look to the biographies of local and regional political leaders shows that they all have begun their political careers or interest in politics at a very young age by helping their father, grandfather, uncle or cousin in the election campaign for the municipal council. This early political socialisation introduced them to the city and to district party politics. During the municipality election which I described previously children actively participated during the election campaign. They helped to produce the election campaign leaflets and they distributed them in the neighbourhood. More importantly they had a clear knowledge of how the electoral process works and why it was important for their *parivars* to win the election. The political scientist Mark Franklin has recently argued that people learn the habit of voting, or not, based on experience of their first elections (Franklin 2004). Elections that do not stimulate high turnout among young adults leave a 'footprint' of low turnout in the age structure of the electorate as many individuals who were new at those elections fail to vote at subsequent elections. Elections with high turnout leave high levels of footprinting. For the Yadavs of Ahir Para Sadar Bazaar certainly their first municipality election left an important 'footprint' that influences their participation into politics for the rest of their lives. And we saw how the high political participation found amongst the Yadavs of Ahir Para partly has its roots in the political 'battles' provoked by the rivalries within the community.

The political mobilisation of caste and the role of kinship

The fact that informants constantly explain 'factionalism' as part of the Yadav 'culture' is certainly intriguing and induced me to investigate whether there was something particular about the social-structure of the Yadav caste/community which determines high levels of factionalism. Indeed in the available literature, rivalries have been described as structurally endemic in communities such as the Ahir/Yadavs, Jats, Gujars and to some extent the Patidars (in Gujarat) and Marathas (in Maharashatra). In western Uttar Pradesh competition is likewise described as endemic: 'As nobody within the caste, and no caste by itself, enjoys pre-eminence, the rivalry is perennially there . . .' (Gupta 1997: 166). The Ahir/Yadavs like the Gujars, Jats, Marathas and Patidars all have a caste/cluster horizontal organisation. They share a pastoral past and a military culture. These warrior-pastoral caste-clusters are usually large, territorially dispersed and importantly informed by strong ideologies of descent coupled with an emphasis on internal equality and brotherhood rather than on the religious language of purity and pollution. Their status is often ambiguous. colonial ethnographers were undecided whether they were 'castes' or 'tribes' and whether they were Rajput (and hence Kshatriya- the warrior category) or Shudra (menial category) (see Tambs-Lyche 1997: 148). The Ahirs, together with Jats, Gujars and Rajputs, were considered to be tribal groups originally who had come under the influence of Hinduism and had then become castes (Kolenda 1978: 21). In this way their tribal customs, which they retained in their internal organisation, were causally explained. A certain kind of kinship and political organisation appears to characterise these 'tribal' castes. Jats, Ahirs, Gujars and Rajputs were divided into patriclans, which were patrilocal, patrilineal and exogamous. More recently Unnithan-Kumar has shown how castes related to a Rajput-like culture '. . . share a centrality of territorially defined lineal kinship in their lives which leads them to experience caste in ways both similar and, at the same time different from caste as we know it generally, i.e., as a set of agnatic and affinal groups dispersed over a wide territory' (Unnithan-Kumar 1997: 3). Similarly, the subdivisions of Kshatriya-like castes are of a different order than other caste communities. They generally have few 'endogamous' subdivisions and, conversely, are divided into numerous 'lines', 'branches' and 'clans' which have an exogamous character. In addition these 'loose structure' castes usually have a high degree of internal graduality (Pocock 1957, 1972) in terms of wealth, power and ritual. However despite class differences amongst these communities, their members maintain that they are all related to one another, however distantly, either by descent or marriage.

The heterogeneity inherent in the Ahir/Yadav caste, in terms of socio-economic and ritual status, has been depicted in many ways by colonial ethnographies and in the petitions and memoranda which historically document the dialogue between the colonial government and Yadav individuals or caste associations (see Michelutti 2008: chapter 3).

The Ahir/Yadavs have been portrayed not as rigid, bounded essentialist groups, but rather as a fluctuating, fluid and internally factionalised social category. Colonial ethnographers left a legacy of hundreds of pages of ethnographic and ethnological details which portray the Ahir/Yadavs as 'Kshatriyas', 'martial', and 'wealthy', or as 'Shudras', 'cowherders, 'milk sellers' and low in status terms. Comments by local officers from 'the field' reveal their inability to define consistent socio-structural patterns within the Ahir grouping. The lack of clear-cut endogamous rules and the imprecise and ambiguous status of the caste as a whole were amongst the main 'problems' that colonial officers seemed to face. Ahirs' recurrent structural ambiguities seem in fact to represent a 'hard task' even for such 'classificatory' masters as the colonial ethnographers. The Ahirs could not be classified as Rajputs because they did not follow the 'prescribed' Rajput codes of conduct, or at least part of the community did not. However, to classify them as Shudra would have neglected some of their 'Kshatriya' customs such as kin-based organisation, hypergamous marriage patterns, martial attitudes and landholding rights.

Such dilemmas were constantly reflected in the preparatory reports for the census and in the documentation related to the implementation of specific policies such as the Female Infanticide Act (1870), or the application of the 'Martial Races' theory that guided the recruiting strategies of the colonial government. The search for 'guilty' and 'criminal' clans, and the search for 'martial' clans within the Ahir community produced a valuable source of information on the nature of the kinship organisation as well as on the status dynamics present within the different Ahir subdivisions.

The critical analysis of these sources shows how, within the Ahir/Yadav caste cluster, although rules of endogamy were present at some levels, the community was mainly united by 'fictitious kinship', i.e. local alliances and affinities that bound groups of Ahirs internally and established links with other subcastes and castes (Rao 1977; 1979). Within the Ahir/Yadav 'caste-cluster', alliances between different segments, or sections of segments, amongst which no specific *real* genealogical relationship or connection existed, were common. Accordingly, the endogamous units within the community were never rigidly bounded and ranked; nor were they ordered following a sharp purity-pollution hierarchy. Rather, subdivisions within the caste were maintained by claiming different patterns of descent and different habits and customs related to territory and political power. In addition, each subdivision was internally characterised by differentiation of status, power and wealth. Such features contributed to the absence of a clear-cut ranking based on the ideology of purity-pollution and, importantly, to the attachment of status not only to endogamous groups but also to exogamous groups and clusters of lineages. Thus, different segments of the Ahir/Yadavs were not of the same order. This social system led to preferential hypergamous marriage patterns and to the breaching of the ideals of endogamy at the lower and higher levels of the caste/community hierarchy. In this system, since nobody within the castes enjoyed ascribed fixed ritual and social status, there was high internal mobility and the battle for economic and political resources was an integral part of it. Rival factions within a lineage or a cluster of lineages led by individual leaders tended to draw their additional political support from adjacent lineages. This created competing alignments in which personal networks of influence and power ran along and across lineages.

This structure is not dissimilar to the one I recorded in Mathura in the late 1990s. Actually, the 'tribal qualities' of the Ahir/Yadav kinship system, recorded in pre-colonial and early colonial times, are still resilient and have found a new vitality in modern caste society. Contemporary Mathura Yadavs place emphasis on 'the community' aspect of their caste rather than on the ideology of purity and pollution. Local processes of aggregation and fusion are legitimised by the assumption that, despite their subdivision and rank, all Ahir/Yadavs had the same origins: the ancestor Krishna and his place of birth, the town of Mathura. It follows that all the Yadavs are brothers. Hence today an increasing number of

Yadavs view themselves as members of a large kin-community which recognises common descent. This widely shared belief works against the internal status and cultural subdivisions which were already historically ill-defined.

By the same token the community is internally highly heterogeneous. Locally, prestige is attached to lineages rather than clans and there are *parivars* which are more prestigious and wealthier than others. Differences in the ritual sphere are not very sharp, so that inequality among local Yadavs is today primarily a product of economic and political conditions. Locally, the members of the different subdivisions are extremely heterogeneous in terms of wealth and power. Yadavs' economic variability is extremely visible. Well-off segments of *parivars* live close to poor ones and their different economic status is reflected in the outside appearance of their houses, in their internal decorations, and in the food they offer to visitors. This visible wealth disparity is supported by economic data collected amongst different Ahir Para Yadav *parivars* during the Mathura Election Study (1999).[10] These data not only show the economic heterogeneity present within the community but also that the Yadavs are amongst the most economically diverse castes in Sadar Bazaar. Brahmans are the richest caste in Sadar Bazaar (43 per cent rich compared with 14 per cent poor), closely followed by Banias (32 per cent rich compared with just 7 per cent poor). The other upper castes are fairly concentrated in the middle category (74 per cent) with relatively few rich and poor, as are the SCs (64 per cent middle), although to a slightly lesser extent. The Yadavs and the Muslims are hence the most economically heterogeneous castes in Sadar Bazaar. The substantial proportion in both the poorest and richest categories illustrates this.[11] Figure 9.1 shows the economic distribution of the Yadavs in Sadar Bazaar.

These data not only show the economic heterogeneity present within the community but also that the Yadavs are amongst the most economically diverse castes in the locality as well as one of the most mobile: a world where everybody wants to be the chief and where in practice everybody can become the boss. Aggregative strategies coupled with an extreme intracaste differentiation and socio-economic mobility have

[10] Mathura Election Study (1999). Survey deposited at the Centre for the Study of Developing Societies.

[11] Interestingly, the majority of the Muslims interviewed belong to the Meo caste community who claim Rajput ancestry and share a similar kinship structure with the Yadavs, Jats and Gujars, see Mayaram (1997: 132).

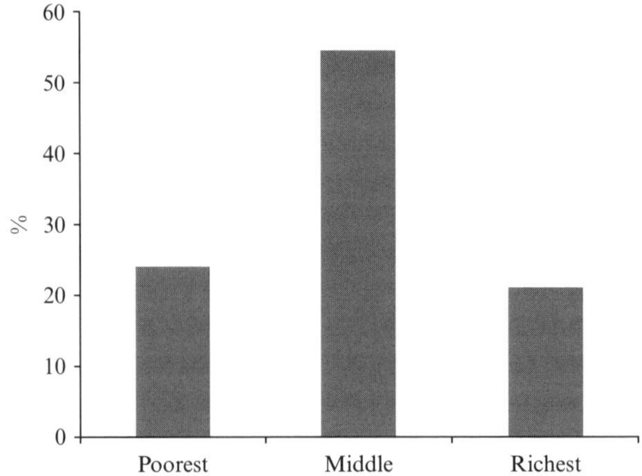

Figure 9.1. Economic distribution of Yadavs, Sadar Bazaar.
Source: Mathura Election Study, 1999.

been considered in the literature as phenomena directly linked to 'modern' processes of substantialisation (see Fuller 1996).

Indeed, today local Yadavs stress the 'uniqueness' of their caste structure by saying that Yadavs are not a *jati* but a *vansh*. When they use English they translate the word *vansh* as 'race'. By describing their community as a *vansh*/race, informants stress the horizontal 'caste-cluster' character of their caste, thereby stressing the idiom of kinship and descent rather than the idiom of religious hierarchy. Andre Béteille (1969: 45) has shown convincingly how the ideas of descent and race (understood in sociological rather than biological terms) are inseparably combined in the concept of *jati*; and in the light of available ethnographic data, I suggest that amongst pastoral 'caste-cluster' communities such a link is stronger than in other castes.[12] The exploration of Rajput-like horizontal cluster organisations leads me to suggest that to understand caste as a perfect segmentary system is an oversimplification which obscures the complexity presented by many caste/communities where a less clear-cut internal hierarchical and vertical social organisation is evident and where there is instead an emphasis on brotherhood and internal mobility. Furthermore, such a perspective conceals how processes of fusion are facilitated within caste/communities which traditionally were informed by

[12] For comparative ethnographic data on Rajputs see Richard Fox (1971); on Marathas see H. Orenstein (1963: 1–9); Lomova-Oppokova (1999) and Hansen (2001); and on the Patidars see Pocock (1972).

horizontal alliances rather than by vertical ones. It is perhaps not a coincidence that the most visible 'substantialised' and politically powerful Indian caste/ communities—the Marathas in Maharashtra, the Patidars in Gujarat, the Yadavs in northern India—have a strikingly similar social organisation and regional character. Thus I suggest that their horizontal cluster type organisation has found a new vitality in a 'modern' caste society that recognises *difference* and *equality* rather than a language of ritual hierarchy as an acceptable manifestation of caste. In addition it is equally plausible to suggest that the horizontal organisation of the Yadav community centred on descent, coupled with a significant amount of economic variability and internal mobility contributes to the high degree of observed factionalism which indirectly contributes to local political socialisation.

The political ethnography of the Yadavs and other comparative material on powerful politicised castes in India shows how some socio-cultural structures and political cultures are more prone to create room for ambiguity, and in so doing facilitate the process of the vernacularisation of democratic politics. Hansen (2001) shows, for instance, how the most effective processes of community identity formation usually occur when the constructed identities are in reality extremely 'imprecise'. He argues that 'the politics of identity is generally driven by the paradox that no identity, no sense of community, and no imputed property of a place ever can be self evident and stable' (ibid.: 2) and that 'The efficacy of a name, and thus an identity, in terms of fixing or accruing of meaning and connotations, depends, therefore, on its constant performance—in authoritative writings, in public speeches, images, songs, rumours and so on' (ibid.: 3). This form of 'political participation', I will add, thrives in communities/societies where socio-cultural structures are ambiguous and imprecise and create scope for rivalry, contestations and competition. These spaces are, in turn, made even more unstable by political democracy and become open to endless contestation.

The Yadav case study hence shows how, in order to understand the nature of caste cleavages in Indian democracy, one also needs to evaluate the local kinship structures and ideologies within which politicians and political parties operate. Political participation and mobilisation are in fact not isolated from socio-cultural processes and it is precisely by studying how they are shaped in spheres which are not 'political' *per se* (like kinship) that anthropologists can best contribute to the understanding of the dynamics of popular democracy (Spencer 1997). Such an approach has the potential to unravel why certain social and political cleavages are more apt to successfully exert their influence within the democratic political system rather than others. But, more generally, it highlights how political ethnographies offer the possibility of unravelling the complex interrelations between caste and politics by looking not only at what culture does to democracy but also at what democracy does to culture and society.

10

A Left Front Election

MUKULIKA BANERJEE

Summary. This chapter provides an electoral ethnography of a campaign in the state of West Bengal. The uniquely continuous electoral victories of the Left Front since 1977 in this eastern state of India throws up the puzzle of how a coalition of parties has achieved this feat in a country where incumbent governments repeatedly suffer electoral defeats. A thick ethnographic description of the campaigning process, tracing the numerous techniques, organisational hierarchies and political messages at every level of the state's population, provides some answers to this conundrum.

Introduction

ELECTIONS IN INDIA are largely met with enthusiasm and participation, especially in the rural areas and among the most disadvantaged sections of society. Over more than six decades, elections have emerged as the most important aspect of India's democratic record and are considered inviolable events that demand the participation of its citizens, who vote both out of a sense of duty and privilege. In short, elections are the most sacrosanct, secular, universal, public rite of modern India.[1] In general, elections are held with unerring punctuality and efficiency by India's Election Commission that is popularly voted the most respected public institution of India.[2] Further, the consensus that exists across all political parties for the EC's 'model code of conduct' during the election period is essential both for the smooth running of elections as well as the high

[1] See Banerjee (2007) for a greater elaboration of the notion of 'Sacred Elections' and for an analysis of popular discourse about them.
[2] NES Survey data.

Proceedings of the British Academy **159**, 243–266.

levels of popular engagement in electoral politics. In this chapter, I shall focus on elections as they have been held in the state of West Bengal between 1996 and 2005, during which the Left Front government has won two state-level elections and contested several parliamentary seats at the national level.[3] This particular government formed by a coalition of Communist parties has a unique track record in the history of Indian democracy of having stayed in power for over three decades by winning a consecutive series of free and fair elections. It is thus something of a conundrum and demands explanation.

Any analysis of how and why the Left Front has managed to stay in power in a country where incumbent governments are repeatedly voted out of power usually throws up a number of possible reasons. First, the most cited charge against the LF's victories is what its detractors call 'scientific rigging'. The term implies that over the years Communist cadres have perfected the art (and science) of bullying voters, having bogus votes cast in their favour, obstructing supporters of opposition parties from casting their votes by overwhelming the queues at polling stations with their own cadres and so on—in short, the LF won by cheating. Second, the LF is seen to win because of its pro-poor policies among which the introduction of the gender-blind minimum wage and registration of sharecroppers are the most significant. This is borne out in the pattern of the LF's vote share where its largest proportion of supporters live in rural areas and belong to the lower rungs of the social hierarchy. The third reason often cited for the LF's untrammelled success is the lack of any alternative as no other political party or coalition can match the LF's organisation or reach in West Bengal. The tussle between the Congress and the Communists in the 1960s and 1970s was replaced in subsequent decades by a tussle within the Congress between the disorganisation of the old Congress Party and the break away Trinamul Congress, whose main and only asset appears to be the whimsical but popular leader, Mamata Banerjee.

While all the reasons cited above are important factors in explaining the Left Front's electoral success, the truth lies in a greater elaboration of each of these. In this chapter, I will focus in some detail on the first reason, namely, the LF's electoral machinery and the charge of 'scientific rigging'. I will examine how the LF plans, manages and executes its election campaigns to examine the basis of this charge. But in order to understand the

[3] For a recently published volume on several ethnographic studies of the 1967 and 1971 Indian elections see Shah (2007).

significance of this account, it is also important to recognise the role of the LF government in West Bengal's life on an everyday basis and in the time that lapses between elections.[4] This also gives us some indication of how it manages opposition from other political parties outside of electoral time so as to reap the benefits of a decimated opposition at the polls.

In the thirty years or so in power the LF government has engaged in both coercion and, increasingly, in what Gramsci would call 'the manufacture of consent'. While its early decade of power may have been characterised by violence, the years of its more recent electoral victories may be said to be characterised by a forced creation of consent. Not necessarily the product of democratic consultation, Gramsci characterises the creation of consensus as an activity of the state, rather than of civil society, and one that is achieved without the use of force. The successful creation of consent ratifies the role of the state and endorses its indispensability in the regulation of social life. Analytically, in Gramsci, consensus is opposed to coercion, that is achieved through force, rather than persuasion. The 'hegemony' that is achieved through the creation or the 'manufacture' of consent, then, allows the state to dominate policy, ideas and activities such that the role of the state is naturalised and seen to be 'just so'. I have shown elsewhere the processes through which the Left Front government in West Bengal has created this consensus using its capillary organisation across the state and the role of its cadres down to the village level, who are entrusted with what I characterise as a sort of 'DIY hegemony' (see Banerjee 2008).

The main features of the LF's career in the past three decades of government can be seen to have passed through at least three distinct phases. In the first 'revolutionary' phase, lasting roughly until the 1980s, Operation Barga was implemented with numerous land grab movements initiated by sharecroppers. Cadres and leaders were created during this phase, as leadership was required to represent the interests of the *bargadar* (sharecroppers, strictly someone who cultivates the land of another person on condition of delivering a share of that produce to that person) against the entrenched power of the landowning classes. The resulting redistribution of land and more importantly the new found self-

[4] See Chatterjee *et al.* (1997) for an account of a Left Front campaign during elections in the 1990s in West Bengal. My account builds on their description as I have tried to systematically show how the Left Front campaign works at every level from a village right up to the party's headquarters located in the capital. My account is also informed by ethnographic knowledge of the party's everyday functioning at the village level, in 'everyday time' outside of elections.

confidence generated through challenging the status quo and redressing old power equations brought the Communists their first wave of support. In the second phase of the 1990s, this support needed consolidation. This was done by isolating all supporters of rival political parties, gathering support among 'the poor' i.e. sharecroppers and daily wage labourers, through a system of incentives and punishments and the takeover of all organisations, whether political or otherwise (e.g. football clubs, *puja* committees, school teacher's unions) such that little that happened in vast parts of West Bengal's public life was allowed to remain outside the gaze of the party.[5] In rural and urban areas alike, the local level comrades manoeuvred themselves (through their DIY hegemonic practices) into occupying positions where they were the sole and indispensable arbitrators in all disputes, applications and demands. Given that each local comrade was also a member of the larger party organisation which in turn controlled the resources of the State and government, the entire machinery of police, developmental grants, employment opportunities, and above all information were all marshalled in supporting this hegemonic capture. This second phase was the most brutal of all, and was repeatedly dominated by *shontrash*, 'terror'. Any opposition, whether through organised political parties or through individuals standing up to the writ of the local comrades, was summarily crushed through the use of violence, humiliation, inflicting personal tragedies on the families of the detractors, withholding all benefits from them and, in extreme cases, such people were simply killed.

After the 2001 state level elections, a newer phase can be said to have emerged when a sixth consecutive victory was won despite the vociferous opposition led by Mamata Banerjee. Most steam was spent on opposition camps; the fledgling units of Trinamul Congress that had sprung up in villages across West Bengal died an early death, crushed under the weight of the juggernaut of the LF's vast machinery. This last period also saw the LF government led by a new chief minister (from 2004), who sought to implement the national consensus across parties for greater private investment in industrialisation, in West Bengal too. This effectively allowed him to achieve three things, or so he hoped. First, attracting new industrial plants to West Bengal would provide much needed employment opportunities; second, it would give the LF a new programme of reforms which it

[5] In rural areas and small towns, even matters internal to families were open to scrutiny and arbitration of the cadres. As people describe it, the cadres kept track of the contents of every cooking pot (*haandhir khobor*).

desperately needed to produce after the twenty years that had elapsed since the introduction of Operation Barga; and finally, it allowed him to make his mark on Left Front politics, which had become virtually synonymous with his illustrious and patrician predecessor.

Outside of the proposed Special Economic Zones and new industrial areas the LF government continued to carry on the work of manufacturing consent in the traditional LF areas. In those areas the everyday violence of cadres was now no longer required, the capture of institutions was complete; rather it was saved only for 'trouble spots' such as in Singur and Nandigram, when any party or group dared to raise its head again or when land had to be forcibly grabbed away from farmers by the Communist government this time for its coveted new industrial plants. Any analysis of elections fought and won by the LF therefore has to be read with this track record in mind. The LF clearly stays in power through a combination of tactics, which in turn evinces a combination of wide ranging emotions from the electorate.[6] While there is much fear and trepidation among voters about the actions of the cadres, there is also much love and identification for the party in the same people. But whatever the emotions, everywhere in West Bengal people agreed that the LF and particularly the Communist Party of India (Marxist) ran a massive and efficient election campaign and it is to this election machinery that I turn my attention next.

I started with the CPI (M) headquarters in Alimuddin Street in Kolkata, where the main campaign strategy was designed. In stark contrast to government offices in Writer's Building, these offices exuded an air of calm efficiency, were clean and well maintained. Portraits of Communist leaders looked down on a computer, four telephones, a telephone directory entitled 'A Ready Reckoner' compiled by their official publication *Ganashakti* that lay next to it, and freshly labelled files containing among other things the detailed itinerary of the fifty to sixty guest speakers who would address campaign rallies across the state occupied a shelf. Twelve men at these headquarters coordinated the election campaign and then delegated work to the district and zonal levels where the real battle was waged. I started with them for it was these twelve generals who kept sight of the big picture, who 'mapped' the state according to estimated levels of 'safe' and 'troubled' seats, they made decisions

[6] See Michelutti (2008), especially pages 186–216 for a contrasting case of 'caste associations' and the role that they play during an election campaign in providing organisational support and in enabling it to make candidates 'visible', in the absence of a well-organised party machine.

regarding the pacing of the campaign, determining which areas needed extra inputs, where the guest speakers should be sent and how their movements could be orchestrated. For instance, it was customary for Politburo members of the CPI (M) to help with the campaigning but several of them being non-Bengali, for instance Harkishan Singh Surjeet (General Secretary in 1999), could be sent only to those areas in Bengal where the audience would follow Hindi.

The overall strategy for the 1999 elections had been to improve the Left Front coalition's performance by gaining two new seats among the 42 contested in addition to maintaining their current position of 33 seats from the 1998 elections.[7] In the 1999 elections, the hottest topic on everyone's lips had been the new alliance between the ruling BJP and the Trinamul ('Grassroots') Congress recently formed by the erstwhile Congress politician Mamata Banerjee. Having broken away from a moribund Congress whose poll prospects looked grim, Mamata had attempted to revive an opposition to the Left Front in West Bengal. The previous winter I had spent several weeks shadowing her activities as she had set about establishing herself as an alternative opposition to the Congress and as a potential candidate for chief minister. In those months she had captured something in the public imagination by her personality, down-to-earthness and her challenge to the seemingly invincible Communists. Her alliance with the BJP prior to the 1999 elections was meant as a tactical measure to marshal some funds into her fledgling campaign. Despite the modest scale of their operations, this small vernal grassroots Congress seemed to have caused a disproportionate ire among the lofty oaks in the Communist camp. 'How can this woman who is nothing but a drama *baaj* and looks like a maid servant challenge all the work we have done!" expostulated one elderly and *bhadralok* functionary when her name was mentioned. The temerity of the Trinamul Congress in challenging the mighty Communists at the polls despite the lack of a party organisation, their amateur efforts at vote rigging and their allegations against local party cadres of bullying their workers caused ridicule and anger. One of the workers brandished a copy of *Ganashakti* for an account of the biased coverage of the national government-controlled television station Doordarshan against the Communists. But minutes later when a journalist dropped in for pictures of the inside of the Communist party headquarters, no doubt impressed by its air of calm efficiency, he

[7] The outcome was not as good as this plan envisaged: in 1999 the Left Front was reduced to 29 seats, and the Trinamul Congress increased its holding from 7 to 8 seats.

was summarily dismissed. 'Why take pictures of us? We are volunteers, workers, we don't want ourselves advertised' was their response. About the blatantly communal agenda of the BJP, the criticism flowed more easily. One of them remarked, with little irony, that doing politics with the birthplace of Ram was for them to do politics with the birthplace of Jyoti Basu (who was chief minister at that time) or Karl Marx. But in response to my line of questioning, this gentleman was quick to modify his argument and he conceded that not all religious people were communal, which is why the Left Front had never stopped anyone from building temples or mosques.

While their criticism of the enemy was harsh, the general confidence in their campaign was undeniable. They were polite to the visitor but, as in all party offices, the guarded distance of these men in power remained. The 'generals' answered all questions with an eye on a vision but with a studied distance from the reality on the ground. Indeed many such strategists had been local party workers, but had proved to possess little crowd appeal, and so had been posted to more intellectual tasks. Elections, for these strategists, were not about the heat and dust of meetings, jostling crowds, about rhetorical speeches or about unexpected twists when a small party could suddenly attract voters in the middle of a campaign or about people changing their minds at the last minute. Rather, an election was about meticulous planning, delegating work through explicit instructions while maintaining their unshakeable belief in their ideology.

A more promising volubility was to be found in a well-known politician whom people had nicknamed the 'Professor of Electoral Engineering'. Curious about the mixed metaphors of erudition and pragmatism, I sought him out in Writers Building, where all ministerial government offices were to be found. He was a cabinet minister and the party sergeant-major par excellence. He enjoyed the reputation of one who could be relied on to ensure that thousands showed up at campaign rallies in Kolkata, and for facilitating voters to show up at the polls; rickshaw pullers for instance were known to vote out of sheer loyalty to this man. A large rough man, he spoke his mind loudly and clearly. The secrets of his popularity, he said, were basically two things: his extraordinary memory (exemplified in his ability to remember nearly 10,000 phone numbers off the top of his head) and his attention to maintaining relations with everyone 'from a cobbler to a Russi Mody'.[8] Describing the

[8] Mody was the Tata chief in Jamshedpur for many years.

forthcoming campaign, the numbers flowed easily from his memory. He explained the party's general strategy with the help of the example of West Bengal's largest parliamentary constituency, whose electoral size was nearly 1.6 million. His assessment of this constituency went thus: he figured that the voter turnout would be about 75 per cent i.e. 1.2 million voters would cast their votes. This meant they had to figure out how many of these 1.2 million votes would go the LF. The largest number of votes the LF had ever won in this constituency was 580,000 i.e. just under 50 per cent of the vote, and in the elections of the previous year, the LF had managed only 490,000. Thus assuming that everyone who had voted for the LF at the last election would vote for them again, there was still a shortage of 90,000 votes from their previous best. The strategy this time was therefore triangular, he explained. Though the Congress had won 120,000 votes the last time, he reckoned this time it would manage only 80,000. This time there was another candidate, an erstwhile independent but now the leader of the BJP in West Bengal. It was reckoned that he would win over 50,000 votes owing to his personal and social ties in the area. Another 20,000 votes would be spoilt votes. This took the number of votes the LF would not win to about 150,000. This left the LF with about 1,000,000 votes to play with, of which they required only 550,000. He concluded his assessment with an enigmatic smile and said, 'I have to ensure that we win those'. Of course the main issue was precisely how he would 'ensure', especially given his party's reputation for 'scientific rigging'. He explained further. Of the required 550,000, he could safely assume that a large part of the 490,000 votes that had gone in their favour would do so again. For, he explained, in the industrial belt of the state, voting was a tradition; 'almost like a superstition and party loyalties are like football loyalties, there is no logic behind this' he added. And he knew, like everyone else, that the most important part of the electorate for the Communists were the most disadvantaged sections of society, who had been the main beneficiaries during their regime. The fight for the rights of the disadvantaged, for humanity, had been the *raison d'être* of their ideology and this was what socialism did best—to serve basic needs, he argued. 'We show our support for the weaker sections and this is what makes them stronger'. But he also added to this lofty observation the rather patronising and widely used phrase among Communist leaders and cadres alike: *bostey diley chutey chai* i.e. if you invite them to sit down, they want to lie down. The implication of this remark was mainly that growing prosperity also changed needs and that people always want more, and that no amount of reforms were ever enough for an ever-demanding and needy population. Given that the Communists in West Bengal are among the very few Communists in the world who have (had to) survived in a robust democratic set-up, their characterisation of the fickle electorate should not come as a total surprise. Rather than being able to assume popular approval, this government had to constantly work harder at winning and maintaining their popular support. And support for the party, even for veterans such as the minister, was as unpredictable as the waves in the sea. To him there were always various undercurrents and it was impossible to predict the next big wave. This was the reason why wooing the 5–10 per cent 'unreliable' voters was so crucial, he argued, because they could swing either way. To prove his point, he cited an example from the previous year when the LF had lost a safe local Panchayat seat in a place where the Municipality had actually done some excellent work. But even he was willing to admit that the incidents of excellent work were extremely uneven across the state, that it had been a while since the party or the government had done anything radically new to challenge the status quo, and that they had no truthful answers for West Bengal's abysmal development record, despite being the highest rice-producing state in the country.

As 'Professor of Electoral Engineering' the minister therefore had to deal with the twin problems of a capricious electorate on the one hand, and a party running out of revolutionary ideas on the other. His solution therefore was to create the grandest spectacle that also carried people with it. This, he felt, could only be achieved by mounting a campaign that reached every voter and overwhelmed the electorate by its sheer and ubiquitous presence, and by having slogans that had an enduring message and carried a commitment behind them. Returning to the example he had used at the start of the conversation, he pointed out that in the forthcoming elections there were 70,000 new voters in this constituency, caused by improved voters' lists and first time voters. Of these, by the cadres' pre-poll estimation ('scrutiny') only 10,000 could be relied upon to vote for the LF. This left 60,000 of the new voters to woo but this would be whittled down to the more realistic figure of 50,000 because of 'erosion' (of party support). 60,000 votes, it will be recalled, was also the shortfall between the guaranteed 490,000 LF voters and the required 550,000 votes in this constituency. After 'scrutiny' of these new voters and their backgrounds by the local cadres of all lists across the seven Assembly constituencies that made up this large parliamentary constituency, it was their assessment that about 40,000 of these votes, if cast, could be theirs, subject of course to the mounting of the 'grand spectacle' of a campaign mentioned earlier. The juggernaut of the party machinery would make this happen he said, but 'It is my job to make sure that these 40,000 voters actually vote'. This, as I observed for myself, was achieved on polling day as a result of weeks of relentless pressure, in subtle and not-so subtle ways, of persuading people to cast their vote. The party hoped that their overwhelming campaign would keep the LF candidate foremost in the mind of the voter.

Concluding the discussion, the minister pointed out to me the irony in his account. 'All this huge election campaign is therefore mounted ultimately for those 40,000 voters', i.e. less than 5 per cent of the electorate, a story that was repeated across the state. And while he admitted that that is what electoral politics was about everywhere, there was also a veiled critique of the party and its policies. To his mind, the party's inability to recognise that they could not take the electorate's gratitude for granted and the need for revolutionary programmes to address people's growing needs was its biggest failure. 'Unless we are able to do this as a philosophy, as an ideology, we will continue to fail'.[9]

This was a remarkably candid observation for a powerful leader of a seemingly invincible party on the eve of a confident campaign. But the Communist Party was also a complex organisation within which most individuals were merely cogs in the wheel. The minister had clearly managed to carve out his niche as the man on the coalface among the more urbane and cultured leaders who desperately needed him to fight the heat of an electoral battle. But his modest ministry, rough manner and place in the campaign also indicated that his career in the Communist Party was limited.[10] While such men were crucial to the functioning of a mass based party such as the CPI (M), there was no room for such a personality in the ranks of its leadership. He must have realised this for his final ruminations were accompanied by a sarcastic smile: 'I can only guarantee that I will make sure our supporters show up to vote, but I cannot guarantee the result of the elections. But what I *can* guarantee are two things: "I cannot save the dead" and "I will never be a big CPI (M) leader".'

[9] This may seem prescient given the LF's poor showing in the 2008 Panchayat elections and the 2009 general election, but it could be argued that other factors were at work then. If anything, the poor judgements over forced industrialisation, using state-led violence, were perhaps equally important factors.

[10] In background and education, he was actually much closer to a politician like Mamata Banerjee, with her rough and ready ways, impulsive manner and ability to make a direct connection with the most common man.

Bolpur constituency

While a well-thought out strategy designed in offices in the headquarters and capital was crucial to a victory, the actual heat of a campaign could only be experienced by moving away from the air-conditioned offices and paperwork, to the streets, to the constituencies, where the actual electoral battle is waged. In a general election, the main battleground is the single-member parliamentary constituency. In Bolpur the incumbent MP was Somnath Chatterjee, a lawyer and a veteran of many campaigns. He was bidding for his sixth win from Bolpur in 1999. His main opponent was from the Trinamul Congress, also a lawyer, who was called Suniti Chattoraj, an erstwhile Congressman like most Trinamul candidates. Chatterjee dismissed Chattoraj as a *bot tola* advocate. This was to describe Chattoraj's rather modest make-shift practice under the large trees (called *bot*) outside the court buildings. Such advocates were known for providing bail payments and guarantees for criminals whom they then help escape the law. Such name-calling was symptomatic of the campaign in general. Chattoraj had been put up as a *bhumiputra* (son of the soil, as he was originally from Birbhum) to counter Chatterjee's origins elsewhere and his cosmopolitan links to Kolkata and Delhi. Like many Trinamul leaders, he had served as a Congress candidate in the past and had now joined Mamata's bandwagon, having given up on Congress's inability to mount a suitable campaign. Trinamul's main strategy for the coming elections had been to register a presence, and try to eat into the vote share of the LF parties. Winning seats was an unrealistic target, but they hoped that winning supporters would add weight to their political presence and give the LF a reality check on their dominance of the political landscape in the state. But in Bolpur, their efforts had been rather less lofty and had started by nicknaming the incumbent a *shaand* (a bull) ostensibly to describe his large frame and dark complexion.

Chatterjee was to be found on the outskirts of the town, camping for the duration of the campaign in a hired bungalow, which he called his 'election bungalow'. As Chairman of the Development Corporation he had access to other residences meant for officers on tours, which helped him travel around whilst campaigning. The MP for Bolpur was no ordinary MP. He had been voted Parliamentarian of the Year, was a veteran of several battles since 1977, and he subsequently went on to become the Speaker of the Lok Sabha in 2004. But even on the eve of his sixth election contest from the Bolpur seat he seemed to continue to relish the coming battle as though it was his first, although he was distinctly assured about his prospects. These were looking good enough for him to relax and ruminate on his career. He was originally from Hooghly district, but in 1977 two prominent leaders of the CPI (M)—Jyoti Basu (chief minister from 1977–2005) and Benoy Choudhury (chief architect of the radical Operation Bargadar)—had personally visited him at home inviting him to contest the difficult Jadavpur seat, rather than stand as an Independent candidate as he had planned. He won in both the 1977 and 1981 elections but then lost to the Congress candidate in 1984, a result he attributed to the pro-Congress effect of Mrs Gandhi's assassination. In 1985, he was rewarded with the vacancy in the Bolpur seat, and won the bye-election. Since then, he had seen his constituency grow from a relatively poor rural area with very little infrastructure to one where more than three-quarters had been electrified. A large part of the constituency was tribal and he seemed keen to target their basic welfare above others. He seemed struck most by the escalation of popular demands: small villages wanted more telephone exchanges spurred by the increasing proliferation of long distance call booths, areas which had no schools for girls fifteen years ago demanded higher secondary education and areas where there had been no roads now demanded 'all weather' ones. But then like his colleagues in Kolkata he felt that people had learnt to make more demands mainly because his government had started to give them something in the first place. *Bostey diley chutey chai* i.e. if you ask them to sit down, they want to lie down, he said, reiterating the minister's words. But thinking as an MP and as their representative he was proud that his constituents always demanded better resources rather than ask for jobs directly. This implied that they were not asking for handouts, but for greater developmental benefits that enabled new opportunities.

When I asked whether this instrumental imperative might have been the reason behind high voter turnouts, he disagreed. He attributed the high levels of turnout, instead, to what he called the 'consciousness raising' work of the cadres of the party, through which the cadres explained the importance of political participation, regardless of the actual party that people supported. But when pushed on whether this notion of participation in the abstract might lead to voters supporting rival parties too, he dismissed Mamata Banerjee's chances emphatically. Going over the well-rehearsed criticisms that were repeated endlessly at countless meetings and conversations, he enumerated the four main criticisms of her politics: communalism (for allying with the BJP), her support to a government in Delhi that had closed industries in Bengal, her support for too many imports, that had in turn led to the closure of mills in Bengal. One might have attributed the clarity of these criticisms to his legal mind, but in truth it was exactly the criticism of Mamata that every member of the party produced, from the generals of Alimuddin Street to a comrade in charge of a small village's activities. The uniformity of the message was striking, and even the order in which the criticisms were listed varied little. But later, watching him on the campaign trail while he spoke at meetings held under a blistering sun in the middle of newly harvested paddy fields, or at a dimly lit street corner meeting late in the evening in Bolpur town, his rhetorical ability to spin out these simple messages into hour-long speeches was in evidence. Like many Communist leaders, his language of erudition, his spotless white clothes, his familiarity with the political world in far away Delhi won him the awe and admiration among the audience of paddy farmers and wage labourers. Earlier while speaking in his rented bungalow, in the middle of delivering a litany of his party's achievements in his constituency, the phone had rung with news of the elections in Maharashtra where polling was in progress, and his excitement on hearing the gossip about fellow parliamentarians had been immediate. This ability to switch registers—from a local street corner meeting, to an audience with a visitor, to the gossip of fellow MPs—was clearly the hallmark of a parliamentarian. That Chatterjee belonged to many constituencies other than the Bolpur constituency that he represented in the elections put him in a different class from the rest of his comrades, and this gave rise to a curious but palpable tension.

This tension was dramatically in evidence in July 2008, when the Politburo of the CPI (M) expelled Somnath Chatterjee from the party. The reason was that he had declined to resign from his post of Speaker of the Lok Sabha in Parliament, despite the party's directive to do so. The Politburo had felt it was inappropriate for Chatterjee to continue as Speaker of a House in which the ruling coalition had lost the support of the Communists, thereby precipitating the trust vote. While this seemed shocking when it happened, it seemed entirely in tune with how the party saw its role in the career of its politicians. The famous debacle of Jyoti Basu (the Chief Minister of West Bengal from 1977–2001) being held back from the prime minister's job was a glaring example (Nigam 2000). But the philosophy of the party, i.e. the party organisation being the ultimate basis (*bhitti*) for all decision-making rather than any one individual, was a message that all cadres everywhere in the state were keen to reinforce. While this philosophy inculcated a strict discipline in the functioning of thousands of workers, there were also high-profile casualties such as Basu and Chatterjee. When I mentioned my meeting with Chatterjee to the comrade in my research villages, he narrated an anecdote that illustrated this belief in the party being the ultimate authority perfectly. The comrade recalled a time when Somnath Chatterjee, during one of his election campaigns, promised a school to a village which had petitioned him for one. Immediately after the meeting and after the petitioners had left, the local comrades (of whom 'our' comrade was one) told him off roundly. They pointed out that all he was permitted to promise, in return for votes, was to look into the matter. He was told that the actual allocation of a school was a decision that only the local party office could take, after consulting with all the local comrades and keeping the party's grand design for the whole district in mind.

This little anecdote revealed much. First and foremost, even 'ordinary' party workers felt they had the authority to tell a politician off, regardless of his stature in India's national parliament. They could do this not out of any personal impertinence but because they spoke on behalf of the party. The extreme egalitarianism that the term 'comrade' at least ideologically implied seemed to be in practice at least in this instance. Further, it was reiterated to Chatterjee (as indeed to his colleagues in Parliament) that while he may have been the man with the education and charisma to become a professional politician and electoral candidate, he was ultimately a pawn in the overall game plan of the party. His public appearances, the length of his speeches, the list of the party's achievements and promises, the mention of special issues local to where he was speaking, were all effectively scripted for him by his local party organisation. Thus at electoral meetings he had to be loquacious without getting carried away, reassuring without being smug, proud of his party's achievements without taking any personal credit—for it was an understanding that he shared with his party colleagues—that they were all in the end only cogs in a giant juggernaut.[11] So my next stop was another step down into the belly of this beast.

The party office

In an office in Bolpur, the biggest town of the parliamentary constituency of the same name, a group of men sat in an open-fronted office on the

[11] This was in marked contrast to the Trinamul candidate, who mostly designed his own campaign. He was supported by enthusiastic workers who met in various hastily rented unfurnished rooms, but these youngsters stuck together mainly through their hatred of the cadres rather than from a clear common ideological agenda.

main street in the bazaar. This was the Communist Party of India (M) office, of the sort that is ubiquitous on the landscape of West Bengal. Every district, town and block had its own office, which served as coordinating centres for the activities of their workers and cadres in each village, block and ward of the towns. In the Bolpur constituency there were 157 Gramanchals, 18 wards in Bolpur town and 5 in the Vishwabharati university area of Shantiniketan. There were 199 polling booths and 149,700 registered voters, and each polling booth covered 1,000 or so voters. To cover this area effectively, booth committees had been formed, 70 offices had been set up such that each ward had located within it two or three offices, thereby covering the catchment area of the 199 polling booths. Nearly 15,000 party workers covered the 199 polling booths and that effectively meant that about 70 workers covered each booth. This implied that about one party worker was assigned to every 12 voters, a breathtaking level of contact with the electorate.[12] It also meant that about 10 per cent of the electorate were themselves working for the party and the members of teachers' councils, student bodies and farmers' unions who pitched in extra hours during an election campaign made this possible. It was these workers who made contact with their assigned voters when the election was imminent to ensure they had their voter ID cards in place, helping them with the paperwork, accompanying them to get these done if need be. In the following weeks, they kept in touch, dropped in for news, brought round dummy Electronic Voting Machines (EVMs) when they were first introduced and chatted with people about their expectations and grudges. While party workers at this level had little influence within the party, this exchange and contact allowed them to serve as eyes and ears of the party and it allowed voters the satisfaction of having had some sort of contact with the party. It made people look forward to elections as the time when they could air their grievances without fear and could even make fresh demands, which the party workers were forced to listen to. Both sides knew that nothing would come of these airings, but it provided the semblance of responsiveness, which could be a crucial factor when the electorate is faced with tall promises from all political parties. As one woman said with a sarcastic smile one evening, after the two party workers had left her home, 'without us they are nothing!'

[12] As Chatterjee *et al.* (1997: 146) note: 'On a conservative estimate, the Left Front mobilizes something like two million campaign workers in the state for an electorate of about forty million.'

On entering the party office that overlooked the busy main street in Bolpur bazaar, I could see that this was a specially rented space underneath their permanent office on the floor above. It had more an air of a field office than regional headquarters, it had no furniture, no pictures of Communists on the walls, which were otherwise common in all CPI (M) offices, and there was no door to walk through. There were several party members, all men, squatting on the hired rugs on the floor and the air was one of calm confidence, as workers relaxed and chatted, surrounded by tied bundles of pamphlets and flyers ready for distribution. They seemed to be engaged in a game of quiz about the margin of victory in particular seats in past elections. Each tried to outdo the other in getting the exact numbers of votes right, as well as details of the particular contest, not unlike men of the same age who show off their knowledge of cricket scores. In the parliamentary constituency of Bolpur this main field office in turn coordinated with block and village level ones. The office also served as an entrepôt for supplies of campaign material, pamphlets and posters, and as a communication room for schedules of future meetings and itineraries. It was a resting camp for party workers who dropped in there once a day during the campaign to gather news from other parts of their constituency and to report on how their own efforts were going. This was the office that determined the pacing of a campaign in a constituency.

Sustaining a campaign for a period of nearly four weeks took meticulous planning. From six months prior to when the elections were likely to be held (and this has been reasonably predictable in a number of Indian states and very much so for West Bengal for at least three decades), workers at the headquarters of the CPI (M) started the process of overall planning and strategising for the state. The LF usually started its campaign at a low intensity but persistent contact with the voters that gradually built up to a crescendo on polling day. Workers at the assembly or parliamentary constituency headquarters, such as the one in Bolpur, mapped out how such a campaign could be adapted to the specific needs of their particular constituency. The campaign was therefore divided into several phases, with each phase associated with specific activities and lasting for a predetermined period of time. In the first phase, soon after elections were announced, a detailed 'scrutiny' of the constituency was done.[13] This involved a 'mapping' of the constituency according to residential patterns of urban, semi-urban and rural areas. The caste and religious profile of each of these areas was then confirmed, as was the

[13] 'Scrutiny', like many other English words such as 'party' and 'vote', has entered Bengali.

gender ratio. New voters were identified as well as those who had passed away since the last elections. Further, the pattern of votes cast at each polling station at the previous elections was scrutinised to identify patterns of potential retractors and supporters according to location, age, gender and community.[14] Added to this assessment was the record of any developmental benefits that the government had provided since the last elections. Also, areas that had made repeated demands for a particular school or hospital were noted as were those that had been recent beneficiaries. The activities of local cadres for the Party were also assessed and compared to others. In this crucial phase of 'scrutiny' and planning, the party cadres found that their year-round involvement in the affairs of their local beats is what gave them an excellent understanding of the particular nature of the area. As two school teachers observed to me, 'We don't know how they know, but the party workers *always* seem to know if we have voted for them. They know from the way we talk, hold ourselves, our general mood, what we are thinking.' Even among their detractors, they were aware of the reasons why people did not vote for them, the reasons for which could vary considerably between classes and men and women. Thus for those 'mapping' their constituencies, the population within was imagined in very specific and idiosyncratic ways such that the information available to them was broken down to the village and ward level for each of the above factors. Thus, for instance, Bolpur town for them was no longer a large urban space but a collection of single wards, identified mainly by their varying degrees of support for the party. This overshadowed any other identification of class or neighbourhood. The workers remapped all areas according to specific criteria aimed only to achieve electoral victory. This initial scrutiny then generated the overall strategy and campaign for the constituency. The mapping at this stage was still done in broad-brush strokes, identifying areas where votes were assured, others where this was not the case, and those in the middle who were undecided. This picture was gradually filled in with greater detail as the work of the campaign began and freshly gathered information during increased contact with the voters themselves was fed back to the

[14] The practice of 'mixing' votes from various polling stations in a constituency has changed several times over past elections. Initially, when paper ballots were used, votes were mixed before counting so as to make it impossible to identify particular local patterns of voting. With the introduction of EVMs it became possible again to disaggregate the constituency vote into those from particular polling stations. In the elections of 2009, the Election Commission reintroduced the system of 'mixing' to avoid the possibility of tracing the provenance of particular votes.

campaign headquarters. This careful mapping then determined the nuances of the campaign. For instance, in 1999, the opposition's political alliance with the Hindu right wing BJP provided an argument for the Muslims to vote against them. Accordingly, particular messages tailor-made for a particular ward with a concentration of Muslims were agreed and used in the door-to-door campaign. In wards where a particular complaint had not been addressed, campaigners were armed with ready answers and palliatives. The phase of increased interaction also revealed which voters did not have the requisite papers and voter identification cards that the Election Commission had made mandatory since the 1990s. Among illiterate voters, cadre members would help them have these made by accompanying them to the local block or municipal office, filling out the forms for them and in generally providing much needed moral support.

The example of the *Shorbo Bharat Ganatantric Mohila Shomiti* (the All India Democratic Women's Association (AIDWA), or women's wing of the Left Front cadres in West Bengal) provides an illustration of the work done by the cadres during this phase. In 2001 I shadowed a particular cell of the AIDWA. The election was still a month away and they were out three times a day visiting various households on their beat. For them, the campaign was an intensification of what they did all year round. In the eighteen Wards covered by them, each ward had a women's committee and teams which visited the homes of their 2,600 members, as well as those who were not yet so. As they canvassed door to door, and talked to people, they asked them questions—about communalism, riots, basic needs. Although they claimed 'We can tell by looking at a house who they vote for', they insisted that they took on board the requests of all, regardless of their party loyalties. Complaints were listed once a month when zonal committees met, and then these were fed back to the party office. Since many such complaints were about domestic problems such as persistent but unsuitable suitors 'harassing' their daughters, the party attempted to solve the problem in the first instance through arbitration. If this did not work, they appealed to the police because, as they said candidly: 'In West Bengal at least, the police listen to us because of party pressure'. As women they felt they had little power in society, but as the women's wing of the party, they experienced a surprising amount of respect from the police. Their efforts were mainly directed towards poorer women who they felt had to be empowered enough to take a stand on issues, become trained and eligible for the increasing quotas available for women to be represented on local Panchayat Committees. Their growing sense of self-respect and their increased personal security—

missing in the early 1970s—was their biggest achievement. They held meetings at regular intervals at various levels of organisation. They had continued to campaign for equal wages for women labourers, and this had won them the loyalty of 90–5 per cent of the large tribal population of the constituency. The Rs. 8 a year membership fee to a union had won them bonuses, maternity leave and medical expenses that made their situation better than women in other places. For large sections of the migrant worker population efforts were concentrated on literacy drives, learning to read numbers so they could identify bus numbers and to sign their names.

It was clear that through their work in this initial phase of the campaign, the members of the AIDWA were sufficiently familiar with the households in their beat to make a realistic assessment of the likely vote pattern in the coming elections. They knew for instance that among the poorer sections the vote was completely polarised: people had already made up their minds whether to vote for them or not. In their reckoning, the few undecided voters were invariably drawn from the middle classes and when they checked this assessment at the Zonal Presidents' meeting, where they had access to the records of previous elections, they found that apart from a few percentage points they were invariably correct. In this particular election, they not only predicted victory, but also the margin of victory. In their assessment, the local MP would improve his vote share by 10,000–15,000, increasing his final tally to about 275,000. They attributed this rise to the increase in subscriptions to the party. Every family was invited to and allowed to contribute only Rs. 1. While the monetary significance of this sum was minor, its symbolic significance was enormous. It made people identify with the party and, more importantly for the campaigners, it helped them make a well-judged assessment of forthcoming electoral support. To provide some idea of numbers, since the last election, in the Bolpur Assembly constituency itself (a part of the larger parliamentary constituency) of the 415,000 families, over 35,000 families had already made a donation to their party. In just one ward (where we happened to be having this conversation) they had managed to raise Rs. 14,000–15,000, a larger figure than in previous years, and they had not yet approached everyone.

In the second phase, the more visible aspect of the campaign came to light: the posters, 'walling'[15] with political murals, buntings and flags. By

[15] 'Walling' is a wonderful Bengali neologism drawn from English roots. Cognate words include 'lining' (electricity) or 'training' (travel by train).

this time, the coordinators would have identified walls suitable for painting murals of political leaders and messages. They commissioned cartoons lampooning the opposition and verses which explained their ideas to the general public and these were painted, stuck and imprinted on every available space across the West Bengal landscape. This involved coordinating artists, painters, handbill stickers, printers and transport. Towards the end of the second phase, the first consignment of handbills and party manifestoes would be distributed at the doorstep and on street corners.

In the final phase of the last two weeks before election day, dummy ballot papers or EVMs, and voters' identification numbers would be distributed during the door to door campaigns, which by this stage in the campaign took place three times a day. During this period the local MP would, over a typical two day period, be required to attend a big public meeting in a village adjacent to the brand new highway built with his support at the centre, where people from surrounding villages would be brought, flag off a cycle rally organised by the youth wing, address another rally in the vast Bolpur Maidan, meet with local intellectuals and journalists in the library of the town hall and at the end of the second day, address a meeting that would be the culmination of four processions from different parts of Bolpur which would converge in the main market centre. The schedule was determined almost entirely by the party organisation and the individual contestant merely followed the programme he was given.

A typical large public rally in West Bengal was similar to such gatherings elsewhere in India. Like village fairs, they were held in open ground with good access routes and thousands of people travelled to them using various means of transport, some walking several kilometres, and even camping overnight with bedding and food. Vendors sold tea, trinkets, and toys and political memorabilia were ubiquitous on the grounds. Political meetings were usually announced to start at a particular time which usually marked the start of a long afternoon and evening, the culmination being the much anticipated speeches by politicians. At one of the Left Front meetings I attended, the incumbent MP of Bolpur, Somnath Chatterjee, was the main speaker. Addressing a crowd of about 3,500, under a blistering sun, dressed in starched white *kurta* and pyjamas, he arrived just as the last of the more raucous and inexperienced preliminary speakers were finishing. His speech immediately established his greater erudition and experience. He started in the quiet, sophisticated tones of the metropolitan lawyer that he was, slowly growing in timbre and volume as he recounted the injustices of all other political parties functioning elsewhere in India, the hegemony of the United States of America in dictating national agendas of all countries in the world, the commitment of his own party and its allies to serving the poor and so on. Not once was his opponent and his political party in the coming election even mentioned. His was meant to be the speech of a patrician politician and that is what he duly delivered.

In the final phases of the campaign, as election day drew even closer, the tension mounted palpably. Meetings were held more frequently, the processions got larger and more prominent, auto-rickshaws, fitted with loudspeakers, traversed roads continually blaring party messages, and the number of visits by cadres to individual households increased during the day. In West Bengal, the presence of the CPI (M) and its allies in the Left Front dominated everything and was inescapable. For the cadres, the elections clearly brought a lot of extra work, but these workers insisted that it also brought excitement. 'An election is like an exam' as the local comrade said to me. 'We work hard for two months to get good results, but we also keep working before that.' These foot soldiers of the party had duties all the year round and the election campaign was an intensification of these existing jobs. What made their work easier, compared to say other political parties, was the clarity of the message they had to carry to the voters. As pointed out earlier in this chapter, there is a remarkable consistency to be found in the interpretation of policy, the linguistic formulation to convey it and sometimes even the body language that accompanies the message down the party organisation. For instance, when faced by some women in a completely dark *busti* (slum) in the middle of Bolpur city who demanded electricity so that their children could their homework, the response of the AIDWA worker was: 'How did you even learn to ask for this much? If we hadn't improved your lives already, you would not even have known about electricity, which of course is now the next step.' After we had left them and were walking to the next settlement, they muttered with ill-concealed disdain: 'these people! *Bostey diley chutey chaye*,' thereby echoing the minister and the MP. This kind of paternalism is the hallmark of the Communist parties and this particular message was repeated at every level of the party organisation: the minister's office, the headquarters in Alimuddin Street, the district level office, down to the block and even to every comrade who lived in the villages of West Bengal. This itself was evidence of a well-organised campaign—the message was undiluted, there was a clear chain of command and every soldier had total loyalty to the party.

Another excellent example of the consistency of the 'party line' was to be found in their formulations about the main opposition leader, Mamata Banerjee. Among the women workers sweating it out in the dimly lit streets of the urban mess of Bolpur on humid evenings, one might have expected a chink in their armour, some secret admiration for a personality such as Mamata, who came from a modest class and background similar to theirs and who spoke their language. Instead what one heard was apoplectic anger, similar to that expressed by their *bhadralok* chiefs in Alimuddin Street. *Bisronkhola*, *unmad*—disorderly, out of control—were the words to describe Mamata. When pushed to consider whether having a woman as a head of a political party had some innate value in itself, they were quick to note that they preferred the fact that their party believed in training and empowering women and implemented the policy of reservation of seats for women in local Panchayat governments and this was infinitely more desirable than merely having a woman at the top. In fact, they were willing to argue the opposite, i.e. that Mamata Banerjee had let women down: her immodest manners did not inspire trust from men. Her biggest failing in the eyes of these obedient, hard-working women was not her political ideas, but her unpredictability and the extraordinary manner in which she expressed her politics. 'Sitting on a minister's car, lying down on the street outside Writers Building! Is this politics?!' they wondered. 'She may dress like us but her behaviour is anything but ordinary. If we had anyone like her in our party she would have been disciplined.' And therein, in a nutshell, lay the difference between the Left Front parties and their electoral opponents. If there was a touchstone that defined this party it was iron discipline and consistency. And it was this consistent and uniform message that the juggernaut hammered home, at every level of the electorate, and every day of the six weeks leading up to election day.

The post-election phase

It is no wonder, then, that the CPI (M) alone wins nearly three-quarters of the votes in some constituencies. In the elections described above, for instance, it won 70,000 of the 103,000 votes cast in Bolpur. But while other parties may rest on accolades, the CPI (M) has a further phase of activity, which is held after the elections, when analyses of election results are carried out, again at a disaggregated level, to identify trends, areas of high and low support and voter turnout. That the workers of the party returned to the doorstep *after* a campaign, even when they had won an election, was probably one of the most important reasons behind the loyalty of their supporters. The usual complaint against political parties nationally has been that they appear only when they need votes before an election and never when the voters need the politicians. Therefore any reappearance of party workers afterwards to thank and greet voters was indeed rare. In this post-election scrutiny, the poll results of each ward and village were gathered, both informally by asking people and from booth-wise results, obtained from the Election Commission. These findings were then aggregated to reconstitute this pixelated picture into overall trends for each constituency. The percentages of all votes were added up and any incremental losses and gains calculated. Assessments of strategies were made, identifying which plans worked better than others, which strategies needed revising and the follow-up actions required for promises made. MPs and speakers were analysed individually, and those who had made rash promises of schools and electricity without first clearing it with the party were reprimanded and damage limitation exercises were planned. While even though in the Indian electoral system vote shares matter less than the number of seats won, the party continued to aspire to win larger and larger sections of the votes. It was as if securing electoral victory was only a means to the end of complete dominance of all politics in the state.

Coda

In 2006 the Election Commission responded to widespread charges of 'scientific rigging' against the Left Front's electoral tactics by political parties in West Bengal and India. The opposition alleged that the LF was able to win every election since 1977 only because it had invented several hidden and 'scientific' tactics to rig the elections. While charges of booth capturing and outright violence were rare, the general sense in the media and the population generally was that the LF used more subtle tactics that were not obviously illegal but were nevertheless irregular. Examples of these methods of rigging were: making sure votes belonging to 'dead' and absent voters were cast for the LF; queues of large numbers of cadres at polling stations in areas where large numbers of opposition sympathisers lived deterred busy voters who had no time to wait; cadres intimidated voters at polling stations by hovering around the polling station in large numbers, and so on. To put these allegations to rest once and for all, the Election Commission decided to hold a different sort of election in West Bengal during its Assembly Elections of 2006. This was to be what it called a 'quiet' election, hitherto reserved for other 'problem states'. A quiet election has strict rules: no campaign materials can be displayed in public places, all political meetings are restricted by number, no 'walling' on private property is permissible, and all printed campaign materials are disallowed, as are amplifiers. From the description of a campaign provided earlier in this chapter, it is evident that this election would have to be an unusually quiet affair that would lack the pomp and circumstance usually associated with a campaign. In voting procedures too, there were strict new rules: voting would be held in five phases to enable minute observation of each phase, the personnel supervising the voting process had to be brought in from outside the state and officials were transferred to neighbouring districts and observers from other states were also brought in. Predictably, the Election Commission's decision was met with outraged indignation by the Communist leadership everywhere and specially in Bengal. The decision to apply rules that the Election Commission had hitherto reserved only for troubled states such as Bihar hurt Bengali pride severely. But despite the protest and having nearly risked a disqualification caused by their vociferous denouncement of the EC, the campaign eventually settled into its usual momentum. It was indeed a quiet election, so much so that if one did not actually know that it was imminent, one could have missed it. Yet, despite the noisy denunciations of the EC by the Communist leadership and cadres, popular support for the EC ran surprisingly high. 'At last we can make up our minds in peace' is how many people put it. People whose huts stood by the highways were thrilled that they did not have to fork out the extra cash to have to paint over LF murals once the elections had passed. The general atmosphere was calm, if a bit tense. But when the results were declared, nearly six weeks after the first vote had been cast, it transpired that the LF had not only won the Assembly Elections for a record seventh time, but it had improved its vote share further. The party had managed a victory again and it remains to be seen whether this trend will continue in the next elections.

In the 2009 general elections, however, the LF suffered a serious reverse. Mamata Banerjee's Trinamul Congress forged an alliance with Congress, its erstwhile parent and opponent. They succeeded beyond all expectations. What went wrong for the CPI (M) will, however, have to be the subject of another paper.

11

The Challenge of Representing the Complex Reality of India

JAMES MANOR

IF YOU ENCOUNTER a neat summation of a wide-ranging set of papers on India like this one, beware. It will mislead you. India—the most complex society and polity on earth—defies tidy summation, and so must any collection of sophisticated studies of it. The question to ask about such a collection is not whether it can be neatly synthesised (it cannot be), but whether it comes close to capturing the diversity of India.

The analyses in this volume go a long way towards that goal. We have here papers by leading authorities on India's society, economy, politics, culture and demography—and their various studies offer plenty of complications and incongruities. These arise less from disciplinary diversity than from the nature of India. *Within* individual chapters, we encounter incongruities in social relations, demographic and economic trends, plus further incongruities between different dimensions of individual problems, and often between levels in the political/administrative system, and between regions. This is true despite the authors' efforts to make their analyses accessible to non-specialists. Complexity and incongruity are inescapable in assessments of India. There are also clear differences *between* chapters. Some inspire optimism, while others are discouraging—and yet both sets of studies ring true. Encouraging and depressing realities coexist. Several chapters here deal with both at the same time. So if this collection leaves you with mixed feelings, then it has done its job and done justice to Indian reality.

To make sense of what appears in this volume, it may be helpful to provide a little context—to complement the other chapters, and to help readers understand why the many variations and incongruities which we find here emerge when serious analysts explore India. By considering these contextual features, we may discern a little more coherence in these studies than is apparent at first glance.

Proceedings of the British Academy **159**, 267–275. © The British Academy 2010.

In India change has long tended to occur gradually, not radically. Much of the explanation for that lies in its history. During the period of British rule, the old socio-economic order broke down in only one, comparatively small region of what we now call India. This occurred in Kerala where the socio-economic institution which provided the then dominant Nayar caste with the basis for its pre-eminence (the matrilinear *tharavad*) could not adjust adequately to the changes wrought by capitalism (see Jeffrey 1976). It is no accident that unusually radical political forces have gained influence in Kerala. But the main point here is that such socio-economic breakdowns did *not* occur in other Indian regions. There, change has come more gradually—and since politicians have developed a taste for incrementalism, politics and public policy have been less radical.

This becomes especially evident if we compare the succession of radical lurches to left and right that have occurred in China since the creation of the People's Republic in 1949 with political and policy adjustments (a much milder word) in India since independence in 1947. China swung sharply—indeed excessively—to the left in the 1950s, culminating in the disastrous Great Leap Forward. Then Mao's opponents forced a marked swing to the right—until 1966 when he countered with an even more extreme leftist campaign, the Cultural Revolution. And then, in reaction, came a similarly extreme turn back to the right after 1979, when market forces were (in their distinctive Chinese way) encouraged—eventually producing extraordinary economic growth and a startling increase in economic inequalities. Indian politics and policies over this period tended to shift back and forth between left and the right in a somewhat similar cyclical pattern. But in every case, we saw more cautious course corrections—gradualism rather than radicalism—which produced less disruption (and less dramatic results) than in China. And these adjustments in India have tended to occur in an uneven, piecemeal fashion which leaves large pockets largely unaffected—adding further to Indian incongruities and its unrivalled complexity.

Thus for example, the liberalisation of India's economy after 1991 was undertaken cautiously and incrementally, often by stealth. (For more details see Jenkins 1999.) It was pursued relentlessly enough between 1991 and 1995 (when it slowed markedly because a national election loomed) to bring about a substantial change that has so far proved irreversible. But by the standards of East and Southeast Asia, economic liberalisation in India has been—and remains—quite limited. This is true partly because coalition governments over the last decade have been forced by parties that have sustained them in power to go slow. But it also owes much to an intense reluctance among leading Indian politicians to trigger what one Southeast Asia specialist has called 'social change in fast forward' which follows from aggressive economic liberalisation[1]—because social dislocation might destabilise politics and threaten their prospects of re-election which are already rather dim (see below).

Leaders at the national level (as opposed to the state level in this federal system) necessarily became more cautious in their overall approach to governing after 1989 when it became impossible for any single party to win a majority of seats in the Lok Sabha (the dominant lower house of India's Parliament). In the years since then, as Oliver Heath and Yogendra Yadav show in their chapter, parliamentary majorities have only been obtainable through the formation of multiparty coalitions. Small, often regional, parties in these coalitions have imposed constraints upon leaders of the main parties in these alliances, forcing them to proceed more cautiously.

We have just noted that the coalition governments which have held power in New Delhi since 1998—led by the *Bharatiya Janata* Party (BJP) and by the Congress Party—have been forced by pressure from parties supporting them to proceed at a snail's pace with economic liberalisation. (Hence the impatience of interests that prefer rapid economic reform, noted in Vijay Joshi's chapter.) But there is more to it than that. The BJP was compelled between 1998 and 2004 to shelve most of its Hindu nationalist agenda because all but one of the twenty-three parties in its ruling coalition were unenthusiastic about it. And even more strikingly, the moderating logic of coalition (and at times, minority) government has curtailed the number of abuses of power committed by Indian prime ministers since 1989. In my view, only once since 1989 has an Indian prime minister been guilty of an abuse of power.[2] That provides a startling contrast with India between 1971 and 1989 when prime ministers with huge parliamentary majorities indulged in frequent abuses—and for that matter, with Britain under both Margaret Thatcher and Tony Blair, where prime ministers committed many more abuses than we have seen in India since 1989.

[1] I owe this phrase to Anne Booth of the University of London. She was referring, in a seminar discussion, mainly to Indonesia.

[2] The occasion was the bribery of Jharkand Mukhti Morcha Members of Parliament to support the government of P. V. Narasimha Rao in 1995.

This caution among political leaders partly explains why so few of India's national elections—only two of fifteen—have hinged upon what the French call an 'issue of regime'.[3] By that they mean an utterly fundamental issue about how a country is to be governed. Such issues only arise when leading politicians take radical action. One 'issue of regime' arose at the election of 1971 when Indira Gandhi—in a dramatic break with past practice—promised to 'abolish poverty' and duly won a landslide victory. Another dominated the next election in 1977 when Mrs Gandhi's failure to deliver on that pledge and her abandonment of democracy during the Emergency (1975–7) triggered another landslide—this time against her. But before and since that pair of elections, no 'issue of regime' has emerged because politicians have been too cautious and equivocating to permit it to happen.

Another key feature of the context for these studies is in part both an outcome and a cause of this cautious approach to politics and public policy. The unparalleled complexity of Indian society gives people there an extremely broad array of identities upon which they might focus at any given time. These include linguistic identities, and sub-identities within them based on dialects; religious identities and sectarian sub-identities within them; three kinds of caste identities (*varnas* or large sub-divisions, *jatis* or endogamous groups, and *jati*-clusters); national, regional and sub-regional identities; plus class, urban/rural, and gender identities. Most of these identities cut across and thus undermine one another. And crucially, most Indians have tended not to fix their attention—fiercely and permanently—on any one of these identities, as people in for example Sri Lanka have done. Indians have tended to shift their preoccupations from one to another, and then another of these identities—often and with great fluidity. (For further details see Manor 1996.)

This mercifully prevents tension and conflict from building up along a single fault line in society. It also prevents politicians who seek to fix people's attention on a single identity from making much headway. This is bad news for Hindu nationalists who emphasise religious identities, and for leftists who stress class. It provides major advantages to parties which are less ideological and which are therefore better able to respond flexibly to fickle shifts in the popular mood. This creates strong incentives for

[3] This number includes the 2009 election which, at this writing in December 2008, is several months in the future. But it is already apparent that no 'issue of regime' will arise at that election. It was the late B. D. Graham who originally called our attention to 'issues of regime' in Indian politics.

politicians to avoid emphases on single, overarching issues—and instead to offer diverse interest groups a similarly diverse array of promises and programmes. These often sit incongruously alongside one another, so that they both respond to and sustain the incongruities and heterogeneities in Indian life which are abundantly documented in this volume. This partly explains why 'issues of regime' seldom emerge, and why social polarisation seldom occurs.[4] Sometimes what does *not* happen is as important as what does.

It is essential—not least because caste is discussed in several chapters here—to note one of the most important changes to occur in India since independence, the declining power of caste hierarchies in rural areas. To say that this is happening is not to argue that caste is wasting away, or that it no longer shapes social relations. People still tend strongly to marry their children within long-standing endogamous caste groups (*jatis*), and to identify with their caste groups. But caste is increasingly coming to denote not hierarchy but difference, as several scholars writing on diverse parts of India—including Dipankar Gupta who addresses a different topic in this book—have been telling us since the mid-1990s.[5] This trend does not emerge from the kind of quantitative analysis of society that we find in the chapter here by Divya Vaid and Anthony Heath. But the qualitative evidence for it is exceedingly strong, and it provides a crucial complement to their study.

The waning power of caste hierarchies has implications in two important spheres which have received attention in many of the studies in this volume: once again, politics and government policy. It is bound to affect political behaviour. It has already triggered more caste conflict, a trend which is likely to gather greater force. This occurs in part because formerly dominant castes kick against their declining influence and lash out at less prosperous groups who no longer defer to them—and because those less exalted caste groups react against the slow pace at which their fortunes are improving, a trend which Divya Vaid and Anthony Heath document so effectively here. And by making society in rural areas—where two-thirds of Indians still live, and where elections are won and lost—less ordered and self-regulating, it may create opportunities for

[4] Note that surveys by *Lokniti* at the Centre for the Study of Developing Societies in Delhi found that only 1 per cent of voters who went to the polls in state elections a few days after the terrorist attack in Mumbai in November 2008 stated that their preferences had been influenced by that vile episode.

[5] See for example Mayer (1996), Karanth and Charsley (1998) and Gupta (2000).

political parties that stress issues other than caste hierarchies to gain more influence. It might, for example, enable parties of the left and/or the Hindu right to fix voters' attention more firmly on their pet themes: class and religious differences, respectively (although at present, there is little evidence that either thing is happening).

The declining power of caste hierarchies is also important when we consider studies here and elsewhere of public policy—because it has major implications for the importance of government programmes in the lives of India's rural majority. In former times, village headmen drawn from the locally dominant caste enjoyed the status and deference to persuade or compel other villagers to join in collective efforts to 'get things done'—minor public works, crucial activities at harvest or sowing time, etc. Today in much of rural India, because of the erosion of hierarchies, those headmen can no longer achieve these things. So to 'get things done', villagers often need to reach beyond the village—upward to higher levels in the political/administrative system where funds, goods, services and managerial/technical assistance can be accessed.[6]

It is just as well, then, as localities have become increasingly dependent upon politicians and administrators at higher levels and on government programmes, that we have witnessed a substantial proliferation of such programmes over the last thirty years. One of India's most perceptive former administrators has said that this proliferation was the most striking change that he had witnessed during his career.[7] Many of these programmes have had limited or perverse impacts, but enough have proved somewhat constructive to make a significant difference. Several of the studies in this collection refer to programmes of both types.

There is another reason for the increased importance of government programmes: nearly all political parties in India lack the organisational capacity to make their influence penetrate downward below the (rather exalted) district level into local arenas. This is true even of the overestimated organisation of the BJP, although it is comparatively strong in other ways (Manor 2005). Only the Communist Party of India (Marxist) possesses such penetrative capacity, but this is true only in the state of West Bengal, in the small state of Tripura, and to a lesser degree in Kerala. This makes the perceptive case study by Mukulika Banerjee in

[6] For important examples of this set of changes, see G. K. Karanth, V. Ramaswamy and R. Hogger, chapters 11 to 14 in Hogger and Baumgartner (2004).

[7] Interview with B. K. Bhattacharya, former Chief Secretary of Karnataka, Bangalore, 7 July 2006.

this volume (which is drawn from West Bengal) exceptional, not typical. Because political parties cannot penetrate effectively to the village level in most parts of India, localities (and politicians higher up who wish to cultivate popular support at the local level) must rely mainly on formal government programmes.

Until fairly recently, this comment offered rather tepid comfort to localities in need (and for that matter, to politicians) because for several years, beginning in the early 1990s, state and central governments were very short of funds for such programmes. But since 2003 that has changed. India has witnessed 'stupendous growth' in official revenues, a '31% compound annual growth rate over the four-year period ending 2007–08—on the back of an economy that grew at 9% a year'.[8] This has enabled state governments to spend far more. And at the national level, the Congress-led government which has held power since 2004 has introduced an array of immensely expensive initiatives. These include a rural employment guarantee scheme (arguably the largest poverty-reduction programme on earth), a quadrupling of spending on basic education, a loan waiver for farmers, and a cluster of six infrastructure programmes under the *Bharat Nirman* label.

That government has taken these steps to address the needs of poor people who—as close readings of the chapters here by Vijay Joshi, Zoya Hasan, Divya Vaid and Anthony Heath, Lucia Michelutti, and finally Patricia and Roger Jeffery indicate—have been left behind by rapid economic growth and globalisation. This is not a response to a revolt of the rural poor at the national election in 2004, a mythical explanation mindlessly peddled by the international media. (The victorious alliance in that election actually did better in urban areas than in rural parts, and the rural poor voted in markedly different ways in different Indian states.) Instead, these new programmes were intended to attract fulsome support (which was lacking the last time round) from the rural poor at the *next* election in 2009. These initiatives are massive enough to have a significant impact—despite serious imperfections in their implementation. They may even bring a little light to the exceedingly dark (and quite accurate) picture which emerges from the study in this volume by the Jefferys.

The surge in government revenues (and spending) may also reverse a trend which has been evident since 1977—the tendency for incumbent governments to be thrown out by voters at election time. Five of the last

[8] *Economic Times*, 6 Dec. 2008.

six, and seven of the last nine national elections have been lost by sitting governments. The pattern is even more striking at the state level. Governments in major Indian states have been ousted about 70 per cent of the time since 1977. If we remove West Bengal (where a left front has been re-elected on every occasion since 1977) from that calculation, the figure approaches 90 per cent. These are spectacularly high rejection rates by international standards—although they are paralleled, somewhat incongruously, by higher levels of support for the democratic process in India than in other consolidated democracies. But now marked increases in spending may be making governments more re-electable. In four state elections in north-central India in November–December 2008 (which came too late to be included in Oliver Heath and Yogendra Yadav's analysis in this book), three incumbent governments were returned to power.

The availability of massive government revenues, if it persists amid the global economic crisis, will help to discredit the ill-founded accusation that when Prime Minister P. V. Narasimha Rao and Finance Minister Manmohan Singh cautiously opened up the Indian economy in and after 1991, they were pursuing *neo-liberal* policies. (This is a charge which Joshi carefully avoids echoing in his chapter here on the economy.) Narasimha Rao rejected this claim. He stated flatly in 1992 that 'I do not believe in trickle-down economics.' His model was 'not Margaret Thatcher but Willy Brandt' who had encouraged market forces in order to achieve economic growth which would yield greater government revenues, so that the state could redistribute more wealth and perform tasks which the private sector would leave unattended.[9]

In other words, even as he introduced marked changes in economic policy, Rao sought to conform to—and indeed, to lend greater substance to—the social democratic traditions of the Congress Party which he led. He saw it as another example of the gradualism which has predominated in Indian policy-making since independence. It took many years for government revenues to take off but, at the time of writing, his intention—which was far from neo-liberal—appears finally to have been realised.

It remains to be seen how much impact this will have on the poverty, inequality and social exclusion—and the imperfections in policy implementation—which are evident in these chapters. Change, as we have seen, occurs gradually in India—but it happens nonetheless, sometimes

[9] Interview with P. V. Narasimha Rao, New Delhi, 11 Feb. 1992.

in fundamental ways. As it does, incongruities—painful ironies amid remarkable achievements—persist. Economic growth has surged, as have (belatedly) government revenues, but poverty remains a vile, daunting challenge. The consolidation of a decidedly genuine democracy occurred decades ago—but it made India a more difficult country to govern, as leaders who have been ousted at successive elections know only too well. The power of caste hierarchies has declined—opening the way to more forceful challenges to injustice, but also to more abrasive social relations and spasms of violence (Varshney 2002). India has become still more complex and fascinating, and yet also more difficult to encompass even in a wide-ranging volume such as this. But we have made a start.

Bibliography

Abbasi, K. (1999), 'The World Bank and world health: Focus on South Asia—II: India and Pakistan', *British Medical Journal*, 318 (7191), 1132–5.

Acharya, S. (2006), *Essays on Macroeconomic Policy and Growth in India* (Oxford: Oxford University Press).

Acharya, S., Cassen, R., and McNay, K. (2004), 'The economy—past and future', in T. Dyson, R. Cassen and L. Visaria (eds.), *Twenty-First Century India—Population, Economy, Human Development, and the Environment* (Oxford: Oxford University Press), 202–27.

Ahluwalia, M. (1998), 'Infrastructure development in India's reforms', in I. J. Ahluwalia and I. M. D. Little (eds.), *India's Economic Reforms and Development: Essays for Manmohan Singh* (New Delhi: Oxford University Press), 87–121.

Ahluwalia, M. (2002), 'Economic reforms in India since 1991: Has gradualism worked?', *Journal of Economic Perspectives*, 16 (3), 67–88.

Ahmad, I. (1973), *Caste and Social Stratification among the Muslims* (New Delhi: Manohar).

Akhtar, R., and Learmonth, A. (1985), 'Resurgence of malaria in India 1965–76', in R. Akhtar and A. Learmonth (eds.), *Geographical Aspects of Health and Disease in India* (New Delhi: Concept Publishing), 107–23.

Alam, J. (2004), *Who Wants Democracy?* (New Delhi: Orient Longman).

Arita, I., Nakane, M., and Fenner, F. (2006), 'Is polio eradication realistic?', *Science*, 312, 852–4.

Arora, N. K., Patwari, A. K., and Lakshman, M. (1999), 'Pulse polio immunization program evaluation 1997–98' (New Delhi: All India Institute of Medical Sciences).

Aylward, R., Acharya, A., England, S., Agocs, M., and Linkins, J. (2003), 'Global health goals: Lessons from the worldwide effort to eradicate poliomyelitis', *The Lancet*, 362 (9387), 909–14.

Bacchetta, P. (1994), 'Communal property/sexual property: On representations of Muslim women in a Hindu nationalist discourse', in Z. Hasan (ed.), *Forging Identities: Gender, Communities and the State* (New Delhi: Kali for Women), 188–225.

Bajpai, R. (2006), 'Redefining equality: social justice in the Mandal debate 1990', in V. R. Mehta and T. Pantham (eds.), *Political Ideas in Modern India: Thematic Explorations* (New Delhi: Sage Publications), 326–39.

Banerjee, M. (2007), 'Sacred elections', *Economic and Political Weekly*, 42 (17), 1556–62.

Banerjee, M. (2008), 'Democracy, sacred and everyday', in J. Paley (ed.), *Democracy: Anthropological Approaches* (Santa Fe: SAR Press), 63–95.

Banthia, J., and Dyson, T. (1999), 'Smallpox in nineteenth-century India', *Population and Development Review*, 25 (4), 649–80.

Barnett, S. A. (1975), 'Approaches to changes in caste ideology in south India', in B. Stein (ed.), *Essays on South India* (Hawaii: University Press of Hawaii), 149–80.

Barnett, S. A. (1977), 'Identity choice and caste ideology in contemporary south India', in K. David (ed.), *The New Wind. Changing identity in South Asia* (Paris: Mouton Publishers), 393–441.

Basile, E., and Harris-White, B. (2000) 'Corporative capitalism: Civil society and the politics of accumulation in small town India', Working Paper No. 38, *QEH*.

Basu, P. (ed.) (2005), *India's Financial Sector: Recent Reforms, Future Challenges* (India: Macmillan).

Basu, A., and Kohli, A. (eds.) (1998), *Community Conflicts and the State in India* (New Delhi: Oxford University Press).

Basu, K., and Maertens, A. (2007), 'The pattern and causes of economic growth in India', *Oxford Review of Economic Policy*, 23 (2), 143–67.

Bayly, S. (1999), *Caste, Society and Politics in India: From the 18th century to the modern age* (Cambridge: Cambridge University Press).

Berry, S., and Kiely, R. (1993), 'Is there a future for Korean democracy?', *Parliamentary Affairs*, 46 (4), 594–604.

Besley, T., and Burgess, R. (2004), 'Can labour market regulation hinder economic performance? Evidence from India', *Quarterly Journal of Economics*, 119 (1), 91–134.

Béteille, A. (1969), *Castes: Old and New: Essays in social structure and social stratification* (London: Asia Publishing House).

Bhagwati, J. (1993), *India in Transition: Freeing the Economy* (New York: Oxford University Press).

Bhagwati, J., and Desai, P. (1970), *India: Planning for Industrialisation* (London: Oxford University Press).

Bhan, G. (2001), 'India gender profile', Report Commissioned for Sida, Report No. 62, *Bridge (Development-Gender)* (University of Sussex, Brighton: IDS). Available from <http://www.bridge.ids.ac.uk//bridge/reports/re62.pdf>

Bhat, M. (1989), 'Mortality and fertility in India, 1881–1961: A reassessment', in T. Dyson (ed.), *India's Historical Demography* (London: Curzon Press), 73–118.

Bhat, M. (1998), 'Contours of fertility decline in India: An analysis of district-level trends from two recent censuses', in G. Martine, M. Das Gupta, and L. Chen (eds.), *Reproductive Change in India and Brazil* (Mumbai: Oxford University Press), 97–131.

Bhat, M. (2001), 'Indian demographic scenario, 2025', *Discussion Paper* (New Delhi: Institute of Economic Growth).

Bhat, M. (2002*a*), 'Maternal mortality in India: An update', *Studies in Family Planning*, 33 (3), 227–36.

Bhat, M. (2002*b*), 'India's changing dates with replacement fertility: A review of recent fertility trends and future prospects', in United Nations Population Division, *Completing the Fertility Transition* (New York: United Nations), 376–91.

Bhat, M. (2002*c*), 'Returning a favour: Reciprocity between female education and fertility in India', *World Development*, 30 (10), 1791–1803.

Bhat, M., Navaneetham, K., and Rajan, I. (1995), 'Maternal mortality in India: Estimates from a regression model', *Studies in Family Planning*, 26 (4), 217–32.

Bhat, M., and Zavier, A. J. (2007), 'Factors influencing the use of prenatal diagnostic techniques and the sex ratio at birth in India', *Economic and Political Weekly*, 42 (23), 2292–303.

Bhattacharya, P. (2006), 'Economic development, gender inequality, and demographic outcomes: Evidence from India', *Population and Development Review*, 32 (2), 263–91.

Bhattacharya, S. (2006), *Expunging Variola: The control and eradication of smallpox in India 1947–1977* (New Delhi & Hyderabad: Orient Longman).

Bhatty, Z. (1996), 'Social stratification among Muslims in India', in M. N. Srinivas (ed.), *Caste, its Twentieth Century Avatar* (New Delhi: Penguin), 244–62.

Bidwai, P. (2006), 'The "merit" fallacy', *Frontline*, 16 June.

Bienen, H., and Herbst, J. (1996), 'The relationship between political and economic reform in Africa', *Comparative Politics*, 29 (1), 23–42.

Billig, M. (1995), *Banal Nationalism* (London: Sage).

Bloom, D., and Canning, D. (2001), 'Cumulative causality, economic growth and the demographic transition', in N. Birdsall, A. Kelley, and S. Sinding (eds.), *Population Matters: Demographic Change, Economic Growth, and Poverty in the Developing World* (Oxford: Oxford University Press), 165–200.

Bloom, D., Canning, D., and Sevilla, J. (2003), 'The demographic dividend: A new perspective on the economic consequences of population change', *Population Matters* (Santa Monica, CA: RAND Corporation).

Bonu, S., Rani, M., and Baker, T. D. (2003), 'The impact of the national polio immunization campaign on levels and equity in immunization coverage: Evidence from rural north India', *Social Science and Medicine*, 57 (10), 1807–19.

Bosworth, B., Collins, S., and Virmani, A. (2007), 'Sources of growth in the Indian economy', in S. Bery, B. P. Bosworth, and A. Panagariya (eds.), *India Policy Forum* (Washington, DC: Sage), Vol. 3, 1–50.

Brass, P. (1965), *Factional Politics in an Indian State: The Congress Party in Uttar Pradesh* (Berkeley, CA: University of California Press).

Breen, R. (1997), 'Inequality, economic growth and social mobility', *The British Journal of Sociology*, 48 (3): 429–49.

Breen, R. (2004), *Social Mobility in Europe* (Oxford: Oxford University Press).

Breen, R., and Jonsson, J. (1997), 'How reliable are studies of social mobility? An investigation into consequences of unreliability in measures of social class', *Research in Social Stratification and Mobility*, 15, 91–112.

Browne, M. N., Frondorf, A., Harrison-Spoerl, R., and Krishnan, S. (2004), 'Universal moral principles and the law: the failure of one-size-fits-all child labor laws', *Houston Journal of International Law*, 27, 1–46.

Buiter, W., and Patel, U. (2006), 'Excessive budget deficits, a Government-abused financial system and fiscal rules', in S. Bery, B. P. Bosworth, and A. Panagariya (eds.), *India Policy Forum* (Washington, DC: Sage), Vol. 2, 1–38.

Butler, D., Lahiri, A., and Roy, P. (1995), *India Decides: Elections 1952–1995* (New Delhi: Books and Things).

Caldwell, J. C., Reddy, P. H., and Caldwell, P. (1983), 'The social component of mortality decline: An investigation in south India employing alternative methodologies', *Population Studies*, 37 (2), 185–205.

Cassen, R. (2002), 'Well-being in the 1990s: Towards a balance sheet', *Economic and Political Weekly*, 37 (27), 2789–94.
Chadha, G. K., and Sahu, P. P. (2002), 'Post-reform setbacks in rural employment: Issues that need further scrutiny', *Economic and Political Weekly*, 37 (21), 1998–2026.
Chakraborty, S. (2002), 'Private health provision in Uttar Pradesh, India', in D. H. Peters, A. S. Yazbeck, R. R Sharma, G.N.V. Ramana, L. H. Pritchett, and A. Wagstaff (eds.), *Better health systems for India's poor: Findings, analysis and options* (Washington DC: World Bank), 257–77.
Chapman, G., and Pathak, P. (2000), 'Indian urbanisation and the characteristics of large Indian cities revealed in the 1991 census', in C. Guilmoto and A. Vaguet (eds.), *Essays on Population and Space in India* (Pondicherry: French Institute of Pondicherry), 97–116.
Chatterjee, P. (1997), 'Introduction', in P. Chatterjee (ed.), *State and Politics in India* (New Delhi: Oxford University Press), 1–40.
Chatterjee, P. (2001), 'On civil and political society in post-colonial democracies', in S. Kaviraj and S. Khilnani (eds.), *Civil Society: History and Possibilities* (Cambridge: Cambridge University Press), 165–78.
Chatterjee, P., Bose, P. K., and Samaddar, R. (1997), 'Discipline and development', in P. Chatterjee (ed.), *The Present History of West Bengal* (Delhi: Oxford University Press), 137–92.
Chibber, P. (1999), *Democracy without Associations: Transformation of the Party System and Social Cleavages in India* (Ann Arbor: University of Michigan Press).
Chibber, P., and Petrocik, J. (1990), 'Social cleavages, elections and the Indian party system', in R. Sisson and R. Roy (eds.), *Diversity and Dominance in Indian Politics Vol 1. Changing Bases of Congress Support* (New Delhi and London: Sage), 104–22.
CHSJ (2007), *Citizens Report: Reviewing two years of NRHM, October 2007* (New Delhi: Centre for Health and Social Justice).
Chung, W., and Das Gupta, M. (2007), 'The decline of son preference in South Korea: The roles of development and public policy', *Population and Development Review*, 33 (4), 757–83.
Ciotti, M. (2006), 'In the past we were a bit "Chamar"': Education as a self- and community engineering process in northern India', *Journal of the Royal Anthropological Institute*, 12 (4), 899–916.
Clark, T., and Lipset, S. M. (1991), 'Are social classes dying?', *International Sociology*, 6(4), 397–410.
Conlon, F. F. (1977), *A caste in a changing world: The Chitrapur Saraswat Brahmans, 1770–1935* (New Delhi: Thomson Press).
Corbridge, S., and Harriss, J. (2000), *Reinventing India: Liberalization, Hindu nationalism and popular democracy* (New Delhi: Oxford University Press).
Corbridge, S., Srivastava, M., Veron, R., and Williams, G. (2005), *Seeing the State: Governance and governmentality in India* (Cambridge: Cambridge University Press).
Cunningham, C. D., and Menon, N. R. M. (1999), 'Race, class, caste . . .? Rethinking affirmative action', *Michigan Law Review*, 97, 1296–1310.

Dalton, R. J. (1984), 'Cognitive mobilization and partisan dealignment in advanced industrial democracies', *Journal of Politics*, 46 (1), 264–84.

Das, N., and Dey, D. (1998), 'Females' age at marriage in India: Trends and determinants', *Demography India*, 27 (1), 91–115.

Das Gupta, M., and Bhat, M. (1999), 'Intensified gender bias in India: A consequence of fertility decline', in M. Krishnaraj, R. Sudarshan, and A. Shariff (eds.), *Gender, Population and Development* (New Delhi: Oxford University Press), 73–93.

Datt, G., and Ravallion, M. (2002), 'Is India's economic growth leaving the poor behind?', *Policy Research Working Paper Series* (Washington: The World Bank Development Research Group Poverty Team).

Datta, N. (1999), *Forming an Identity: A social history of the Jats* (New Delhi: Oxford University Press).

Datta, P. K. (1999), *Carving Blocs: Communal ideology in early twentieth-century Bengal* (New Delhi: Oxford University Press).

De Long, J. B. (2003), 'India since Independence: An analytic growth narrative', in D. Rodrik (ed.), *In Search of Prosperity: Analytic narratives of economic growth* (Princeton, NJ: Princeton University Press), 184–204.

Deaton, A. (2003), 'Regional poverty estimates for India, 1999–2000', *Research Program in Development Studies* (Princeton: Princeton University).

Deaton, A. (2004), 'Health in an age of globalisation', *Research Program in Development Studies* (Princeton University: Center for Health and Wellbeing), 46.

Deaton, A., and Drèze, J. (2002), 'Poverty and inequality in India: A re-examination', *Economic and Political Weekly*, 37(36), 3729–48.

Deaton, A., and Kozel, V. (2005), 'Data and dogma: The great Indian poverty debate', *World Bank Research Observer*, 20 (2), 177–99.

Desai, N. (2007), 'Growth and employment', *Business Standard*, 15 November.

Deshpande, L., Sharma, A. N., Karan, A. K., and Sarkar, S. (2004), *Liberalisation and Labour: Labour flexibility in Indian manufacturing* (New Delhi: Institute for Human Development).

Deshpande, S. (1999), 'Mapping a distinctive modernity: "Modernisation" as a theme in Indian sociology', *Institute of Economic Growth: Occasional Papers in Sociology*, 1.

Deshpande, S. (2002), 'Assets versus autonomy? The changing face of the gender–caste overlap in India', *Feminist Economics*, 8 (2), 19–35.

Deshpande, S. (2004), *Contemporary India: A Sociological View* (New Delhi: Penguin).

Deshpande, S. (2006), 'Exclusive inequalities: Merit, caste and discrimination in Indian higher education today', *Economic and Political Weekly*, 41 (24), 2438–44.

Deshpande, S. (2008), 'Quota sans creamy layer in education?', *Economic Times*, 16 April.

Deshpande, S., and Deshpande, L. K. (1999), 'Gender discrimination in the urban labour market', in T. S. Papola and A. N. Sharma (eds.), *Gender and Employment in India* (New Delhi: Vikas Publishing), 223–48.

Dev, S. M., and Ravi, C. (2007), 'Poverty and inequality: All-India and states, 1983–2005', *Economic and Political Weekly*, 42 (6), 509–21.

Devarajan, S., and Shah, S. (2004), 'Making services work for India's poor', *Economic and Political Weekly*, 39 (9), 907–19.

Dhanagare, D. N. (1968), 'Political elite and caste association: A comment', *Economic and Political Weekly*, 3 (48), 1852.

Dirks, N. B. (2001), *Castes of Mind: Colonialism and the making of modern India* (Princeton and Oxford: Princeton University Press).

Dix, R. H. (1989), 'Cleavage structures and party systems in Latin America', *Comparative Politics*, 22 (1), 23–37.

Dollar, D., and Collier, P. (2001), *Globalization, Growth, and Poverty: Building an inclusive world economy* (Washington DC: The World Bank & Oxford University Press).

Drèze, J., and Khera, R. (2008), 'From accounts to accountability', *The Hindu*, 6 December.

Drèze J., and Murthi, M. (2001), 'Fertility, education, and development: Evidence from India', *Population and Development Review*, 27 (1), 33–63.

Drèze, J., and Sen, A. (1995), *India: Economic Development and Social Opportunity* (New Delhi: Oxford University Press).

Drèze, J., and Sen, A. (2002), *India: Development and participation* (New Delhi: Oxford University Press).

Dumont, L. (1980 [1966]), *Homo Hierarchicus: The caste system and its implications* (Chicago: University of Chicago Press).

Dyson, T. (1984), 'India's regional demography', *World Health Statistics Quarterly*, 37 (2), 200–31.

Dyson, T. (1989), 'The historical demography of Berar, 1881–1980', in T. Dyson (ed.), *India's Historical Demography* (London: Curzon Press), 150–96.

Dyson, T. (2001*a*), 'A partial theory of world development: The neglected role of the demographic transition in the shaping of modern society', *International Journal of Population Geography*, 7 (2), 67–90.

Dyson, T. (2001*b*), 'The preliminary demography of the 2001 census of India', *Population and Development Review*, 27 (2), 341–56.

Dyson, T. (2003), 'HIV/AIDS and urbanization', *Population and Development Review*, 29 (3), 427–42.

Dyson, T. (2004), 'India's population—the future', in T. Dyson, R. Cassen, and L. Visaria (eds.), *Twenty-First Century India—Population, Economy, Human Development, and the Environment* (Oxford: Oxford University Press), 74–107.

Dyson, T., and Moore, M. (1983), 'Kinship structure, female autonomy, and demographic behavior in India', *Population and Development Review*, 9 (1), 35–60.

Dyson, T., and Murphy, M. (1991), 'Macro-level study of socio-economic development and mortality: Adequacy of indicators and methods of statistical analysis', in J. Cleland and A. Hill (eds.), *The Health Transition: Methods and Measures* (Canberra: Health Transition Centre, Australian National University), 147–64.

Dyson, T., and P. Visaria (2004), 'Migration and urbanization: Retrospect and prospect', in T. Dyson, R. Cassen, and L. Visaria (eds.), *Twenty-First Century India—Population, Economy, Human Development, and the Environment* (Oxford: Oxford University Press), 108–29.

Dyson, T., Cassen, R., and Visaria, L. (eds.) (2004), *Twenty-First Century India—Population, Economy, Human Development, and the Environment* (Oxford: Oxford University Press).

Editorial (2009), 'Acceptance of corruption', *Economic and Political Weekly*, 44 (5), 5.

Eisenstadt, S. N. (2000), 'Multiple modernities', *Daedalus*, 129 (1), 1–29.

Erikson, R., and Goldthorpe, J. H. (1987), 'Commonality and variation in social fluidity in industrial nations', *European Sociological Review*, 3 (2), 145–66.

Erikson, R., and Goldthorpe, J. H. (1992), *The Constant Flux: A study of class mobility in industrial societies* (Oxford: Clarendon Press).

Erikson, R., and Goldthorpe, J. H. (2001), 'Trends in class mobility: The post-war European experience', in D. B. Grusky (ed.), *Social Stratification: Class, race and gender in sociological perspective* (Oxford: Westview Press), 344–72.

Evans, G., and Whitefield, S. (1993), 'Identifying the bases of party competition in Eastern Europe', *British Journal of Political Science*, 23 (4), 521–48.

Fanselow, F. S. (1996), 'The disinvention of caste among Tamil Muslims', in C. J. Fuller (ed.), *Caste Today* (New Delhi: Oxford University Press), 202–26.

Featherman, D. L., Jones, F. L., and Hauser, R. M. (1975), 'Assumptions of mobility research in the United States: The case of occupational status', *Social Science Research*, 4 (4), 329–60.

Fox, R. G. (1971), *Kin, Clan, Raja and Rule: State–hinterland relations in pre-industrial India* (Berkeley: University of California Press).

Franklin, M. N. (2004), *Voter Turnout and the Dynamics of Electoral Competition in Established Democracies since 1945* (Cambridge: Cambridge University Press).

Franklin, M. N., Mackie, T. T., and Valen, H. (eds.) (1992), *Electoral Change: Responses to evolving social and attitudinal structures in Western countries* (Cambridge: Cambridge University Press).

Frederiksen, H. (1968*a*), 'Malaria control and population pressure in Ceylon', in D. M. Heer (ed.), *Readings in Population* (Englewood Cliffs, NJ: Prentice-Hall), 69–73.

Frederiksen, H. (1968*b*), 'Determinants and consequences of mortality trends in Ceylon', in D. M. Heer (ed.), *Readings in Population* (Englewood Cliffs, NJ: Prentice-Hall), 74–80.

Fuller, C. J. (1996*a*), *Caste Today* (New Delhi: Oxford University Press).

Fuller, C. J. (1996*b*), 'Introduction', in C. J. Fuller (ed.), *Caste today* (New Delhi: Oxford University Press), 1–30.

Fuller, C. J., and Harriss, J. (2000), 'For an anthropology of the modern Indian state', in C. J. Fuller and V. Bénéï (eds.), *The Everyday State and Society in Modern India* (New Delhi: Social Science Press), 1–30.

Galanter, M. (1984), *Competing Equalities: Law and the backward classes in India* (Berkeley, Los Angeles, London: University of California Press).

Ganzeboom, H. B. G., Luijkx, R., and Treiman, D. (1989), 'Intergenerational class mobility in comparative perspective', *Research in Social Stratification and Mobility*, 8, 3–84.

Ghosh, J. (2004), 'Income inequality in India', *People's Democracy*, 28 (7).

Ghosh, J. (2006), 'Case for caste-based quotas in higher education', *Economic and Political Weekly*, 41 (24), 2428–32.

Giridharadas, A. (2006), 'A college education without job prospects', *New York Times*, 30 November.

Gist, N. P. (1954), 'Caste differentials in south India', *American Sociological Review*, 19 (2), 126–37.

Goldthorpe, J. H. (1992), 'Employment, class, and mobility: A critique of liberal and Marxist theories of long-term change', in H. Haferkamp and N. J. Smelser (eds.), *Social Change and Modernity* (Berkeley: University of California Press), 122–46.

Goldthorpe, J. H., Llewellyn, C., and Payne, C. (1980), *Social Mobility and Class Structure in Modern Britain* (Oxford: Clarendon Press).

Goldthorpe, J. H., and Mills, C. (2004), 'Trends in intergenerational class mobility in Britain in the late twentieth century', in R. Breen (ed.), *Social Mobility in Europe* (Oxford: Oxford University Press), 195–224.

Gould, W. (2002), 'Congress radicals and Hindu militancy: Sampurnanand and Purushottam Das Tandon in the politics of the United Provinces: 1930–1947', *Modern Asian Studies*, 36 (3), 619–55.

Government of India (1955), 'Report of the Backward Classes Commission', Volume 1 (Chairman Kaka Kalelkar).

Government of India (1980), 'Report of the Backward Classes Commission', Volume 1, 1980 (Chairman B. P. Mandal).

Goyal, S. (1989), 'Social background of officers in the Indian administrative service', in F. R. Frankel and M. S. A. Rao (eds.) *Dominance and State Power in Modern India: Decline of a social order* (New Delhi: Oxford University Press), 425–33.

Greenough, P. (1995*a*), 'Global immunization and culture: Compliance and resistance in largescale public health campaigns: Symposium introduction', *Social Science and Medicine*, 41 (5), 605–7.

Greenough, P. (1995*b*), 'Intimidation, coercion, and resistance in the final stages of the South Asian smallpox eradication campaign, 1973–1975', *Social Science and Medicine,* 41 (5), 633–45.

Griffiths, P., Hinde, A., and Matthews, Z. (2001), 'Infant and child mortality in three culturally contrasting states of India', *Journal of Biosocial Science*, 33 (4), 603–22.

Grusky, D. B., and Hauser, R. M. (1984), 'Comparative social mobility revisited: Models of convergence and divergence in 16 countries', *American Sociological Review*, 49 (1), 19–38.

Guha, R. (2007), *India after Gandhi: The history of the world's largest democracy* (Basingstoke and Oxford: Macmillan).

Guilmoto, C. Z. (2000), 'The geography of fertility in India (1981–1991)', in C. Z. Guilmoto and A. Vaguet (eds.), *Essays on Population and Space in India* (Pondicherry: French Institute of Pondicherry), 37–53.

Guilmoto, C. Z., and Rajan, I. (2001*a*), 'Spatial patterns of fertility transition in Indian districts', *Population and Development Review*, 27 (4), 713–38.

Guilmoto, C. Z., and Rajan, I. (2001*b*), 'Geographic patterns in fertility changes', in K. Srinivasan and M. Vlassoff (eds.), *Population-Development Nexus in India* (New Delhi: Tata McGraw-Hill), 88–109.

Gulati, A. (1998), 'Indian agriculture in an open economy', in I. J. Ahluwalia and I. M. D. Little (eds.), *India's Economic Reforms and Development: Essays in Honour of Manmohan Singh* (New Delhi: Oxford University Press), 122–46.

Gupta, A. (1993), 'Blurred boundaries: The discourse of corruption, the culture of politics, and the imagined state', *American Ethnologist*, 22 (2), 375–402.

Gupta, C. (2002), *Sexuality, Obscenity, Community: Women, Muslims, and the Hindu public in colonial India* (New Delhi: Permanent Black).
Gupta, C., and Sharma, M. (1996), 'Communal constructions: media reality vs real reality', *Race and Class*, 38 (1), 1–20.
Gupta, D. (1997), *Rivalry and Brotherhood* (New Delhi: Oxford University Press).
Gupta, D. (2000), *Interrogating Caste: Understanding hierarchy and difference in Indian society* (New Delhi: Penguin).
Gupta, D. (2001), *Mistaken Modernity: India between worlds* (New Delhi: HarperCollins India).
Gupta, D. B., and Gumber, A. (2002), 'External assistance to the health sector and its contributions: Problems and prognosis', Working Paper No. 88 (New Delhi: Indian Council for Research on International Economic Relations).
Gupta, M. (1988), 'Women in the industries and service sector in India', *Equal Opportunities International*, 7 (4/5), 26–35.
Gwatkin, D. (1979), 'Political will and family planning: The implications of India's Emergency experience', *Population and Development Review*, 5 (1), 29–59.
Hanchate, A., and Dyson, T. (2004), 'Prospects for food demand and supply', in T. Dyson, R. Cassen, and L. Visaria (eds.), *Twenty-First Century India—Population, Economy, Human Development, and the Environment* (Oxford: Oxford University Press), 228–53.
Hansen, T. B. (2000), 'Governance and myths of state in Mumbai', in C. J. Fuller and V. Bénéï (eds.), *The Everyday State and Society in Modern India* (New Delhi: Social Science Press), 31–67.
Hansen, T. B. (2001), *Wages of Violence: Naming and identity in postcolonial Bombay* (Princeton and Oxford: Princeton University Press).
Hanson, J., and Kathuria, S. (1999), *India: A financial sector for the twenty-first century* (New Delhi: Oxford University Press).
Hardgrave, R. L. (1968), 'Caste: Fission and fusion', *Economic and Political Weekly*, 3, Special Number, 1065–70.
Hardgrave, R. L. (1969), *The Nadars of Tamilnadu: The political culture of a community in change* (Berkeley: University of California Press).
Hardgrave, R., and Kochanek, S. (2008), *India: Government and Politics in a Developing Nation* (New York: Harcourt Brace Jovanovich).
Harriss-White, B. (2003), *India Working: Essays on society and economy* (Cambridge: Cambridge University Press).
Hasan, R., Mitra, D., and Ural, B. (2007), 'Trade liberalisation, labour market institutions and poverty reduction', in S. Bery, B. P. Bosworth, and A. Panagariya (eds.), *India Policy Forum* (Washington, DC: Sage), Vol. 3, 71–110.
Heath, A. F. (1981), *Social Mobility* (London: Fontana Paperbacks).
Heath, A. F., and Payne, C. (2000), 'Social mobility', in A. H. Halsey and J. Webb (eds.), *Twentieth-Century British Social Trends* (Basingstoke: Macmillan), 254–78.
Heath, A., and Yadav, Y. (1999), 'The united colours of Congress: Social profile of Congress voters 1996 and 1998', *Economic and Political Weekly*, 35 (34 & 35), 2518–28.
Heath, A., Glouharova, S., and Heath, O. (2005), 'India: two-party contests within a multiparty system', in M. Gallagher and P. Mitchell (eds.), *The Politics of Electoral Systems* (Oxford: Oxford University Press), 137–56.

Heath, O. (1999*a*), 'The fractionalization of Indian parties', *Seminar*, 480, 66–71.
Heath, O. (1999*b*), 'Anatomy of BJP's rise to power: Social, regional and political expansion in the 1990s', *Economic and Political Weekly*, 34 (34 & 35), 2511–17.
Heath, O. (2005), 'Party systems, political cleavages and electoral volatility in India: State-wise analysis 1998–1999', *Electoral Studies*, 24 (2), 177–99.
Heuzé, G. (1990), 'Workers' struggles and indigenous Fordism in India', in M. Holmstrom (ed.), *Work for Wages in South Asia* (New Delhi: Manohar), 160–72.
Holmstrom, M. (1985), *The Social Anthropology of Indian Labour* (Cambridge: Cambridge University Press in Association with Orient Longman, Mumbai).
Holmstrom, M. (ed.) (1990), *Work for Wages in South Asia* (New Delhi: Manohar).
Hogger, R., and Baumgartner, R. (eds.) (2004), *In Search of Sustainable Livelihood Systems* (New Delhi: Sage).
Hout, M. (1983), *Mobility tables* (Beverly Hills: Sage).
Hout, M., Brooks, C., and Manza, J. (1995), 'The democratic class struggle in U.S. Presidential elections: 1948–1992', *American Sociological Review*, 60 (6), 805–28.
Inden, R. (1990), *Imagining India* (London: Blackwell).
Inglehart, R. (1990), *Cultural Shift in Advanced Industrial Society* (Princeton, NJ: Princeton University Press).
Institute of Applied Manpower Research (2005), *India Yearbook 2004: Manpower Profile* (New Delhi: Concept Publishing House).
International Institute for Population Sciences (IIPS) (1995), *National Family Health Survey (MCH and family planning)—Uttar Pradesh, 1992–93* (Bombay: International Institute for Population Sciences).
International Institute for Population Studies (IIPS). (2005). Facility Survey (Under Reproductive and Child Health Project) Phase II, 2003: Mumbai: International Institute for Population Sciences, <http://www.rchiips.org/PRCH-2.html>, accessed on 5 January 2009.
International Institute for Population Sciences (IIPS) and ORC Macro (2000), 'National Family Health Survey (NFHS-2) 1998–99: India' (Mumbai: IIPS), <http://www.nfhsIndia.org/pnfhs2.html>, accessed 26 September 2006.
International Institute for Population Sciences (IIPS) and Macro International (2007), 'National Family Health Survey (NFHS-3), 2005–06: India' (Mumbai: IIPS), <http://www.nfhsIndia.org/nfhs3_national_report.html>, accessed 19 January 2008.
Jacob, P. (2001), 'Magnitude of the Women Workforce in India: An Appraisal of the NSS Estimates and Methods', *Sarvekshana*, 86, 1–8.
Jaffrelot, C. (1996), *The Hindu Nationalist Movement and Indian Politics 1925 to the 1990s* (London: Hurst).
Jaffrelot, C. (2000), 'The rise of the Other Backward Classes in the Hindi belt', *The Journal of Asian Studies*, 59 (1), 86–108.
Jaffrelot, C. (2003), *India's Silent Revolution: The rise of the lower castes* (London: Hurst & Company).
Jaffrelot, C., and Kumar, S. (eds.) (2009), *Rise of the Plebeians?* (London: Routledge).
Jaoul, N. (2007), 'Political and "non political" means in the dalit movement', in S. Pai (ed.), *Political Process in UP: Identity, economic reform and governance* (New Delhi: Pearson), 142–68.

Jeffery, P., and Basu, A. (eds.) (1998), *Appropriating Gender: Women's activism and politicized religion in South Asia* (New York: Routledge).
Jeffery, P., and Jeffery, R. (1996), *Don't Marry me to a Plowman! Women's everyday lives in rural north India* (Boulder and New Delhi: Westview Press & Vistaar).
Jeffery, P., and Jeffery, R. (2006), *Confronting Saffron Demography: Religion, fertility and women's status in India* (New Delhi: Three Essays Collective).
Jeffery, P., and Jeffery, R. (2008), '"Money itself discriminates": Obstetric emergencies in the time of liberalisation', *Contributions to Indian Sociology*, 42 (1), 61–93.
Jeffery, P., Jeffery, R., and Jeffrey, C. (2008), 'Disputing contraception: Muslim reform, secular change and fertility', *Modern Asian Studies*, 42 (2 & 3), 519–48.
Jeffery, P., Jeffery, R., and Lyon, A. (1989), *Labour Pains and Labour Power: Women and childbearing in India* (London: Zed Books).
Jeffery, R., and Jeffery, P. (1997), *Population, Gender and Politics: Demographic change in rural north India* (Cambridge: Cambridge University Press).
Jeffery, R., Jeffery, P., and Rao, M. (2007), 'Safe motherhood initiatives: Contributions from small scale studies', *Indian Journal of Gender Studies*, 14 (2), 285–94.
Jeffrey, C., Jeffery, P., and Jeffery, R. (2008), *Degrees Without Freedom? Education, masculinities and unemployment in North India* (Stanford, CA: Stanford University Press).
Jeffrey, R. (1976), *The Decline of Nayar Dominance: Society and politics in Travancore, 1847–1908* (New Delhi: Vikas Publishing).
Jenkins, R. (1999), *Democratic Politics and Economic Reform in India* (Cambridge: Cambridge University Press).
Jesani, A. (2003), 'Social objectives of health care services: Regulating the private sector', in K. Seeta Prabhu and R. Sudarshan (eds.), *Reforming India's Social Sector: Poverty, nutrition, health and education* (New Delhi: Social Science Press), 205–20.
Jhabvala, R., and Subrahamaniya, R. K. A. (eds.) (2000), *The Unorganized Sector: Work Security and Social Protection* (New Delhi: Sage).
John, R. M., and Mutatkar, R. (2005), 'Statewise estimates of poverty among religious groups in India', *Economic and Political Weekly*, 40 (13), 1337–45.
John, T. J. (2006), 'Polio eradication: A national commission required', *Economic and Political Weekly*, 41 (51), 5229–34.
Joshi, V. (1998), 'Fiscal stabilisation and economic reform', in I. J. Ahluwalia and I. M. D. Little (eds.), *India's Economic Reforms and Development: Essays in honour of Manmohan Singh* (New Delhi: Oxford University Press), 147–68.
Joshi, V. (2003), 'India and the impossible trinity', *The World Economy*, 26 (4), 555–83.
Joshi, V. (2004), 'Myth of India's outsourcing boom', *Financial Times*, 16 November.
Joshi, V. (2008), 'Convertibility now? No, thanks', in R. Kumar and A. Sen Gupta (eds.), *India and the Global Economy* (New Delhi: Academic Foundation and NCAER), 285–304.
Joshi, V., and Little, I. M. D. (1994), *India: Macroeconomics and Political Economy, 1964–1991* (Washington, DC: World Bank; and New Delhi: Oxford University Press).
Joshi, V., and Little, I. M. D. (1996), *India's Economic Reforms 1991–2001* (Oxford: Oxford University Press).

Joshi, V., and Sanyal, S. (2004), 'Foreign inflows and macroeconomic policy in India', in S. Bery, B. Bosworth and A. Panagariya (eds.), *India Policy Forum* (Washington, DC: Brookings Institution; and New Delhi: NCAER), Vol. 1, 135–79.

Karanth, G. K. (1996) 'Caste in contemporary rural India', in M. N. Srinivas (ed.), *Caste—its Twentieth Century Avatar* (New Delhi: Penguin), 87–109.

Karanth, G. K., and Charsley, S. R. (eds.) (1998), *Challenging Untouchability: Dalit Initiatives and Experiences from Karnataka, South India* (New Delhi: Sage).

Karve, I. (1953), *Kinship Organisation in India* (Madras: G. S. Press).

Kerr, C., Dunlop, J. T., Harbison, F. H., and Myers, C. A. (1960), *Industrialism and Industrial Man: The Problems of Labour and Management in Economic Growth* (Cambridge: Harvard University Press).

Khilnani, S. (1997), *The Idea of India* (London: Hamish Hamilton).

Kingdon, G., Cassen, R., McNay, K., and Visaria, L. (2004), 'Education and literacy', in T. Dyson, R. Cassen, and L. Visaria (eds.), *Twenty-First Century India—Population, Economy, Human Development, and the Environment* (Oxford: Oxford University Press), 130–57.

Kishwar, M. (1996), 'Introduction', in M. Kishwar and R. Vanita (eds.), *In Search of Answers: Indian women's voices from Manushi* (New Delhi: Manohar), 1–49.

Koenig, M. A., Foo, G. H. C., and Joshi, K. (2000), 'Quality of care within the Indian family welfare programme: A review of recent evidence', *Studies in Family Planning*, 31 (1), 1–18.

Kohli, A. (1987), *The State and Poverty in India* (Cambridge: Cambridge University Press).

Kolenda, P. (1978), *Caste in Contemporary India: Beyond organic solidarity* (London: Benjamin/Cummings).

Kolenda, P. (2003), 'Caste in India since Independence', in P. Kolenda (ed.), *Caste, Marriage and Inequality: Essays on North and South India* (New Delhi: Rawat Publications), 390–412.

Kolff, D. (1990), *Naukar, Rajput and Sepoy: The ethnohistory of the military labour market in Hindustan* (Cambridge: Cambridge University Press).

Kothari, R. (1964), 'The Congress "System" in India', *Asian Survey*, 4 (12), 1161–73.

Kozel, V., and Parker, B. (2002), 'Poverty in rural India: The contribution of qualitative research in poverty analysis' (Washington, DC: World Bank).

Krishna, A. (2006), 'Pathways out of and into poverty in 36 villages of Andhra Pradesh, India', *World Development*, 34 (2), 271–88.

Kumar, S., Heath, A., and Heath, O. (2002*a*), 'Determinants of social mobility in India', *Economic and Political Weekly*, 37 (29), 2983–7.

Kumar, S., Heath, A., and Heath, O. (2002*b*), 'Changing patterns of social mobility', *Economic and Political Weekly*, 37 (40), 4091–6.

Kundu, A. (1999), 'Trends and pattern of female employment: A case of organised informalisation', in T. S. Papola and A. N. Sharma (eds.), *Gender and Employment in India* (New Delhi: Vikas Publishing), 52–70.

Kundu, A., and Gupta, S. (2000), 'Declining population mobility, liberalisation and growing regional imbalances, the Indian case', in A. Kundu (ed.), *Inequality, Mobility and Urbanisation* (New Delhi: Manak Publications), 257–74.

Kundu, A., and Sharma, A. N. (eds.) (2001), *India: Perspectives and Policies* (New Delhi: Institute for Human Development).
Labonte, R., Schrecker, T., and Sen Gupta, A. (2005), *Health for Some: Death, disease and disparity in a globalizing era* (Toronto: CSJ Research and Education).
Leonard, K. I. (1978), *The Social History of an Indian Caste: The Kayasths of Hyderabad* (Berkeley and London: University of California Press).
Lerner, D. (1962), *The Passing of Traditional Society: Modernizing the Middle East* (Glencoe: The Free Press).
Lerner, D. (1968), 'Social aspects of modernization', in T. Parsons and D. L. Sills (eds.), *International Encyclopaedia of the Social Sciences* (New York and London: Macmillan), 386–94.
Liddle, J. (1988), 'Occupational sex segregation and women's work in India', *Equal Opportunities International*, 7 (4/5), 7–25.
Liddle, J., and Joshi, R. (1986), *Daughters of Independence: Gender, caste, and class in India* (New Delhi: Kali for Women).
Lieten, G. K. (2003), 'Development priorities: Views from below in UP', in R. Jeffery and J. Lerche (eds.), *Social and Political Change in Uttar Pradesh: European perspectives* (New Delhi: Manohar), 55–75.
Lipset, S. M., and Rokkan, S. (1967), 'Cleavage structures, party systems, and voter alignments: An introduction', in S. M. Lipset and S. Rokkan (eds.), *Party Systems and Voter Alignments: Cross-National Perspectives* (New York: The Free Press), 1–64.
Lobo, L. (1989), 'Koli Kshatriya of North Gujarat', *The Eastern Anthropologist*, 42 (2), 171–92.
Loevinsohn, B., Aylward, B., Steinglass, R., *et al.* (2002), 'Impact of targeted programs on health systems: A case study of the polio eradication initiative', *American Journal of Public Health*, 92 (1), 19–23.
Lomova-Oppokova, M. (1999), 'Marathas: The role of kinship relations in the social and political life of Maharashtra', in I. Glushlova and R. Vora (eds.), *Home, Family and Kinship in Maharashtra* (New Delhi: Oxford University Press), 185–98.
Ludden, D. (ed.) (1996), *Contesting the Nation: Religion, Community, and the Politics of Democracy in India* (Philadelphia: University of Pennsylvania Press).
Maddison, A. (2007), *Contours of the World Economy 1–2030 AD: Essays in Macro-Economic History* (Oxford: Oxford University Press).
Mandelbaum, D. G. (1970), *Society in India* (Berkeley: University of California Press).
Manor, J. (1996), '"Ethnicity" and politics in India', *International Affairs*, 72, 459–76.
Manor, J. (2005), 'In part a myth: The BJP's organisational strength', in K. Adeney and L. Saez (eds.), *Coalition Politics and Hindu Nationalism* (London: Routledge), 55–74.
Mayaram, S. (1997), *Resisting Regimes: Myth, memory, and the shaping of a Muslim Identity* (New Delhi, New York: Oxford University Press).
Mayer, A. C. (1960), *Caste and Kinship in Central India: A village and its region* (Berkeley: University of California Press).
Mayer, A. C. (1996), 'Caste in an Indian village: Change and continuity, 1954–1992', in C. J. Fuller (ed.), *Caste Today* (New Delhi: Oxford University Press), 32–64.

McMillan, A. (2005), *Standing at the Margins: Representation and electoral reservation in India* (Oxford: Oxford University Press).

McNay, K., Arokiasamy, P., and Cassen, R. (2003), 'Why are uneducated women in India using contraception? A multilevel analysis', *Population Studies*, 57 (1), 21–40.

McNay, K., Unni, J., and Cassen, R. (2004), 'Employment', in T. Dyson, R. Cassen, and L. Visaria (eds.), *Twenty-First Century India—Population, Economy, Human Development, and the Environment* (Oxford: Oxford University Press), 158–77.

McNicoll, G. (1984), 'Consequences of rapid population growth: Overview and assessment', *Population and Development Review*, 10 (2), 177–240.

Mehta, P. B. (2007), 'Let them have scholarships', *Indian Express*, 3 April.

Michelutti, L. (2004), '"We (Yadavs) are a caste of politicians": Caste and modern politics in a North Indian town', *Contributions to Indian Sociology*, 38 (3), 43–72.

Michelutti, L. (2008), *The Vernacularisation of Democracy: Politics, Caste and Religion in India* (London and New Delhi: Routledge).

Michelutti, L. (Forthcoming), 'The magic appeal of muscular politics in Indian popular democracy', in P. Price and A. Ruud (eds.), *Power and Influence in South Asia: Bosses, Lords, and Captains* (New Delhi and London: Routledge).

Ministry of Finance, Government of India (2004), 'Central Government Subsidies in India: A Report', *National Institute of Public Finance & Policy* (New Delhi: Department of Economic Affairs).

Ministry of Finance, Government of India (2006) *Economic Survey 2005–6* (New Delhi: Government of India).

Ministry of Finance, Government of India (2007) *Economic Survey 2006–7* (New Delhi: Government of India).

Ministry of Finance, Government of India (2008), *Economic Survey 2007–8* (New Delhi: Government of India).

Ministry of Health and Family Welfare, Government of India (2006), 'Janani Suraksha Yojana—features and frequently asked questions and answers as in October 2006' (New Delhi: Government of India) <http://mohfw.nic.in/dofw%20website/JSY_features_FAQ_Nov_2006.htm>, accessed 9 April 2007.

Ministry of Health and Family Welfare, Government of India (2007), 'National Family Health Survey (NFHS-3), 2005–06, NFHS HIV, Measurement Process and Prevalence', <http://mohfw.nic.in/NFHS-3%20HIV%20Prevalence.ppt>, accessed January 2008.

Mishra, P., Rastogi, S. R., Kanitkar, T., Ramesh, B. M., Roy, T. K., Arnold, F., Feeney, G., Govindasamy, P., and Retherford, R. D. (1995), *National Family Health Survey (MCH and family planning)—Uttar Pradesh, 1992–93* (Bombay: Population Research Centre, Lucknow University and International Institute for Population Sciences).

Mishra, S. (2005), 'Public health scenario in India', in K. S. Parikh and R. Radhakrishna (eds.), *India Development Report 2004–05* (New Delhi: Oxford University Press, for the Indira Gandhi Institute of Development Research), 62–83.

Mission Document (2005), *National Rural Health Mission (2005–2012)* (New Delhi: National Rural Health Mission).

Mitra, S. K., and Singh, V. B. (1999), *Democracy and Social Change: A Cross Sectional Analysis of the Indian Electorate* (New Delhi: Sage).

Molund, S. (1988), *The Koris of Kanpur: Between caste and class* (Stockholm: Stockholm Studies in Anthropology).

Mosse, D. (2003), 'On Binaries and Boundaries', in K. Sivaramakrishnan and A. Agrawal (eds.), *Regional Modernities: the Cultural Politics of Development in India* (Stanford: Stanford University Press), 329–37.

Müller, A. R., and Patel, R. (2004), 'Shining India? Economic liberalization and rural poverty in the 1990s' (Oakland, CA: Institute for Food and Development Policy/Food First).

Narayan, D., and Pettesch, P. (eds.) (2002), *From Many Lands: Voices of the poor* (Washington, DC: World Bank and Oxford University Press).

NASSCOM (2006) 'Indian ITES-BPO Industry: NASSCOM Analysis', *Indian ITES-BPO Industry—Fact Sheet.*

National AIDS Control Organization (2000), 'Surveillance for HIV infection/AIDS cases in India', <http://www.naco.nic.in/vsnaco/indianscene/update.htm#8.htm>, accessed February 2000.

National AIDS Control Organization (2006), 'Facts and figures', <http://www.nacoonline.org/facts.htm>, accessed August 2006.

National Commission for Enterprises in the Unorganised Sector (2007), *Report on the Conditions of Work and Promotion of Livelihoods in the Unorganised Sector* (New Delhi: Government of India).

Nayyar, D. (2006), 'Economic growth in independent India: Lumbering elephant or running tiger?', *Economic and Political Weekly*, 41 (15), 1451–8.

Ní Bhrolcháin, M., and Dyson, T. (2007), 'On causation in demography: Issues and illustrations', *Population and Development Review*, 33 (1), 1–36.

Nichols, D. P. (1997), 'What kind of contrasts are there?', *From SPSS Keywords* 63 (UCLA: Academic Technology Services, Statistical Consulting Group), <http://www.ats.ucla.edu/stat/SPSS/library/contrast.htm>.

Nichter, M. (1995), 'Vaccinations in the third world: A consideration of community demand', *Social Science and Medicine*, 41 (5), 617–32.

Nigam, A. (2000), 'Logic of failed revolution', *Economic and Political Weekly*, 35 (17), 1414.

Nijhawan, N. K. (1969), 'Inter-generational occupational mobility', *Economic and Political Weekly*, 4 (39), 1553–7.

Nortman, D. (1978), 'India's new birth rate target: An analysis', *Population and Development Review*, 4 (2), 277–312.

Office of the Development Commissioner, Ministry of Micro, Small and Medium Enterprises (2008) *The Micro, Small and Medium Development Act 2006*, S.O. 1642 (New Delhi: Government of India).

Office of the Economic Adviser, Department of Industrial Policy and Promotion, Ministry of Commerce and Industry (2005), *Handbook of Industrial Policy and Statistics 2003–5* (New Delhi: Government of India).

OECD (2007), *Economic Survey of India 2007* (Paris: OECD).

Oommen, T. K. (2004), *Nation, Civil Society and Social Movements: Essays in Political Sociology* (New Delhi: Sage Publications).

Orenstein, H. (1963), 'Caste and the concept of 'Maratha', in Maharashtra', *The Eastern Anthropologist*, 16 (1): 1–9.
Osella, C., and Osella, F. (2006), 'Once upon a time in the West? Stories of migration and modernity from Kerala, South India', *Journal of the Royal Anthropological Institute*, 12 (3), 569–88.
Osella, F., and Osella, C. (2000), 'The Return of King Mahabali: The politics of morality in Kerala', in C. J. Fuller and V. Benei (eds.), *The Everyday State and Society in Modern India* (New Delhi: Social Science Press), 137–62.
Panagariya, A. (2004), 'India's trade reform', in S. Bery, B. P. Bosworth and A. Panagariya (eds.), *India Policy Forum* (Washington, DC: Brookings Institution and New Delhi: NCAER), Vol. 1, 1–57.
Panagariya, A. (2008), *India: the Emerging Giant* (New York: Oxford University Press).
Pandey, G. (1990), *The Construction of Communalism in Colonial North India* (New Delhi: Oxford University Press).
Panini, M. N. (1996), 'The political economy of caste', in M. N. Srinivas (ed.), *Caste—Its Twentieth Century Avatar* (New Delhi: Penguin), 28–68.
Papola, T. S., and Sharma, A. N. (1999), *Gender and Employment in India* (New Delhi: Indian Society of Labour Economics and Institute of Economic Growth in association with Vikas Publishing).
Parekh, B. (2004), 'Limits of the Indian political imagination', in V. R. Mehta and T. Pantham (eds.), *Political Ideas in Modern India: Thematic Explorations* (New Delhi: Sage), 437–58.
Parsons, T. (1960), *Structure and Process in Modern Societies* (Glencoe: The Free Press).
Patil, S. (1990), 'Should "class" be the basis for recognizing backwardness?', *Economic and Political Weekly*, 25 (50), 2733–44.
Patnaik, U. (2007), *Republic of Hunger and Other Essays* (New Delhi: Three Essays Collective).
Paul, Y. (2006), 'Polio eradication programme: A failure', *Economic and Political Weekly*, 41 (43 & 44), 4538–40.
Phookan, M. (2004), 'A brief market report on the cosmetics and toiletries market in India', in *Customized Market Research* (Washington, DC: US Foreign Commercial Service and US Department of State).
Pierik, R., and Houwerzijl, M. (2006), 'Western policies on child labour abroad', *Ethics and International Affairs*, 20 (2), 193–218.
Pinch, W. R. (1996), *Peasants and monks in British India* (Berkeley: University of California Press).
Pingle, V. (2003), 'Caste', in S. Ganguly and N. DeVotta (eds.), *Understanding Contemporary India* (London: Lynne Rienner Publishers), 231–54.
Planning Commission, Government of India (2002*a*), 'India Economic Road Map: the Next Five Years 2002–2007' (New Delhi: Government of India).
Planning Commission, Government of India (2002*b*), 'Draft tenth five year plan', Volume III (New Delhi: Government of India).
Planning Commission, Government of India (2002*c*), 'Tenth Five Year Plan 2002–2007', Vol. 2 (New Delhi: Government of India).

Planning Commission, Government of India (2002*d*), 'Vision 2020' (New Delhi: Government of India).

Planning Commission, Government of India (2005*a*), 'Approach to the mid-term appraisal of the tenth plan (2002–07)' (New Delhi: Government of India).

Planning Commission, Government of India (2005*b*), 'Mid-term appraisal of the tenth five year plan (2002–2007)' (New Delhi: Government of India).

Planning Commission, Government of India (2007), 'An Approach to the eleventh five-year plan' (New Delhi: Government of India).

Planning Commission, Government of India (2008), 'Report of the high-level group on the services sector' (New Delhi: Government of India).

Pocock, D. F. (1957), 'Inclusion and exclusion: A process in the caste system of Gujarat', *Southwestern Journal of Anthropology*, 13 (1), 19–31.

Pocock, D. F. (1972), *Kanbi and Patidar: A study of the Patidar community of Gujarat* (Oxford: Clarendon Press).

Pocock, D. F. (1973), *Mind, Body and Wealth. A study of belief and practice in an Indian village* (Oxford: Basil Blackwell).

Press Trust of India (2007), 'Mayawati sacks 7,400 more cops', Rediff India Abroad 2007, <http://www.rediff.com///news/2007/sep/30maya.htm>, accessed 28 October 2008.

Pritchett, L., and Murgai, R. (2007), 'Teacher compensation: Can decentralisation to local bodies take India from the perfect storm through troubled waters to clear sailing?', in S. Bery, B. P. Bosworth, and A. Panagariya (eds.), *India Policy Forum* (Washington, DC: Sage), Vol. 3, 123–68.

Purfield, C. (2006), 'Mind the gap—Is economic growth in India leaving some states behind?', *IMF Working Paper*, WP/06/103.

Puri, A. (2007), 'Meet your new DM', *Outlook*, 7 August.

Qadeer, I. (1998), 'Reproductive health: A public health perspective', *Economic and Political Weekly*, 33 (41), 2675–84.

Ram, F., Paswan, B., and Ladu Singh, L. (2005), 'India: facility survey (under Reproductive and Child Health Project)', Phase II, 2003 (Mumbai: International Institute for Population Sciences), <http://www.rchiips.org/PRCH-2.html>, accessed 5 January 2009.

Raman, A. (2007), 'Keep it skimmed', *Outlook*, 16 April.

Ramaswamy, E. A. (1990) 'Indian trade unionism: The crisis of leadership', in Mark Holmstrom (ed.), *Work for Wages in South Asia* (Delhi: Manohar Books). 160–72.

Randall, V. (2001), 'Party systems and voter alignments in the new democracies of the Third World', in L. Karvonen and S. Kuhnle (eds.), *Party Systems and Voter Alignments Revisited* (London: Routledge), 238–60.

Rao, M. S. A. (1977), 'Rewari kingdom and the Mughal Empire', in R. Fox (ed.), *Realm and Region in Traditional India* (New Delhi: Vikas Publishing), 79–89.

Rao, M. S. A. (1979), *Social Movements and Social Transformation: The study of two Backward Classes Movements in India* (New Delhi: Macmillan).

Reddy, K. S., and Sivaramakrishnan, K. (2006), 'Unmet national health needs: Visions of Public Health Foundation of India', *Economic and Political Weekly*, 41 (37), 3927–33.

Registrar General, India (1998), *State Profile 1991 India* (New Delhi: Government of India).

Registrar General, India (1999), *Compendium of India's Fertility and Mortality Indicators 1971–1997 Based on The Sample Registration System* (New Delhi: Government of India).

Registrar General, India (2006), *Census of India 2001*, <http://www.censusindia.net/results/2001census_data_indx.html>, accessed July 2006.

Registrar General, India, in collaboration with Centre for Global Health Research, University of Toronto, Canada (2006), *Maternal Mortality in India, 1997–2003: Trends, causes and risk factors* (New Delhi: Registrar General, India).

Reserve Bank of India (2007), *Handbook of Statistics on the Indian Economy* (Mumbai: Rekha Misra).

Rishyasringa, B. (2000), 'Social policy and reproductive health', in R. Ramasubban and S. Jejeebhoy (eds.), *Women's Reproductive Health in India* (Jaipur and New Delhi: Rawat Publications), 418–45.

Roberts, K. (2003), 'Social correlates of party system demise and populist resurgence in Venezuela', *Latin American Politics and Society*, 45 (3), 35–56.

Rodrik, D., and Subramanian, A. (2005), 'From 'Hindu Growth' to the productivity surge: the mystery of the Indian growth transition', *IMF Staff Papers*, 52 (2).

Rudolph, S. H., and Rudolph, L. I. (1967), *The Modernity of Tradition: Political development in India* (Chicago and London: University of Chicago Press).

Sachar, R. (2006), *Social, Economic and Educational Status of the Muslim Community in India* (New Delhi: Cabinet Secretariat, Government of India).

Said, E. W. (1978), *Orientalism: Western Conceptions of the Orient* (New York: Pantheon).

Sarvekshana, National Sample Survey Organisation (2001–2002), 'An integrated summary of employment and unemployment survey results 55th round', 25 (2 & 3), 87th Issue.

Sathyamala, C., Mittal, O., Dasgupta, R., and Priya, R. (2005), 'Polio eradication initiative in India: Deconstructing the GPEI', *International Journal of Health Services*, 35 (2), 361–83.

Scully, T. (1995), 'Reconstituting party politics in Chile', in S. Mainwaring and T. Scully (eds.), *Building Democratic Institutions: Party Systems in Latin America* (Stanford: Stanford University Press), 100–37.

Searle-Chatterjee, M., and Sharma, U. M. (1994), 'Introduction', in M. Searle-Chatterjee and U. M. Sharma (eds.), *Contextualising Caste: Post-Dumontian approaches* (Oxford: Blackwell), 1–24.

Shah, A. M. (ed.) (2007), *The Grassroots of Democracy: Field studies of Indian elections* (New Delhi: Permanent Black).

Shariff, A. (1995), 'Socio-economic and demographic differentials between Hindus and Muslims in India', *Economic and Political Weekly*, 30 (46), 2947–53.

Singh, M. (2002), 'Liberalization: Opportunities for social action', in A. Maharishi (ed.), *A common cause: NGOs & civil society* (New Delhi: National Foundation for India), 24–8.

Sivaramakrishnan, K., and Agrawal, A. (2003), 'Regional modernities in stories and practices of development', in K. Sivaramakrishnan and A. Agrawal (eds.),

Regional modernities: the cultural politics of development in India (New Delhi: Oxford University Press), 1–62.

Spencer, J. (1997), 'Post-colonialism and the political imagination', *The Journal of the Royal Anthropological Institute*, 3 (1), 1–19.

Srinivas, M. N. (1962), *Caste in Modern India and Other Essays* (Bombay: Asia Publishing House).

Srinivas, M. N. (1996), *Caste, its Twentieth Century Avatar* (New Delhi: Penguin).

Srinivas, M. N. (2003), 'An obituary on caste as a system', *Economic and Political Weekly*, 38 (5), 455–9.

Srinivasan, S., and Bedi, A.S. (2009), 'Tamil Nadu and the diagonal divide in sex ratios', *Economic and Political Weekly*, 44 (3), 56–63.

Srinivasan, T. N. (2005), 'Comments on Dani Rodrik and Arvind Subramanian, From "Hindu growth" to productivity surge: The mystery of the Indian growth transition', *IMF Staff Papers*, 52 (2).

Srivastava, D. K., Bhujanga Rao, C., Chakraborty, P., and, Rangamannav, T. S. (2003), 'Budgetary subsidies in India: Subsidising social and economic services', *National Institute of Public Finance and Policy* (New Delhi: Planning Commission, Government of India).

Srivastava, N. (2003), 'And promises to keep: The challenge of gender disparities in India's economic development', *Indian Journal of Economics*, 84 (332), 123–46.

Sopher, D. (1980), 'The geographical patterning of culture in India', in D. Sopher (ed.), *An Exploration of India* (London: Longman), 289–326.

Subramanian, A. (2007), 'The Evolution of Institutions in India and its relationship with Economic Growth', *Oxford Review of Economic Policy*, 23 (2), 196–220.

Tambiah, S. J. (1997), *Levelling Crowds: Ethnonationalist Conflicts and Collective Violence in South Asia* (Berkeley: University of California Press).

Tambs-Lyche, H. (1997), *Power, Profit and Poetry. Traditional society in Kathiwar, western India* (New Delhi: Manohar).

Tarlo, E. (2003), *Unsettling Memories: Narratives of the Emergency in Delhi* (London: Hurst and Co.).

Tata Services Limited (2007), *Statistical Outline of India* 2006–7 (Mumbai: Tata Services Limited).

Taylor, C. E., Cutts, F., and Taylor, M. E. (1997), 'Ethical dilemmas in current planning for polio eradication', *American Journal of Public Health*, 87 (6), 922–5.

Tharamangalam, J. (1996), 'Caste among Christians in India', in M. N. Srinivas (ed.), *Caste, its Twentieth Century Avatar* (New Delhi: Penguin), 263–91.

Treiman, D. J. (1970), 'Industrialisation and social stratification', in E. O. Laumann (ed.), *Social Stratification—Research and Theory for the 1970s* (Indianapolis: Bobbs-Merril), 207–34.

Turnbridge, J. E., and Ashworth, G. J. (1996), *Dissonant Heritage: The management of the past as a resource in conflict* (Chichester, New York: J. Wiley Press).

UNDP (2008), *Human Development Report 2007/08. Fighting Climate Change: Human solidarity in a divided world* (New York: Palgrave Macmillan).

UNICEF (2006), *The State of the World's Children 2007* (New York: United Nations Children's Fund).

United Nations (2005), *World Population Prospects: The 2004 Revision Population Database* (New York: United Nations).

Unnithan-Kumar, M. (1997), *Identity, gender and poverty: New perspectives on caste and tribe in Rajasthan* (Oxford: Berghahn Books).

USAID (2008), 'Pre-solicitation notice, RFI#386–07–004', <www.usaid.gov/in/Pdfs/RFI_386–07–004.pdf>, accessed 30 January 2008.

Vaid, D. (2007), 'Class Mobility of Women and Men in India', Unpublished D.Phil. thesis (Nuffield College, Oxford University).

Vanaik, A. (1990), *The Painful Transition: Bourgeois Democracy in India* (London: Verso Books).

Van Hollen, C. (1998), 'Moving targets: Routinisation of IUD insertion in maternity wards in Tamil Nadu, India', *Reproductive Health Matters*, 6 (11), 98–106.

Van Hollen, C. (2003), *Birth on the Threshold: Childbirth and modernity in south India* (Berkeley & Los Angeles: University of California Press).

Varshney, A. (2002), *Ethnic Conflict and Civic Life: Hindus and Muslims in India* (New Haven: Yale University Press).

Venkatesan, V. (2006), 'Legal backing', *Frontline*, 23 (8), 22 April–5 May.

Vicziany, M. (1983), 'Coercion in a soft-state: The family planning programme of India', *Pacific Affairs*, 55 (3 & 4), 373–402 & 557–92.

Vira, B., and Vira, S. (2004), 'India's urban environment', in T. Dyson, R. Cassen, and L. Visaria (eds.), *Twenty-First Century India—Population, Economy, Human Development, and the Environment* (Oxford: Oxford University Press), 292–311.

Vira, B., Iyer, R., and Cassen, R. (2004), 'Water', in T. Dyson, R. Cassen, and L. Visaria (eds.), *Twenty-First Century India—Population, Economy, Human Development, and the Environment* (Oxford: Oxford University Press), 312–27.

Virmani, A. (2004), 'India's economic growth: from socialist rate of growth to Bharatiya rate of growth', *Working Paper No. 122* (New Delhi: ICRIER).

Visaria, L. (2004*a*), 'Mortality trends and the health transition', in T. Dyson, R. Cassen, and L. Visaria (eds.), *Twenty-First Century India—Population, Economy, Human Development, and the Environment* (Oxford: Oxford University Press), 32–56.

Visaria, L. (2004*b*), 'The continuing fertility transition', in T. Dyson, R. Cassen, and L. Visaria (eds.), *Twenty-First Century India—Population, Economy, Human Development, and the Environment* (Oxford: Oxford University Press), 57–73.

Visaria, L., and Visaria, P. (1982), 'Population (1757–1947)', in D. Kumar and M. Desai (eds.), *The Cambridge Economic History of India, Volume II: c.1757–c.1970* (Cambridge: Cambridge University Press), 463–532.

Visaria, P. (1997), *Women in the Indian Working Force: Trends and differentials* (Pune, India: Gokhale Institute of Politics and Economics).

Visaria, P. (1999), 'Level and pattern of female employment, 1911–1994', in T. S. Papola and A. N. Sharma (eds.), *Gender and Employment in India* (New Delhi: Vikas Publishing), 23–51.

Visaria, P. (2000), 'Urbanization in India', unpublished manuscript (New Delhi: Institute of Economic Growth).

Washbrook, D. A. (1975). 'The development of caste organisation in South India, 1880 to 1925', in C. J. Baker and D. A. Washbrook (eds.), *South India. Political Institutions and Political Change 1880–1940* (Delhi: Oxford University Press), 150–203.

Weber, M. (1920/1958), *The Religion of India* (New York: Free Press).

Williamson, J. G. (2001), 'Demographic change, economic growth, and inequality', in N. Birdsall, A. Kelley, and S. Sinding (eds.), *Population Matters—Demographic Change, Economic Growth, and Poverty in the Developing World* (Oxford: Oxford University Press), 106–36.

Wilson, C., and Dyson, T. (1992), 'Family systems and cultural change: Perspectives from past and present', in E. Berquó and P. Xenos (eds.), *Family Systems and Cultural Change* (New York: Oxford University Press), 31–45.

Wilson, D., and Purushothaman, R. (2003), 'Dreaming with the BRICs: The Path to 2050', Goldman Sachs, Global Economics Paper No. 99.

World Bank (2000), *Project appraisal document: On a proposed IDA credit in the amount of SDR 106.5 million (US $ 142.6 million equivalent) to India for an immunization strengthening project* (Washington, DC: Health and Nutrition and Population Sector Unit, South Asia Region).

World Bank (2000), 'Uttar Pradesh fiscal and governance reform loan project' (Washington, DC: The World Bank).

World Bank (2003), *Supplemental Credit Document, International Development Association, Proposed Settlement Credit of SDR 59.5 million (US $ 83.4 million equivalent) to India for the Immunization Strengthening Project* (Washington, DC: Human Development Unit, South Asia Region).

World Bank (2007), *World Development Indicators* (Washington, DC: World Bank Publications).

Xie, Y. (1992), 'The log-multiplicative layer effect model for comparing mobility tables', *American Sociological Review*, 57 (3), 380–95.

Yadav, K. C. (1994), *India's Unequal Citizens: A study of other backward classes* (New Delhi: Manohar).

Yadav, Y. (1996), 'Reconfiguration in Indian politics: State assembly elections 1993–95', *Economic and Political Weekly*, 31, 95–104.

Yadav, Y. (1997), 'Reconfiguration in Indian politics: State assembly elections 1993–1995', in P. Chatterjee (ed.), *State and politics in India* (New Delhi: Oxford University Press), 117–207.

Yadav, Y. (2000), 'Understanding the second democratic upsurge: Trends of Bahujan participation in electoral politics in the 1990s', in F. R. Frankel, Z. Hasan, R. Bhargava, and B. Arora (eds.), *Transforming India: Social and Political Dynamics of Democracy* (New Delhi: Oxford University Press), 120–45.

Yadav, Y. (2004), 'The elusive mandate of 2004', *Economic and Political Weekly*, 39 (51), 5383–98.

Zwart, F. (2000), 'The logic of affirmative action: Caste, class and quotas in India', *Acta Sociologica*, 43 (3), 235–49.

Author Index

Subject Index